Age in Love

Early Modern Cultural Studies

SERIES EDITORS

Carole Levin
Marguerite A. Tassi

Age in Love

Shakespeare and the Elizabethan Court

Jacqueline Vanhoutte

UNIVERSITY OF NEBRASKA PRESS

© 2019 by the Board of Regents of the University of Nebraska

A short version of chapter 1 appeared in *Explorations in Renaissance Culture* 37 (2011): 51–70. An early draft of chapter 2 appeared in *English Literary Renaissance* 43.1 (2013): 86–127 (© 2013 by English Literary Renaissance Inc.). Thanks to these journals for their permission to reuse these materials.

All rights reserved

∞

Library of Congress Cataloging-in-Publication Data
Names: Vanhoutte, Jacqueline, 1968– author.
Title: Age in love: Shakespeare and the Elizabethan court / Jacqueline Vanhoutte.
Description: Lincoln: University of Nebraska Press, 2019. | Series: Early modern cultural studies | Includes bibliographical references and index.
Identifiers: LCCN 2018051867
ISBN 9781496207593 (cloth: alk. paper)
ISBN 9781496214539 (epub)
ISBN 9781496214546 (mobi)
ISBN 9781496214553 (pdf)
Subjects: LCSH: Shakespeare, William, 1564–1616—Political and social views. | Shakespeare, William, 1564–1616—Characters—Queens. | Elizabeth I, Queen of England, 1533–1603—Relations with courts and courtiers. | English literature—Early modern, 1500–1700—History and criticism. | Older men in literature. | Courts and courtiers in literature. | Great Britain—Court and courtiers—History—16th century.
Classification: LCC PR3024 .V36 2019 | DDC 822.3/3—dc23
LC record available at https://lccn.loc.gov/2018051867

Set in Garamond Premier by Mikala R. Kolander.
Designed by N. Putens.

To the memory of my beloved grandmother,
Emma Dethier Vandenberghe (1914–2009).
I have seen some majesty and I know it.

CONTENTS

List of Illustrations
ix

Acknowledgments
xi

Introduction
1

1. *Endymion* at the Aging Court
33

2. Falstaff among the Minions of the Moon
77

3. Remembering Old Boys in *Twelfth Night*
121

4. Antony
159

Epilogue
205

Notes
209

Bibliography
259

Index
281

ILLUSTRATIONS

1. Geoffrey Whitney,
A Choice of Emblemes (1586)
7

2. Portrait of Robert Dudley, Earl of
Leicester, by William Segar (1587)
49

3. *Discours de la Vie Abominable, Ruses,
Trahisons... Desquelles a Usé et Use
Journellement my Lorde de Lecestre* (1585)
54

4. Title page of Arthur Golding's
translation of Ovid's *Metamorphoses* (1584)
88

5. George Gascoigne, *The Noble Arte of
Venerie or Hunting* (1575)
108

6. Rainbow Portrait of Elizabeth I,
attributed to Marcus Gheeraerts the
Younger (1600–1602)
170

ACKNOWLEDGMENTS

This book would not have been possible without the unfailing support and intellectual generosity of my husband, Alex Pettit. His confidence in my work sustains me when my own flags. Marrying him is the best career choice I made. I'm deeply grateful as well to John Coldewey, who introduced me to the joys of early drama and who passed away as I was finishing the manuscript. After all this time, I still write for him, my kind, witty, charming, and exacting first reader. My daughter Claire, who is fourteen, patiently put up with this book for the majority of her life. She brought me joy and much-needed relief. Carole Levin has been a model, a mentor, and an inspiration for my entire career. Her trailblazing scholarship paved the way for so many women in the field, including myself. I have also benefited greatly from Catherine Loomis's learned comments, her wise counsel, and her vast knowledge of the period. I am grateful to Marguerite Tassi, Jo Carney Eldridge, and Alisa Plant for their faith in the book, and to the anonymous reviewers who have contributed important insights over the years. My chairs, David Holdeman and Robert Upchurch, encouraged and funded my research, as did others at the University of North Texas. Amanda Kellogg, Heidi Cephus, and Christa Reaves assisted me at various stages. Thanks are due as well to my friend and colleague Jeff Doty, with whom I discuss my ideas about Renaissance drama at length. Faith Lipori, Corey Marks, Amy Taylor, Nicole Smith, and Paul and Jacqueline Vanhoutte provided crucial emotional support. Miranda Wilson gave me important feedback and thirty-seven years of friendship—for this, much thanks. Paul Menzer and Doug Bruster kindly lent their support at the end. My work reflects conversations with numerous other friends, students, and colleagues, including the members of the Elizabeth I Society and the attendees of the Blackfriars Convention in Staunton. Thanks also to the two long-eared souls who spanieled me at the heels throughout the writing process, Emma and Cleopatra.

INTRODUCTION

I take the title of this book from Shakespeare's Sonnet 138, a poem about an aging male speaker who, by virtue of his sexual entanglement with the dark lady, "vainly" performs the role of "some untutor'd youth" (138.2–5).[1] As his theatrical metaphor indicates, the speaker views his desire for the lady as a violation of generational roles. The sonnet establishes equivalences between the speaker's senescent sexuality and female sexual promiscuity by paralleling his lies about his age with the lady's lies about her fidelity. The claim that these are transgressions of the same order may strike modern readers as disingenuous or hysterical. After all, in the era of Viagra, we tend to applaud aging men in the role of lovers: the sexual activity of our old men signals their transcendent virility, their triumphant conquest of time. In the era of the Virgin Queen, this was not the case. Lust was the proper purview of those of "stripling age," a period roughly corresponding to adolescence and young adulthood, not those of "olde age," which might begin as early as the forties or fifties.[2] Instead of indulging in "days of love, desire, and vanitie," as the sonnet speaker does, Sir Walter Ralegh believed that older men had to grow "to the perfection of [their] understanding."[3] Those who continued to conceive sexual desires as they aged defied social expectations regarding appropriate behavior, exposing themselves to the judgment of others. No wonder, then, that Shakespeare's speaker "loves not t' have years told" (138.12).[4]

Although the gap in age between the sonnet speaker and his love objects is of obsessive concern in the sequence, coloring "almost every motive and action in the relationships to which the *Sonnets* refer," critics have been largely silent about its implications.[5] This silence is all the more striking given that Shakespeare's decision to embrace the perspective of a lover whose "days are past the best" (138.6) is not an aberration. Rather, we might think about the poetic persona of the sonnets as a kind of signature, an overt admission on Shakespeare's part of his enduring fascination with the amorous experiences of older men. The pattern that I am calling "age in love" pervades Shakespeare's mature works, informing his experiments in all dramatic genres. Many of his most memorable characters—Bottom, Othello, Claudius, Falstaff, and Antony, to name a few—share with the sonnet speaker a tendency to flout generational decorum by assuming the role of the "young gallant" (*Merry Wives of Windsor*, 2.1.22). These superannuated lovers supplement their role-playing through costume changes: Bottom takes on an ass's head, Malvolio dons his stockings and garters, Falstaff and Antony dress like women. Hybrids and upstarts, cross-dressers and shape-shifters, comic butts and tragic heroes, Shakespeare's old men in love turn in boundary-blurring performances that probe the multiple categories by which early modern subjects conceived of identity. The ways in which these protean characters draw attention not just to gender distinctions (as do the androgynous heroines of the romantic comedies) but also to generic and generational ones make them flexible vehicles for a range of social, political, philosophical, and aesthetic inquiries. In the chapters that follow, I show that questions that we have come to regard as quintessentially Shakespearean—about the limits of social mobility, the nature of political authority, the transformative powers of the theater, the vagaries of human memory, or the possibility of secular immortality—receive indelible expression through his artful deployment of the age-in-love trope.

The courtliness in which Shakespeare cloaks this ancient trope matters: what drew him to the old man in love, I argue, is not just the timelessness of this figure but also its timeliness. Leslie A. Fiedler points out that "myths of old men in love" are "as ancient as the culture of what we call the West."[6] These myths took on a culturally specific cast in late Tudor England because of the composition of the Elizabethan court. While the accession of Elizabeth I in 1558 enabled the meteoric rise of some young

INTRODUCTION

men, including Robert Dudley (later Earl of Leicester), thereafter "new blood entered" the Elizabethan court "only when vacancies were created."[7] According to Keith Thomas, the "median age of Privy Counselors" at the Elizabethan court "was never less than fifty-one."[8] In 1588, when the court dramatist John Lyly first staged his influential *Endymion*, a play about aging courtiers, average life expectancy at birth was thirty-seven; those who made it to twenty-five might expect to live to their early fifties.[9] Sir Christopher Hatton was forty-nine, the Earl of Leicester fifty-five, Sir Francis Walsingham fifty-six, and William Cecil, Lord Burghley sixty-nine at the time—all elderly men by early modern standards. Shakespeare's pose as an aging lover in his most courtly work identifies him with the court's "fairest creatures," many of whom had failed in their aristocratic duty to produce biological "increase" (1.1).

While Elizabeth followed precedent set by her male forebears in surrounding herself with older men, her expectations regarding their behavior were distinctive. As Hillary Clinton's running mate Tim Kaine observed, traditionally the idea of the "strong man" does not include serving a "strong woman" in a supportive role.[10] Elizabeth's exceptional status as the female monarch of a patriarchal system, and her strategies for maintaining that status, required the men around her to make exceptions as well. None did so more spectacularly than her elder favorites, Leicester and Hatton. By parlaying their subservient brand of sexual charisma into political capital and social status, these two violated their culture's gendered ideals, which insisted on sexual restraint and male dominance as crucial components of masculinity.[11] Through the queen's favor, Hatton, a member of the lesser gentry, rose to the position of lord chancellor of England, while Leicester, arguably descended from "a tribe of traitors," became "the one man in England who ... approached a king's estate."[12] Although Castiglione's proposition that "the thoughts and ways of sensual love are most unbecoming to a mature age" garnered wide agreement in the period, these men continued to perform the role of the lover regardless of age.[13] Their deviations from gender and generational norms called attention to other deviations, like the failure to secure timely marriages or produce legitimate heirs, and helped render Hatton and Leicester subjects of unprecedented gossip and public scrutiny. In her groundbreaking study of contemporary responses to Elizabeth I, Carole Levin identifies rumors about the queen's love affairs as signs of widespread discomfort with female rule—an argument that can be expanded to include responses to the queen's alleged lovers, whose unorthodox behavior was sometimes difficult to reconcile with their dignified status as royal counselors.[14] A rich cultural discourse, in a variety of media—rumors, images, unpublished and published poems and treatises, plays and performances—sprang up around these elder minions, making them celebrities avant la lettre.[15] According to Michael L. Quinn, "the first requisite for celebrity is public notoriety," which helps convert individuals into "representatives of the character traits most revered (or feared) by the community."[16] Hatton and, to a much greater extent still, Leicester came to play such a representative role, embodying communal fears, anxieties, and fantasies about the transformational powers of female rule.[17] At a time when all politics were personal, the incessant chatter about these men was a form of political speech, a sign of people's interest in state matters that were technically the purview of elites. That the Elizabethan regime was alert to the dangers of this phenomenon is evident from the fact that they passed new laws, criminalizing various forms of speech.[18]

Despite the government's best efforts, the collective conversation about the queen's men found its way into print, where it assumed conventional patterns. Allusions to Ovid's Circe framed sexual submission to Elizabeth as a form of male degeneration, for example, and references to bearbaitings, law courts, or hell and the Last Judgment expressed a desire to see the queen's favorite men punished for their perceived transgressions. These satiric discourses generated distorted images of public figures with a tenuous connection to the men themselves. As the favorite target of contemporary invective, for example, Leicester acquired an unshakable reputation for lechery and drunkenness, even though his biographer assures us that the earl was an "abstemious man."[19] By making the debate about the queen's eldest favorites audible again, I am able to show that theatrical representations of libidinous elderly courtiers drew on its characteristic tropes, thus shedding light on problems that have long vexed

INTRODUCTION

Shakespeare scholars, like the nature of the relationship between *The Henriad* and *The Merry Wives of Windsor* (chapter 2). I am also able to identify new sources for major characters, like Malvolio (chapter 3), forge connections among major works rarely discussed together, like *Hamlet* and *Antony and Cleopatra* (chapter 4), and propose new readings of these works. Ultimately, I demonstrate that Elizabeth I and her court shaped Shakespeare's plays in unexpected and previously undocumented ways.

The many references to lecherous older courtiers in plays offer one gauge of how the conduct at court conflicted with broader expectations regarding gender- and age-appropriate behavior. The publication of *Endymion* in 1591 launched a veritable vogue for the *senex amans* that lasted into the Jacobean period, with Thomas Middleton's *Revenger's Tragedy* (1607) and Shakespeare's *Antony and Cleopatra* (1608) marking the final wave of the phenomenon for my purposes. On stage, the "limited performances" of "old men lustful" openly alluded to the Elizabethan court; Lyly's Cynthia, Shakespeare's Cleopatra, and Middleton's Gloriana are all objects of senescent lust modeled on the queen's public personae, for example.[20] Surveying the preponderance of "old man's venery," one stage character explains that the behavior that was "rather an emblem of dispraise . . . in Monsieur's days"—the days of Elizabeth's last official suitor—had by the time of James's accession grown to "a fashion."[21] As this metaphor indicates, the figure of "age in love" evokes forces of change and innovation for early moderns, however counterintuitive it might seem to us to embody such forces in randy old men. The timeframe for the phenomenon, meanwhile, identifies it with what historians refer to as the second reign of Elizabeth I, when the possibility of the queen marrying had vanished and the sexualized protocols of the court were therefore played out "vainly."[22] Under such conditions, the desire to "make the old fellow pay for's lechery" gives dramatic expression to a range of controversial impulses.[23] It is no accident that attacks on "treacherous, lecherous" older men (*Hamlet* 2.2.581) often double as gestures of independence from dominating and adulterating women in Renaissance plays.

By offering sexualized portrayals of fictional characters that glanced

5

at historical figures, the theatrical "fashion" for "old men's venery" participated in the rise of "embodied writing" that Douglas Bruster argues transformed society in the final decades of Elizabeth's reign, ushering in an early modern version of the public sphere.[24] Depictions of "old men lustful" offered cover for political commentary, adapting to artistic and polemical purpose a rhetorical strategy favored by Tudor dissidents, who preferred to take aim at the queen's counselors rather than at the queen herself.[25] This strategy of indirection is particularly effective against a female ruler (or, as the 2016 American election showed, a would-be female ruler) because it reduces her to an object of masculine discourse and manipulation, thus enforcing rhetorically the patriarchal norms that she violates politically. To cite a pertinent example, the widely circulated Catholic pamphlet known as *Leicester's Commonwealth* (1584) relied on such tactics in its seminal (an irresistible word, under the circumstances) representation of Leicester as an oversexed old man. Although its authors, a group of anonymous Catholic expatriates, objected to policies that the queen had approved, they limit direct attacks to Leicester and his henchmen.

The earl was an obvious target for malcontents and dissidents: not only did he enjoy a privileged relationship with the queen, but he was also the leader of the Protestant faction at court, and a major patron and protector of radical Protestants. Leicester conducted his affairs, including his courtship of the queen, in a shockingly public fashion, moreover. Relying on traditional modes of aristocratic self-display, he ordered matching portraits showing himself and the queen for the 1575 festivities at Kenilworth, for example. According to Elizabeth Goldring, these gestured toward "a future in which Leicester is no longer an earl, but a prince consort or a king."[26] Leicester was also among the first statesmen to turn to the printing press to court "popularity," a word that Jeffrey S. Doty shows gained traction during this period and which referred to the cultivation of popular favor and to the public pitching of political arguments.[27] Straddling old and new methods of publicity, the earl relied on his extensive patronage network to circulate flattering images of himself—at times quite literally, in that some books included a portrait of the

THE SECOND PARTE
OF EMBLEMES,
AND OTHER DEVISES,
gathered, Englished, and moralized,

And diuerse newlie deuised, by
Geffrey Whitney.

FIG. 1. Dudley Bear and Ragged Staff, Geoffrey Whitney, *A Choice of Emblemes* (1586), O1R. By permission of the Folger Shakespeare Library.

handsome aristocrat.[28] Others reproduced the Dudley bear and ragged staff, an aristocratic "insignia" of the sort Jürgen Habermas associates with the "representative" publicity of pre-print culture.[29]

While Leicester and his older brother Ambrose, Earl of Warwick, had adopted the badge to advertise their (matrilineal) descent from the fifteenth-century Beauchamp Earls of Warwick, the badge now signaled Leicester's official imprimatur in printed books sold to a burgeoning population of readers instead. The epistolary dedications of these books presented the earl as the embodiment of Protestant and humanist ideals; he was a man "upon whose wisedome, foresight, trustinesse, pollicie, & stoutness, God hath ordained the securitie of our most gracious soveraigne Lady, & of her Maiesties Realme and subiectes" as well as "of his owne Religion."[30] Leicester deserved promotion to the highest places not because he had the right aristocratic credentials but because he had all the right "qualities of the mind, and . . . qualities of the bodye." Thomas Blundeville proposed others might look to the earl as a "glasse" showing these qualities, and that "those that Honors woulde atcheeve / and Counslers eke desire to bee" should take him as their model.[31] Years later, Francis Bacon would affirm Blundeville's wisdom, by advising the turbulent Earl of Essex to imitate his stepfather when addressing the queen.[32]

All this humanist puffery had unintended consequences, however. While the idea that Leicester's career offered a reproducible blueprint for upward mobility was exciting to some, it proved alarming to others. The earl had in effect invited these others to discuss their reservations by going public with arguments about his own merits. Taking the cue, *Leicester's Commonwealth* represents itself "a debate or conversation" about the earl, illustrating "the relationship operating between rumour, manuscript and print."[33] Although he presumably came to regret it, Leicester had initiated this conversation. Where his clients found a paragon of excellence, his critics saw "an aspiringe minde . . . tristinge after dignities, swaie and authoritie" far beyond those afforded by his place. Not only was the earl an ambitious upstart, according to these naysayers, but he was also an aging voluptuary "loste in lawless luste" and "base and filthy luxurie."[34] Leicester achieved unprecedented notoriety, becoming the most discussed member of the regime after the queen. His defenders wondered at his detractors, who found "new & strange kinds of rancor and venim (more then all the *Poets* from the beginning of the worlde could ever invent from the description of *Envie*, & the *Furies* themselves) wherewith to... empoison their most outragious slaunders, breathed out against him."[35] Because the Dudley bear and ragged staff was a frequent target, these "new & strange" attacks became identified with the sport of bearbaiting (see chapter 1).

There are, in other words, specific historical reasons that the "volumes of report" on the "doings" of the great sound like the "false, and most contrarious quest" of barking dogs to Shakespeare (*Measure for Measure*, 4.1.59–61), or that he developed a "strong if unconscious association between sex and publicity."[36] Shakespeare's earliest reference to bearbaiting takes the form of a figurative assault on an earl proud of his badge; Clifford, playing on Warwick's "rampant bear chain'd to the ragged staff," threatens to "rend" the "bear / And tread it underfoot with all contempt, / Despite the bearard that protects the bear" (*2 Henry VI*, 5.1.203, 208–10). Although it lacks sexual overtones, this exchange links bearbaiting tropes to attacks on the bear and ragged staff badge, a visual symbol that Londoners would have identified with the Elizabethan Earl of Leicester. Plays like *Merry Wives of Windsor* and *Twelfth Night* exploit audience interest in such court connections in more subtle fashion, by casting their aging lovers as the bear-like objects of public scorn. In its first chapter, this book traces Shakespeare's enduring fascination with the *senex amans* through Lyly's *Endymion* to the Catholic exiles who first used bearbaiting tropes to portray the Elizabethan court as a hotbed of geriatric sexuality. Subsequent chapters show that Shakespeare addresses a range of timely subjects through the timeless figure of the old man in love, including the problems attendant on the succession (in *Twelfth Night*), the relation of Elizabeth I to the country that she governed (in the Falstaff plays), and the nature of the queen's powers over male subjects (in *Antony and Cleopatra*). His lusty old men thus testify to the complicated pleasures afforded by the playwright's exploitation of court scandal, as well as to his tendency to extend to his audiences the tools for political judgment.[37]

INTRODUCTION

Although they participate in a "fashion," Shakespeare's contributions to the age-in-love tradition are distinguished by his self-consciousness about the commercial, political, and artistic implications of this figure. Metatheatrical devices underscore how the spectacle of a highly placed older man succumbing to erotic impulses produces debate among lower-placed beholders (e.g., the opening scene of *Antony and Cleopatra*). Insofar as this debate occurs among inferiors about superiors, and alludes to real as well as imaginary figures, it confirms that the theater is a "place of judgment," to which "even the worste sorte of people" are admitted as "the judges of faultes there painted out," a process that the antitheatricalist Stephen Gosson argues is "neyther lawfull nor convenient" but constitutes "a kinde of libelling, and defaming."[38] Gosson, who takes special exception to the lampooning of public figures on stage, was right; in an absolute monarchy, "private men, and subjects" had no "lawfull authoritie . . . to judge" the men that the sovereign had raised to public office.[39] Yet Shakespeare shows us private subjects—including his Windsor wives—modeling such behavior repeatedly. By peddling the fantasy of calling a powerful man to "accompt . . . to see what other men could say against him," Shakespeare embraces the democratizing functions of the theater, and positions his audiences as "adjudicating" publics, a rhetorical strategy that Peter Lake and Steven Pincus find characteristic of the emergent Post-Reformation public sphere.[40]

As Lake, Doty, Bruster, Paul Yachnin, Stephen Wittek, András Kisery, and others have argued, early moderns turned to the theater to satisfy cravings generated by changing modes of publicity, like the desire for "news" or for the political competence that might produce social prestige.[41] Works about the court supply these cultural goods in abundance. The "new & strange" stories about Leicester were considered "news," for example, since many believed them true (like participants in today's internet culture, participants in early modern print culture were not always able to distinguish real from fake news). The "growing news consciousness" that marked Elizabethan culture was a top-down affair; in plays and pamphlets alike, "news" means "news at the court" (*As You Like It*, 1.1.97) and more specifically still news about "who's in, who's out" of favor at the court (*King Lear*, 5.3.15).[42] While it privileged sexual morality and social decorum over more political concerns, the late Elizabethan conversation about court favoritism was conducted among "private persons" about the public figures who ruled them.[43] Theatrical representations of lecherous old courtiers contributed to this phenomenon by inciting audiences to laughter, considered in the period a form of judgment. In the *Book of the Courtier*, laughter performs the same work of enforcing social norms as "praising or censuring." Not only does Castiglione discuss how to provoke laughter, but his courtiers also express their decorous "regard for time and place" by laughing together at manifest absurdities, like the idea of "old men [in] love."[44] The judgments encouraged by the theatrical fashion for old men's venery were not valid because they conformed to the edicts of reason, as in the Habermasian ideal of the public sphere. Rather, these were social judgments, based on commonly held criteria regarding appropriate sexual and generational behavior, which put into play emotions of shame, envy, desire, disgust, embarrassment, and resentment. By making, in Henry Wotton's memorable phrase, "greatness very familiar, if not ridiculous," theatrical portraits of deviant elderly courtiers also distinguished moral status and social prestige from class rank, thereby granting audiences a measure of ascendancy over their nominal betters.[45]

Since perceptions of Elizabeth's favorites impinged on perceptions of her legitimacy, these scathing portraits implicated the regime as a whole. Ultimately, the target was the queen herself. A commonplace of post-Machiavellian political thought held that subjects could judge monarchs by the company they keep. Blundeville argues, for example, that if counselors "be well chosen, the Prince is judged as well of straungers as of his owne subjects to be wise and carefull of his common wealth" but "in preferring will before reason" a prince risks "rather to be called a tyrant than a Prince."[46] Such views made relations of love or friendship fraught for all monarchs, who in showing affection for one subject risked alienating others.[47] A female ruler whose promotions reflected "private affection and respect, or partialitie" incurred the additional risk of confirming that women were natural tyrants who privileged "will before reason."[48] Under such conditions, Sir Philip Sidney believed that "who goes about to undermine" Leicester's good name "resolves withal to overthrow" the queen.[49] Curtis Perry's "dream of the impersonal monarch" first appeared during Elizabeth's reign because it gave expression to gendered longings.[50] The protopublic sphere may have been politically radical and democratizing, as Doty, Kisery, Lake, and others have argued, but it was also socially conservative. It enforced gender and generational hierarchies and gave rise to the modern idea that "to be properly public required that one rise above, or set aside, one's private interests and expressive nature." Michael Warner's language here points to the constitutive role that social decorum—always a gendered phenomenon—plays in framing notions of publicity. By conjuring "affects of shame and disgust" through satiric depictions of elderly courtiers devoted to queens, plays helped redefine "proper" publicity in terms of traditional masculinity.[51]

As a group, late Elizabethan and early Jacobean playwrights were intent on exploiting the democratizing and misogynistic implications of "age in love" figures. Where Jonson or Middleton invariably present lecherous older men as sources of ridicule, Shakespeare's aging lovers often produce more nuanced reactions, however. The critical tradition on Falstaff or Antony bears ample witness to these characters' ability to elicit a range of responses beyond condemnation, including powerful emotions of loss, sympathy, and identification.

One explanation for Shakespeare's distinctive approach can be found in the network of social relationships connecting Elizabeth's most talented subject to her favorite subject. When Jonson and Middleton began writing plays, Leicester had been dead for years; neither playwright is thus likely to have had much exposure to the queen's elder favorite. In contrast, Shakespeare, eight years older than Jonson and sixteen years older than Middleton, came of age when Leicester was still the premier theatrical patron in the country. Leicester died in 1588, at the beginning of Shakespeare's career as writer, when the public theater was a fledgling institution, just starting to wean itself from court patronage. The founder of the Theatre where Shakespeare's plays were first staged, James Burbage, had been a liveried member of the earl's famous traveling troupe, as had the clown Will Kempe. Leicester was also instrumental in putting together the Queen's Men, the company of elite players created for Elizabeth I in 1583, which included several more of Shakespeare's future colleagues. One scenario for Shakespeare's "lost years" has him starting his career with either Leicester's players or with the Queen's Men, which needed an actor when it visited Stratford in 1587.[52] Even if he did not learn his craft under the earl's protection, as so many of his colleagues did, Shakespeare must have taken a lifelong interest in Leicester, who was the local magnate in Warwickshire. The playwright's boyhood coincided with the earl's long public courtship of the queen, which had culminated in the legendary 1575 entertainments at Kenilworth, near Stratford. Some biographers believe Shakespeare to have attended these entertainments, alluded to in several plays.[53] Had Leicester succeeded in his matrimonial ambitions, Warwickshire as a whole might have reaped the benefit.[54] If the earl's hopes of preferment were always pinned on pleasing the queen, Shakespeare's hopes must have at one time been pinned on pleasing the earl.

Throughout his career, the homology between theatrical artist and royal favorite gave Shakespeare a way to orient himself in relation to the extraordinary woman who ruled the country. Already in *Love's Labor's Lost* Berowne berates the "allow'd" Boyet for being "some please-man, some trencher-knight, some Dick / That smiles his cheek in years and knows the trick / To make my lady laugh when she's disposed" (5.2.478, 464–66). The aging upstart's gift for "jesting merrily" with the Princess of France turns her aristocratic suitor's show to a stale "Christmas comedy" (5.2.462–77). The idea that royal favorites were usurpers of aristocratic privilege who resembled actors or jesters is not new to Shakespeare. Those who resented the queen's men often described them in theatrical terms. Robert Naunton reproduces a classic bit of gossip from the period, for example, when he claims "Hatton came to the court ... as a private gentleman of the Inns of Court in a masque, and for his activity and person (which was tall and proportionable) taken into the Queen's favor."[55] When wielded by less favored subjects, the analogy to theatrical artists highlighted violations of divinely sanctioned class and gender hierarchies. Elizabeth's alleged proclivity for handsome and entertaining men—"Daunsers ... [who] please her delycate Eye"—made mincemeat out of traditional criteria for judging masculine excellence, installing in pride of place a lowly "vegetable" like Hatton or a consummate hypocrite like Leicester, who knew how "to play his part well and dexterously."[56] According to one observer, the queen always surrounded herself with "very tall, fine strong men ... so that I never in my life saw their like."[57] Critics proposed that the queen's preference for such charismatic and attractive men threatened to undermine the hierarchical order over which she presided.

The emphasis on the favorites' theatricality reflects anxiety about the destabilizing effect of the queen's elective powers, which Shakespeare at times shares, as do the modern critics and historians who reproduce these unflattering stereotypes about Hatton and Leicester.[58] But throughout his career Shakespeare also relishes the possibility that gifted artists who brought a bit of "sport" to court, and who knew how to "please ... the ladies" might become "made men" (*A Midsummer Night's Dream*, 3.1.10–12, 4.2.17–18). Louis Montrose characterizes Bottom's experiences in *A Midsummer Night's Dream* as "an outrageous theatrical realization of a personal fantasy" common among Elizabethans.[59] A handful of privileged men had realized this fantasy, or so many Elizabethans believed. In addition to being the subjects of envy and slander, Hatton and Leicester were aspirational models of sorts, who had achieved what Tom MacFaul describes as the "highest point to which a subject might aspire."[60] Their careers were a major source for the dream of social mobility that haunts Elizabethan culture, and that, in Shakespeare's works, so often takes the peculiar form of election, on the grounds of sexual merit or personal attraction, by a regal woman. Bottom, Malvolio, Falstaff, Claudius, Othello, and Antony play out (or attempt to play out) different versions of this scenario, which revises orthodox humanist fantasies about meritocracy along unorthodox sexual and gendered lines.

The homology between theatrical artists and royal favorites shapes the age-in-love figures that concern me in this book, and helps to provoke the incompatible impulses—the desire to punish and the desire to emulate—that account for the complexity of Shakespeare's lusty old men. In a political setting, the royal favorite's resemblance to a theatrical artist evokes negative associations, prompting retaliation, like the verbal beatings that Hatton and Leicester endured, or the stage violence visited on characters like Claudius, Falstaff, or Malvolio. In a theatrical setting, where audiences share Elizabeth's notorious "partialitie" for amusing performances, the same likeness can also conjure the adulterating emotions of pleasure and admiration that modify colder judgments. The obloquy reserved for lecherous older men in early modern culture thus allows Shakespeare to test his own faculties of suasion, his uncanny ability to turn apparent transgression into artistic transcendence. The playwright inherited a fundamentally satiric trope from classical authors like Plautus, which been adapted by earlier Elizabethan writers to convey a critical attitude toward Elizabeth I and her court. He experimented with this received material in a range of generic modes—submitting it to the self-reflective conventions of the sonnet or to the synthesizing tendencies of tragicomedy, for example. These experiments in turn produced new perspectives on the court and on the idea of artistry. Shakespearean age-in-love figures share a tendency to suppress "simple truth" (138.8) in favor of the lies, dreams, and "rare vision[s]" (*A Midsummer Night's Dream*, 4.1.205) of the con artist and the artist. That these visions are often inspired by a "great fairy" (*Antony and Cleopatra*, 4.8.12) tells us something about the strong toil of Elizabeth I's grace on Shakespeare's imagination.

In taking up the topic of Shakespearean superannuated male sexuality, this book builds not just on recent scholarship about the Post-Reformation public sphere, but also on emergent interest in premodern constructions of aging, as manifested by the slew of books and essays that have appeared on the subject in the last decade. Perhaps the question of how Elizabethan subjects represented the descent into "the vale of years" (*Othello*, 3.3.266) has remained unexplored until recently because, as Keith Thomas puts it, "of all divisions in human society, those based on age appear the most natural and the least subject to historical change." Thomas goes on to argue that this appearance blinds us to the variant cultural meanings attached to aging. Tudor society was organized along the gerontocratic premise that old men should rule and young men should serve; at all levels, from parish to playhouse to palace, age and seniority helped determine rank.[61] This arrangement reflected the common belief in older men's superior powers of discernment and self-government.[62] An extensive discourse, which drew on classical works like Cicero's *Cato Maior: De Senectute*, elaborated on the gerontocratic ideal, legitimating the authority of elders by reference to their acquisition of the qualities necessary to governance, including "counsaile, wisedome, authoritie and pollicie."[63] Since good health and long life were considered the product of good judgment, moderation and self-regulation, Cicero argued, reaching a certain age constituted in and of itself a credential for authoritative office.[64] Such beliefs explain the preponderance of elderly counselors in plays, like *Hamlet*'s Polonius or *Coriolanus*'s Meninius. Still, the benefits that older men enjoyed were contingent on their ability to retain control over themselves and over their material circumstances. The most privileged class had arrived at the first stage or onset of old age, sometimes described as the "green and spirited" old age, a category which overlaps with our notion of the middle-aged, and to which all of Shakespeare's aging lovers, with the possible exception of Falstaff, belong.[65] The positive valuations of the elderly were also offset by ancient prejudices inherited from the warrior societies of the past, which placed a high value on the physical abilities of hale male bodies.[66] Such factors have led scholars like Thomas, Nina Taunton, Christopher Martin, Philip Collington, and Anthony Ellis to find that Tudor society was beset by a "paradox of old age," in which the idealizing constructions of official discourses conflicted with actual practices, or with "gerontophobic" representations in poetry and drama.[67]

Although they might appear gerontophobic, the satiric representations of lecherous older men that concern me in this book enforce behavior consistent with gerontocratic ideals.[68] Considerations of age determined what constituted natural behavior, shaped perceptions about gender and sexuality, and influenced relations among individuals. Alexandra Shephard calls attention to this often ignored "generational dimension of patriarchy," arguing that age was a key determinant of masculine status and privilege.[69] As Shakespeare's Rosalind reminds us, "boys and women" were considered "for the most part cattle of" the same "color." Rosalind's metaphor is revealing: "changeable, effeminate ... inconstant," lacking control over their bodies and the ability to regulate their emotions, boys were like women *and* domestic animals in requiring the supervision of adult males (*As You Like It*, 4.4.410–14). Under such conditions, full manhood was "a distinct phase in life," not a condition enjoyed by all men at all times. One corollary is that "patriarchal imperatives . . . constituted attempts to discipline and order men as well as women."[70] The proscription on sex after a certain age protected the privileged category of the older man by defining appropriate conduct. Given that "the race and course of age is certayne," men should observe a decorous progression: "For even as weakenes and infirmytie is incident to yonge Chyldren, a lustinynes and braverie to younge men, and a gravitye when they come to rype years; soe lykewyse the maturitye or rypenes of old age, hathe a certain speciall gifte, geeven and attrybuted to it by nature, which oughte not to bee neglected, but to bee taken in hys due tyme and season when it cometh."[71] For a mature man to take the role of the lover constituted an unnatural regression, which would return him to the effeminate condition of the boy, or reduce him to the state of a domesticated animal (sheep, asses, black rams, Barbary horses, and Bartholomew boar-pigs, to name a few relevant examples).[72]

Having waited to attain the perfection of full manhood, older men had to guard against aspects of aging to maintain it. Aging was considered a cooling process, in which "the natural heat, which is the source of the body's vitality, gradually diminished, consuming the natural moisture."[73] Insofar as this cooling meant that men—and women—became less subject to animal passions, it heightened their capacity for judgment and wisdom; according to the French physician Laurent Joubert, "youthful fury has run its course" in the old man, making him "wiser and more prudent."[74] Castiglione deems "old men" better equipped to transcend sensual desire and experience spiritual love than young men on similar grounds.[75] According to Hamlet, even women might benefit from the cooling effects of aging; "at your age," he tells Gertrude, "The hey-day of the blood is tame, it's humble / And waits upon the judgment" (3.5.68–70). Although the attrition of vital heat helped cooler heads prevail, if left unchecked, it became a source of concern for men because it threatened

INTRODUCTION

to make them like women and children.[76] Cicero, a major proponent of the virtues of aging, stresses the need to conserve "the memorie and reasonable parte of man, whyche is the mind," comparing it to "a Lampe, if to muche oyle bee infused into it, burnethe not brightly . . . soe likewise the mind is a like dulled & blunted, when the body is either overcharged wyth syperabooundance and surfette."[77] Sexual "surfette" was treacherous because it expended vital heat in vain. Older men were sometimes believed incapable of engendering sons, one reason perhaps that the sonnet speaker emphasizes the futility of his desire in Sonnet 138.

Although medical authorities disagreed about many aspects of senility, they agreed that sexual activity hastened its advent, a correlation conveyed through the word "dotage."[78] The destabilizing effects of erotic desire compounded that of advancing years, so that frequent sex might turn even young men old: "whoredome . . . dimmeth the sight, it impaireth the hearing . . . it exhausteth the marow, consumeth the radicall moysture and supplement of the body, it riveleth the face" and "induceth olde age."[79] Treatise after treatise urged men to delay senility by refraining from "immoderate venerie," which "hastneth on old age and death." For "an olde man to fall to carnal copulacion," one treatise claimed, meant "he doth kill a man, for he doth kill him selfe."[80] Cicero counseled men who wished to age gracefully not to "go against nature" lest they precipitate their decrepitude or demise; "let us therefore bid adieu to al such youthly prankes," he proposes, which belong to "lustye and greene headed Gallantes . . . agitated and pricked with the fervent heate of unadvised adolescencye."[81] When Shakespeare's aging males play the parts of untutored youths or young gallants, their language echoes the philosophical and medical discourses that policed senescent sexuality.

Superannuated lovers were an affront not just to nature, but also to society. Cicero supplements his allusions to natural cycles with theatrical metaphors, which signal a violation of social decorum, a refusal to "handle and playe" the "parte" appropriate to one's age.[82] Castiglione shares this preoccupation with age as a problem of decorum, devoting many passages to the question of how older men ought to behave. There is something unseemly about owning to sexual desire after the "young affects" had become "defunct," as Shakespeare's Othello acknowledges (*Othello*, 1.3.263–64). In his scene of judgment, Othello is primarily concerned with refuting implications of sexual incontinence, and for good reason.[83] Premodern decorum insisted on rigid protocols of age-appropriate behavior. Aging men had to maintain what Thomas calls "a dignified exterior" at all times, which meant avoiding "sexual competition with younger men. Lust in the elderly was an infallible occasion for ridicule and censure."[84] This condemnation recurs in all types of premodern works, from ballads, proverbs, epigrams, poems, and plays to scientific, philosophical, and moral treatises. The age limit beyond which carnal desires became suspect for men was low, moreover. Barthomolaeus Anglicus thought the proper time to father children was before age thirty-five, Sir Thomas Wyatt said his farewell to love before dying at age thirty-nine, and Petrarch placed himself at age forty in the tradition of the *puer centum annorum*, or the hundred-years-old boy, whose "most notable folly . . . was his desire to continue to have love affairs."[85] Since age was thought about in relative rather than absolute terms and sexual incontinence accelerated the processes of aging, the context of an active sexuality produced especially low chronological tresholds for categorizing men as old.

Even the fear of being cuckolded—a defining emotion for many Shakespearean males, including the sonnet speaker, Othello, and Antony—reflects anxieties about age-related social judgments, since cuckoldry was an experience to which older men were prone.[86] Joubert argues against the notion that old men could not bear sons to defend couples constituted of a young wife and an elderly husband from charges of cuckoldry and adultery. Although he notes that the wife's reputation suffered in these situations, Joubert focuses on beliefs about the aging husband's sexuality, the provoking offense.[87] Mark Breitenberg views the premodern obsession with cuckolding as a sign of patriarchal "regulation and scrutiny of women's sexuality."[88] This obsession also reflects a perceived need to regulate the behavior of aging males. By insisting that a young wife will turn to an age-appropriate lover, cuckolding scenarios imaginatively restore a natural, moral, and social order that the old husband's lust has violated. Such scenarios are a mainstay of classical and medieval literature, where the *senex amans* is an old husband who arrogates (or tries to arrogate) a desirable young woman to himself, as Chaucer's January does. Older husbands with young wives usurped a role that society had reserved for younger men—they did not restrict themselves to their proper "parte." Long before Shakespeare's aging speaker imagines himself playing the role of an "untutor'd youth" in an erotic triangle with an unchaste woman and a younger man, this behavior had been established as unacceptable, inviting all manner of retaliation, including the ridicule meted out in the fabliau tradition, the shaming enacted by charivaris, or the public disgrace that followed on accusations of cuckoldry.[89]

Although Shakespeare's theatrical representations of the *senex amans* diverge in telling ways from the traditional May-December marriage plot—Malvolio and Falstaff are bachelors, Claudius and Antony choose age-appropriate partners—they retain the emphasis on senescent male sexuality as a theatrical usurpation of youthful prerogative, a form of social transgression that incites public punishment.[90] This censorious attitude reflects the gerontocratic orientation of premodern society. If old age "hath in it so greate aucthoritye, that it is muche more to bee esteemed and is farre moore woorthe, then all the vaine pleasures of headye and rashe Adolescency," for an older man to behave like a young one amounts to a form of madness—a point taken up in some detail by *Twelfth Night*. Of course, some older men did give into "beastly, savage, and furious" lust, rather than give it up, as Cicero advised them to; actual behavior does not necessarily conform to prescriptive ideals, or there would be no need for such ideals.[91] Under normal circumstances, however, these men had little reason to expect that their sexual activity would lead to rewards other than momentary pleasure and they had every reason to expect that it would bring disastrous consequences, ranging from diminished social status to failing health to premature death. The older man wishing to indulge in the "expense of spirit" did indeed bring "a waste of shame" on himself (Sonnet 129.1), as Falstaff, Malvolio, and Antony find out.

The last two decades of Elizabeth's reign suspended these normal circumstances for the most visible and privileged men in the country. Her courtiers' abdication of conventional gender and generational roles had brought them what Hatton called the "singular blessings and benefits" normally associated with conformity to these roles—titles, land, high office, vast influence, great political authority.[92] In a remarkable 1572 letter advising Hatton to diverge from traditional masculine behavior, the courtier Edmund Dyer urged his friend "to consider with whom you have to deal, and what we be towards her; who though she do descend very much in her sex as a woman, yet we may not forget her place, and the nature of it as our Sovereign."[93] Leicester and Hatton took advice like this to heart, compromising on their "place" first as men and then as older men—delaying or forgoing marriage or remarriage, failing to produce heirs, playing the role of the lover—to accommodate Elizabeth's contradictory "place" as woman and sovereign.

That this unorthodox strategy proved successful challenged what Charles Taylor calls "the social imaginary": "the ways in which people imagine their social existence, how they fit together with others ... the expectations that are normally met, and the deeper normative notions and images that underlie these expectations."[94] Indeed, the singular virulence of anti-Leicestrian discourses—as D. C. Peck notes, "other counsellors were slandered but with nothing like the same enthusiasm, imagination, and perseverance"—suggests that the earl's continued hold on Elizabeth provoked *more* public concern than did that of younger men like Ralegh or Essex.[95] Like the man who dresses in women's clothes, the older man who plays the merry gallant disturbs sanctioned hierarchies by descending from a privileged "place" to a less privileged one. Shakespeare's sonnet speaker acknowledges as much when he places himself structurally on par with an unchaste woman. His self-awareness reminds us that deviance, viewed from a certain angle, can become defiance, and apparent futility a kind of triumph. Through its oscillations in meaning, Sonnet 138 executes a precarious balancing act, simultaneously condemning and celebrating its speaker's unorthodox sexuality. As such, it forms the perfect introduction to Shakespeare's fascination with the fraught figure of the old man in love, inspired in part by the Elizabethan court's experimentation with gendered and generational roles.

INTRODUCTION

In highlighting the influence on Shakespeare of the "great Planets" who orbited the monarchical moon, this book supplements historicist readings of Shakespeare that focus on what Susan Frye calls "the power struggle for the meanings surrounding the queen's female body."[96] This approach, which derives from the work of Stephen Greenblatt and Louis Montrose, has dominated accounts of the queen's impact on literary phenomena for three decades and highlights the anxiety and resistance that Elizabeth I provoked in her male subjects. Montrose's assertion that the queen's "pervasive cultural presence" was a "condition" of the imaginative possibilities explored by Elizabethan writers remains an enabling one, on which I premise my argument.[97] But I agree with Katherine Eggert that the new historical emphasis on masculine anxiety sometimes results in reductive readings, in which Elizabeth's "queenly influence" is met with "either authorial resistance" (good) or "authorial capitulation" (bad).[98] Elizabeth did not just cause "anxieties about male privilege up and down the line."[99] She also prompted some men to experiment with unconventional ways of extending their level of privilege. Like the Renaissance lyrics examined by Catherine Bates, the drama abounds in "figures who appear by choice to defy the period's model of a phallic, masterly," and rational "masculinity."[100] The fact that these characters expect their deviance to result in social, political, or even spiritual reward can be attributed to Elizabeth's queenship, which unleashed radical possibilities that we have yet fully to investigate. The negative views of Elizabeth's effect on the men around her prevail because of a critical preference for one kind of evidence over another: the scorn of the queen's detractors over the praise of her panegyrists, the career of the Earl of Essex over that of the Earl of Leicester, Shakespeare's *A Midsummer Night's Dream* over his *Antony and Cleopatra*. Indeed, the high value that new historicists place on political dissidence often aligns their arguments with the perspectives of the queen's disgruntled male subjects at the risk of extending the "venerable tradition of misogyny" that Montrose identifies as a dominant mode of opposition to Elizabeth.[101]

By returning men like Hatton and Leicester to their place in the story, I aim to highlight evidence of innovative cooperation between the queen and her male subjects instead. Judging by the characters I examine in this book, this cooperation sometimes strikes Shakespeare as a form of collusion and sometimes as a form of collaboration. A compromised figure, "age in love" is also a figure of compromise, valued by Shakespeare for the ability to find a midway between extremes. Shakespeare's lusty old men are all go-betweens: the sonnet speaker has one foot in the theater and one in court, Falstaff one in court and one in the tavern, Antony one in Egypt and one in Rome. The nuanced perspective afforded by these characters enables Shakespeare to move beyond the extremes of praise and blame endemic to early modern (and modern) discourses about Elizabeth I, to consider instead the emotional and aesthetic responses that the queen inspired. Writing about *A Midsummer Night's Dream*'s investment in art's "utopian potential," Hugh Grady contrasts the critical view of the play as "performing local and power-accommodating work in deference to the Queen" to his own. These are not mutually exclusive propositions; the same queen who prompted Shakespeare to "power-accommodating work" inspired his utopian fantasies.[102] To go from Bottom to Antony, as I do in this book, is to chart the gradual elevation of the age-in-love figure in Shakespeare's canon, an elevation that I argue reflects his growing appreciation of the Elizabethan court.

Throughout this introduction, I have used words like "debate" and "conversation" to highlight a fundamental premise of my argument, namely that Shakespeare's view of public figures is always in dialogue with that of others. Crucial among these is Lyly, who had a gift for the kind of diffuse political allegory that encourages speculation and discourages reprisals.[103] Maurice Hunt argues Lyly's court comedies "provide the only sustained dramatic precedent for Shakespeare's critique of Queen Elizabeth by means of allegorical mirror images."[104] While "critique" does not convey the range of perspectives on Elizabeth examined in this book, I share Hunt's conviction regarding the centrality of Lyly's influence on Shakespeare. An acknowledged source for *Midsummer Night's Dream* and *Merry Wives of Windsor*, *Endymion* sets a theatrical precedent for all the lecherous old men that concern me, which is why my first chapter focuses on it.[105] Shakespeare learned from this play how to fuse real and

INTRODUCTION

fictional figures, thereby inspiring what the prologue to *Endymion* calls "pastimes," a word that links what we refer to as the topical component of plays to other pleasures afforded by the theater.[106] As Lyly reminds us, allusions to political persons, events, or patterns do not necessarily reflect the writer's desire to align himself with certain factions, criticize certain policies, or intervene in public affairs. They also have entertainment value. Eager for the "journalistic news and topical comment" purveyed by plays, London audiences enjoyed playing at politics.[107] For the price of admission to the theater, even the disenfranchised might become knowledgeable consumers of political material, who "voted on what they liked or did not like."[108] In *Bartholomew Fair* (1614), Jonson's mocking scrivener draws up "Articles of Agreement" between spectators and authors that describe applause as a form of "suffrage." While granting spectators "their free will of censure," he also tries to prevent "any state decipherer or politic picklock" from searching out "who was meant" by various characters.[109] As this caveat—or is it an invitation?—suggests, early moderns tended to read "plays . . . analogically, often 'applying' quite exotic fictions to contemporary persons and events."[110] Playwrights may have had incentive to provide grist for their audience's interpretative mill, but catering to a taste for "pastimes" was risky, as Jonson and Thomas Nashe found out when their provocatively entitled *Isle of Dogs* (1597) led to Jonson's imprisonment.[111] In the aftermath of this affair, the Privy Council ordered "the common playhouses" struck down because of "lewd matters that are handled on the stages."[112] Although this order was never enforced, the council pursued a policy of tighter control over performances in the late 1590s, with "mixed success" and perhaps mixed motives.[113] Writers for the public theaters had ample reason to balance the commercial value of staging politically loaded material against the risk of offending their courtly patrons. Lyly's veiled allegories offered a model for attaining such a balance, which accounts for their enduring popularity with Elizabethan and Jacobean playwrights. Shakespeare, Jonson, and Middleton all recycle materials from Lyly's plays, including a bit of stage business from *Endymion*, in which a male favorite collapses on stage before his lady. This tantalizing pattern ran afoul of authorities only when Jonson abandoned the normal caution and made the lady "Elizabeth I" and not "Cynthia," "Gloriana," "Titania," "Cleopatra," or an unnamed fairy queen.[114]

Shakespeareans are often reluctant to allow "pastimes," because they believe censorship prevented playwrights from referring to specific persons or they are wary of following the "inglorious" path of forebears like N. J. Halpin, whose ham-fisted "equating of dramatic characters with historical personages" has not aged well.[115] Although this reluctance originates in mid-twentieth-century formalist approaches to literature, which sought to establish the timeless nature of Shakespeare's work by purging its timeliness, it has persisted even in the wake of the new historicism.[116] Taking David Bevington's cue, historicist critics prefer to find evidence of "ideas or platforms"—or, nowadays, political ideologies and discursive practices—in Shakespeare's plays over references to "personalities."[117] While few critics would, after Leah Marcus and Louis Montrose, contend that a Titania or a Joan offer no comment on Elizabeth I, many continue to approach the idea that Shakespeare's plays glance at public figures other than Elizabeth with suspicion.[118] Even Matthew Steggle, who argues that theatrical "personation . . . was a point of contention" throughout the period, cites critical consensus to exclude Shakespeare's plays from consideration.[119]

This resistance is rooted in values that have little to do with early modern politics, in which platforms or positions were invariably tied to personalities (as, for example, a radical Protestant agenda or an interventionist policy in the Netherlands was tied to Leicester). Nor does it reflect what we know about Renaissance aesthetics. Given that Jonson set himself the task to write plays "near and familiarly allied to the time," his famous praise of Shakespeare as "not of an age, but for all time," which continues to exert undue influence over Shakespeare's literary reputation, may have been tinged with irony.[120] Certainly Hamlet, who commends players for being "abstract and brief chronicles of the time," shares in Jonson's theatrical values; his warning to Polonius that the "ill report" of players should be avoided "while you live" (2.2.526) identifies court figures as proper targets for satiric representation on stage. Not surprisingly, the clearest statement of anxiety about theatrical personation in the period is from a high-ranking member of the court, Elizabeth's last favorite, the disgraced Earl of Essex, who worried in 1600 that "they shall play me in what forms they list upon the stage."[121] The earl's anxieties were well-founded. The representation of actual "gentlemen of good desert and quality that are yet alive under obscure manner" did occur.[122] If Jonson denounces the allegorical readings of "narrow-eyed decipherers," he also provides them with plentiful fodder for speculation.[123]

In this introduction as in the rest of this book, I draw on the early modern vocabulary for describing the timely content of plays, because this vocabulary helps to elucidate the nature and function of theatrical allusions. Richard Dutton sensibly proposes that the problem with most topical readings is that they insist on too precise a correspondence, when theatrical analogies were "incomplete, titillatingly so."[124] As his adverb indicates, ambiguous allusions to contemporary persons have a stimulating effect on audiences, then as now. While Téa Leoni's character in the television show *Madam Secretary* is not Hillary Clinton, she confronts similar situations, prompting comparisons to her historical counterpart. These comparisons are integral to the pleasure we experience in watching the show, a pleasure fundamentally cognitive in nature. When, as happened during the 2017 season of *Madam Secretary* or the 1624 run of *A Game at Chess*, an actual figure takes offense at a fictional representation, the relationship between the two may be more one of identity. The early modern "personate" implies such a one-on-one correspondence between fictional character and historical person. Other expressions, like "sport," "device," "glance," and "pastime" suggest more complicated processes are at work, however. The verb "glance," for example, means "to strike obliquely," to "pass by without touching," or "to allude or refer to obliquely or in passing, usually by way of censure or satire; to hit at, reflect upon."[125] "Glance" conveys an almost imperceptible touch (as opposed to a heavy-handed identification), a skewed perspective, and motivations that range from playfulness to aggression. An inferior discussing a superior in public might only "glance" for fear of repercussions; so Shakespeare's Adriana "in company often glanced" at her husband's abusive behavior (*Comedy of Errors*, 5.1.66).

INTRODUCTION

As this example suggests, early modern expressions for personal allusions emphasize a social dimension and consider their effect on real or imagined audiences (Adriana's "company"), including those constituted by authorities. When glancing at persons in an "obscure fashion," playwrights eager to avoid repercussions could apply principles of selection or concentration, thus making what Hamlet calls an "abstract." They could also fragment their target into multiple "forms," to use Essex's locution, or conflate several different targets into one form. Hamlet describes Luciano in the *Murder of Gonzago* not as brother to the murdered king but as nephew to the king (3.2.244): a reflection of Claudius's past actions, of Hamlet's future actions, and of the incestuous and murderous practices of the Danish court more generally. Hamlet can assert that the play contains no offense because it is not a perfect match for his intentions or for Claudius's crimes—ultimately, like all plays using glancing allusions, it allows its author to claim that "it touches us not" (3.2.242).[126] Glancing allusions are a form of *"functional* ambiguity," to borrow Annabel Patterson's phrase; they capitalize on the arousing effects of timely content while avoiding "directly provoking or confronting the authorities."[127]

Such allusions also encourage audiences to bring anterior knowledge to bear on matters set before them by the play. No matter what topic they point to, extratextual references stimulate an audience's cognitive functions, including those involving memory, asking members to participate in the play. References to analogic interpretation as a "sport" or "pastime"—the bearbaiting trope comes to mind, as we will see—suggest that such participation provided playgoers with an extra measure of pleasure. Like Castiglione's courtiers, whose ambiguous references to real persons provoke knowing laughter, playgoers express a shared understanding of proper regard for "time and place" when laughing. Positioned as competent interpreters, auditors can speculate about a range of possibilities and collaborate in the construal of meanings.[128] Where a one-one correspondence asks the audience to accept a playwright's criticism or praise of a historical figure, a more diffuse resemblance prompts comparative thinking; weighing how a particular character both is and is not like that public figure, audience members learn to form judgments of their own. Hamlet, eager to secure a judgment of Claudius, does not have his actors play the murder of his father. Instead, he has them play "something like the murther of my father" (2.2.595). The relationship between Shakespeare's age-in-love figures and actual Elizabethan courtiers also tends to be one of evocative likeness, the "fat meat" (*2 Henry IV*, epilogue, 27) on which such speculative judgment feeds, rather than absolute identity, food only for censorship.

When glancing references provoke communal "sport" or collective laughter, audiences are transformed into publics, joined together not just by shared emotions and experiences in the theater but also by the shared cultural memories that produce those emotions and experiences. As Marvin Carlson puts it, when we laugh at theatrical parody "the parallel response by our fellow audience members is evidence that they share our memory of the material whose comic iteration we are witnessing."[129] Carlson's emphasis on evidence indicates that participating in a theatrical public involves both feeling together and thinking together. What he calls the "memory machine" aspect of the theater, especially powerful in repertory theatres with continuity in personnel and audiences like Shakespeare's, replicates in theatrical terms the reflexive "circulation of texts among strangers" over time that Michael Warner argues constitutes publics.[130] For Warner public-making is a print-based phenomenon. As his emphasis on reflexivity suggests, however, human memory plays a fundamental role in linking texts over time. The theatrical "fashion" for "age in love" drew on printed pamphlets and books, and it drew on theatrical and cultural performances, prompting audiences to remember these varied "texts" and to compare them to one another, thus generating the common ground that brought them together as a public. Shakespeare's uncanny survival as an artist may derive from his ability to secure an enduring public by reproducing these effects within his own canon. When modern audiences watch Falstaff, they might catch a glimpse of Bottom's ghost, especially if the same actor has played both parts (as Will Kempe likely did). Early modern playgoers had a far richer series of predecessors to draw on, from plays, pamphlets, poems, and other sources.

INTRODUCTION

By reconstructing this context, I hope to shed light on how Shakespeare transformed timely material into timeless art.

The Earl of Leicester is a key figure in this book because he embodied a pattern of courtly behavior (of the erotic and upwardly mobile variety) for his contemporaries, who left an extensive written record of their reactions to him.[131] By the time Shakespeare joined in the debate about royal favoritism, both Leicester and Hatton had died. Leicester had made such an impact on the collective memory, however, that the "new" and "strange" conversation about him continued unabated long after his death. Shakespeare's attraction to these haunting and haunted materials reflects his interest in afterlives—in what makes certain events, patterns, or individuals so memorable that they earn "a place i' th' story" (*Antony and Cleopatra*, 3.13.46).

By remembering the extraordinary performances of the queen's suitors, Shakespeare's plays capitalize on their audience's conscious and unconscious associations for a variety of purposes. While we cannot know with certainty whom the playwright meant to catch with his "unsavory similes" (*1 Henry IV*, 1.2.79), it is possible to speculate responsibly about how these worked, especially given the metatheatrical moments that guide interpretation. Shakespeare's allusions often work in unexpected ways. They do not plead on behalf of a particular court faction or promote a particular political agenda so much as they encourage an expanded and expanding public to laugh, to take pleasure in reflecting on the Elizabethan regime, or to think through the ramifications of new modes of publicity. Taken together, the plays that concern me in this book also constitute Shakespeare's career-long meditation on the memorializing functions of the theater, a process that endows past individuals with a kind of secular immortality. While no eyewitness report testifies to the validity of connections that I make, three generations of playwrights reproduce a set of interlinked patterns with remarkable consistency. If I worry at times that I am becoming too much like Jonson's "narrow-eyed decipherers," I am comforted by the fact that I am in good company, since Shakespeare read Lyly's age-in-love tropes analogically and Middleton read Shakespeare's that way.

INTRODUCTION

Chapter 1 sets the stage for the rest of the book by situating the *senex amans* in the context of the Elizabethan court, where it came to accumulate the culturally specific meanings on which Shakespeare later drew. I examine the ways in which Elizabeth I's approach to rule caused her favorites to deviate from normative standards of behavior, thereby triggering unprecedented public concern. Opposition tracts like *Leicester's Commonwealth* and Cardinal Allen's *Admonition to the Nobility and People of England and Ireland* (1588) exploited these anxieties by depicting the queen's favorites as threatening, buffoonish, or animalistic figures. I propose that the scandal to which Lyly's *Endymion* refers is the crisis of publicity that ensued on the circulation of these slanderous materials to a broad public. Leicester in particular became subject to "all vulgar relations" and to the "libels" generated by "men in passion and discontent."[132] These attacks on the earl alarmed members of Elizabethan government, who felt that they compromised the regime as a whole. Where other critics contend that *Endymion* either praises or criticizes the queen, I argue that Lyly's "tale of the Man in the Moon" responds to "libels" about Elizabeth's courtiers, and that its main focus is on their behavior, which it aims to reform through its didactic portrayal of old men in love. Lyly's theatrical treatment of senescent male sexuality proved influential; despite their divergent approaches and affiliations, later playwrights and pamphleteers all present "old men lustful" as theatrical creatures, who in "show[ing] like young men" threaten normative values.[133] They also associate generational violations with other forms of usurpation, including that of class privilege and of monarchical authority.

Shakespeare's amorous older men dominated the public stage for over a decade after the publication of *Endymion*. In the second chapter, "Falstaff among the Minions of the Moon," I argue that Hal's favorite knight offers a provocative reflection of Elizabeth's favorite knights. My argument is rooted in posthumous descriptions of Leicester, who died in 1588, but had achieved a kind of cultural immortality. By repurposing key aspects of anti-Leicestrian materials, Shakespeare endows his fat favorite with the haunting qualities that have ensured his survival over the centuries. Of particular significance to the characterization of Falstaff are satiric depictions of the earl as a bear baited for his lechery. Although the baiting pattern is consistent across the three plays that feature Falstaff, it is most explicit in *The Merry Wives of Windsor*, where Shakespeare is uninhibited in his solicitation of "pastimes." The established connections among the queen, her aging favorite, and the theater also help Shakespeare make the lecherous old man a device for situating his plays in relation to the Elizabethan court. By encouraging comparative analysis, the Falstaff plays urge audiences to make political and aesthetic judgments, and thus to usurp the sovereign's position.

The third chapter argues that Falstaff's ghost haunts *Twelfth Night*. In this late comedy, Shakespeare experiments with the same materials in a different generic register, reflecting in the process on the consequences of the fat man's success. Multiple allusions to *Endymion*, the Falstaff plays, Ben Jonson's satirical comedies, and Sir John Harington's *A New Discourse on a Stale Subject, or the Metamorphosis of Ajax* (1596) establish *Twelfth Night*'s preoccupation with "th'unmuzzled thoughts" (3.1.118) of satirists. While *Twelfth Night* participates in the discursive processes it examines, it also records misgivings about doing so. The play strains against the conventions of satire by giving us a surfeit of amorous old men; where the portrayal of Malvolio accords with popular forms of anticourt satire, Shakespeare offers an emended portrait of the *amans senex* in Orsino. A new Endymion, Orsino embodies the generative and artistic potential of this protean figure by his nostalgic aestheticism.

The concluding chapter draws on preceding chapters to reconsider the relation between *Antony and Cleopatra* and the court of Elizabeth I. Although Antony is not often considered in the company of the other lecherous old drunks I examine, he is made of the same stuff. I propose that *Antony and Cleopatra* is a kind of eulogy in dramatic form, which conjures present emotions in an effort to intervene in cultural narratives about the transformative effect of queens on men. While Shakespeare hews to the facts in Plutarch's "The Life of Marcus Antonius," he does not encourage the conventional contemptuous attitude toward those facts. His Romans echo the antigovernment propaganda of the 1580s and 90s in finding that their general's "dotage o'erflows the measure" (1.1.1) and in characterizing the queen he loves as witchlike, but the play itself pushes us to more complicated and emotional reactions to its central characters. The nobility of Shakespeare's "mutual pair" (1.1.37)—upheld if the play is felt to be a tragedy and the protagonists deserving of the elevation that tragic status implies—counters prevalent attitudes toward gender, aging, and sexuality. Four years after Elizabeth's death, defect had begun to look a lot like perfection to Shakespeare.

CHAPTER 1

Endymion at the Aging Court

The modern critical focus on Elizabeth I's superannuated sexuality produces the odd impression that she had grown old alone; until the last decade of her reign, however, her most important courtiers and councillors were near contemporaries. The sense of misrecognition that comes with aging is central to the court dramatist John Lyly's *Endymion*, first performed for the fifty-five-year-old Elizabeth I in 1588.[1] Its hero awakes from a forty-year sleep mystified by his own transformation: "that this should be my body I doubt; for how could my curled locks be turned to grey hairs and my strong body to a dying weakness, having waxed old and not knowing it?"[2] Endymion's predicament—he is literally unconscious of his own aging—heightens the common phenomenon of "having waxed old" unawares, in a way that must have resonated with courtiers who had grown gray in the queen's service. Endymion continues to play the lover long after the role has ceased to be appropriate, moreover, a behavior that makes him the theatrical equivalent of mutton dressed as lamb. As this cliché suggests, those who fail to calibrate their actions and clothing to their age invariably invite ridicule, even if age-appropriate behavior and costume vary from culture to culture. For a variety of reasons—court protocols were set when everyone involved was young and the queen may have retained her sexual charisma into the 1580s and 1590s—Elizabeth's favorites found themselves assuming the indecorous role of the old man in love as the sixteenth century waned. Men like Robert Dudley, Earl of Leicester, and Sir Christopher Hatton thus drew unprecedented attention to the question of senescent male sexuality, and the widely held prejudices about age and sexuality described in the introduction of this book came to color perceptions of Elizabeth's court.

From the beginning of her reign, the queen had construed her relationship to her subjects in eroticized terms. Hannah Betts explains that the cult of Elizabeth was not a "performance confined to its star player"; instead, it "invited, indeed depended upon, a supporting cast of subjects, each defining himself as suitor to his monarch."[3] In this political drama, favorites like Leicester and Hatton modeled ideal reactions to the queen's presence, affirming her power through public displays of their own susceptibility to it. Leicester was represented, for example, as the holly bush Deep Desire, "furnished on every side with sharpe pricking leaves to prove the restlesse prickes of his privie thoughts," in George Gascoigne's description of the 1575 Kenilworth entertainments, which was reprinted in 1587.[4] The connotations of the word "pricke" left little doubt as to the nature of the deep desires that moved the elegant earl.[5] The only Englishman whom Elizabeth considered marrying, Dudley had publicly assumed the role of her lover in 1559, and he sustained it, with a few notable lapses, for nearly three decades until his death in 1588. He performed the role with singular verve and to singular effect, accumulating the lands, titles, monopolies, and offices that transformed him, the fifth son of an executed traitor, into one of the most powerful men in the country.[6]

Although favorites like Leicester and Hatton shared the traditional ambitions of the ruling class, their innovative approach to upward mobility outraged many contemporaries. The perception that these men deviated from normative standards of masculinity became more pronounced as they got older. In 1588, when a twenty-five-year-old man might expect to live to his late forties or early fifties, both Hatton and Leicester had entered the period of life known as green old age, which was considered most suited to governmental office. According to Cicero, aging well involved being delivered "out of the yoke of . . . sensuall lustes and voluptuous appetites," which made the "unripe administracion of unskillful yong men" hazardous to commonwealths. Older men were better equipped to govern than young ones because "prudence and pollicye" were the hallmarks of "old age" and because old age "dothe not esteeme nor care" for the "bestiall pleasures, and voluptuousness of the bodye" that move youth.[7] Since sexual desire was such a degrading experience for older men, the continued commitment of the queen's courtiers to the lover's role rekindled anxieties expressed earlier in the reign by John Knox, namely that "where women reigne or be in authoritie" men experience "suche a metamorphosis and change ... as poetes do seyn was made of the companyons of Ulisses."[8] For early moderns "unmanly degeneration" involved "a distinct hierarchy of descent from man to woman to beast," a trajectory dramatically enacted by the slippage of an older man from his position of supreme privilege on the scale of earthly beings.[9] These views explain the renewed allure of certain Ovidian figures as the Elizabethan age waned. Late sixteenth-century representations of "age in love" refer to Circe and Diana, charismatic goddesses associated with the transfiguration of men into animals, or Circe's niece Medea, the witch who turned the "furrowed wrincles" of Aeson into "yong and lustie flesh."[10] That these myths circulated in a printed translation by Leicester's protégé Arthur Golding, which was dedicated to the earl and bore his device of the bear and ragged staff on the title page, may have abetted the identification of mythic figures with court personalities.[11] While testifying to Elizabeth's enduring attractiveness, these allusions to Ovid also record misgivings about the transformational nature of her powers.

Opposition tracts like the anonymous pamphlet known as *Leicester's Commonwealth* (1584) and Cardinal William Allen's *Admonition to the Nobility and People of England and Ireland* (1588) certainly played on such motifs in their depiction of Elizabeth's relationship to her courtiers. Insofar as these works seek to appeal to "all true Englishmen," they cite not just their own "holie intentions" but a range of "just groundes" for resistance to the Elizabethan government.[12] Borrowing from the regime's own arsenal of tools, dissident writers sought to conjure something like a court of public opinion, defined in opposition to the royal court.[13] Descriptions of the "unspeakable and incredible variety of luste" indulged at court become one impetus to judgment, encouraging "all the worlde, and namely our owne nation and people"—not just fellow Catholics—to "judge" Elizabeth's "desertes."[14] In their efforts to discredit the queen, these tracts single out her greatest favorite, depicting Leicester as an elderly Lothario whose "carnal beastliness" surpasses that of Emperor Heliogabalus (infamous, not coincidentally, for cross-dressing).[15] Elizabeth's attachment to this allegedly ignoble creature shows by implication her failure in exercising good judgment and meeting standards of good rule. Contemporaries were quick to get these implications; one pro-government pamphlet terms the slanders about Leicester "seditious" and reminds Elizabeth's "subjectes" that they had no such "authoritie over her, as to bee judges of her just or unjust dealing, much lesse to make themselves correctors, or executors of justice against her upon their owne judgement, and at their owne pleasure."[16]

Although the attempts by exiled Catholic dissidents to have Leicester "called publicly to trial" failed to produce the hoped-for regime change, their portrayal of the earl nevertheless struck a chord.[17] By the late 1580s, the topic of Leicester's sexual and political activities had become something of a "flash-point," popular and provocative enough to incite attempts at government censorship.[18] Lyly's depiction of Endymion as an overreaching lover who fails to recognize the advent of old age borrows from this controversy. As Sara Deats notes, *Endymion* identifies "love with deformity"; in one case, a male character's love-induced "sleep results in senescence, in the other, bestiality."[19] Since senescent male sexuality registered as a form of bestiality, the two are in fact versions of the same degrading experience. By indulging in behavior appropriate to youths, Elizabeth's aging favorites showed the "certain deformity" that Castiglione argues is a primary "source of the laughable."[20] The controversies surrounding these men inform Lyly's representation of Endymion as a "poor gentleman," who has developed "grey hairs," "wrinkled cheeks," and "decayed limbs" while in Cynthia's "service" (4.3.78–80), and whose fidelity and love are called into question by the malice of slanderers.[21] While age does not diminish the queen's appeal in *Endymion*, her attractiveness risks placing men around her in positions unbecoming to their years, in a way that recalls yet another Ovidian figure, Tithonus, Aurora's aging lover.[22] Lyly offers Elizabeth's courtiers, confronted with an extraordinary crisis of publicity, a choice: they can emulate his protagonist, who learns to sublimate his passion for Cynthia. Or they can, like Corsites and Sir Tophas, reject the Neoplatonic solution and persist in "thinking that all that suits young men suits [them]."[23] In his treatment of Sir Tophas, Lyly adapts the satiric elements of the age-in-love trope to theatrical purpose, presenting superannuated male sexuality as a form of generational cross-dressing. The acerbity of Lyly's satire offers one measure of how high anxieties on the subject ran at the court of the Elizabeth I. Its influential nature—in the wake of *Endymion*'s publication in 1591, a horde of lusty old men took over the public stages—reveals that calling royal favorites to "accompt" did not just appeal to a minority of Catholic propagandists.[24]

That age was a loaded topic in the late 1580s and in the 1590s is hardly news: critics—especially male critics—have long claimed Elizabeth's aging mortal body strained her royal image. According to Steven Mullaney, for example, the eroticized discourses that shaped the queen's relationship to her subjects faltered when confronted with "the conundrum of the aging female body, with its over-determined registers of sexuality and death."[25] French ambassador André Hurault de Maisse's description of the sixty-five-year-old queen, in which he details her gaudy clothes, yellowed teeth, and wrinkled throat or bosom, has become a critical set piece, guaranteed to reproduce in modern readers the "contempt" that Louis Montrose claims characterized Elizabethan reactions to the queen's aging. The "theme of *mundus scenescit*" did pervade late Elizabethan political culture; however, even the most derogatory references to aging planets did not isolate Elizabeth for criticism.[26] Cardinal Allen asserts that most English men "will never adore the sun setting, nor folow the declininge fortune of so filthie, wicked and illiberall a Creature." But he also takes to task those "base and dishonorable" men who do "adore the sun setting," the "infamous amorous Apostats and heretikes" surrounding the queen, whose "insatiable covetousnes and concupiscence" has "made lamentable havoke, waste, and destruction." According to Allen, the Elizabethan "courte" is "a trappe" where for some "thirtie years together" the queen has through her "damnable and detestable arte... intangle[d] in sinne" gentlemen and nobles alike, giving England the reputation for "effeminate dastardie." Construing Elizabeth as a modern-day Circe, Allen testifies to her enduring power to cast spells: she holds her noblemen, her councillors and "the verie parliament itself" in "a wonderfull thralldo[m]."[27] The exiled cardinal does not show contempt for Elizabeth so much as fear—an important distinction, since contempt poses a far greater threat to authority than fear, as the queen herself realized.[28] Allen designates as the proper object of contempt those men entrapped by the queen who, Endymion-like, have remained frozen in their position of amorous adoration for years. Such men, the cardinal's allusions to the mythic sorceress contend, are not really men at all.

In 1588, when Allen's tract and Lyly's *Endymion* first appeared, Elizabeth had ruled for thirty years. Despite divergent perspectives, the queen's detractor and her panegyrist present the survival of her charisma as a sign of her supernatural power over men. What one calls defect, the other casts as perfection; Allen's Circe becomes Lyly's Cynthia. Perhaps the late Elizabethan moon cult, which *Endymion* popularized, emerged in response to contaminating images of the aging court like Allen's. Although Philippa Berry finds planetary imagery "unproblematic" because it does not "focus attention on the gender of the monarch," this imagery can evoke aging processes.[29] If Sir Walter Ralegh's *Ocean to Cynthia* presents Elizabeth as "eternally youthful," for example, the Tithonus-like speaker is subjected simultaneously "to his own old age and to the agelessness that he beholds."[30] Lyly's planetary allegory offers an alternative version of these themes. Far from denying that Cynthia is in the "latter minute of her age," Endymion paradoxically adduces her "ripe years" as evidence that "time cannot touch" her (1.1.60, 67). Montrose and Mullaney might find in Cynthia the dramatic equivalent of the paint that Elizabeth allegedly used to disguise her wrinkles.[31] But it matters that Lyly's praise depends on acknowledging, not on suppressing, the queen's age. In this regard, *Endymion* reflects Elizabeth's own rhetorical strategies more comprehensively than do modern portraits of her as a ludicrous old woman, whose "verbal, visual, and sartorial rhetoric" vainly attempted to project a youthful image.

Arguments that the queen's rhetoric could overcome neither her "inevitable natural aging" nor the "cultural perceptions regarding the impact of time and age upon a monarch who was an unmarried woman" are compelling because they blame the late Elizabethan malaise on the queen's aging body, thus endorsing our own "cultural perceptions regarding the impact of time and age."[32] We tend to view aging as a problem for women, specifically. This perception influenced Shekhar Kapur's decision to cast the thirty-seven-year-old Cate Blanchett as Elizabeth in the recent movie on the "Golden Age" (2007), opposite Clive Owen's forty-something Sir Walter Ralegh. By rectifying the age imbalance, the director suppressed the troubling evidence that much younger men like Ralegh addressed the fifty-five-year-old queen as their "true fantasy's mistress."[33] New historicists and historians often handle the difficulty that Elizabeth's age poses in a different way, assuring us that love is not love but disguised ambition.[34] "Later Elizabethan royal panegyric" was "pervaded by a distinctly cynical air," they claim, while praise of the queen's beauty was a "fiction," which became "harder to sustain" as the years passed.[35] The dominant scholarly view on late Elizabethan sexual politics preserves a modern sense of decorum by proposing that the typical male courtier swore that he was made of truth, and lied, so that his queen might think herself an untutored youth. The reluctance to allow the possibility that Elizabeth remained attractive, and that her courtiers remained attracted, thus reveals far more about modern "embarrassment" and "discomfort at the thought of the aging Elizabeth flirting" than about the dynamics of the Elizabethan court, or the perceptions of Tudor subjects on the matter.[36]

As we saw in the introduction, premodern authorities emphasized the incompatibility of senescence with male, rather than with female, sexuality. Medical handbooks did advise older people generally to refrain from sexual activity.[37] But in humoral theory aging was a cooling process that was more traumatic for men, whose superior heat distinguished them from women, than for women, who were naturally cold.[38] According to some models, menopause had a drying effect on women, moreover, which meant that older women gained in heat and became more like men, a theory that helped explain Elizabeth's continued vitality.[39] Where women's status was confirmed or even ameliorated by the changes that age wrought, men risked losing theirs. Accordingly, treatises describe aging as an exclusively male problem: they advise men who wish to "waxe yonge again" to avoid "overmuch venery" and other carnal excesses in order to conserve the "naturall hete" that distinguished them from their inferiors.[40] Not only did lecherous old men risk categorical degradation, they also violated social decorum; according to Castiglione, such "senseless fools" deserve "with perpetual infamy to be numbered among the unreasoning animals." Although this is rarely noted, Pietro Bembo devises his scheme of Neoplatonic love to help old men retain their masculine status by "check[ing] the perversity of sense with the bridle of reason." "The Courtier may be permitted to love sensually while he is young," Bembo argues, "but if later, in more mature years, he chances to conceive such an amorous desire" without sublimating it he "deserve[s] more blame than compassion." Old men who conceived sexual desire—and mental susceptibility was sufficient cause—demoted themselves to the status of boys, who found the ladder of love "hard to travel"; women, for whom it was "impossible"; or "unreasoning animals."[41]

While old men who failed to calibrate age and sexuality were judged severely, aging queens elicited more generous responses then than now. Modern scholars often encourage contempt for Elizabeth I by emphasizing the delusional quality of her feminine vanity. The discrepancy between the queen's actual age and her apparent age in famous portraits forms a cornerstone of these arguments, which derive from Sir Roy Strong's observation that this "withered, vain old lady of seventy" was painted with an "astoundingly rejuvenated face."[42] Like Christopher Martin, I think the focus on "the 'mask of Youth' convention" has "come to overdetermine modern judgments."[43] The adjective "vain," with its implications not just of excessive pride but also of futility, recurs with such frequency that it has become an epithet.[44] Yet, Janet Arnold demonstrates, the hard evidence fails to substantiate this charge: "the story of Elizabeth's vast wardrobe turns out to be one of careful budgeting and good organization, not wild extravagance and vanity."[45] And if Elizabeth's "visual ... rhetoric" sometimes did endow her with the "mask of youth," her verbal rhetoric conveyed a different picture, acknowledging and taking pride in her age.[46] In response to a 1586 parliamentary petition urging the execution of Mary, Queen of Scots, Elizabeth finds that she has "lived many years" but that after "twenty-eight years' reign I do not perceive any diminition of my subjects' good love and affection towards me." In such moments, she construed her advancing age as an asset.[47]

Indeed, Elizabeth routinely and with evident self-satisfaction called attention to the length of her reign. Her correspondence with male suitors often refers to her age. She self-deprecatingly describes herself to the Duke of Alençon as "the poor old woman who honors you"; she threateningly reminds James VI of Scotland that "we old foxes can find shifts to save ourselves by others' malice"; she gently admonishes the Earl of Essex that "eyes of youth have sharp sights, but commonly not so deep as those of elder age."[48] Elizabeth also deployed her age to rhetorical purpose with foreign dignitaries, including the Polish Ambassador whom she rebuked in Latin for his—and his king's—youthful presumption. This particular occasion in 1597 prompted much admiration from English courtiers. Montrose cites the line about how "the Queen was cankered, and that her mind had become as crooked as her carcass," attributed to the Earl of Essex by his rival Sir Walter Ralegh, as evidence of contempt for the aging Elizabeth.[49] Here is Essex, on the same body and mind, in a different tone: "what a princely triumph she had of [the Polish ambassador] by her magnanimous, wise and eloquent answer!... And sure her majesty is made of the same stuff of which the ancients believed their heroes to be formed: that is, her mind of gold, her body of brass ... when other metals break and rust and lose both form and color, she holds her own—her own pure colors which no other of nature can match or of art imitate."[50] Essex's assertion that other metals would have rusted by now references Elizabeth's advanced age, even as it records her transcendence of it. We are here in the realm of Lyly's Cynthia, "a mistress of ripe years and infinite virtues, great honours and unspeakable beauty ... whom time cannot touch because she is divine" (1.1.59–67). Such paradoxical praise acknowledges the queen's age, only to dismiss it as irrelevant to the force of her charisma, conveying an altogether different reaction to

Elizabeth's aging than do the more frequently quoted statements, which involve either the fictitious suppression of her age or the contemptuous insistence on it.

The latter are not representative of what we might call more immediate reactions to the queen.[51] To be sure, her courtiers were well aware that "despite the majestie and gravitie of a scepter, borne 44 yeare," it pleased the queen "to be told, that shee looked younge." When, in 1596, Bishop Rudd, calculating her age at sixty-three, "enterlard[ed]" his sermon with "some passages of Scripture, that touche the infirmities of Age," she was not pleased with his "arithmetick." Elizabeth recovered quickly, though, and found "the good bishop was deceaved in supposing she was so decayed in her limbs and senses, as himselfe, perhaps, and others of that age are wont to be."[52] Her contemporaries bore frequent witness to her extraordinary vitality; in 1600, the hunting queen, intent on killing "many stags and bucks," challenged her attendants because her "body endures more travel that they can."[53] Most contemptuous comments about Elizabeth's age are mediated by distance (the exiled Allen's tract), time (famous comments made by Ben Jonson, Francis Bacon, Godfrey Goodman, or John Clapham after her death), or third parties (the words that Ralegh and others attributed to Essex).[54] While Elizabeth's death may have licensed a franker discussion of the depredations that age had inflicted, these posthumous anecdotes also show a tendency toward revisionism, influenced perhaps by the events surrounding Essex's rebellion. Although Elizabeth's age exacerbated concerns about the succession, it does not seem to have inspired contempt until the "troubles" with Essex "waste[d] her muche."[55] In 1599, Thomas Platter reported that the queen "was most gorgeously appareled, and although she was already seventy-four, was very youthful still in appearance, seeming no more than twenty years of age. She had a dignified and regal bearing."[56] Platter's comment is typical in drawing attention first to the queen's advanced age (ironically, Elizabeth was only sixty-six at the time) and then to her successful transcendence of it by means of her splendid "bearing."

Although modern critics often find that the queen's age poses an insurmountable obstacle to continued attractiveness or enhanced authority, those around her did not necessarily find the "fiction" of love hard to sustain as the Elizabethan age, and its brightest star, waned. The "language of love ... [that] strengthened the bonds of affective allegiance" between the queen and her subjects had always been inseparable from the "demonstration of her fitness to rule."[57] While Elizabeth's long reign may have eroded her physical charms, it bore compensatory witness to her political acumen, a factor that accounts for the expressions of affection that she continued to inspire. The ever-astute Sir John Harington yoked the queen's ability to provoke affective responses in her subjects—to keep them in Allen's "wonderfull thralldom"—to the soundness of her political judgment:

> When she smiled, it was a pure sun-shine, that every one did chuse to baske in, if they could; but anon came a storm from a sudden gathering of clouds, and the thunder fell in wondrous manner on all alike. I never did fynde greater show of understanding and lerninge, than she was bleste with.

The first sentence is sometimes quoted as evidence of the queen's capriciousness even though Harington construes her "show" as evidence of acumen. Where Harington doubts the authenticity of Elizabeth's emotions, he is categorical about the emotions she inspired: "we did all love hir, for she said she loved us, and muche wysdome she shewed in this matter." Nor did these feelings preclude an erotic dimension. Harington records one occasion in 1594, when the "Queene stoode up, and bade me reache forthe my arme to reste her thereon. Oh what swete burden to my nexte songe!—Petrarcke shall eke out good matter for this businesse."[58] Judging by the "swete" confusion that she inspired in the caustic Harington, Elizabeth knew how to turn her frailty into erotic and political advantage.[59]

A self-described old fox, Elizabeth may have been something of a cougar avant la lettre. Perhaps the best evidence of the queen's enduring appeal, and of her own attitude toward her age, is to be found in the journals of Ambassador de Maisse—the source that critics rely on to generate their unflattering portraits of the aging queen. Montrose notes with wonder that, despite the queen's "bizarre" and age-inappropriate erotic provocations, de Maisse "eschews the opportunity for maliciously misogynistic commentary that his private medium allowed him."[60] This is an understatement. Not only do the journals avoid the judgments that Montrose makes, they testify to Elizabeth's lasting charisma. The journals clarify that the queen did not strive to pass herself off as young; rather, they show Elizabeth's "larger refusal to surrender to prejudice" about the impact of age "on her person or capacities."[61] Elizabeth never disguised her age from de Maisse: "she often called herself foolish and old," he recounts, "saying she was sorry to see me there, and that, after having seen so many wise men and great princes, I should at length come to see a poor woman and a foolish."[62] Anna Riehl argues that de Maisse understood this self-denigration to be an invitation to praise.[63] Instead of denying the queen's age, as we might expect, the ambassador urged the well-established correlation of age to wisdom. Pleased, Elizabeth replied "it was but natural that she should have some knowledge of the affairs of the world, being called thereto so young, and having worn that crown these forty years." These are not the words of a woman striving to pass herself off as younger than she is. If Elizabeth used age to trump gender in the matter of wisdom, she also exploited both age and gender for their association with vulnerability: she begged de Maisse "to consider the position in which she was placed; that she was a woman, old and capable of nothing by herself." Whatever the queen made of her age, she insisted on it, and on shaping de Maisse's perceptions of it to her own advantage.

Aware of the queen's rhetorical manipulation, de Maisse nonetheless fell under her spell. His familiarity with Elizabeth bred not contempt but admiration; the longer he stayed in England, the more unequivocal his praise of its queen became. Here is a typical passage: "When anyone speaks of her beauty she says that she was never beautiful, although she had that reputation thirty years ago. Nevertheless she speaks of her beauty as often as she can. As for her natural form and proportion, she *is* very beautiful" (emphasis added). On another occasion, he notes, "It is a strange thing to see how lively she is in body and mind and nimble in everything she does... She is a very great princess who knows everything." Still later, he tells her "that she did wrong to call herself old so often as she did" and notes to himself that "verily, save for her face, which looks old, and her teeth, it is not possible to see a woman of so divine and vigorous disposition both in mind and body."[64] The signs of age are recorded but subordinated syntactically and conceptually; what matters is Elizabeth's "divine and vigorous disposition both in mind and body."

The queen's reminders of her age prompted the French ambassador to consider her transcendence of the limitations that age imposes. Machiavelli holds that "princes become great when they overcome the difficulties and obstacles that are imposed on them," and that, if necessary, a "wise prince" eager to acquire "prestige" will contrive such problems in order to crush them.[65] By figuring her age as an obstacle, Elizabeth preempted criticism and generated an impression of her own greatness. Ever her student, Shakespeare adapted this strategy for his Richard III, who first labels his body as inadequate for wooing and then overcomes that obstacle when he woos his enemy's widow. The impression of greatness produced by such means depends on the politics of presence—on the virtuosity of the physical performance, on the audience's willingness to overlook, as it were, the visible infirmities of the body and to "see ... a vigorous disposition" instead. These transactions entail a willing suspension of disbelief, the successful suppression of simple truth (the queen's actual age) in favor of more complex truths (her ability to act "no more than twenty years of age"). The paradoxical praise that Elizabeth earned from a range of men suggests that this theatrical strategy, far from being vain, was effective at least some of the time. Like Enobarbus at the court of Shakespeare's Cleopatra, or Endymion at the court of Lyly's Cynthia, de Maisse found that age could not wither this queen, even though she described herself as wrinkled deep in time.

The same cannot be said for the men around the queen, and de Maisse notes with discomfort the advanced age of Lord Burghley, the most powerful man in the country, who, in contrast to the vigorous dancing queen, had to be carried around in a chair.[66] Celebrations of Elizabeth's transcendent beauty often mention her aging attendants by way of contrast, in a way that brings to mind Ovid's Tithonus. In Christopher Marlowe's popular translation, this "aged swain" complains that the goddess of dawn flees his bed, whilst "the moon sleeps with Endymion every day."[67] Although Ovid's Endymion remains eternally youthful, Elizabeth's lovers were not so lucky. An epilogue attributed to Shakespeare and performed before Elizabeth in 1598 praises her ability to make "new when old are gon," and imagines "the children of these lordes / sitting at [her] counsell bourdes" turning "grave & aeged" in her presence, for example.[68] Francis Davison's "Ode to Cynthia" similarly claims that "Times yong houres attend her still," while "All her lovers old do grow, / But their hearts they do not so."[69] Where Davison allows Elizabeth the wisdom of age in a youthful-seeming body, her male "lovers" retain youthful emotions even as they age, a far more problematic proposition, or so Marlowe's elegy suggests. Even a cursory survey of the relevant court literature indicates that the "conundrum" of the aging male body proved as challenging to court discourses as that of the aging female body. To cite a relevant example, Lyly departed from his sources to make his Endymion initially as vulnerable to the passing of time as Marlowe's Tithonus. Like Ralegh, who complained about having given up "our youth, our joys, and all we have" to be repaid with "age and dust," Endymion sacrifices his "golden years in hopes, waxing old with wishing" (2.1.23–24).[70] The charge of vanity—leveled against Elizabeth I by modern scholars—is often reserved for such aging courtly lovers, whose "long pursuit and vain assay" defy orthodox conceptions of masculine virtue.[71]

The disjunction between superannuated male bodies and the youthful feelings they harbored was a topic that critics of the court also broached in detail. Courtiers like Leicester and Hatton had always been vulnerable to slanders that characterized their promotions as violations of social hierarchies.[72] As they aged, their "services" transgressed other hierarchies as well. Allen's tirade against Elizabeth's "cheif councellers," guilty of "publike piracie and robberie bothe by sea and lande," culminates, for example, in an indictment of that speciall extortioner, whom she tooke up first of a Traitor & woorse then naughte, only to serve her filthy luste, whereof to have the more fredom and intrest, he (as may be presumed, by her consent) caused his owne wife cruelly to be murthered, as after warde for the accomplishement of his like brutishe pleasures with an other noble dame it is openly knowne he made awaie her husband; who now of an amorous minion advaunsed to highe office, degree, & excessive welthe, is becum her cheife leader in all her wicked and unwonted course of regiment.

In the Cardinal's view, the upstart earl owed his social standing to his prolonged devotion to the "filthy luste" of his queen. Although the "amorous" Leicester's behavior is excessive, it is also representative, since the queen has "abused her bodie" with "divers others." As "cheife" minion, the earl epitomizes the "brutishe" sexuality endemic at court.[73]

That an effeminate and animalistic subjection to women's desire could result in social and political elevation is one of the fundamental paradoxes of Elizabethan political life. Leicester embodied that paradox for a number of reasons, including biographical ones. The position of "male favourite to a virgin queen was without precedent," as Simon Adams puts it, so that Elizabeth and Leicester wrote the "job description . . . between them."[74] Although there is a tendency nowadays to distinguish Leicester from more obviously arriviste favorites like Hatton or Ralegh, the earl owed his status as a member of the nobility to the queen's "favor and countenance," a point not lost on the contemporaries who doubted that he was a "mette man" for high office and categorized him as an arrogant upstart.[75] These critics pointed out that Leicester was "noble only in two descents and both of them stained with the block."[76] And indeed, Leicester's father and grandfather—Edmund Dudley (ca.1462–1510) and John Dudley, Duke of Northumberland (1504–1553)—were among the so-called "new men" promoted by Elizabeth's father and grandfather. When angered, Elizabeth reminded Leicester of his dependence on her favor, describing him contemptuously as "a creature of our own . . . that hath always received an extraordinary portion of our favor above all other subjects even from the beginning of our reign."[77]

The queen gave all her favorite creatures animal names (Leicester was her robin, Hatton her sheep, and Ralegh her fish), a rhetorical move by which she monopolized the category of the human, thus trumping normative gender hierarchies and establishing herself as dominant.[78] Burghley, whom she nicknamed her "Spirit," was the one major courtier allowed the emblematic victory over animal passions crucial to the successful maintenance of early modern masculine identity.[79] But even his status was subject to revision. When he complained about other courtiers, Elizabeth teased her "Sir Spirit," noting that "your kinde (they say) have no sense, but I have of late seen ... that if an ass kicke you, you feele it too soone. I will recant you from being my spirit, if ever I perceive that you disdaine not such a feeling."[80] The habitual and often comical references in court letters to the queen's monikers indicate that her practice was well publicized (not unlike that of a recent American president). Her disgruntled subjects followed suit by deploying animal "comparisons" to produce the derisive laughter described by Castiglione.[81] The counterfeiter John Pole allegedly described Leicester as "the common bull of the Courte," for example, and numbered him with Ralegh and Hatton among the "carped [carpet] knights" who earned their keep because they "coulde doe beste & have been best weaponed."[82] As the bovine metaphor suggests, in the fevered imagination of less favored subjects, Leicester became an incongruous mixture of the hypermasculine and the submasculine. Age tilted the balance toward the latter view; by the late 1580s, English subjects had compared the earl to a whole menagerie of beasts, including bulls, robins (because of the queen's nickname), and bears (because of the Dudley family crest of the bear and ragged staff; see figure 1).

That the years were hard on Leicester did not help his case. Robert Naunton claims that having been a "goodly person" in his youth, "toward his latter end ... he grew high colored and redfaced."[83] In 1585, the French ambassador reached a similar conclusion: Leicester, once a "most handsome gentleman," had "become quite plump," an observation substantiated by William Segar's 1587 portrait of the earl.[84]

As the earl became old and grew fat, the lover's role he had espoused increasingly became a liability. Those eager to mock Leicester portrayed

FIG. 2. Portrait of Robert Dudley, Earl of Leicester, by William Segar (1587). By permission of Hatfield House Library and Archives, Hatfield, Hertfordshire, England.

him not just as "lecherous, treacherous, brutal and cunning" but also, more damningly, as bestial and "foolish."[85] The inconsistencies between Leicester's youthful ambitions and his actual achievements helped tarnish his public image. By the time Elizabeth agreed to a more activist policy in the Netherlands, and charged Leicester with the execution of it in 1585, he was old (at least by the standards of the day) and failed miserably.[86] Leicester accepted the title of governor-general of the Netherlands in 1586, thereby confirming allegations of misplaced ambition and earning himself a public reprimand from the queen. According to various sources, his stay in the Netherlands consisted, moreover, mainly of banquets and entertainments.[87] The combination of hubristic overreaching, sensual overindulgence, and military fiasco proved rich fodder to critics, who characterized the earl as a vain old man who had long promised far more than he could deliver, a "noble lecher / that used art to provoke," a "valiant soldier / that never drew his sword."[88] Summarizing a long tradition of such comments, Naunton claims the earl knew "to play his part well and dexterously, but his play was chiefly at the foregame"; in the matter of "his lance," he "had more of Mercury than of Mars, and . . . his device might have been . . . *Veni, vidi, redivi*."[89] The phallic innuendos, the emphasis on age and vanity, the conflation of (failed) sexual, military, and theatrical performance became staples of anti-Leicestrian lore.

The incongruous discrepancy between the earl's aging body and his indefatigable libido was first established by *Leicester's Commonwealth* in 1584. It depicts a ruthless and duplicitous man, comically given over to every behavior that, according to doctors, accelerated the processes of aging: excessive eating, excessive drinking, and "overmuch venery."[90] As Sir Philip Sidney observes, Leicester's detractors thought nothing of representing the "same man extremely weak of body, and infinitely luxurious."[91] One memorable passage describes the earl as a man who like

> old adulterers is more libidinous at this day than ever before, more given to procure love in others by conjuring, sorcery, and other such means. And albeit for himself, both age and nature spent do somewhat tame him from the act, yet wanteth he not will, as appeareth by

the Italian ointment procured not many years past by his surgeon or mountebank of that country, whereby (as they say) he is able to move his flesh at all times, for keeping of his credit, howsoever his inability be otherwise for performance; as also one of his physicians reported to an earl of this land, that his Lordship had a bottle for his bedhead of ten pounds the pint to the same effect.[92]

The artificial means—"conjuring, sorcery" and "Italian ointment[s]"—that hold up Leicester's flagging "flesh" so he can "move" according to his "will" establish his sexuality as a violation of both "age and nature." A theatrical prop of sorts, the ointment allows the earl temporarily to overcome his "inability" to turn in the sexual "performance" of a younger man.

To portray the queen's favorite as an aging man of giant proportions and appetites, *Leicester's Commonwealth* also offers up playful renderings of the Dudley bear and ragged staff, among the most common visual symbols in the period. This ubiquitous device originated with the Beauchamp-Neville Earls of Warwick, relatives of the Dudleys through female descent. The badge connected the earl's upward mobility with his matrimonial ambitions, since he assumed it shortly before being ennobled, at a 1562 meeting of the Knights of the Garter, when a majority of the Knights petitioned the queen to marry her favorite subject.[93] Meant to advertise his connection to the legendary King Arthur, the bear and ragged staff adorned Leicester's belongings, from books to buildings, from linens to letters, from servant's liveries to the earl's ceremonial armor. The device also appeared in the printed works by his many clients, and featured prominently in his courtship of the queen. In a 1570 letter to Elizabeth, for example, Leicester imagines himself her bear, "tied to your stake... in the bond-chain of dutiful service," begging her not to "muzzle" her "beast."[94] A gift that Leicester gave Elizabeth in 1573 made similar use of the muzzled bear to signal his devotion; it was "a fanne of white fethers, sett in a handell of golde... and on each side a white beare and twoe perles hanging, a lyon ramping with a white moseled beare at his foote."[95] In the splendid entertainments at Kenilworth two years later, considered his final bid for the queen's hand, Leicester included an actual bearbaiting (this event produced the most complete description we have of the sport).[96] Because of such factors, the heraldic Dudley bear came to refer to the earl in his aspect as the queen's lover.

Leicester's Commonwealth capitalizes on the familiar bear badge in a number of ways. It depicts Leicester as a predatory hypocrite who "feedeth ... upon our differences in religion, to the fatting of himself and ruin of the realm." The badge also proves a rich source of fat jokes: "you know the bear's love ... is all for his own paunch." And it helps recast Leicester's "service" in sexual terms, most notably when "the Bear shalbe taken to her Majesty's hand and fast chained to a stake, with muzzle-cord, collar, and ring, and all other things necessary, so that her Majesty shall bait him at her pleasure without all danger of biting, breaking loose, or any other inconvenience whatsoever." Used by the earl to signal his loyalty to Elizabeth I, the muzzled bear comes to signify instead his beastly subjection to the queen's "pleasure."[97] The bearbaiting episode reconfigures the earl's social transgressions as natural transgressions, thus highlighting the ways in which the sexual politics of the Elizabethan court violated "deep and unwritten rules about the kinds of behavior and eroticism that are appropriate to the public."[98] In its satiric recasting of the favorite-as-royal-pet motif, this passage also articulates a central paradox about Leicester, a "subject without subjection" who was at once immensely potent and publicly emasculated. The authors avoid direct criticism of Elizabeth I, enjoining her only to "turn her countenance aside" from her lecherous minion so that he might be brought to trial.[99] By depicting the queen as a Circean dominatrix, however, they present her unorthodox relationship with this "old adulterer" as a source of both threat and titillation.

The unprecedented popularity of *Leicester's Commonwealth* suggests that others enjoyed its portrayal of Leicester as an oversexed old man.[100] As Peter Lake notes, the tract presented itself as a rational debate among "loyal Englishmen of different religious persuasion," thus modeling "a discussion between men of good will" accessible to all.[101] The authors' surmise that "many subjects ... otherwise most faithful" bore the earl a "great mislike" because of "the excessive favor showed to this man so many years without desert" turned out to be accurate.[102] Even those who shared

Leicester's political commitments found the pamphlet's guilty pleasures irresistible; the Earl of Ormond caught Sir John Harrington reading it in secret and teased him about it in front of Leicester.[103] By spawning multiple imitations, *Leicester's Commonwealth* put into circulation what the ever-perceptive Sidney calls a "dictionary of slanders" about the earl.[104] The public chatter about the "musseled" bear who led "the princly lion anie waie semes best to his owne luste and liking" endowed the famous badge, inscribed with the Garter motto "*Honi Soit Qui Mal Y Pense*," with a peculiar irony.[105] As if in acknowledgement of this phenomenon, the 1585 French translation of *Leicester's Commonwealth* includes a frontispiece of the bear, chained to his staff, and baited by multiple figures, both high (the hand of God) and low (a peasant).[106]

William Camden confirms "that evill speakers tooke occasion to tugge and teare at [the earl] continually . . . by defamatory libels."[107] The frequently reproduced image of a great bear beset by barking dogs, which became a mainstay of anti-Leicestrian discourse, conveys the hierarchical nature of the attacks and the high level of public noise these generated.[108] Strikingly, the earl's "evill speakers" came from different backgrounds but shared a common vocabulary of ridicule. Critics of the earl's behavior in the Netherlands opined, for example, that the "bear he never can prevail / to lion it, for lack of a tail." And shortly after Leicester died in 1588, his theatrical troupe reported the cobbler William Storage for "leawd woordes utteryd ageynst the raggyd staff."[109] Storage was imprisoned for his offense, one indication that authorities saw such remarks as a threat, even when (especially if?) they came from a cobbler.

Elizabeth I's other councillors made common cause with the earl because they felt that the slanders against Leicester exposed the regime in its entirety to public judgment. Francis Walsingham pronounced *Leicester's Commonwealth* "the most malicious written thing that ever was penned sithence the beginning of the world," warning that its malice would taint all, including the queen.[110] Similarly, a government proclamation ordering the suppression of antigovernment tracts argued that works like *Leicester's Commonwealth* tried to make Elizabeth's government "odious and hateful" by inciting "obloquy and hatred" for "her majesty's principal

AV LECTEVR SVR
cette image.

Et Ours (Amy lecteur) que tu vois tant syl-
uestre,
Outrageux & felon, rempli de Cruauté,
C'est le Comte inhumain, le Comte de Lecestre,
Qui surpasse les Ours par sa ferocité.

FIG. 3. *Discours de la Vie Abominable, Ruses, Trahisons ... Desquelles a Usé et Use Journellement my Lorde de Lecestre* (1585), 2r. RB606530, The Huntington Library, San Marino, California.

noblemen, councillors, judges, and ministers of justice."[111] Picking up on the dissidents' desire "to bark at the Bear that is so well britched," Sidney pointed out in defense of his uncle that "the wolves that mean to destroy the flock hate most the truest and valiantest dogs" and that those who "persecuted . . . councillors" never ceased "before they had as well destroyed the kings themselves."[112] Sidney never published this document, probably because the government was anxious about further printed "disputation on the subject of the Earl's morals."[113] The Privy Councillors thought, in other words, that the public debate about one of their own posed in and of itself a threat to the queen's authority.

The authors of anti-Leicestrian tracts had put the earl on "trial" for his "deserts towards his country," encouraging their readers to pass judgment and thus to participate in what Michael Warner calls "the being of the sovereign."[114] Appalled, the Elizabethan regime resorted to prohibition and censorship to regain control of the conversation. On December 16, 1584, the government tried and failed to get a bill against "scandalous libelling" through the House of Lords. The following March it tried and failed to get similar legislation passed in the House of Commons.[115] A few months later, in June 1585, the Privy Council issued a letter demanding still stricter suppression of the "seditious and traitorous books and libels," in which "her Majesty" took specific exception to the "slanderous and hateful matter against [her] very good lord the Earl of Leicester" and "declare[d] . . . his innocence to all the world." Tellingly, the letter imagines the "malicious, false, and slanderous" accounts of the earl widely "dispersed and spread abroad" by "contemptuous persons" to the general public. The Privy Council framed the controversy about Leicester as a new kind of crisis, in which an explosive and transformative mode of political communication ("the slanderous devices against the said Earl") encouraged an infinite public ("all the world") to think itself more discerning than "her Majesty," who in retaining the earl's services had allegedly "failed in good judgment and discretion." The word "devices," used to convey the proliferation of these slanderous materials, evokes both the mechanical reproduction associated with print technology and the heraldic emblem satirized in the attacks on Leicester.[116]

Lyly's *Endymion* ends on a parable about "a man walking abroad, the wind and sun [striving] for sovereignty." Although the wind blows hard, tearing at the man's coat, he is forced to concede victory to the sun, whose warmth succeeds where the wind's bluster failed. The wind, the epilogue hastens to explain, is a "storm" instigated by the "malicious that seek to overthrow us." The "sun" is the Aurora-like Elizabeth I, the "dread sovereign" whose "favourable beams" cause all, court and cast alike, to kneel submissively at her feet (1–16). Although other versions of this parable exist, Lyly's interpretation of it—his association of the wind with the spiteful rumors, "tattling tongues" (4.1.22), and "wolves barking at . . . Cynthia" (5.1.132) referenced in the play, of the sun with the transformative qualities of the queen's favor, of the contest between them as one over sovereignty—is unique.[117] At least one reader of *Endymion* latched on to this interpretation; when he imagines turning his "storm-beaten face" to the sun, Shakespeare's speaker reproduces the parable's association with sexual "disgrace" and "shame" (*Sonnets*, 34.6–9).[118] Scholars have long noted that Lyly's play seems prompted by a court-related scandal, although efforts to connect the play to specific events have faltered thus far.[119] If Lyly's prologue coyly invites the very "pastimes" it rejects as inappropriate (7), the epilogue, by echoing the documents relating to the suppression of *Leicester's Commonwealth* and other pamphlets, points to a relevant "pastime": the controversies that attended the court's alleged defiance of "age and nature."[120] In Endymion, Lyly provides a model for silencing the howling of the wolves, the pervasive gossip that *Leicester's Commonwealth* characterized as "the tempest of men's tongues, which tattled busily" of Leicester's "actions and affairs."[121] Endymion is a figure of "age in love," reclaimed and redeemed from scurrilous conjecture or "spite" (4.3.158), fortified against "the malicious" tongues who do "but stiffen our thoughts and make them sturdier in storms" (epilogue, 11–13). Kneeling before Elizabeth, speaking in the first person plural, the actor delivering the epilogue insists on the representative nature of Endymion's experiences, while his phallic metaphors assert, against the "wind" (9) of rumor, the compatibility of masculine virtue and service to the queen.[122]

While *Leicester's Commonwealth* made Leicester an embodiment of "age in love" to a broad reading public, matters were more complicated at court, where the earl's contemporaries also played the role of lover in vain, and where the problem of aging male sexuality needed to be addressed with corresponding delicacy. The queen's "lovers" were all still alive in 1588, when *Endymion* was staged at court: Hatton was forty-nine, Leicester fifty-five, Walsingham fifty-six, and Burghley sixty-nine. The Earl of Oxford, Lyly's patron, was thirty-eight—younger than the others, but by no means a spring chicken, at least by the standards of Tudor England, where the average life expectancy at birth was thirty-seven.[123] The cast of Lyly's play reflects the preponderance of aging men at court; it calls for at least five, and arguably more, old men.[124] Despite (or perhaps because of) the prologue's disavowal of topical allusion, scholars have expended much energy in trying to link these male characters with historical persons.[125] An "ancient man" who appears to Endymion in a dream, for example, might represent Lord Burghley.[126] Geron could be the Earl of Shrewsbury, and Eumenides the Earl of Sussex.[127] Sir Tophas, the braggart soldier whose amorous adventures constitute the subplot, has been associated with Gabriel Harvey and Philip II of Spain.[128] Corsites, the captain who first guards and then marries Tellus, Cynthia's rival and double, may be Sir Henry Lee, the queen's old champion, who first guarded and then bedded Anne Vavasour; or Sir Amyas Paulet, who last guarded but most assuredly did not bed Mary, Queen of Scots.[129] Endymion himself might refer to James IV of Scotland, Leicester, or Oxford.[130] In short, everyone who was anyone in late Elizabethan England had reason to see himself in the gray-bearded boy actors of Lyly's play.

As the general nature of his allegory suggests, Lyly extends the trope of "*mundus scenescit*" to the collective plight of aging Elizabethan courtiers. That rival arguments identify Endymion with Leicester and Oxford reveals just how capacious Lyly's mirror is, for these two were from different generations, belonged to distinct court factions, and had different religious affiliations (even if Leicester had allegedly enjoyed Oxford's feminine "leavings").[131] The details of Endymion's case—he loves Cynthia, he makes a mistake, he falls out of favor, he spends time in exile, he returns to Cynthia's good graces—accord with the contours of most courtly careers, including Leicester's, Oxford's, Hatton's, Ralegh's, and Lee's.[132] Given this indeterminacy, Sallie Bond argues that Lyly's hero functions as an "Everycourtier," "prisoner of his own emotional role" as Petrarchan lover.[133] But Endymion's *cri de coeur* to Cynthia—"Have I not spent my golden years in hopes, waxing old with wishing, yet wishing nothing but thy love?" (2.1.23–25)—expresses frustration not just with having to play the role of the lover but also with having to play it into his sunset years.

Growing old posed an occupational hazard for Elizabeth's favorites, who could not heed medical advice to make "an ende of bodily luste" despite their need to secure a reputation for "good counsaille."[134] Noting that Cynthia's "wavering, waxing, and waning" (1.1.39–40) does not affect her dazzling beauty, Lyly's play concentrates instead on how her senescent courtiers might "cease off . . . to feed so much upon fancies" and avoid a "dotage no less miserable than monstrous" (1.1.28–30). According to Cicero, "libidinous volupte" is a quality "founde in younge men" but when "this folishnes . . . entangleth and captivateth the senses of old men" who are "light witted, & keep not them selves within the limittes of reason" it "is commonly called Dotage."[135] When applied to Endymion's feelings for Cynthia, the word emphasizes the convergence of senility and sexual infatuation, casting aging as a problem for the men attracted to the moon goddess, rather than for the moon goddess herself. Lyly turns to Castiglione's Bembo, who holds that the elderly courtier can be "inflamed with those loves that are sweet without bitterness," for a solution: his hero narrowly avoids a "monstrous" fate by pursuing an "unspotted" and age-appropriate love (5.4.167) for Cynthia, thereby abiding by court protocols without violating generational decorum.[136]

Although scholars often attribute Lyly's choice of myth to his interest in arcane philosophical allegories, the Endymion myth also served Elizabethans to comment on the adulterating intimacy between monarchs and their favorites. At least one tradition emphasized carnal interpretations of the central relationship.[137] In what may be the first Shakespearean allusion to this myth, Alice Arden testifies to its associations with upward mobility and sexual favoritism when she compares Endymion to her lover, the upstart Mosby: "Had chaste Diana kissed him, she like me / Would grow lovesick, and from her wat'ry bower / Fling down Endymion and snatch him up."[138] The disparity in status between the moon goddess and the shepherd recalled that between Elizabeth and her "amorous minions," especially those perceived as "base and unpure persons" awarded "the highest honors and most profittable offices of her courte and cuntrie."[139] Elizabeth's courtiers themselves used the myth to comment on patterns of disgrace and return to favor. In the wake of the Vavasour affair, the elderly Lee played a sleeping knight awakened by the queen in a 1592 entertainment at Ditchley, for example. Other subjects relied on the myth to speculate about the queen's preferences for certain lower-born male courtiers. So Spenser imagines a "Cinthia" who once "didst love / though now unthought, / And for a fleece of woll, which privily, / The Latmian shepherd once unto thee brought / His pleasures with thee wrought."[140] The oblique allusion is to a version in which Endymion and the moon consummate their relationship and produce children—and to prevalent rumors about Elizabeth's children by Leicester, or, given the "fleece of woll," by Hatton, whom she had nicknamed her bellwether or sheep.[141]

Sir Francis Bacon certainly saw Endymion's story as a "fable" about princes and their favorites:

> For princes... do not easily admit to familiar intercourse men that are perspicacious and curious, whose minds are always on the watch and never sleep; but choose rather such as are of a quiet and complying disposition, and submit to their will without inquiring further, and shew like persons ignorant and unobserving, and as if asleep; displaying simple obedience rather than fine observation. With men of this kind princes have always been glad to descend from their greatness, as the moon from heaven.

Endymion's sleep stands not for philosophical contemplation, here, but for the willing abdication of masculine prerogative, the adoption of an unreasoning position of submission, in exchange for royal "favours."[142] Bacon associates the waking state with rationality, curiosity, and perspicacity, while sleep connotes a descent into ignorance, a return to what Garrett Sullivan calls "vegetable and animal life."[143] As Bacon construes the part, moreover, the ideal favorite acts like the ideal woman—he is "quiet," "complying," "ignorant," and "obedient."[144]

Lyly has more empathy and admiration for "men of this kind" than does Bacon. Like all royal favorites, Endymion finds early in the play that his thoughts are "stitched to the stars . . . much higher . . . than I can reach" (1.1.5–7). Eumenides regards Endymion's amorous ambitions as "vanities" (1.1.34), since "things immortal are not subject to affections" (1.1.9–10), but the play compares its hero favorably to his friend. Where one has "greatness of . . . mind," the other's "fortunes . . . creep on earth" (1.2.18; 1.1.84). Endymion's "greatness" exacts a price, however, since "traps" await those who love "one that all the world wondereth at," making them "unfortunate" (1.2.90–94). *Endymion* highlights the sacrifices demanded of favorites, including their renunciation of normal masculine prerogatives, like the right to marry and produce heirs. When scandalous rumors cause him to fall out of favor, Endymion asks the absent Cynthia,

> Wouldst thou have me vowed only to thy beauty and consume every minute of time in thy service? Remember my solitary life, almost these seven years. Whom have I entertained but my own thoughts and thy virtues? What company have I used but contemplation? Whom have I wondered at but thee? Nay, whom have I not contemned for thee?
> (2.1.14–19)

Endymion's questions are rhetorical; like Elizabeth, Cynthia expects her favorite to forgo all others. Although she assures Endymion that her "princely favour" (5.4.168) will bring its own benefits—"thou shalt find that Cynthia shineth not on thee in vain" (5.4.186–87)—these do not include the traditional rewards of comedy, namely legitimate children and marriage, since Endymion is excluded from the festive weddings at play's end.

Cynthia's disclaimer notwithstanding, the favorite's commitment to the "solitary life" struck many as a "vain" form of sexuality, a perception exacerbated by the passing years. "Great princes' favorites" are "but as the marigold at the sun's eye," in Shakespeare's telling metaphor (25.5–6). "In favor with their stars," they can boast of "public honour and proud titles" but leave no children behind (25.1–2), which is why the speaker urges the young man to emulate the reproductive habits of the rose instead. Marriage and begetting children were "essential to the achievement of patriarchal manhood in early modern England."[145] Allen appeals to this view when he writes with scorn about the men who committed to the "single lyfe to the danger of their soules, and decay of their famelies, to attend her [that is, Elizabeth's] pleasure."[146] Although *Endymion* lacks Allen's contemptuous emphasis on waste and futility, it highlights the same deviations from masculine norm. The "restored" Endymion secures the right to bask in Cynthia's favor only by becoming the exception to the comic rule that has "all parties pleased" through marriage (5.4.211–12).

The concerns that *Endymion* raises regarding the "solitary life" of the favorite target certain members of the play's original court audience. Hatton might have stood model for Endymion in that he had "divorc[ed] himself . . . from the amiableness of all ladies" to feed on his monarch's "favour" (2.1.44–47): "I have most entirely loved your person and service," he wrote to Elizabeth, "to the which . . . I have everlastingly vowed my whole life, liberty, and fortune . . . God knoweth I never sought place but to serve you."[147] Although this decision brought him considerable status, Hatton had no children who might benefit from his success. By cultivating the queen's favors, Elizabeth's favorites assured their social and political elevation but risked canceling out other aspects of their identity. The queen's men were aware of the risks they took "to attend her pleasure." Explaining to his mistress, Lady Sheffield, why he could not marry her, Leicester noted that

> you must think hit ys some marvelous cause that forceth me thus to be cause almost of the ruyne of my none [own] howse . . . yf I shuld marry I am seuer never to have favor of them that I had rather yet never have wyfe than lose them, yet ys ther nothing in the world next that favor that I wold not gyve to be in hope of leaving some children behind me, being nowe the last of our howse.[148]

The demand that he give up "hope of leaving some childern behind" ultimately proved too much; in 1579, the earl secretly married Lettice,

Countess of Essex, cousin and look-alike of his queen. Leicester was devastated when his young son, born of that union, died in the summer of 1584, shortly after the publication of *Leicester's Commonwealth*. Acknowledging that the "love of a child be dear," Hatton reminded Leicester in his letter of condolence that "of men's hearts you enjoy more than millions," given his status as "a grave and faithfull Councillor; a pillar of our long-continued peace; a happy nourisher of our most happy Commonwealth."[149] In his response Leicester pronounced himself a "true and faithful man to [Elizabeth] for I have lived and so will die only hers."[150] It is habitual to read such hyperbolic statements cynically, but Leicester had nothing to gain by portraying himself as the queen's devoted lover to Hatton, who also portrayed himself that way. Rather, their letters suggest that a camaraderie developed between these men who had started out as rivals, born of the sacrifices that they had made for their "marvelous cause."[151] Elizabeth might have been, like Lyly's Cynthia, "jealous . . . careless, suspicious, and secure," but Hatton and Leicester nevertheless reckoned themselves, like Endymion, her "fish . . . which at [her] waxing is as white as the driven snow and at [her] waning as black as the deepest darkness" (2.1.31–37).

Or Hatton reckoned himself her flesh and Leicester her fowl. Ralegh was her fish. While Lyly's animal similes are often viewed in terms of his stylistic innovations, they also mimic court discourse in their allusions to Elizabeth's pet names for her favorites.[152] When Hatton felt eclipsed by Ralegh, Elizabeth reassured the older man that "the water, and the creatures therein, do content her nothing so well as you ween, her food having been ever more of flesh than fish," and she pronounced Hatton, her "*pecora campi*" far "more contenting to her than any waterish creatures."[153] At court, the representation of a moon goddess whose "authority commandeth all creatures" had a way of implicating actual individuals (1.2.34).[154] When Sir Tophas's "honour" compels him to declare war on the "monster *ovis*"—"a black enemy with rough locks—it may be a sheep, and *ovis* is a sheep" (2.2.96–98)—courtiers surely thought of the swarthy Hatton, who described himself in letters as her "Majesty's sheep and most bound vassal" or, more prosaically, as her "Mutton."[155] To an audience attuned to "analogical reading," the conflict between Sir

Tophas and the "monster *ovis*" must have parodied the rivalries between Elizabeth's favorites.[156]

When the "bewitched" (1.1.88) Endymion identifies himself as Cynthia's tamed fish, or when Sir Tophas proposes to do battle with his "black and cruel enemy" (2.2.88), we might not only hear an allusion to Ralegh, Leicester, or Hatton, but also to Circe, the mythic sorceress who transfigures men into animals. Tellingly, Lyly compares the position of the courtier to that of a domesticated animal, like a squirrel carried by a gentlewoman "in a chain"—strange "what things are made for money" (2.2.148–50).[157] Cynthia's vocabulary of power draws on the process of domestication; she threatens, for example, to "tame" the "tongues" and "thoughts" of unruly subjects (3.1.17–18). Reacting to Semele's failure to submit, Cynthia also resorts to verbal brutality, with the promise of actual brutality to follow: "Speaks the parrot? She shall nod hereafter with the signs. Cut off her tongue, nay, her head, that ... will not be persuaded!" (5.4.224–27). Like Elizabeth, who was fond of bridling, muzzling, and collaring metaphors, Cynthia uses animal metaphors as a rhetorical means of securing her own authority, while ensuring what Bacon calls a "complying disposition" in her courtiers.[158] Cynthia's palace thus resembles "Circes dwelling place," where "Lyons, wolves and beares" welcome visitors with "gentle looke," "fawning feete," and "wanton tails."[159] In its depiction of its dominating and dehumanizing moon goddess, *Endymion* flirts with the construction of Elizabeth as Circe found in tracts like Allen's.[160]

The affinity of Cynthia to Circe attests to the queasy "proximity" of "praise and blame" in Elizabethan political discourse, a consequence of the queen's transformation of apparent weaknesses like age or gender into political assets.[161] This affinity marks a fault line, where the representations of loyal subjects converge with those of treasonous critics. George Chapman's "Hymnus in Cynthiam" offers a case in point. It denies that Cynthia's interest in Endymion is carnal, noting that she affects him "for his studious intellect." But it also concludes with a request that Cynthia "execute a Magicke miracle: / Slip everie sort of poisond herbes, and plants, / and bring the rabid mastiff to these hants." As Helen Hackett notes, Chapman's dream here becomes a "nightmare," which casts Elizabeth as a Circe-like enchantress surrounded by "rabid mastiffs"—the dogs used, not coincidentally, in bearbaitings.[162] In their attempt to mobilize all "true Englishmen" against the Elizabethan regime, anticourt polemicists had, it seems, expressed concerns about the queen's transformative "favour" shared by even her most devoted courtiers. So Leicester's planned entertainments at Kenilworth included a play that figured Elizabeth as a type of Diana but concluded with a more ominous Ovidian vision of the queen who had "turned and converted" various courtiers, including her host, "into most monstrous shapes and proportions. As some into fishes, some other into foules."[163] Hatton, in a similar vein, opined that "The Queene did fishe for men's souls, and had so sweet a baite, that no one coude escape hir network"; in truth, Harington explains, "she knew every one's parte, and by this *fishing* . . . she caught many poor fish, who little knew what snare was laid for them."[164] Like Shakespeare's Cleopatra, Elizabeth used a "bended hook" to draw up her male favorites, transforming these "Tawny-finned fishes" in the process (*Antony and Cleopatra*, 2.5.13–14). Wielded by Elizabeth's favorites, the "poor fish" susceptible to her charms and traps, transfiguration metaphors celebrate the queen's power while expressing lingering anxieties regarding its effects.

The passing years can only have exacerbated the experience of deformity or degradation associated with being Elizabeth's "fish." It was one thing for Leicester to present himself as "Deep Desire," who had undergone "a strange and cruel metamorphosis" at the queen's hand in 1575. It was quite another thing for this image of Leicester to circulate again in 1587, when Gascoigne's description of the "pleasures" at Kenilworth was reprinted. The claims that no "delay could daunt [the earl], no disgrace could abate his passions" had by then acquired unpleasant new connotations.[165] The reappearance of the "Princely Pleasures" must have abetted widespread perceptions of the earl's vanity, since the hopes it expressed—that the queen might marry and might marry the earl—had proved decisively futile. "The stately cedar whose top reacheth unto the clouds" had by then indicated her intention never to bow her "head to the shrubs that grow in the valley" (2.2.104–6).[166] Insofar as Leicester was still presenting himself as Deep Desire, he had, like Endymion, slept "out his youth and flowering time and become dry hay before" he knew himself "green grass" (2.3.37–39).

The late Elizabethan moon cult channeled the anxieties generated by the exceptional position of men at the aging court in a productive fashion, emphasizing the control that these men could exert in reshaping their responses to their confounding queen. While it may be true that works like *Endymion* portray "the victimisation of the male courtier" at the hands of "the unnatural woman at the centre" of Elizabethan culture, they do not present these courtiers as "powerless."[167] Instead, the moon cult translated into the court's own idiom the Neoplatonic injunction that elderly courtiers learn how to "check the perversity of sense with the bridle of reason." Ralegh draws on a number of related concepts when he distinguishes Elizabeth/Diana from Circe, for example: "A knowledge pure it is hir [Diana's] woorth to know, / With Circes let them dwell, that thinke not so."[168] His contrast implies a basis for comparison; the difference between Diana and Circe does not inhere in the goddesses but in male reactions to and perceptions of them. Ralegh's oblique allusion to Actaeon reminds us that Diana, like Circe, can turn men into beasts, a scenario courtiers avert by policing their thoughts, sublimating their sexual impulses, and restricting their ambitions to "knowledge pure."

In her classic essay on Petrarchan uses of the Actaeon myth, Nancy J. Vickers describes the myth in Freudian terms, as revealing the anxieties that "powerless men (male children)" feel "in relation to powerful women (mothers)."[169] In Elizabethan England, the political applications of the myth dominated the familial ones, endowing the "dismemberment" that might follow on transgressive desire with a measure of literalness. Actaeon's illicit gazing at Diana made him an exemplum of lust; as Golding explains in his dedicatory letter to Leicester, the dogs "with greedie teeth and griping pawes their Lord in peeces dragge" to punish him for his "foule excess of chamberworke."[170] Golding's bestseller prominently displayed the Dudley bear badge in its front matter, helping to promote the association of Actaeon with transgressive courtiers baited by dogs for their excesses of "chamberwoorck," like the earl.[171] Even the queen used the myth to warn male courtiers about the consequences of such unchaste overreaching.

The garden at Nonesuch Palace included "a grove (lucus) named after Diana, the goddess," featuring a "basin" which portrayed "the story of how the three goddesses took their bath naked and sprayed Actaeon with water, causing antlers to grow upon his head, and of how his own hounds afterwards tore him to pieces." The grove also contained a small temple, with marble tables inscribed with related mottos, reminding passers-by that "the goddess of chastity gives no unchaste councils, she does not council disgrace, but avenges it," and that "from an unclean fountain impure springs, from an unpleasant mind a sight defiled."[172] Combined with these mottoes, the myth impressed on courtiers the need to police themselves, lest they suffer Actaeon's fate.

Working with these same Ovidian allusions, *Endymion* strives to make the same distinctions between pure and impure responses to the queen. Lyly assigns aging a crucial role in this process of differentiation by emphasizing the maturation of his hero, an antitype of Actaeon who keeps the rabid dogs at bay when he prefers the "unspotted" attractions of Cynthia to the sensual allurements of Circe. Lyly brings the latter figure on stage as Tellus, the would-be enchantress who yearns for the power to turn "lovers into beasts" (1.2.74).[173]

As I mentioned above, the court dramatist alters the classical myth, in which Endymion remains eternally young, to have his hero change perceptibly over the course of the play. Other characters comment on this transformation: Endymion's "golden locks" become "silver hairs," his "chin, on which scarcely appeareth soft down" becomes "filled with bristles as hard as broom" (2.3.34–41). Lyly surrounds his sleeping hero with four other aging or aged male lovers, moreover—Geron, Corsites, Sir Tophas, and, arguably, Eumenides. The play's preoccupation with superannuated male sexuality elicits little critical commentary, perhaps because critics are reluctant to consider the possibility that *all* the male characters get older. While acknowledging Endymion's "visible signs of age," for example, David Bevington finds that "almost surely, the other members of the court have not aged visibly along with him, despite plentiful evidence of a long lapse of time." Perhaps the theory that Lyly's play employs a "double sense of time" developed as a palatable alternative to the idea of a stage full of aging lovers.[174] In fact, the play insists that everyone but the immortal Cynthia is subject to time. Even the sapling next to which Endymion falls asleep in act 2 grows into a tree by act 5. While some characters, like Geron, are old when introduced, others, like Eumenides, age along with Endymion. When the baffled Endymion wakes up from his long sleep, he fails not just to recognize his own aged body but also that of his best friend. Gazing on Eumenides' altered face as in a mirror, Endymion theorizes that his "affection is old and [his] appetite cold" (5.1.174–75). Eumenides has become an old man, a state that Endymion finds, in accordance with the medical and philosophical authorities of the time, incompatible with a hot sensual appetite.

In contrast to earlier versions of the myth, which focus on the moon's susceptibility to human beauty, Lyly's revision also focuses on Endymion's susceptibility to feminine beauty.[175] Lyly's hero endures his fate because of his sexual misbehavior, unlike his classical analogue, whose sleep is a gift from the gods. This alteration reflects the common association of sleep to lust; according to Sullivan, "passionate excess and immoderate sleep" were considered "states of being over which reason has no restraining influence . . . sleep and the passions each mark humans as functionally the same as beasts."[176] When they mock Endymion, the children of the subplot remind us that sensual love is emasculating: it "taketh men's stomachs away that they cannot eat, their spleen that they cannot laugh, their hearts that they cannot fight, their eyes that they cannot sleep, and leaveth nothing but livers to make nothing but lovers" (2.2.9–13). Despite the risk of dismemberment and emasculation, Lyly's hero cannot resist the "allurements of pleasure" or his "loose desires" (1.2.46–50) for Tellus. Topical readings have identified Tellus, who plays earth to Cynthia's heaven, with Lettice Knollys, Douglas Sheffield, Anne Vavasour, or Mary, Queen of Scots.[177] While these ladies certainly drew attention to the problem of courtly male sexuality (all four have cameos in *Leicester's Commonwealth*), the logic of Lyly's allegory also makes Tellus a dark reflection of Elizabeth's body natural.[178]

Lyly splits his queen in two, presenting her body politic as Cynthia, the "more than mortal" object of platonic adoration (1.2.19). The earthly

Tellus yearns for adoration of a different sort, recalling polemical accounts of a queen whose enchanting ways made men choose the "single lyfe . . . to attend her pleasure." As Curtis Perry points out, the subject of royal favoritism "focuses attention on the gap between the king's two bodies" because political rewards are allotted according to personal preference.[179] What renders Cynthia superior to Tellus is the fact that "Cynthia governeth all things" (1.2.29–30); her politic "majesty" distinguishes her from her more natural counterpart (2.3.18). Tellus, meanwhile, recalls Allen's Elizabeth/Circe. She intends to "entangle" Endymion in a "sweet net," catching him by means of "witchcraft" (1.2.44, 82), forcing him to use "his sharp wit . . . in flattering of [her] face and devising sonnets in [her] favour," and encouraging him to spend "the prime of his youth and pride of his time . . . in melancholy passions, careless behaviour, untamed thoughts, and unbridled affections" (1.2.64–67).[180] Tellus even proffers the empty promises to suitors that, according to Allen, caused the "sum of the nobility" to remain unmarried for Elizabeth's sake (see 4.1.60–64).[181]

In this reading, Endymion's forty-year sleep—induced by Tellus, with the help of the witchlike Dipsas—signifies his surrender to fleshly lust for the queen (and not, as is sometimes argued, for other women), which renders him vulnerable to malicious tongues. "It is an old saying," Eumenides observes, "that a waking dog doth afar off bark at a sleeping lion" (3.1.10–11). Hackett argues that "dream-settings" like the one in *Endymion* were popular at court because they "enabled erotic plots to be constructed around Elizabeth."[182] The possibility that Tellus and Cynthia represent two facets of the same entity resolves the apparent contradiction between the claims that Endymion makes regarding his "solitary life" and evidence of his ongoing relationship with Tellus. The play implies that this relationship has been consummated—Tellus has "yielded" to Endymion (5.4.79)—and it may even imply, in its references to Tellus having made a "picture of Endymion" (5.4.264), that the union produced a child.[183] These rumors swirling about Tellus and Endymion recall the ones about Elizabeth and her favorites, like the claims "that Lord Robert kept her majesty" and that he "hath had five children by the queen."[184]

Within the framework of the play, these rumors are the only ones that can account for the "many wolves barking at Cynthia."

While the feelings of lust that Tellus inspires might be tolerable in a young man, Castiglione's Bembo would find them reprehensible in an old one. Aging gracefully requires the sublimation of erotic passion into platonic admiration. In Lyly's peculiarly Elizabethan revision of these Neoplatonic motifs, it requires Endymion to forgo Tellus (the queen's body natural) in favor of Cynthia (the queen's body politic), for whom "all things must be not only without lust but without suspicion of lightness" (4.1. 75–76). Only when the hero's "fair face" has "turned to withered skin," does he learn to bring these "thoughts within the compass of [his] fortunes" (4.3.86). Cynthia rewards him with the chaste Neoplatonic kiss that wakes him up, a kiss that "may be said to be the joining of souls rather than of bodies," and that thus is allowed even to old men.[185] To be sure, the moon goddess remains concerned that "eating immoderately or sleeping again too long" will cause her favorite "to fall into a deadly surfeit or into his former sleep" (5.1.155–56). By echoing Renaissance treatises on aging, which emphasized the nefarious effects of "surfette" on "the memorie and reasonable parte" of the aging male, Cynthia establishes herself as an antitype of Medea, whose sexual rejuvenation of the aged Aeson made her "an emblem of unnatural desire" in the period.[186] Although Cynthia does magically rejuvenate Endymion by play's end, his metamorphosis hinges on his love becoming "unspotted" by sexuality. A kind of logic, deriving from humoral accounts of the body, informs this final transformation. Having made an "ende to bodily lust," Endymion conserves his vital heat and so is able "to waxe yonge agayne," thus overcoming his resemblance to Tithonus.[187] Lyly's hero achieves the mentality of an old man in the body of a youth, neatly reversing the age-in-love figure that he embodied earlier in the play, and becoming the masculine counterpart of Cynthia/Elizabeth. Under such conditions—and only under such conditions—Cynthia can allow Endymion to persevere in his feelings for her, rewarding them with royal "favour" (5.4.177).

Lyly's play might thus be seen as a recuperative, didactic effort directed at Elizabeth's aging favorites, who had since their youth expressed their desire for the queen in eroticized terms, and who were now subject to unprecedented public ridicule for remaining incongruously trapped in the posture of the lover. *Endymion* offers these courtiers a choice: they can model themselves after the protagonist, who wakes up to his gray hairs in time to adjust his behavior, who gives up all claim to a physical relationship with Cynthia, and who learns to take "more pleasure in [his] aged thoughts than ever [he] did in [his] youthful actions" (5.4.1175–76). Or they can, like the other old men in the play, continue to expose themselves to public mockery. Through his depiction of Sir Tophas and Corsites, Lyly clarifies that he shares in the contempt for senescent male sexuality that pervaded the works of anticourt polemicists. The main plot of *Endymion* shows how courtiers might avoid the "perpetual infamy" associated with such "monstrous dotage." The subplots show what such infamy might look like by ridiculing the "certain deformity" and "wonderful thralldom" of aging males.

Tophas and Corsites are both foils for Endymion, although Corsites is more obviously so, since he falls for the same witchy woman. Charged with guarding Tellus, he succumbs to her charms instead. When giggling fairies pinch him so that "spots" run "o'er all his flesh" (4.3.43), the punishment marks Corsites as a lecher. Black spots were associated with leprosy, a disease allegedly brought on by an overabundance of lechery, and punningly alluded to by Zontes, who observes that Corsites seems "more like a leopard than a man" (4.3.89).[188] As this comment indicates, Tellus has made good on her desire to turn her lovers into animals. The fairies also construe Corsites's lust for Tellus, which causes him to intrude on the sleeping Endymion, as a "trespass" against Cynthia in their song: "Saucy mortals must not view / What the Queen of Stars is doing" (4.3.42, 33–34).[189] Corsites becomes a version of Actaeon, punished for wanton prying into the queen's mysteries. Cynthia's reprimand reinforces this network of connections by targeting Corsites for ridicule: "You may see, when warriors become wantons, how their manners alter with their faces. Is it not a shame, Corsites, that having lived so long in Mars his camp, thou should'st now be rocked in Venus's cradle?" (4.3.125–28). As her metaphor underscores, Corsites's spotted desire for Tellus is a "shame" because it involves the violation of an age barrier, reducing the old captain to the status of a napping infant.

The play's condemnation of aging male sexuality is even more acerbic in its treatment of the "vainglorious" Sir Tophas, a character to whom "report hath been prodigal," since it left him "no equal" (2.2.85, 118–19). A braggart soldier who becomes the willing victim of two aging witches, Tophas bears the unmistakable imprints of both Roman comedy and English political culture. His name derives from Chaucer's Thopas, a would-be knight noted for pleasing women, dreaming of fairy queens, and being "Yborn . . . in Flaundres."[190] By the time Sir Thomas Wyatt wrote his satires, Thopas had already become a figure for courtly excess.[191] In keeping with this trend, Lyly's *miles gloriosus* seems to have waddled straight out of anticourt propaganda. Where the change from Sir Thopas to Sir Tophas calls Sir Christopher Hatton to mind, the associations with Flanders glances at Leicester, whose exploits in the Low Countries were a frequent source of ridicule.[192] The huffing and puffing knight is markedly corpulent: "more than a man," as his page Epi comically asserts (1.3.41–42), and less than a woman, as the ensuing action demonstrates. Tophas also suffers from a discrepancy between his desires and his ability to perform them; where Leicester was "more Mercury than Mars," Tophas aspires to be "Mars and Ars" but achieves only "mass and ass" (1.3.96–97). His preposterous claims to military prowess are further undermined by his confusion of battling and banqueting; as his page observes, "other captains kill and beat, and there is nothing you kill but you also eat" (2.2.71–73). Although his thoughts "swell" (2.2.80) like Endymion's, the cowardly Sir Tophas remains mired in flesh, a ludicrous and lubricious figure of "surfeit" (2.3.144).

Bevington argues that Tophas is "a vehicle for a thoroughly English satire directed at social climbing, affected Petrarchan posing . . . and other mannerisms of the courtly hanger-on."[193] I would add that categories of age figure prominently in Lyly's satire, giving it a topical edge that has gone largely undetected (Plautus's *miles gloriosus* was neither old nor fat). As sensual desire—that "great platter of plum-porridge of pleasure" (5.2.9–10)—returns the old man to the status of a child and an animal, the subplot plays out the Ovidian scenarios averted in the main plot. Tophas at first disclaims interest in sensual love, which he "disdain[s] as a thing childish and fit for such men as can digest nothing but milk" (2.2.139–41). He soon finds, however, that "love hath, as it were, milked my thoughts" (3.3.23). The "amorous knight" (3.3.94) falls in love first with Dipsas and then with Bagoa, two old hags. Epiton explains that his "master loveth antique work" (5.2.34–35), glancing perhaps at Leicester's patronage of antiquarians and his similar preference for "argumentum at antiquitate."[194] In the grips of his infatuation, the old soldier "doth nothing but make sonnets" (4.2.23), expressing his preference for old wine and old conies and old matrons:

> Epi, I feel all Ovid *de Arte Amandi* lie heavy at my heart as a load of logs. What a fine thin hair hath Dipsas! What a pretty low forehead! What a tall and stately nose! What little hollow eyes! What great and goodly lips! How harmless she is, being toothless! Her fingers fat and short, adorned with long nails like bittern! In how sweet a proportion her cheeks hang down to her breasts like dugs, and her paps to her waist like bags! . . . How virtuous is she like to be, over whom no man can be jealous! (3.3.53–64)

We laugh, here, not only at the aptly named Dipsas, but also at her lover, whose Ovidian allusions and Petrarchan blazon reveal his ridiculously inappropriate erotic longings.

"Love" is indeed a "lord of misrule" (5.2.5) when it makes old men behave like young ones, a comment that at the Elizabethan court was not without political implications. G. K. Hunter assures us that "the love which Sir Tophas expresses for Dipsas does not in any way modify the view we take of Endimion's love for Cynthia," but it is hard not see in this ridiculous old man who "ventureth on her whom none durst undertake" (3.3.74–75) a grotesque reflection of the play's hero.[195] Overcome by his passion (and by the wine he consumes in large quantities), Tophas falls asleep on stage. Where Endymion wakes up in time to control his sensual desires, Sir Tophas's lust has made him an "amorous ass / who loves Dipsas" (3.3.120–21).[196] As readers of Castiglione might expect, he exposes himself to the mockery of the children on the stage, who bark at him and propose to "let bandogs shake him" awake (3.3.131). Bandogs are mastiffs, the preferred breed for bearbaitings.[197] Although Lyly never stages this baiting of the old man, he invites us to imagine it. Diane Purkiss persuasively argues that Dipsas figures "Elizabeth's obsolescence as a vehicle for maternity."[198] Tophas in turn embodies the vain, impotent, and theatricalized sexuality of the queen's aging courtiers. His willingness to accept Bagoa as a substitute for Dipsas, when the latter turns out to be unavailable—"so she be a wench, I care not" (5.4.293–94)—shows him to be a "Lord . . . nothing squeamish for satisfying of his lust," who can "be content (as they say) to gather up crumbs when he is hungry."[199] Here, then, is a fit embodiment of the "insatiable couetousnes and concupiscence" that Cardinal Allen and others found at Elizabeth's aging court.

By showing Tophas's conversion from *miles gloriosus* to *senex amans*, Lyly capitalizes on the latent theatrical metaphors used to describe the inappropriate sexual performances of old men. Cicero thought decorous old age entailed being "contented wyth the space & tyme, whych god graunteth," just as a "Stageplaier . . . muste so expresselye handle and playe his parte, that he maye wynne prayse and commendacion."[200] Far from being contented with the "parte" assigned to him, Tophas sets about playing one more properly belonging to a younger man. Unable to "stand" without a woman, Tophas gives up his sword, shield, gun, and "pike" (3.3.19, 37), the theatrical props of masculinity, to devote himself to his two "old matrons" (5.3.101). The fat knight's transformation into a would-be gallant is effected through an actual costume change; "discover me in all parts," he commands his page, "that I may be like a lover, and then I will sigh and die. Take my gun, and give me a gown" (3.3.27–29). He even considers changing his beard to complete his impersonation, although he confesses himself unsure as to whether he should sport the "bodkin beard or the bush" (3.3.35). Epiton's quip—"Will you be trimmed, sir?" (3.3.34)—clarifies that Tophas's plans involve a wholesale categorical demotion, tantamount to castration (Epiton's name means "to cut short").[201] By cross-dressing as a young lover, the aging Sir Tophas literally takes himself "a hole lower" (3.3.89).

As moments like this show, Lyly's child actors played up the "natural tension between the child himself and the adult he is imitating."[202] Much of the comedy in *Endymion* self-consciously calls attention to the distinction between men and children.[203] The numerous references to the beards that help the boys signal advanced age emphasizes their blurring of generational categories: the boy actor who took on the role of Tophas donned a gray beard to play an old man criticized for behaving like a boy. Hunter argues that the "incapacity of the boys to represent adult passions" helped Lyly offer "portraits" of the court "which avoid any personal implication."[204] While this may be true of Cynthia, whose character remains untainted by the references to age-inappropriate behaviors, the same cannot be said for Endymion or Sir Tophas. By highlighting one contradiction (the old man cross-dressed as the lover) by means of its inverse (the boy cross-dressed as an old man), Lyly's metatheatrical references construe aging male sexuality as a categorical regression. To draw on one of its favorite metaphors, the play thus holds up a mirror to the courtiers who have "waxed old" without "knowing it."

I do not know whether Elizabeth and her elderly courtiers recognized themselves in Lyly's pointedly mocking portrait of an old man enamored of old meat.[205] I do know that Lyly never obtained the preferment he had hoped for from the queen, and that the Earl of Oxford withdrew his patronage later in the same year that *Endymion* was performed at court.[206] And I know that when Shakespeare decided to stage versions of this scene, he made *his* amorous asses in love with enchanting and dominating fairy queens. Sir Tophas is the prototype for all the aging Shakespearean males who preposterously cause the "reversal of priority, precedence, and ordered sequence" by acting on sexual urges, to quote Patricia Parker. Because age was as important a factor as "gender and social place" in the "right ordering" of early modern society, the preposterous figure of "age in love" signaled categorical degradation, the violation of natural sequence, and the subversion of natural hierarchies.[207] To bring this point home to an aging court, Lyly bends generational categories in *Endymion* as adeptly as he bends gender categories in *Gallathea*. His theatrical treatment of superannuated male sexuality—Lyly imagines it as a kind of acting against type, where an elderly male character literally takes on the costume and the role of an "untutor'd youth" (Sonnet 138.3)—influenced Shakespeare, who made the old man in love a favorite of the public stages. To those reading Lyly's play in the nineties, as Shakespeare did, senescent male sexuality presented itself as the definitive problem confronting the late Elizabethan court. Representations of amorous old men in later Elizabethan and early Jacobean literature invite a range of reactions to the perceived sexual transgressions of elderly courtiers like the Earl of Leicester, from uneasy amusement to savage contempt to empathetic embrace. By their variety, these responses suggest just how ambivalent Elizabeth's subjects felt about the men who surrounded the Virgin Queen, and whose unorthodox means to power challenged notions of masculinity and class hierarchy.

CHAPTER 2

Falstaff among the Minions of the Moon

In the long cultural tradition that has sought to relate Elizabeth I and her most talented subject, Sir John Falstaff plays a starring role.[1] Anecdotal evidence suggests that the queen intervened repeatedly in Shakespeare's shaping of this character. So, according to his eighteenth-century biographer Nicholas Rowe, Shakespeare wrote *The Merry Wives of Windsor* (1597) because Elizabeth "was so well pleas'd with that admirable Character of Falstaff... that she commanded him to continue it for one Play more, and to shew him in Love."[2] A previous generation of scholars used this posthumous "tradition" of royal interference to speculate that the inconsistencies between Falstaff in *The Henriad* (1596–99) and his "impostor" in *The Merry Wives of Windsor* resulted from artistic compromises made to an unperceptive royal command.[3] We might consider these stories as evidence of a different sort. Regardless of their veracity, anecdotes like Rowe's bear witness to a vestigial connection between the Virgin Queen and Shakespeare's fat knight in his aspect as a senescent lover. Although recent critics have shown little interest in this association, Falstaff does introduce himself as one of "Diana's foresters, gentlemen of the shade, minions of the moon... men of good government, being govern'd, as the sea is, by our noble and chaste mistress the moon, under whose countenance we steal" (*1 Henry IV*, 1.2.25–29).[4] The old man's fondness for such euphuisms is no accident; a web of references binds Shakespeare's plump Jack to Elizabeth's "minions" and "men of good government" as they were described in antigovernment tracts or represented in John Lyly's *Endymion*

77

(1588)—especially the greatest minion of them all, Robert Dudley, Earl of Leicester. Shakespeare's Falstaff is, among many other things, a vehicle for thinking about the sexual and generational transgressions of the late Elizabethan court.

The word "minion" referred to the male favorites of sovereign princes.[5] Given the prevalence of the moon cult in the 1590s, Falstaff's opening invocation of Diana invites audience members to consider his relationship to Elizabeth I. Although David Scott Kastan argues that Falstaff's self-description does not signal "a submission to authority but an authorization of transgression; he serves not the monarch whose motto . . . was '*semper eadam* alwaies one,' but only the changeable moon," the moon cult allowed for and indeed celebrated the paradoxical concept of constancy-in-change.[6] The eponymous hero of *Endymion*, a source for *Merry Wives*, defends his beloved Cynthia against charges of inconstancy, for example, by praising her ability to wax and wane while keeping "a settled course." Elizabeth embraced the identification, and had herself portrayed as Cynthia in the famous Rainbow Portrait (ca. 1600; see figure 6). The moon's properties helped court writers portray a queen who claimed constancy, but whom they perceived as an agent of transformation. Most famously, Sir Walter Ralegh used lunar imagery to describe Elizabeth's adulterating effect on his watery speaker in "The Ocean to Cynthia": a change in "Belphoebe's course" here converts the smooth "ocean seas" into "tempestuous waves" there.[7] When Falstaff compares himself to a sea, influenced by his "noble and chaste mistress the moon," he identifies himself, and his transgressions, with the men about the Virgin Queen.

As a royal favorite "fat-witted with drinking of old sack" and given to taking "purses . . . by the moon and the seven stars," Falstaff evokes the picture of the "moon's men" (*1 Henry IV*, 1.2.2, 14, 31) not just as it was drawn by adherents of the court but also as it was drawn by its most assiduous detractors. In 1584, the authors of *Leicester's Commonwealth* had asked that Elizabeth grant their "lawful desire and petition" to try Leicester in court, because of the earl's "intolerable licentiousness in all filthy kind and manner of carnality," and because he was guilty of theft, not only by spoiling and oppressing almost infinite private men, but also whole towns, villages, corporations, and countries, by robbing the realm with inordinate licenses, by deceiving the crown with racking, changing, and embezzling the lands, by abusing his prince and sovereign in selling his favor both at home and abroad... in which sort of traffic he committeth more theft oftentimes in one day than all the waykeepers, cutpurses, cozeners, pirates, burglars, or other of that art in a whole year within the realm.

The earl, the authors opined, was a figure of misrule who should be arraigned under the same "laws" that Elizabeth used "daily to pass [judgment] upon thieves."[8] Cardinal Allen concurred, qualifying Leicester's military activities in the Netherlands as "publike robberies," and arguing that under the earl's leadership English soldiers had become "companions of theeves and revenous woolves: and publike enimies of al true Kinges and lawful Dominion." From the perspective of Elizabethan dissidents, the queen was not a "noble and chaste mistress" but a changeable moon, a monarch who had countenanced the multiple robberies of her "amorous minion," the "cheife leader" of her "wicked and unwonted course of regiment."[9]

By echoing these attacks on the queen's favorite while showing us an unruly favorite in the company of his prince, the second scene of *1 Henry IV* positions its audience to think about the loaded topic of monarchical judgment generally and Elizabeth I's judgment more specifically. Machiavelli, who was in the revolutionary business of defining the criteria by which one might judge princes, held that "the first thing one does to evaluate the wisdom of a ruler is to examine the men that he has around them." Thomas Blundeville agreed that "the sufficiency of the manne" was an accurate gauge of "the choyse of the Prince."[10] Falstaff, well-versed in politic authors, endorses this logic when he claims that "it is certain that either wise bearing or ignorant carriage is caught, as men take diseases, one of another; therefore let men take heed of their company" (*2 Henry IV*, 5.1.75–77). Under such conditions, the "Inclination of Princes to some men, and their Disfavour towards others" might indeed become "fatal," as William Camden averred, in reference to the great favor that Elizabeth I showed the Earl of Leicester.[11] Because "mignonnerie" captured "the straying king personally," Laurie Shannon thinks it "posed a constitutional conflict" for royal advisors and for "the monarchy itself, as embodied in a king who always has the capacity to act 'unkingly.'"[12] A royal favorite reputed a thief, a drunk, and a lecher was also "fatal" in that people might be persuaded the monarch's lack of judgment offered "just cause" for rebelling, when subjects technically were, as the pro-government pamphlet *A Briefe Discoverie of Dr. Allen's Seditious Driftes* (1588) insists, "private men, and subjects, and therefore can have no lawfull authority . . . to judge."[13]

This pamphlet describes the "infamous libels" aimed at Leicester, examined in the previous chapter, as part of an innovative assault on Elizabeth I's prerogative. The author's fear that "private men" might arrogate to themselves the place of "judge, corrector, and executioner of Iustice" substantiates Curtis Perry's claim that "debates about court favoritism" laid "the groundwork for larger transformation of the kind theorized by Habermas."[14] Shakespeare's contemporaries were aware of these changes, even if they lacked the critical vocabulary to describe them. Habermas defines the bourgeois public sphere, which he sees as emerging in the eighteenth century, as constituted of "private people come together as a public" to engage "in a debate over the general rules governing relations"; what is at stake is in part the rights of the private subject to pass judgment on the sovereign.[15] The development of a public sphere had roots in earlier phenomena, including Machiavelli's secular approach to historiography; according to Michel de Certeau, "When the historian seeks to establish, for the place of power, the rules of political conduct"—like those that govern the selection of political advisors—"he *plays the role* of the prince that he is not."[16] De Certeau's metaphor imagines this as a form of theatrical usurpation. By construing Leicester as a "carped . . . knight" who had "never had merited . . . to be so highly favored of [her Majes]tie," the earl's detractors urged "private men" to pass judgment on Elizabeth's judgment, a necessary preliminary to playing the prince by passing judgment on the sovereign herself.[17] In the first play of the *Henriad* Shakespeare signals his interest in this process by having Bolingbroke preface his usurpation and deposition of Richard II with the execution of two royal favorites who have "misled a prince, a royal king" (3.1.8). Although *Richard II* does not pursue the implications of this sequence of events, granting little stage time to the king's favorites, the Bishop of Carlisle's related question—"What subject can give sentence on his king?" (4.1.121)—haunts the rest of the tetralogy in the form of a fat old man.

The issue of the prince's fallible judgment, as manifested in the injudicious treatment of favorites, is raised explicitly in *1 Henry IV* when Falstaff admonishes Hal, "Do not thou, when thou art king, hang a thief" (1.2.62). This admonition is self-interested; as soon as Hal is crowned, his "fat rogue" of a minion (1.2.187) intends to emulate Leicester in letting "his gredy appetite" range free.[18] Even though critics like Kastan equate transgression with resistance to monarchical authority, the fascination exerted by Elizabeth's eldest minion shows unruliness came in other forms than political dissidence for Tudor subjects. In his eagerness to have "England ... give him office, honor, might," Leicester was accused, as Falstaff is, of committing "the oldest sins the newest kind of ways" (*2 Henry IV*, 4.5.126–29), and committing them "upon her Majesty's favor and countenance towards him."[19] That Hal appears at first willing to "countenance" the "poor abuses of the time" (*1 Henry IV*, 1.2.156) in Falstaff thus raises all manner of questions, for, as Falstaff asks of Poins, "if men were to be sav'd by merit, what hole in hell were hot enough for him?" (1.2.107–8).[20] By casting these questions in the familiar terms favored by Catholic dissidents, Shakespeare places his "most comparative, rascalliest, sweet young prince" (1.2.80–81) in relation to his own prince, and his "lugg'd bear," the subject of "the most unsavory similes" (1.2.74, 79), in relation to the queen's "Bearwhelp," the subject of "all pleasant discourses at this day throughout the realm."[21]

The Falstaff plays allude to the recent past to constitute their audiences as a "remembering public." By always leaving us wanting "one Play more," Falstaff is the poster boy for theatrical "ghosting"—the recycling of actors, plots, props, patterns, allusions and so on that, according to

Marvin Carlson, encourages audiences "to compare varying versions of the same" material.²² Such "base comparisons" (*1 Henry IV*, 2.4.250) engage faculties of judgment, and, when they involve historical persons, prompt what Castiglione calls "words of severe censure, of modest praise, and of cutting satire."²³ *A Briefe Discoverie* objects to Allen's "offering a comparison betweene *the D. Parmaes glorious exploits*, and his Lordships [that is, Leicester's] *famous factes* . . . as though his vertues were so farre inferiour, to the others" on precisely these grounds. Similarly, when anti-court polemicists likened Leicester to Richard II's favorites, they were implicitly comparing Elizabeth I to a monarch deposed for showing "too much favor towards wicked persons."²⁴ Elizabeth's famous identification with Shakespeare's Richard II betrayed her well-founded anxiety about the provocative function of such analogic "pastimes," made particularly dangerous, perhaps, by a theatrical setting. In *1 Henry IV*, Henry IV attributes Richard's downfall to his taste for "shallow jesters" and his consequent vulnerability to "every beardless vain comparative" (3.2.61, 67) before castigating his own son: "For all the world / As thou art to this hour was Richard then" (3.2.93–94). The king's censure places Hal in the same comparative relation to Richard II as the authors of *Leicester's Commonwealth* had placed the queen. As such comparisons show, to go from evaluating the merits of a royal favorite to evaluating the merits of the prince is but a short step—and one abetted by Shakespeare's introduction of a measure of contrast into comparative relations. The Falstaff plays encourage their audiences to take this step by doing what no dissident pamphlet could do. They provide theatrical substitutes for Elizabeth I, who shine more brightly than she does. The audience is asked to weigh these substitutes' "*glorious exploits*" against Elizabeth's "*famous factes*," at least in the matter of countenancing an "old fat man, a tun of man" as chosen "companion" (*1 Henry IV*, 2.4.448).

The ways in which Falstaff's multiple transgressions prompt "discourses" is key to these comparative processes. Gossip, slander, and rumor follow Falstaff at the heel, a sure indication of his public notoriety and of his hold on collective memory. In an argument that highlights Falstaff's connection to the figure of Rumor, Harry Berger Jr. proposes that Falstaff stands for judgment, in that he both represents judgment and asks to be judged.[25] Like Berger's Falstaff, Leicester was a knowing collaborator in his prince's project, "growne so far" in her "Majesties favor" as to inspire "much talke . . . muttered in [every] corner, [and] much whisperinge."[26] Although commentators disagreed in their assessment of the earl, they agreed that he generated compulsive chatter and found themselves retelling his story in an effort to substantiate their judgments. The attacks of the 1580s had initiated a series of responses and imitations over the next few decades—an unprecedented phenomenon that the theorist Michael Warner might identify as the "concatenation of texts through time" that conjures a public.[27] This public was not organized around the ideological values of the exiled Catholics who helped call it into being: several of the texts concerned came out of court circles, show signs of Protestant affiliation (e.g., the anonymous *News from Heaven and Hell*), or reflect the mixed motivations of theatrical entrepreneurs (e.g., *The Henriad* and *The Merry Wives of Windsor*). What the audiences for these works did have in common was a taste for satiric representations of fat, vain, thieving, lecherous, cowardly, lubricious, hypocritical old men: the kind whom "men of all sorts take a pride to gird at," the ones who are "the cause that wit is in other men" (*2 Henry IV*, 1.2.6, 10).

By situating Falstaff in the context of anti-Leicestrian discourses, I show that Shakespeare's old knight is a vehicle not just for thinking about the Elizabethan court, but also for thinking about the public theater's relation to that court and the society it governed. In making Falstaff, Shakespeare transformed the raw materials of Leicester's "black legend" through his distinctive modes of theatricality, self-reflection, and showmanship.[28] Like his own "honey-tongued Boyet," Shakespeare is in this "wit's pedlar," retailing courtly "wares" while "grac[ing them] with such show" that he outperforms his models (*Love's Labour's Lost*, 5.2.317–34). I mention Boyet not only because Berowne's description articulates in Shakespeare's own terms the "populuxe" appeal, subversive impact, competitive motivations, and commercial value of early modern theatricality, but also because Boyet is the resented servant of a convention-defying princess. *Love's Labour's Lost* (1594–95) thus calls attention to a category of analysis—gender—often disregarded in public sphere approaches to Shakespeare's works but crucial to the evaluation of Elizabethan political phenomena.[29] Falstaff is more closely associated in the critical tradition with the transcendent "agency of [Shakespeare's] theater itself" than any other character, with the possible (and significant) exception of Cleopatra.[30] To take seriously Falstaff's contention that he is Diana's minion is to accept Elizabeth's central influence on the transformative powers of Shakespeare's art. This chapter traces one aspect of that influence, the way that the unconventional and scandalous relationship between the aging queen and her elderly favorite contributed to a Shakespearean theater that sought sport and profit from exposing political material to public evaluation.

Among Falstaff's salient features in this regard is his unparalleled ability to incite judgment and thereby to induce "other men," including playgoers, into a community defined by the willingness to engage in critical dialogue: what matters about the old knight is not so much that he is witty in himself but that he is the cause of wit in others.[31] The radical impulses that critics identify with Falstaff—his so-called "resistance to the totalizations of power"—inhere in this effect.[32] There is something democratizing about a process that unites and elevates "men of all sorts" in the intellectual baiting of a figure associated with Elizabeth I. There is also something gendered at work in this process. The exercise of wit and judgment, faculties that, as Castiglione's emphasis on them shows, were associated with elite masculinity, compensates for and even averts the threat of erotic and political subjugation that the lecherous old man embodies.[33] The age-in-love trope has the potential to catalyze horizontal exchanges as well as vertical ones, since it moves people to discriminate according to age and gender rather than class. Shakespeare seizes on this potential in his unforgettable portrait of "an old fat man" who looks to be made "either earl or duke" (*1 Henry IV*, 5.4.142) by rendering dubious service to his prince (in the *Henriad*) or his mistresses (in *Merry Wives*).

That Shakespeare's dissolute favorite glances at Elizabeth's deceased favorite is not as much of a stretch as might at first seem. Leicester died eight years before the first Falstaff play was staged, of "continuall burning Feaver," or what Mistress Quickly calls "a burning quotidian tertian" (*Henry V*, 2.1.119).[34] But the earl had by then achieved a lasting impact, due to his dual status as the period's preeminent patron and its favorite target of invective. The form this celebrity took was all the more unprecedented for being diachronic; even postmortem, Leicester continued to represent certain feared, despised, and admired traits in the English imaginary.[35] Writing about this long afterlife in seventeenth-century political discourses, Perry shows that "the changing uses of the image of Leicester provide an excellent case study of the longevity"—and, I would add, the commercial viability—"of topical reference."[36] Notably, Shakespeare highlights the issue of Falstaff's afterlives. All three plays featuring the old knight ask us to compass his death and to imagine him at his final judgment. By recycling the motifs of Leicester's posthumous reputation, these aspects of Falstaff's characterization exploit the "perpetual infamy" that Castiglione ascribed to the old man in love, and that Leicester embodied for his contemporaries.[37]

Leicester's self-promotion laid the groundwork for his lasting cultural cachet. While his was in some ways a traditional sense of politics, the earl relied on newfangled methods to pursue his ends.[38] Like the "*popular* breeches" described in Jonson's *Cynthia's Revels* (1600), a satiric comedy about court favorites, Leicester was "not content to be generally noted in court" but did "press forth on common stages and brokers' stalls to the public view of the world."[39] He did so by commissioning frequent and frequently copied portraits of himself, and by accepting the dedications of over a hundred printed books, available for purchase in "broker's stalls."[40] For Jonson as for Jeff Doty the word "popular" designated "communicative acts that subjected political matters to the scrutiny of 'the people.'"[41] Because of the personal nature of Elizabethan politics, the matter that the earl most often sought to communicate about was himself. Jonson attributes to the "common stages" a role in the popularization of court materials, thinking perhaps of the enterprising earl. Leicester had patronized a traveling troupe of players from the moment he took office as Master of the Horse in 1558 to the moment he died in 1588, and helped launch the careers of James Burbage, Will Kempe, John Heminge, and possibly Shakespeare himself.[42] These actors, who would go on to found the Lord Chamberlain's Men, valued the connection with Elizabeth's eldest favorite enough that in 1572 they requested and were granted the right to become his liveried household retainers.[43] The earl spent copiously on clothes for his actors, including livery shirts adorned with the Dudley bear badge and ragged staff, meant to advertise the troupe's relationship to him. As Ann Rosalind Jones and Peter Stallybras remind us, "memories and social relations were literally embodied" in such garments.[44] When others uttered "leawd words ... ageynst the raggyd staff," the earl's players took umbrage because their own identities were at stake.[45] As long as audiences remembered Leicester's men, these players could no more shed their employment history than they could shed their skin.[46] Like Jonson's pants, the actors carried their courtly past onto the "common stages," inviting the ghost of their old patron to haunt their performances. The theatrical metaphors that became part of the evaluative lore on the earl reflect his long-standing association with players of all kind, including those at the Globe, and conveyed a widespread perception that he was an inherently theatrical person.

Not content to show himself only on stages, Leicester was also a pioneer when it came to using the new modes of publicity afforded by the printing press. Entertainments like the ones he hosted at Kenilworth helped shape Shakespeare's imagination not just because they were spectacular, but also because they found their way into print, and so into the stalls of booksellers. As we saw in the last chapter, George Gascoigne's *Princely Pleasures* was reissued in the late 1580s, when Shakespeare was in his mid-twenties, so that it continued to "advertise [the earl's] position as the queen's favorite" for years after the original performance. Although some scholars speculate that Shakespeare attended the entertainments as a boy, it is more likely that he read about them in works like Gascoigne's.[47] Other books pressing the earl's case also found their way into the playwright's hands. Gascoigne's *The Noble Arte of Venerie or Hunting* (1575) includes a woodcut of the kneeling earl, offering the choice part of a deer to the queen during a hunting party at Kenilworth.[48] Spenser's *The Faerie Queene* (1590, 1596) glances at the earl in the character of Arthur, an association that Leicester had promoted at Kenilworth and that might explain the Hostess's insistence that the dead Falstaff is "not in hell" but "in Arthur's bosom" (*Henry V*, 2.3.9–10). Arthur Golding's translation of Ovid's *Metamorphoses* (1576), the source for multiple allusions describing the effects of lust on older Shakespearean males, displays the Dudley bear and ragged staff on its title page, and includes a long dedicatory letter to "the ryght Honorable and... singular good Lord, Robert Erle of Leycester." Most pertinently, perhaps, the major source for Shakespeare's history plays, Holinshed's *Chronicles* (1587), offers up a long description of the earl's banqueting in the Netherlands, as well as a treatise establishing his aristocratic credentials, including his descent from the Beaufort Earls of Warwick.[49] By the mid-1590s, when Shakespeare began writing the Falstaff plays, he had to look no further than his bookshelf for the "famous factes" about the earl.

The malicious gossip about Leicester proved as enduring as his efforts at self-promotion. Through the 1590s, commoners continued to be brought before the authorities for claiming "my lord of Leicester had four children by the queen's majesty."[50] In 1592, Nashe's *Pierce Penniless's Supplication to the Devil* recalled a time when "the beare... being chiefe burgomaster of all the beastes under the lyon, gan thinke with himself how hee might surfet in pleasure."[51] As such references show, where Leicester had pursued popularity, he obtained notoriety; this "pathological version of fame" was an unintended effect of forces that he had sought to harness to his own ends—"emergent capitalism" and "textual and theatrical reproduction."[52] The proliferation of "millions of impieties "sith [the earl's] death," abusing "the people by their divelish fictions... all to bring" Leicester's "vertues & person in popular hatred," prompted an impassioned posthumous defense, "The Dead Mans Right," in 1593.[53] Coy about the precise nature of the multitudinous slanders involved (the anonymous author only notes that these made his ears blush), the tract nevertheless suggests that the materials derived from *Leicester's Commonwealth* continued to shape the earl's public image long after he died.[54]

The xv. Bookes of
P. Ouidius Naso,
Entituled, Meta-
morphosis.

A worke verie pleasant and delectable.

Translated out of Latin into English meeter
by Arthur Golding Gentleman.

With skill, heed, and iudgement this worke must be read,
For else to the Reader it stands in small stead.

AT LONDON,
Printed by Iohn Windet, and Thomas Iudson.
Anno Domini. 1584.

FIG. 4. Title page of Arthur Golding's translation of Ovid's *Metamorphoses* (1584). By permission of the Folger Shakespeare Library.

Meant to alarm, *Leicester's Commonwealth* had succeeded in entertaining. As Perry points out, plays ranging from *The Spanish Tragedy* (ca. 1587) to *The White Devil* (ca. 1612) continued to assume "a ready familiarity" with its slanderous contents.[55] While these tragedies allude to Leicester's reputation as a Machiavellian politician, other works show the late earl as "the noble lecher / that used art to provoke."[56] The recurrent pun on lecher/Leicester confirms that the "nascent public sphere of the Elizabethan era involved identity and decorum more than rationality or policy, and was often irreverent rather than somber."[57] Playing on the bear and ragged staff, the more salacious entries in Leicester's "black legend" expose the earl explicitly to mocking social judgments. One poem rejoices, for example, that

> The stately Bear that at the stake would stand
> 'Gainst all the mastiffs stout that would come forth
> Is muzzled here and ringed with our hand...
>   Great Robin, whom before all could not take,
>   Is here by shepherd's curs made for to quake.
> Thus may we learn, there is no staff so strong
> But may be broken into shivers small
> No beast so fierce the cruel beasts among
> But age or cunning gins may work his fall.[58]

The poem reflects conventions established by *Leicester's Commonwealth* in relating the earl's bear badge, his upstart ambition, his bestial nature, and his failing genitals. But it also outdoes its source by envisaging the "staff so strong" reduced to "shivers small" by "shepherd's curs." Emphasizing the class differential between the bear and his pursuers, the poem endows these curs with the homegrown courage of the celebrated English mastiff.[59] The "fall" of the earl's "staff," meanwhile, stands for the moralistic and socially conservative admonition "to be content and not desire / For all do fall that do aspire."[60] In this way, the earl's impotence becomes the inevitable consequence of his social mobility and sexual opportunism. Shakespeare mines this same vein of humor in his representation of Falstaff.

Nowhere are the salient aspects of Leicester's posthumous reputation more entertainingly on display than in *News from Heaven and Hell*, an unpublished satire written by an anonymous adherent of the court sometime after the earl's death in 1588. In its competitive escalation of inherited materials, the little-known *News* sets a precedent for Shakespeare's conversion of Leicester's black legend to theatrical purpose. Among other things, this satire makes elaborate and equal opportunity fun of both the earl's "ragged" and his "Stewardes staff."[61] The anonymous author evokes a theatricalized world, in which Heaven is a kind of castle, as in the morality tradition, and hell the domain of vice-like fiends. *News*'s "quandam Earle of Lescester" is a lover of the moon, who shares multiple traits with *Endymion*'s Sir Tophas, including a rotund physique, a fondness for having "a page" carry a "bole of wine to refresh him," and a tendency to lecherous and animalistic behavior (144, 146). By devising condign punishments for this elderly lover, *News* shows the figure of Leicester-in-lust remained attractive to writers because it authorized their political judgments. The satire thus corroborates the suspicions of pro-government thinkers that the "slanderous inveighing" against the queen's great favorite contributed to a usurpation of royal prerogative, which might result in "private subjects" allocating to themselves "the power of setting up and putting downe Princes."[62] That such power is a source of great pleasure is implied by the frankly pornographic bent of the narrative.

News signals its participation in a broader and ongoing discussion about the earl by its self-conscious orientation toward a remembering public familiar with anti-Leicestrian lore and eager to hear "the last reporte... brought by the post" of the earl's adventures (158). Although it never saw print, *News* thus shows the reflexivity and attention to temporality that Warner defines as characteristic of public-making texts.[63] In addition to engaging in the "traffic in news" about the earl, *News* invites debate by construing its readers as members of a jury, instructing them to "waye" with their "charytable wisdomes" what the earl deserves (155), and elevating them to the level of St. Peter and Pluto, the authorities passing judgment within the narrative.[64] Its legalistic account of the earl's postmortem travails capitalizes on the notion first aired in *Leicester's Commonwealth* that Leicester has "a conscience loaden with the guilt of many crimes, wherof he would be loth to be called to accompt or be subject to any man that might by authority take review of his life and actions when it should please him."[65] The author introduces Leicester's ghost on his way to Final Judgment, clad in "a fine white shirte wrought with the beare and the ragged staffe," with "his Stewards staffe of office in his hande," trying "with shewes to delude the worlde there as he had done here" (144). Where in life the earl's "vaine pompe" (144) fooled the powers-that-be, including Elizabeth I, in his imagined afterlife "*Munsur Fatpanche*" (146) meets with a more discerning public, alerted to the pleasures that await by the coy references to the bear badge. *News* recycles old material for its "corpulent" (145), lubricious, and theatrical antihero but also adds new touches, endowing the ghost with such a propensity for "much sweating," that his embossed "shirte" becomes "all wet" (145–46), a nod to the mysterious fever that killed Leicester, and to the fiery torments that await him.

In its depiction of these torments, *News* reconfigures the familiar device of bearbaiting to draw attention to Leicester's violations of gender and generational norms. The author's tongue-in-cheek construction of heaven as situated near the "orb of the moone" equates Leicester's failure to enter the pearly gates with his misguided attempts to enter the "bewtifull venirus dames" who had "dazeled him on earth" (146). Escorted by Sarcotheos, the god of flesh whom he worshipped in life, "*Munsur Fatpanche*" finds himself put on "triall" by St. Peter for his lechery and his "wantonnes of flesh" (148–49). Where the portly ghost repents other sins—the author offers a lengthy list of these, including various murders and "the robbing and stearving of pore souldiers" in the Netherlands (152)—he confesses that he holds lechery "no sinne": "it was so swete and I accustomed to it even from my youth" that he "could never repent me of it nether in youth nor age" (154). After clarifying that he disdains the conventional distinction between youthful "lustynes" and the "gravitye" proper to old age, the ghost volunteers for castration to avoid damnation. He begs "to have the member only punnished that hath only offended" (154).[66] Instead, St. Peter has this "bellye claper marked with an L"; far from signifying that "he had bene a great lorde," it brands Leicester a lecher (154). The pun on Leicester's name designates the earl's conversion of sexual service into political capital as his supreme offence.

Chained by his branded member to an "iron brake," his "privites" made to "enduere" such abuse that he made a "dolfull sight for any his beawtifull ladies... to have beheld," his "Robinships" is then carried off to hell, where

> a naked feind in the forme of a lady with the supported nose should bend this bere whelp in an iron cheane by the middle and... she should be so directly placed against him that the gate of hir porticke conjuntcion should be full oposit to the gase of his retoricke speculation, so that he could not chose but have a perfit aspect of the full pointe of her bettelbroude urchin in the triumphant pride and gaping glory thereof. Now there was no doubte made but that this pleasant sight, togeather with the remembrance of his wounted delight, would make his teath so to water and geve him such an edge that he could not forbeare... to geve a charge with his lance of lust against the center of her target of proffe, and rune his ingredience up to the hard hiltes into the unserchable botome of her gaping gullfe.... Thus was his paradice turned into his purgatory, his fine furred gape into a flaminge trape, his place of pleasure into a gulfe of vengeance, and his pricke of desire into a pillor of fier. (155–58)

This scene of pornographic bearbaiting translates into infernal terms Castiglione's contention that those who give in to "unbridled desire" soon return to it, experiencing once more "that furious and burning thirst."[67] Where most early modern scenarios of sexual abandon focus on the transgressions of the female partner (e.g., Spenser's Acrasia), this one highlights the male's culpability. With his head below the fiend's "bettelbroude urchin," the ghost reenacts his violation of normative heterosexual relations in which the man functioned as the head to the woman's body.

By depending on familiarity with preexisting materials for its humor, *News* illustrates the ways in which satire "near and familiarly allied to the time" draws on its readers' memories to constitute them as an "adjudicating public."[68] The ghost's "pricke of desire," for example, glances back at the Kenilworth entertainments, where Leicester had presented himself as the holly bush Deep Desire, animated by "the restlesse prickes of his privie thoughts."[69] That this same "pricke" is now turned to a "pillor of fier" frames the earl's courtship of the queen as a cause of damnation. Although the identity of the "lady with the supported nose" is ambiguous, paradoxical references to her demonic double's "gaping g[u]llfe" and "bottomeless barrell of virginnitye" evoke the woman who was ever the "center" of Leicester's ambitious and amorous designs; who had costarred in the bearbaiting in *Leicester's Commonwealth* (see chapter 1); and who had endured controversy about her own "gaping gulf" (157).[70] Multiple allusions to the Dudley badge further establish the earl's bestial nature, while singling out his phallus—described in prosthetic terms, as a pillar, lance, or staff—for condign forms of punishment. The discursive detachment of the earl's penis from his body proper culminates in his fiery castration, an emasculation reinforced by the ghost's narrative status as the feminized object of the readers' gaze and the satiric butt of the readers' laughter. By provoking derisive laughter, the author positions his readers as knowing and authoritative collaborators in the castigation of the deceased earl. *News from Heaven and Hell* offers a compensatory fantasy of empowerment, in which the sexual and generational inversions of the Elizabethan court are avenged through the immolation of this old lecher/Leicester, forced "to offer dayly to his god Priapus ... a burnd sacrifice," and reduced in the process to a mere "feminine suppository" (157).

As *News* shows, Leicester's death, far from quieting his critics, reenergized them. Elizabeth's councillors were right to think that far more was at stake (so to speak) in "the slanderous devices against the said Earl" than the personal animosity and angry grumblings of a Catholic minority.[71] A. N. McLaren argues that Elizabeth I's gender helped men like Leicester arrogate unprecedented power. It also made them vulnerable to the chastening attacks of inferiors. The perceived sexual subjection of the queen's aging favorites authorized other subjects to speak against and about them by virtue of their own conformity to gender and generational norms, a process that contributed to the emergence of a public sphere during this period. Leicester's "legend" belongs to the "gossip about public figures" better described as scandal, in that it circulates among strangers and "has both reflexivity... and timeliness."[72] Knowing references to the earl as a man whose "experience in chamberwoorck exceeded his practize in warr" survived him for many years.[73] The longevity of Leicester's "black legend"—the paradox of its enduring timeliness—indicates that it addressed a range of concerns about early modern government, as Perry shows. The age-in-love trope contributed to this phenomenon by drawing the unseemly body of the queen's "amorous minion" into public discourse for the purposes of ridicule, a process that encouraged subjects to think themselves more discerning than their queen, and that established the authority of communally held social norms over that of the monarchy. Such factors explain why as late as 1593 the author of "The Dead Mans Right" accused the "ungratefull Malecontents" who spread "rebellious and seditious Libells" about the dead earl of having "an aspiring minde," and felt an obligation to defend the queen, who had "wisely judged of [Leicester's] vertues, and worthily rewarded his loialtie and paines."[74] Notably, the last installment of the Elizabethan tradition, *Leicester's Ghost* (ca. 1602–04, printed in 1641), reproduces the usual charges about the lascivious earl, who used "strange drinks and Oyntments... [to make] dead flesh to rise" when he "waxed old."[75] Loath to let such fat meat go, writers imagined the elderly Leicester/lecher postmortem, like so much dead flesh irrepressibly rising from the beyond.

Polemical works on Leicester show how a masculine, disembodied ideal of public life emerges in response to the embodied and sexualized modes of publicity at the Elizabethan court.[76] Although the buffoonish figure of Leicester-in-lust first appeared in works opposed to the Elizabethan government on ideological grounds, it proved portable and entertaining enough to cross the divisions that separated the Catholic authors of *Leicester's Commonwealth* in Paris from the Protestant author of *News at court* (*News* makes scoffing references to the Pope and papists that establish its Protestant bona fides). The cultural mobility of this figure indicates that, rather than conveying narrowly partisan positions, the age-in-love trope had a catalytic effect, encouraging those who encountered it to form and voice opinions of their own. In describing an old ghost damned in hell for being lecherous, *News* emphasizes the politic pleasures attendant on debating Leicester's transgressions. Pluto gathers a "solemn assembly," whose members model deliberative processes by discussing the earl's punishment: "sum were of opinion that his harte should be pressed through," while "sum that his hands and fete should be loked in a paier of stokes and manackels which should be made all fiery, of purpose becase his handes had bene always geven to rapine," and still others that hot sulfur be poured down his throat, that "gaping gulfe of all gluttony, drunkenness, and riott" (156). *Leicester's Ghost* also references such a divergence of opinion by noting objections to its narrator's claims; in familiar terms, he denounces those "Doggs that at the *Moone* doe fondly barke."[77] Joining the conversation initiated by *Leicester's Commonwealth,* these later tracts imagine themselves as contributing to an ongoing and highly entertaining debate about the controversial earl (one that allows, moreover, for surreptitious glancing at other royal favorites). The "slanderous devices" aimed at Leicester by the polemicists of the 1580s had conjured a public eager to consume satiric representations of their government, a public whose members enjoyed discussing and passing judgment on the sexual misbehavior of their superiors. This phenomenon was bound not just to erode the authority of the ruling class but also to attract the notice of playwrights like Shakespeare, "whose main business," according to Paul Yachnin, consisted of "marketing popular versions of elite cultural goods to public audiences."[78]

The association of the surfeiting old man in love and the Elizabethan court was fostered on the common stages by the publication, in 1591, of Lyly's *Endymion*, which advertised on its title page that it had been performed "before the Queen's Majesty at Greenwich," and which is an acknowledged source for Shakespeare's *A Midsummer Night's Dream* (1595–96), as well as for the Falstaff plays.[79] Bottom, Falstaff, Malvolio, Orsino, Claudius, and Antony all follow Endymion in lusting after female characters modeled on Elizabeth I.[80] And several of these characters follow Sir Tophas in being hybrids of the *miles gloriosus* and the *amans senex*, who violate gender and generational boundaries.[81] Where Lyly offers distinct idealized and satiric representations of Elizabeth's favorites, Shakespeare often confounds the two modes, presenting us with characters who defy easy categorization and who challenge our faculties of judgment. In privileging problems of sovereignty and judgment, Shakespeare's experiments with aging male characters engage the later tradition on Leicester, and come to altogether different conclusions about the theatrical possibilities inherent in the figure of the lusty old man than his theatrical predecessor did. If, as I argue above, age-in-love tropes function as vehicles for the political empowerment of "aspiring minde[s]," they also provide aspiring playwrights with a means for artistic self-assertion. Indeed, Shakespeare's repurposing of this inherited material is deeply competitive—he embraces the escalation inherent in anti-Leicestrian discourse by outperforming his models.

An early version of this tendency to confound, recycle, synthesize, escalate, and aestheticize is discernible in *A Midsummer Night's Dream,* where Bottom's amorous encounter with a fairy queen make him into something more than "an ass" (3.1.120). Leonard Barkan argues that the precedent for the meeting between Bottom and Titania is "the story of dangerous eye contact between Diana and Actaeon," a myth that, as we saw in the previous chapter, came preloaded with courtly associations.[82] Like the Leicester of antigovernmental lore, and like Lyly's Tophas, Bottom deceives himself into thinking that all parts suit him, including that of the lover. The object of his amorous attentions is an infantilizing fairy queen who charms her lover to sleep on a flowery bank: a combination of Spenser's Gloriana and Lyly's Cynthia, who shares a name and a taste for "lion, bear, or wolf, or bull" (2.1.180) with Ovid's Circe.[83] In his depiction of this mercurial queen bestowing "sweet favors" on a "hateful fool" (4.1.49), Shakespeare alludes to Elizabeth's alleged preference for theatrical upstarts and her tendency to emasculate her courtiers. The incongruous "meddling monkey" on which Titania might dote (2.1.181) even recalls one of the queen's more controversial pet names. Although Ovid's Circe has no simian creatures dancing attendance on her, Elizabeth had dubbed Jean de Simier, the go-between in her last courtship with the Duc d'Alençon, her monkey. The "sweet favors" she showed that meddling gentleman had enraged a jealous Leicester, causing tongues to wag throughout the country.[84]

Like Diana and Circe, the Fairy Queen appears in works connected with Leicester's courtship of Elizabeth, including the Kenilworth entertainments and the Woodstock entertainments (1575, published in 1585).[85] Because of such factors Stephen Greenblatt endorses the critical tradition that casts the entertainment at Kenilworth as the inspiration for *A Midsummer Night's Dream*, which he characterizes as a "gorgeous compliment to Elizabeth." If Shakespeare's play attends to "the charismatic power of royalty," however, it also manifests an abiding interest in those touched, translated, or "transported" (4.2.4) by that power.[86] The phallic image of "Cupid's fiery shaft, / Quench'd in the chaste beams of the wat'ry moon" (2.1.161–62) pays a Lylean compliment to Elizabeth, praising her ability to raise and to stay male desire.[87] But it also reformulates in high poetic terms the lurid image of Leicester's "pillor of fier" vainly drowning itself in the "gaping g[u]llfe" and "bottomeless barrell of" female "virginnitye." And, more intriguingly still, in its attention to the swerve of Cupid's "bolt," which falls on the "little western flower, / Before milk-white, now purple with love's wound" (2.1.166–67), it locates the origins of Oberon's transformative magic in erotic energies misdirected at the Virgin Queen. As we have seen, Leicester was associated with "ointment[s]" meant to "provocke ... filthy luxury," similar in kind if not in effect to the "juice" that Oberon uses to make "man or woman madly dote / Upon the next live creature that it sees" (2.1.170–71).[88] *A Midsummer Night's Dream*, by replaying such familiar motifs in a higher register, renders ambiguous homage to Leicester, relating his role as the queen's failed lover to his role as the patron who commissioned Golding's translations of Ovid, the poet renowned for confounding misplaced erotic desire and the "desire with externall fame above the starres to mount."[89]

The unorthodox suggestion that the rechanneling of vain desires for the queen enabled a flowering of magical or creative powers—that brutish sleep might lead to a substantial dream—is confirmed by Bottom's experiences in the play. An ass who falls asleep on stage as Lyly's Tophas does, and who dreams up an erotic encounter with a fairy queen as Spenser's Arthur or Chaucer's Thopas do, Bottom also expresses desires and ambitions that Shakespeare shared. By revising the Actaeon myth to have Bottom's physical transformation precede his visionary experience, Shakespeare fuses "metamorphic exaltation and degradation into a single, causally connected act."[90] The transformation becomes the enabling condition of Bottom's "rare vision" of the Fairy Queen, which inspires him "to write a ballet of this dream" entitled "'Bottom's Dream,' because it hath no bottom" (4.1.214–16). *A Midsummer Night's Dream* thus parallels Bottom's experiences with the playwright's own, encouraging us to find artistic value in the amorous ambitions that the Fairy Queen inspires. Bottom's encounter with bottomlessness produces radically different results than Munsur Fatpanche's; to "have been the lover of the Fairy Queen" in this play, Helen Hackett explains, is to have had "a metaphysical experience, a transformatory revelation."[91] Bottom is not, or not only, a satiric butt, since the behaviors that he renders ridiculous are rewarded with improved status by play's end, when he becomes a "made" man (4.2.18).[92] Richard Dutton finds in *A Midsummer Night's Dream* "a perfect allegory of relations between the acting companies and the court" at century's end.[93] In Bottom this allegory conflates the role of the actor-playwright with that of the royal favorite. Bottom may become "the privileged vessel" of aesthetic "experience," but only because he willingly subjects himself to the degraded and degrading desires of a queen.[94]

Not coincidentally, Bottom is the play's most memorable character. Shakespeare himself remembers Bottom throughout his career, and endows the characters that derive from Bottom with the same haunting quality, the result of their preposterous violations of social expectations on the one hand and their status as reconstructions of preexisting materials on the other. These two functions are related; according to Patricia Parker, the "Shakespearean preposterous," a category in which she includes both Bottom and Falstaff, is a means of "breaching" the topic of "responsibility for actions in the past or what had gone *before*."[95] *A Midsummer Night's Dream* concerns itself with conflicted reactions generated by the queen's leading favorites, the hateful fools who had risen to preeminence by preposterously humbling themselves to please court ladies. Having, in the popular imagination, traded sexual services for high political status, these men were as much a contradiction to the Elizabethan "sex/gender system" as the queen herself.[96] *A Midsummer Night's Dream* emphasizes the role that individual perception plays in the evaluation of such protean creatures; as Barkan puts it, "that the Fairy Queen sees Bottom as the incarnation of beauty transforms him upward just as surely as the physical change imposed by Puck transforms him downward."[97] Although many, like Francis Bacon, recoiled from "men of this kind," Shakespeare found that the strange mixture of praise, condemnation, and mockery they elicited made for theatrically compelling material.[98]

That Shakespeare found much to say on behalf of the men made, or remade, by his queen is best evidenced by his "corpulent" and narcoleptic knight, Falstaff (*1 Henry IV*, 2.4.422), to whom we are now ready to return. Fat, sweaty, cowardly, drunken, lecherous, hypocritical, and eager to exploit his status as a royal favorite to social advantage, Shakespeare's "reverent Vice, that grey Iniquity . . . [and] vanity in years" (*1 Henry IV*, 2.4.453–54) is constituted of the same materials as the Leicester of opposition literature, that greedy figure of "intolerable licentiousness" who became "old in iniquitie."[99] A lying "round man," who disregards the safety of the soldiers under his command, and who urges his prince to become "for recreation sake . . . a false thief" (2.4.140, 1.2.155–56), Falstaff has been given short shrift by recent literary critics interested in stage representations of royal favoritism, presumably because Hal terminates the relationship when he ascends the throne.[100] For the length of two plays, however, Falstaff's fantasies of social elevation by means of his prince's ill-judged favor are given free play: "the laws of England are at my commandment," he gloats when Hal is crowned, "Blessed are they that have been my friends, and woe to my Lord Chief Justice!" (*2 Henry IV*, 5.3.136–38). When Hal at last turns his countenance from "that vain man" (*2 Henry IV*, 5.5.44), Hal's own past is not the only "foil" that sets off his "reformation" (*1 Henry IV*, 1.2.213–15). Shakespeare's prince accomplishes a task at which Shakespeare's queen had signally failed.

The possibility that Shakespeare's surfeiting "town bull" (*2 Henry IV*, 2.2.158) glances at the "common bull of the court" need not preclude other well-established "pastimes," including the identification of Falstaff with Lord Cobham, or his connection to the Marprelate controversy.[101] On the contrary, the layering of possibilities contributes to the celebrated richness of Falstaff's character. A quintessentially theatrical creature, Falstaff never fails to generate "the uncanny but inescapable impression... that *'we are seeing what we saw before.'*"[102] Throughout the Falstaff plays, Shakespeare urges audiences to recognize that they are revisiting familiar ground. Falstaff famously refers to the recent kerfuffle over his original name (offensive to Cobham because Oldcastle was an ancestor by marriage), for example, when he assures us that Oldcastle is "not the man" (*2 Henry IV*, epilogue, 32), in effect publicizing the Cobham reading while quashing it.[103] He also encourages further speculation regarding the intended target: if Oldcastle is not the man, who is? Meanwhile, the new name signals a renewed emphasis, in the wake of the Cobham affair, on the conjunction in Falstaff of the amorous minion and the "aged counselor."[104] Where "Oldcastle" evokes an elderly courtier (as in the phantom reference to "my old lad of the castle" [*1 Henry IV*, 1.2.41–42]), "Falstaff," with its familiar pun on detumescence, highlights that character's sexuality, the subject of knowing jokes in the plays that feature him.[105]

The characterization of Falstaff as a hypocritical Protestant is consistent with both the Cobham controversy and the materials of Leicester's black legend. In *A Briefe Discoverie*'s view, the "infamous libels" about the earl "secretly cast out and spred abroad" were motivated by the fact that he was "one of the greatest, & principall patrons of true religion."[106] Perhaps, then, Shakespeare turned to Oldcastle, the proto-Protestant leader accused of treason, because of his commonalities with Leicester, another Protestant leader accused of treason.[107] Consider the woodcut in Foxe's *Actes and Monuments*, which shows Oldcastle chained to the gallows, yet another sweaty old man subjected to fiery baiting.[108] The "image of the grotesque puritan" that Falstaff evokes, while popularized by the Marprelate controversy, first gained currency when Leicester was depicted as an "icon of bacchanalian revelry," given to "overmuch attending his pleasures" and excessive "drinking and belly chere," nearly a decade before Shakespeare's fat knight disgraced the English stage.[109]

A "roasted Manningtree ox" (*1 Henry IV*, 2.4.452), a "whoreson little tidy Bartholomew boar-pig," who needs to leave "foining a' nights" and "patch up" his "old body for heaven" (*2 Henry IV*, 2.4.231–33), Falstaff appears destined to suffer a familiar fate for his defiance of age and nature. When he recoils from "remember[ing]" this promised "end" (*2 Henry IV*, 2.4.235), his odd locution suggests a kind of textual déjà vu, as if the self-conscious fat man remembers always already being dismembered.

Over the course of the three plays in which he appears, the entire "dictionary of slanders" devised for Leicester is leveled at Falstaff.[110] The correspondences between "*Munsur Fatpanche*" in *News* and Shakespeare's "fat paunch" (*1 Henry IV*, 2.4.144) are numerous: both sweat copiously enough to stain their shirts (*2 Henry IV*, 1.2.208–10, 5.5.24–25; *News*, 146); both are "greasy" (*1 Henry IV*, 2.4.228; *News*, 148); both are likened to a "Flemish drunkard" (*Merry Wives of Windsor*, 2.1.23; *News*, 148); and both stand accused of "gluttony, drunkenness, and riot," as well as lust. Although we never see Falstaff in hell, we are repeatedly asked to imagine him there, by Hal's references to him as a "devil" or an "old white-bearded Sathan" (*1 Henry IV*, 2.4.447, 463), or by his own wistful musings that "If to be old and merry be a sin, then many an old host that I know is damn'd" (*1 Henry IV*, 2.4.471–72).[111] Even Falstaff's telltale name evokes anti-Leicestrian discourses: not only does *News* make jokes about the ubiquitous bear and ragged staff, it also imagines Leicester's ghost letting "fall [his] staffe" of office for fear of being sent to hell (150). The falling staff was a favorite symbol for what we would now call Leicester's erectile dysfunction—a tactic that Shakespeare exploits in his depiction of his "wither'd elder," whose "naked weapons" form the constant object of his own as well as other men's wit. "Is it not strange," Poins asks Hal as they observe the old man flirting "that desire should so many years outlive performance?" (*2 Henry IV*, 2.4.258, 207, 260–61).[112]

At the theater, such verbal resonances were substantiated, quite literally, by the actor who likely personated Falstaff: the clown Will Kempe, who had been a member of Leicester's troupe, and whom Sir Philip Sidney referred to familiarly as "my Lord of Lester jesting plaier."[113] Kempe's Bottom must have shaped the reception of Kempe's Falstaff, prompting returning spectators to compare Falstaff's relationship with Hal (or with the merry wives) to Bottom's relationship with Titania.[114] Shakespeare exploits Kempe's past in other ways, too. Hal draws attention to the clown's former employment when he notes "how ill white hairs becomes a fool and jester" (*2 Henry IV*, 5.5.48). Kempe had been with Leicester at his court in the Netherlands (according to *News* and other sources, a carnivalesque place of "quaffing" [148], more like a tavern than a place of business), where the earl used the clown to entertain local magnates fond of drinking, gaming, and rioting.[115] Spoken by this former servant, the remark about knowing an old host (or an old ghost, in the alternate reading of this line) damned for being merry thus takes on a topical cast. References of this sort served as "the animating spark" of early modern clowning, and, according to Robert Hornback, Kempe had developed a special knack for satirizing the puritans associated with his former employer.[116]

Even the garments Kempe wore may have evoked his deceased patron for members of the original audience. A conversation between Falstaff and Pistol in the crucial moments before Hal's rejection calls repeated attention to what Falstaff's clothing "doth infer" or "show" (*1 Henry IV*, 5.5.13–14). As Jonson's "popular breeches" show, old clothing repurposed as theatrical costume carried its history on to the stage, where it could materialize relations with court figures, thus exposing these to the audience's collective judgment. Such old clothes inferred a "world of social relations," carrying with them memories which had the power to "mold and shape" the wearers "both physically and socially."[117] Actors were alert to these powers and used them to produce certain effects. Henry Wotton felt that Globe actors who showed like "Knights of the Order with their Georges and garters," for example, made "greatness very familiar, if not ridiculous."[118] When Falstaff dreams about having "new liveries" made (5.5.11) as he stands "stained with travel, and sweating with desire to see [Hal], thinking of nothing else, putting all affairs else in oblivion, as if there were nothing else to be done but to see him" (5.5.24–27), we are made to take special note of his costume.[119] Alluding to Elizabeth's motto—"'Tis '*semper idem*'" (5.5.28)—Pistol frames the tableau of the devoted old knight in his sweaty shirt as a reenactment of previous events, a staged memory. Did Kempe don his old livery garments, adorned with the Dudley bear and ragged staff, to play Shakespeare's fat favorite?[120] And did the clown in staging the dream "of such a kind of man, / So surfeit-swell'd, so old, and so profane" (*2 Henry IV*, 5.5.49–50) put on the manners of his ex-patron, a man infamous for embodying these traits, notorious for his breach of generational decorum, known to have been killed, as Falstaff fears that he will be, both with "hard opinions" and "a sweat" (*2 Henry IV*, epilogue 30–31)? Whatever the answer to these questions, we might see in Leicester's jester playing Falstaff the embodiment of the theater's commodification of court materials.

Leicester was a natural candidate for such treatment, not only because of his notoriety, but also because of his deep associations with the theater in general and fools in particular. According to his critics, the earl was a man "full of colors, juglinges, and dissimulations" who had earned the queen's favor through his talent for "shewes" (*News*, 156, 144), and who therefore had an affinity for "harlotry players" (*1 Henry IV*, 2.4.395–96).[121] These constructions of the earl as a man of the theater had, as we have seen, a basis in fact. Leicester had presided over key events in the development of the theater as an institution, including the grant of the first royal license in 1574. In this document, the queen awarded special privileges to Leicester's troupe in exchange for "the recreation of oure loving subiectes [and] for our solace and pleasure."[122] The man accused of elevating himself by serving the queen's "filthy lust" thus procured the social elevation of actors, so that they could serve the queen's "pleasure."[123] Leicester also furnished Elizabeth with her official fool, Richard Tarleton, who served the queen's pleasure so efficiently that he became Groom of the Chamber and Master of the Fence.[124] The licensed fool and the licentious favorite occupied similar positions in relation to the queen: both agreed to humiliate themselves to elevate themselves. The homology between earl and actor, favorite and fool, struck observers, like the author of *News*, who makes "Tarlton his ruffin" a member of the earl's seedy entourage in hell (155). Critics have long linked elements of Falstaff's characterization to the foolery of Tarleton and Kempe.[125] Falstaff's taste for histrionics and his talent for self-promotion—he hopes to translate his talent for counterfeiting into an earldom or a dukedom and to immortalize himself in printed ballads with his "own picture on the top" (*2 Henry IV*, 4.3.48–49)—reflect their enterprising former patron as well. Collapsing the distinction between fool and favorite, Shakespeare gives us in Falstaff a "ruffin" (*2 Henry IV*, 4.5.124) who is both Leicester and jester, a royal minion confident of his ability to please "the gentlewomen" but understandably more anxious about his reception with men (*2 Henry IV*, epilogue, 23–24).[126]

The network of connections tying Leicester to the theater must have registered differently with Shakespeare and his colleagues than with the authors of opposition tracts, a factor that helps account for the ambivalence and ambiguity in the character of Falstaff. When polemical writers made a taste for histrionics a component of the earl's notorious identity, they meant no praise to the earl or to the theater: in their hands, "age in love" is an antitheatrical trope, which conflates dramatic performance with categorical transgression, attributing both to the queen's Circean powers. If the incident with William Storage offers any indication, in 1588 members of the earl's troupe viewed attacks on his "raggyd staffe" as attacks on themselves: they identified their professional fortunes with his reputation, which they defended.[127] Nearly a decade later, with Leicester dead and that reputation destroyed, and with the theater staking out a new and more independent position for itself, matters had gotten more complicated. Whatever Shakespeare and Kempe were up to with their "Sir John Paunch" (*1 Henry IV*, 2.2.66), they were not in the business of defending or attacking the historical Earl of Leicester. Like Joseph Roach's Betterton, the multiply-ghosted figure of Leicester's jester playing Falstaff may have functioned instead as a kind of "effigy" to "gather in the memory of audiences."[128] Leicester's notoriety showed "perpetual infamy" to be a hot commodity; "loud Rumor," a "pipe / Blown by surmises, jealousies, conjectures" upon whose "tongues continual slanders ride" (*2 Henry IV*, prologue, 2–16), seems always to leave people wanting more. Strikingly, Shakespeare's unholy goddess figures slander as a kind of political "news," brought by "the wind, [her] post-horse," to an eager public which spreads "from the orient to the drooping west" (*2 Henry IV*, prologue, 38, 3–4).

The metaphor of the wind, which, as we saw in the last chapter, was used by Lyly and Sidney to describe verbal assaults on Leicester, conveys the boundlessness associated with the circulation of slanderous materials among potentially infinite strangers. Thanks to the invocation of Rumor, for the duration of *2 Henry IV*, the audience in Shakespeare's theater is made coterminous with this virtual public of "open ... ears," eager to be stuffed with "false reports" (prologue, 1, 8). All become avid consumers of Rumor's news, who taste of the "contempt" that she inspires and assume the feelings of "moral superiority" that she retails.[129]

Although the queen's councillors worried about notoriety and wise individuals tried to avoid it, Shakespeare harvested its perpetuating and leveling energies to theatrical ends.[130] He is predictably self-conscious about this development. When Poins and Hal secretly observe, laugh at, and pass judgment on the "strange" disjunction between Falstaff's age and his sexual desires, the metatheatrical device highlights a shared, voyeuristic fascination with the clownish spectacle of senescent male sexuality. This self-reflective moment illustrates the process by which a violation of sexual and generational norms transforms individual spectators into a critical public, defined and elevated by its collective adherence to rules of social and moral decorum. According to Hobbes, laughter on such occasions results from "the *sudden glory* arising from some sudden *conception* of some *eminency* in ourselves, by *comparison* with the *infirmity* of others." Earlier thinkers, too, had commented on the emancipatory force of communal laughter; in a passage decrying the tendency of plays to extend "judgement" to "the worste sorte," Stephen Gosson rebukes defamatory depictions of real people that provoke the "wonderfull laughter" of the "commen people."[131] Even Falstaff comments on the socially productive force of laughter, which he relies on to secure his position with Hal: "I will devise matter enough of this Shallow to keep Prince Harry in continual laughter" (*2 Henry IV*, 5.1.78–80). *2 Henry IV* dramatizes the power of the theater to unite and elevate its audience through "continual laughter." Made privy to the conversation between Hal and Poins, the audience is invited to pass judgment by laughing with the prince. The common work of enforcing social norms through laughter suspends class divisions, so that Shakespeare's audience momentarily participates by means of theatrical proxy in the "being of the sovereign."[132]

As Poins's offer to "beat" Falstaff "before his whore" (*2 Henry IV*, 2.4.257) suggests, the figure of the old man in love also instills a desire for more spectacles, of a distinctly punitive kind. There was a vogue for such spectacles at the turn of the sixteenth century: *Merry Wives*, *Twelfth Night* (1601–2), *Hamlet* (1600–1601), *The Revenger's Tragedy* (1607), and *Antony and Cleopatra* (1608) are all extended exercises in beating old men before their whores. By dwelling on the sexual subjection of their elders, and reducing these bloat men to "huge hill[s] of flesh" (*1 Henry IV*, 2.4.243), Hal, Poins, Hamlet, Octavius, and Vindice claim the masculine authority associated with disembodiment for themselves. Barbara Freedman wonders why "Shakespeare was interested ... in writing about clownish male sexual humiliation and punishment."[133] One answer is that this theatrical pattern appealed to disenfranchised, second-generation Elizabethan men, weary of (or eager to reflect on) their double subjection to the queen and her aging minions. Like Poins, who remembers with pleasure "how the fat rogue roar'd" when Hal describes Falstaff "sweat[ing] to death" (*1 Henry IV*, 2.2.108–9), or the writer of *News*, who fantasizes "*Munsur Fatpanche*" subject to eternal fiery torment, these younger men must have enjoyed watching their elders burnt in effigy.

While Hal's "I know thee not, old man" (*2 Henry IV*, 5.5.47) may mark a collective reaction to the Elizabethan regime, it had more intimate implications for Shakespeare and his colleagues. The age-in-love trope helped them not just to capitalize on but also to distance themselves from their own institutional past, tainted by the very condition that glamorized it: service to the moon's pleasure. In this context, Falstaff's desire for new livery signals a shift in institutional allegiance from the patronage system to the public theater. His old shirt, soon to be discarded, becomes a reminder of the duty, obedience, and service owed the infamous earl. The parricidal themes that attend Hal's rejection of Falstaff suggest Shakespeare's adulterating awareness of the treachery involved in this process. The Falstaff plays coincide with a period of transition in the history of the theater, which culminated with the 1598 edict "allowing" only the Lord Chamberlain and the Lord Admiral's men, a "watershed" event that Richard Dutton argues changed the status of shareholders in these companies, lifting them from a vagabond state to a "privileged position."[134] Before they secured this position, the artisans of the newly professionalized theater had occasion to reflect on their ambiguous status in relation to the court. Although their former patron had become a target of widespread satire, he may have also functioned as an aspirational model for these theatrical artists, who, like Falstaff and Bottom, sought to translate their histrionic talents into social and material advantage. Kempe playing Falstaff is, among other things, a servant parodying his deceased master to secure the patronage of a new one, the paying audiences of the public stage: at once an image of a kind of petty treason, an eloquent and multifaceted figure of love and betrayal, and a poignant reminder of how close the "harlotry players" had once been to the celebrated queen.

In his final moment in the histories, Falstaff conveys the ambiguity of his position by kneeling, "before you"—that is, the mixed audiences of the theater—"but indeed, to pray for the Queen" (*2 Henry IV*, epilogue, 16–17). In this posture Falstaff recalls iconic representations of courtly submission, like the Leicester pictured in Gascoigne's *Noble Arte*, or the epilogue of *Endymion*, who encourages the entire audience to "not only stoop, but with all humility lay both our hands and hearts at Your Majesty's feet" (15–16).

Submitting to the audience of the public theater instead, Falstaff highlights the ways in which Shakespeare's customers have usurped a place of authority formerly reserved for the queen. Falstaff goes on to note that "all the gentlewomen here have forgiven me" (*2 Henry IV*, epilogue, 22–23), a comment that conflates the women in the audience with that queen, implicitly inviting men to reach a different conclusion.[135] By emphasizing the function of gender in the exercise of good judgment—only "good wenches" would place Falstaff among the "men of merit" who "are sought after" (*2 Henry IV*, 2.4.375)—the history plays call the queen's qualification for good rule into question. At the same time, however, Shakespeare shares in Elizabeth I's fondness for self-dramatizing old men, since his

FIG. 5. George Gascoigne, *The Noble Arte of Venerie or Hunting* (1575), 133. By permission of the Folger Shakespeare Library.

Sir John Paunch is no mere "Munsur Fatpanche." A strong toil of affect (guilt, melancholy, nostalgia, admiration) modulates what had been, until Shakespeare came to it, a straightforward satiric trope. Even the coldly rational Hal finds that "were't not for laughing" he "should pity" Falstaff (*1 Henry IV*, 2.2.110). Shakespeare turned the national pastime of baiting courtly old men into a profitable theatrical venture, a process that involved a recalibration of the theater's relation to the structures of power and to the concepts of recreation and pleasure. Falstaff is the self-identified "lugg'd bear" who facilitates this transaction, but whose fecund charm, self-conscious wit, and inexhaustible talent for "shewes" also threaten to undermine it. Since drama, unlike polemics, thrives on ambiguity and conflict, this tension made for a successful stage formula. If early responses offer an indication, Falstaff achieved instant immortality, becoming a prime mover in establishing his author's reputation and conjuring the enduring public to which we—along with Elizabeth I—belong.[136]

Often disregarded in analyses of Falstaff, *Merry Wives* best illustrates Shakespeare's conversion of scandalous material into renewable forms of theatrical pleasure. Perhaps the Cobham controversy emboldened the playwright to develop features of his knight left latent in *1 Henry IV*. Although Falstaff eats and drinks to excess in that play, the erotic aspects of his surfeit are subsumed in a series of jokes and in his Endymion-like propensity for napping on stage. The Circe/Elizabeth figure associated with the age-in-love pattern is relegated to the margins of the play, where she takes the shape of the Welsh lady, whose speech is "as sweet as ditties highly penn'd / Sung by a fair queen in a summer's bow'r" (3.1.206–7).[137] In his perceptive analysis of *1 Henry IV*, Garret Sullivan argues that the Circe myth haunts Shakespeare's representation of the relation between Hal and Falstaff. While Sullivan contends that Falstaff plays "*both* tavern Circe and dangerous male favorite" to Hal, Falstaff himself casts Hal as the enchantress, at least if we take his observations that he is "bewitch'd with the rogue's company" and that "the rascal" has "given me medicines to make me love him" (2.2.17–19) as referring to the young prince.[138] Falstaff's associations with bestiality, effeminacy, and idleness identify him, meanwhile, as a stereotypical victim to the classical goddess.[139] Hal further emphasizes this pattern by bestowing animal monikers on his favorite and by categorizing Falstaff as a "latter spring" (*1 Henry IV*, 1.2.158), a preposterous old man who, having failed to observe the natural "race and course of age," espouses lusty behavior inappropriate to "hys due tyme and season."[140]

The patterns marking Falstaff as an aging lover in *1 Henry IV* are concretized in *2 Henry IV* and amplified in *Merry Wives*. Where in *1 Henry IV* identifies Falstaff as "a whoremaster" (2.4.469), who "went to a bawdy-house not above once in a quarter—of an hour" (3.3.16–17), *2 Henry IV* stages the lecherous (Leicesterous?) aspect of the royal favorite, and provides him with a "quean" who loves him "better than . . . e'er a scurvy young boy of them all" (2.4.272–73). And *Merry Wives* gives the amorous aspect of its aging antihero free reign: a "greasy knight," "well-nigh worn to pieces with age," Falstaff nevertheless determines to play the "young gallant" (2.1.108, 21–22). The command to show Falstaff in love (whether or not Elizabeth issued it) is thus far more perceptive, and the characterization of Falstaff more consistent, than critics normally allow.[141] The farce returns the old man in lust to the context of female domination: the "female-controlled plotting . . . parallels the Queen-dominated court politics," while magnifying "the pattern of provocation, deferral, prohibition, and frustration found in the cult of Elizabeth." This is the context in which Falstaff—like the queen herself "inclining to threescore" (*1 Henry IV*, 2.4.425), and, as W. H. Auden remarks, way too old to be *Hal's* favorite—belongs.[142]

From its opening conversation about upstarts and coats of arms, laced with sexual and bestial innuendoes, to its allusions to the Actaeon myth and the Order of the Garter, to its final restaging of the paradigmatic bearbaiting scene, *Merry Wives* tightens the connections between its antihero and Elizabeth's amorous minions. Falstaff no longer operates at the safe remove of history: worried about appearing ridiculous to the "fine wits" and "the ear of the court" (4.5.100, 95), he blurs the distinction between the action on- and offstage, encouraging the audience to indulge in "pastimes." The setting and the language of the play abet this process by situating the characters in comparative relation to offstage courtly figures, including Leicester, who had been "constable" (4.5.119) of Windsor from 1562 until his death, and the "radiant Queen" (5.5.46) who often resided in its castle, the seat of the Knights of the Garter. When he imagines one female target as "a region in Guiana, all gold and bounty" (1.3.69), Falstaff likens his amorous ambitions to those of Ralegh and Leicester, who had parlayed their status as royal minions into profitable new world ventures.[143] The fat knight also imagines playing the "cheaters," or escheater, to the wives' "exchequers" (1.3.70–71), framing his sexual opportunism as a lucrative form of royal service. Elsewhere, Mistress Quickly asks us to judge Falstaff's preposterous courting style against that of "the best courtier of them all (when the court lay at Windsor) who could never have brought her to such a canary; yet there has been knights, and lords, and gentlemen, with their coaches... they could never get her so much as sip on a cup with the proudest of them all, and yet there has been earls, nay (which is more) pensioners" (2.2.61–77). Even her malapropism—"canary" for "quandary"—recalls the specific earls and pensioners, who for all their "alligant terms" and "wine and sugar" (2.2.68), failed to secure the lady's agreement: Leicester and Essex, who translated their courtship of the queen into the right to farm customs on the Mediterranean wines of which Falstaff is so fond.[144] *Merry Wives* imagines Falstaff as one in a long line of such amorous and ambitious "knights, and lords, and gentlemen" who court in vain, arguably the most memorable, and certainly the largest, Elizabethan embodiment of "age in love."

As Shakespeare's promiscuous layering of allusions and references indicates, his repurposing of the age-in-love trope in *Merry Wives* does not weigh in on particular conflicts among courtiers. Rather, the play's handling of this trope, and of the bearbaiting motif associated with it, clarifies that it became bound up for Shakespeare with broader issues of memory, judgment, empowerment, and recreation. While all the Falstaff plays imagine the transgressive old man as a baited animal, in *Merry Wives* this baiting structures the plot.[145] Falstaff's first appearance follows an extended reference to bearbaiting, a "sport" Slender loves well (1.1.290), which sets the scene for the "public sport" of punishing the "old fat fellow" (4.4.13–14) in the final act. Slender prides himself on having "taken" an actual bear "by the chain" (1.1.295–96) but the play awards the honor to its middle-class wives, who are immune to Falstaff's courtship, discerning in their judgment of him, and resourceful in administering punishment.

Like *News*, *Merry Wives* baits the courtly old bear loosed on Windsor not just for his "lust and luxury" but also for aspiring "higher and higher" (5.5.94–98)—for seeking, that is, to translate his sexual services into material advantage. For this violation of norms, Falstaff is both effeminized and dehumanized. The public nature of Falstaff's punishment—other characters enact a play, in which he is dressed up, chained, beaten, pinched, and burned with fiery tapers—is important, and not just because it comically and hyperbolically combines the punishments meted out in Lyly's *Endymion* and in the anti-Leicestrian tradition. Ever the cause of wit in others, Falstaff encourages the play's characters to develop their powers of discernment. The tonic effect he has on the critical skills of these characters may be observed in their incessant attempts to categorize him and to devise appropriate infernal torments for him; like the members of Pluto's assembly in *News*, Mistress Ford wishes that the "wicked fire of lust" would melt "him in his own grease" (2.1.67–68).[146] Falstaff's love of "gallimaufry"—his failure to distinguish between "young and old," "high and low," and male and female (2.1.113–15)—generates in others a corresponding need to make and enforce distinctions. In their unanimous condemnation of the amorous old courtier in their midst, the middle-class citizens of Windsor discover themselves, with a little help from the theater, as an adjudicating public.

For some members of the original audience, the pleasures of watching Falstaff play "the lecher" (3.5.144) must also have resided in the clever overhauling of motifs by now as worn as the old knight himself. As Falstaff himself observes, the materials out of which he is constituted test people's ability to "invent anything that intends to laughter more" (*2 Henry IV*, 1.2.8). In *Merry Wives*, Shakespeare consciously challenges the virtuosity of his predecessors, inviting audiences to judge his inventiveness even as they judge his character. Like Sir Tophas and "Munsur Fatpanche,"

Shakespeare's fat man retains a page but the tiny foil is a "little gallant" (3.2.1) named Robin: an early modern Mini-Me. In *Merry Wives*'s rich trove of fat jokes and fantasized final judgments, the "gross wat'ry pumpion" (3.3.41), the sweating "Dutch dish," "half stew'd in grease" (3.5.119), finds himself "damn'd in hell" (2.2.10) in ever more ways and for ever more reasons. "Old, cold, wither'd" (5.5.153) Falstaff rivals Sir Tophas in his taste for old women and Ovidian hyperbole ("O powerful love that in some respects makes a beast a man; in some other, a man a beast" [5.5.4–6]). Where Lyly's *miles gloriosus* pursues two matrons seriatim, the polyamorous Falstaff thinks nothing of trying for two at once. Their husbands fail to register as obstacles; recalling the allegedly homicidal impulses of the "best courtier of them all," Falstaff wishes that Mrs. Ford's "husband were dead" (3.3.50). In another knowing wink at Leicester's black legend, the transformation of Falstaff into a lover goes so against the grain of nature that he requires chemical assistance in the form of "kissing-comfits, and snow eringoes" (5.5.20). Eager to suit himself up as a lover, Falstaff ends up cross-dressed as both a woman and a beast—the wives of Windsor disguise him first as "a witch, a quean, an old cozening quean" (4.2.172) and then as a "male deer" complete with horns (5.5.17). When the assignation with his paramours ends with the arrival of some faux fairies and their "radiant Queen" (5.5.46), Falstaff is beaten as Corsites was in *Endymion*. Falstaff then lies down on stage with eyes tightly shut, a parody of Sir Tophas's parody of Endymion. Thus is Falstaff, like his precursors on stage, and like the queen's amorous "bere whelp," "made an ass" in front of his women (5.5.119).

The concluding images of Falstaff as a baited animal or "brib'd-buck" (5.5.24) chained by an oak showcase Shakespeare's synthetic, accretive, and relentlessly analogical mode of characterization. As an emasculated man dismembered by dogs, Actaeon is an analogue of the baited bear that the audience has been lead to expect ever since the barking dogs prompted Slender to wonder whether "there [be] bears i' th' town" (1.1.287). The allusions to Ovid trigger comparative readings of this scene, since the Actaeon myth was associated with courtiers given to "foule excesse of chamberworcke, or too much meate and drink," to quote from Golding's letter to his patron, that "Knyght of the most noble Order of the Garter."[147] Leicester's taste for the *Noble Arte of Venerie* and ignoble acts of venery made Ovid's "unluckie knight" (3.225) a natural point of comparison, moreover. The parallels became if anything more pronounced after Leicester died, since the death of Golding's Actaeon inspires "much muttering" among survivors: "some thought there was extended / A great deale more extremitie than neded" while others "commended Dianas doing." As was the case with Leicester, these incompatible judgments, which lead "eche partie" to "applie / Good reasons to defende their case" (3.308–9), result in a communal compulsion to revisit Actaeon's story, who is thereby immortalized.

The Fairy Queen reinforces such analogic "pastimes" not only through her presence, which reintroduces the Circe/Diana figure to the central position she normally occupies in age-in-love tropes, but also through her long speech about the Order of the Garter. In it, she frames the tableau of the fat knight, crouching on "bending" knees, with the telltale chain around his neck, and surrounded by the fairies who beat him with fiery tapers, in heraldic terms. The fairy dance, she claims, is "like to the Garter's compass," containing the chained and baited Falstaff (5.5.65). Such a "ring" (5.5.66) was a familiar sight in London—knights of the Garter, including Essex, Leicester, and Hatton, adorned their arms, badges, and persons with it (in his many portraits, Leicester wears jewels emblazoned with the Garter motto). If we take the Fairy Queen's speech as a stage direction, the fairies complete their provocative picture—the theatrical equivalent of what the Privy Council called a "slanderous device"—by writing "*Honi soit qui mal y pense*" using "flow'rs for their charactery" (5.5.69, 73).[148] This tableau lampoons aristocratic devices generally and the infamous bear device specifically, cementing the relation elaborated in all three Falstaff plays between Shakespeare's fat knight and Elizabeth's favorite knights.[149] Given the Order of the Garter's legendary origins in a judgment passed on the sexual indiscretions of a monarch, Shakespeare realizes in Falstaff's "trial" (5.5.89) a long-standing Elizabethan fantasy: to call a royal minion to public "accompt... to see what other men could say against him" (*Leicester's Commonwealth*, 186). With characteristic dexterity, the playwright invokes the Garter motto's retributive properties to engage the failsafe mechanism of satire, reminding those who judge that they are implicated in their judgments.[150]

As befits a play about wit, discrimination, and judgment, *Merry Wives* is written in the comparative mode: its multiple allusions and its metatheatrical moments suggest that "Fat Falstaff" has a "great scene" (4.6.16–17) because it is an incrementally *better* scene than previous ones. The play thus solicits aesthetic judgments as eagerly as it solicits political ones; by positioning Falstaff against a stage tradition that includes Bottom, Endymion, and Sir Tophas, Shakespeare encourages his audience to develop a discriminating appreciation for his evolving artistry. He is not just retailing courtly wares, but improving on them, turning the "public sport" of his theater into a vehicle for his empowerment as an author. When Falstaff is beaten for getting into the clothes of an old "quean", more than one courtly old bear is baited. A master of the forms that Lyly pioneered, Shakespeare marks his superiority to the earlier playwright, whose works suffer by comparison from their exaggerated subjection to the queen's "solace and pleasure." Ben Jonson, who might be faulted for his lack of generosity but never for his lack of perceptiveness, saw just "how farre" Shakespeare did "our Lily out-shine."[151] Although he is a foundational figure of English drama, whose contributions Shakespeare spent years honing, Lyly is not treated with the critical respect accorded the younger generation of Elizabethan playwrights. His status as the queen's chief theatrical panegyrist has something to do with that. We have learned to see unqualified praise of Elizabeth—of any monarch, perhaps—as unmanly and undignified, and we have been taught to want more from our plays. We want the pleasures attendant on judgment; no longer pleased to gaze on sovereignty, we expect to participate in it.

The standards for judgment extended by *Merry Wives* encourage audiences to reflect on the ways in which the Elizabethan court distinguished itself from the rest of English society with regard to gender and generational norms. In the history plays, Hal's unlikely proclivity for a licentious old man, a cowardly "fool" who pretends to be a "valiant lion" (*1 Henry IV*, 2.4.227, 274) and likes to play at being "a perfect king" invites similar comparisons.[152] Throughout, Falstaff assumes that he will become "Fortune's steward" (*2 Henry IV*, 5.3.130–31), confident of "the countenance that [Hal] will give" him (5.5.7–8). The Falstaff plays go out of their way to solicit anxieties about the "man that sits within a monarch's heart / and ripens in the sunshine of his favor" and who abuses "the countenance of the King" (*2 Henry IV*, 4.2.11–13). Shakespeare takes up the Catholic opposition's fantasy of an anarchic England rent by a predatory royal favorite, "A Bearwhelp" who "will overturn all if he be not stopped or muzzled in time," by playing on the fears that "the fift Harry" will "from curb'd license pluck / The muzzle of restraint, and the wild dog / Shall flesh his tooth on every innocent" (*2 Henry IV*, 4.5.130–32).[153] But Hal ultimately refuses to countenance his minion's hopes of preferential treatment or social advancement. The decision to "muzzle" Falstaff marks the way in which Shakespeare's ideal (young, male) prince differs from his actual (old, female) one, who had allowed her "unmoseled" bear to feast at will.[154] In contrast, Hal baits his fat favorite himself; in one of his prescient moods, Falstaff complains, "The young prince hath misled me. I am the fellow with the great belly, and he my dog" (*2 Henry IV*, 1.2.145–46). While the *Henry IV* plays tell "the story of the weaning of the prince from his dangerous male favorite," as Sullivan puts it, they also glance askew at another story, that of a female prince unable to wean herself from hers.[155] Hal's dismissive comment about the presumably dead Falstaff—"I should have a heavy miss of thee / If I were much in love with vanity"—might even comment on the queen's long-lived grief for her "fat . . . deer" (*1 Henry IV*, 5.4.105–7), whose final letter she kept by her bedside until the day she died. When Hal rejects Falstaff, he seals himself "into a steely performance as a king whose private affections appear to have been extinguished completely"—the kind of masculine monarch about whom disgruntled Elizabethans dreamed.[156]

Insofar as audiences caught these comparative "pastimes," they were put in the delicious position of passing judgment on the "best courtier of them all," a position that Elizabeth had tried and failed to reserve for herself. They were also invited to pass judgment on the queen, and to fantasize about her replacement, by a young man like Hal, who demonstrates his "right wits" and "good judgments" when he "turn[s] away the fat knight with the great belly doublet" (*Henry V*, 4.7.47–48).[157] In this way, the wish for God to "send the Prince a better companion" always already entails the wish for God to "send the companion a better Prince" (*2 Henry IV*, 1.2.199–201). The members of the audience share in the vicarious pleasures of de Certeau's historiographer, becoming virtual princes in the process.[158] The theater's usurping ambitions are made explicit in the final scene of *Merry Wives*, when an actor dresses up as the Fairy Queen to subject Falstaff to his final baiting. While the Queen of England could not bring herself to turn her countenance from her minion, her Shakespearean substitute, like Hal, shines brightly in the exercise of newfound authority.[159]

Although Falstaff's long association with Elizabeth's pleasure suggests that some first responders were alert to these political resonances, they need not have made the specific connection to Leicester for Falstaff to have his effect, since Shakespeare recreates the conditions of the controversy within the plays. Falstaff is a paradox in this regard: a fully detachable and timeless amalgam of timely materials—one reason perhaps that he always seems "outside of time."[160] In all three plays Shakespeare represents Falstaff as an already known quantity—an effeminate courtier, a creature of luxury, a "pampered glutton," an opportunistic upstart, the rhetorical target of prince and commoner alike.[161] To show this courtly bear baited is to call attention to how the phenomenon of notoriety, by encouraging "base comparisons," "continual slander," and "unsavory similes" (*1 Henry IV*, 2.4.250; *2 Henry IV*, induction, 6; *1 Henry IV*, 1.2.79), inspires broad-based participation in the political nation. Judging by contemporary anecdotes, Shakespeare's audiences were quick to avail themselves of the tools that he had provided. Several high-ranking Elizabethan courtiers, including the Earl of Essex, used Falstaff to comment mockingly on the behavior of their peers. The Countess of Southampton wrote to her husband (Shakespeare's patron) with the titillating gossip that "Sir John Falstaf is by his Mrs Dame Pintpot made father of a godly milers thumb, a boye that's a heade and very litel body," sounding for all the world like one of Shakespeare's judicious wives.[162] *Merry Wives* extends powers of participation to its female characters, provided they observe the social norms that Falstaff violates. Shakespeare's depiction of his transgressive knight is at once politically radical and socially conservative, in other words—although, in the moments that Falstaff generates sympathy, Shakespeare also flirts with being politically conservative and socially radical.

As might be expected, given my claim, Falstaff's self-consciousness about his own state of publicity is nearly unparalleled in the canon (only Cleopatra has a more developed sense of herself as a subject of public representation). The target of incessant rumors, Falstaff also threatens to resort to publicity to blacken Hal's reputation through "filthy tunes" (*1 Henry IV*, 2.2.45–46). Hal claims that Falstaff is "known as well as Paul's" (*1 Henry IV*, 2.4.526); Falstaff, meanwhile, wishes he knew where to find "a commodity of good names" (*1 Henry IV*, 1.2.82–83). Moments like these identify Falstaff's perpetual infamy as a commodity, like Jonson's "popular pants" or the books dedicated to Leicester sold at Paul's. Falstaff himself represents his relation to the prince as a matter of public speculation: "here I stand," he announces winningly, "Judge, my masters" (*1 Henry IV*, 2.4.439). That Shakespeare stages the loaded question of Falstaff's rejection metatheatrically, as a matter enacted before a critical audience, speaks volumes about the role that he envisages for his theater, a role which aligns it with the new pleasures associated with the printing press, the device for continual reproduction that was changing the conditions of publicity in England. The analogy that Shakespeare posits between the treatment of Falstaff and the baiting of bears indicates that the playwright considered the sport of taking potshots at a public figure a lucrative form of entertainment.

As the long history of commentary on Hal's rejection of Falstaff demonstrates, Shakespeare's comparatives do not always lead to easy judgments, however. Rowe notes that Shakespeare gives Falstaff "so much Wit as to make him almost too agreeable; and I don't know whether some People have not, in remembrance of the Diversion he had formerly afforded 'em, been sorry to see his Friend Hal use him so scurvily."[163] Like the bears to which he is compared, Falstaff has always conjured empathy from the burgeoning publics come to see him baited.[164] What attracted Shakespeare to the figure of "age in love," perhaps, is not just the way that this figure incited particular judgments, but also the ways in which it could be made to invite multiple judgments, and thereby defy or defer final judgment, generating instead a desire for more: one more insult, one more punishment, one more book, one play more, more debate, more analysis, more interpretation.[165] Part Leicester, part Kempe, part Tophas, part Corsites, part Bottom, part Actaeon, part bear, and part woman, Falstaff is also uniquely himself, just like the "old, cozening" queen who allegedly wanted to see him, and all the old men around her, in love. That Falstaff has transcended the circumstances of his invention should not blind us to the topical overtones that align him with that other paradigmatic figure of "grey Iniquity" (*1 Henry IV*, 2.4.453–54), the Earl of Leicester. For one thing, these can illuminate old critical problems, including the question of why Falstaff is fat. Tending to these "pastimes" also allows us a glimpse into how that acquisitive, competitive, and synthesizing intelligence we know by the name of Shakespeare transformed the raw materials of an age into artistic products that have endured for a very, very long time.

CHAPTER 3

Remembering Old Boys in *Twelfth Night*

At the end of *2 Henry IV*, Shakespeare makes a promise he does not keep—"to continue the story, with Sir John in it, and make you merry with fair Katherine of France" (epilogue, 28–29). The absence of reference to Henry V hints at an alternate version of history, a comic fairy tale in which Falstaff, and not the king, makes us merry by ending up with the princess of France. In actuality Shakespeare dispatches Hal's favorite much less glamorously, with what amounts to an accidental hand job from a "quean" (*2 Henry IV*, 2.1.47). Mistress Quickly reports that she felt the ailing Falstaff's feet, and then his knees, and then "up'ard and up'ard" but could not raise him, for "all was as cold as any stone" (*Henry V*, 2.3.23–26). Evidently, she lacks the powers of Lyly's Cynthia to rejuvenate her favorite. The ending that Shakespeare devises for his lecherous old knight revises the ending of *Endymion* (1591) to conform to the most satiric strain of anticourt polemics. The status of Falstaff's death as reported news, the quips about his lubricity, the jokes about his failing phallus, the debate about whether he is "in heaven or in hell" (2.3.8): all rehearse familiar material. Most damningly perhaps, like the "report" on the dead Earl of Leicester proffered by *News from Heaven and Hell*, Mistress Quickly's description of Falstaff's death reduces an old man fond of "handl[ing] women" to an inanimate object handled by women (2.3.36). George Bernard Shaw approved heartily, since in his view such is the fate of all old "soldiers broken down by debauchery."[1]

If Shakespeare was hoping thereby to contain his uncontainable creation, to "move on" as we say nowadays, the hope in which he dressed himself was drunk. No sooner does Mistress Quickly conclude but a spirited discussion breaks out among the characters concerning Falstaff's habits and vices. Their need to "remember" Falstaff (2.3.40) is taken up by the play itself, which seems loath to give up altogether on his "jests, and gipes, and knaveries, and mocks." Fluellen may have forgotten the name of the "fat knight" but Gower recalls it: "Sir John Falstaff" (4.7.48–51). While the memory of a great man may not outlive him by half a year, the memory of a funny one fares better in Shakespeare's plays (even Hamlet has more to say about Yorick than about his father). The flurry of remembrances that attends Falstaff's demise heralds his achievement of a peculiar immortality, of which Shakespeare must already have been aware.[2]

In the wake of the Falstaff plays, other playwrights capitalized on Shakespeare's success, creating derivative characters like the elderly braggart-soldier-turned-whoremonger Captain Shift, also known as "Master Apple-John," in Ben Jonson's *Every Man Out of His Humour* (1599).[3] The original ending of that controversial play, likely censored by court authorities, mocks a scenario familiar from *Endymion*, *The Merry Wives of Windsor* (1597), and *The Henriad* (1596–99). Macilente encounters "a player impersonating Queen Elizabeth" and falls down onstage, "dumb and astonished." The "lean Macilente" then imagines himself basking in the audience's approval, becoming "as fat as Sir John Falstaff" (*Every Man Out*, SD 5.6, 5.6.134.)[4] *Every Man Out* was performed at the Globe by the Lord Chamberlain's Men, on the same stage and by the same actors as the Falstaff plays. According to Marvin Carlson, dramatists draw on audience's memories of previous performances in this manner "to measure themselves against work of the past or to establish their position within a tradition."[5] Macilente's "ghosting" of Falstaff is consistent with Jonson's other attempts at antiquating his older rival, like his turn to Aristophanic "*Vetus Comoedia*" (*Every Man Out*, induction, 226). In what sounds like an outright challenge to Shakespeare, Jonson rejects old-style new comedies whose "argument .... might have been of some other nature, as of a Duke to be in love with a Countess, and that Countess to be in love with the Duke's son" in favor of new-style old comedy "near and familiarly allied to the time" (*Every Man Out*, 3.1.406–11).[6] Only "autumn-judgments"

(3.1.411), Jonson contends, would prefer the former to the latter. Jonson's generational jockeying for position was successful, in that critics still praise the innovativeness of his comical satires and minimize the continuities between these and Shakespeare's plays.[7] Far from being "completely new," however, Jonson's timely satires develop strains of comedy pioneered by Lyly and perfected by Shakespeare.[8]

Not to be outdone, and certainly not by Jonson, Shakespeare reincarnates his old knight, in a retrospective comic fairy tale about a competition among several men for the "favor" of a "fair princess" (*Twelfth Night*, 2.3.122, 3.1.97). Phebe Jensen argues that "Falstaff haunts *Twelfth Night*," finding in the "play's consideration of Puritan satire, Catholic satire, the history of festivity and revelry . . . a return to the not-quite-dead Oldcastle controversy."[9] Shakespeare does indeed remember Falstaff by dismembering him, scattering fragments of the fat knight throughout his courtly comedy. The "not-quite-dead" controversy to which *Twelfth Night* returns, however, is the one first staged by Lyly's play about love among old men. As allusions to *Endymion*, to his own Falstaff plays, to Jonson's *Every Man Out of His Humour* and *Cynthia's Revels* (1600), and to Sir John Harington's *A New Discourse on a Stale Subject, or the Metamorphosis of Ajax* (1596) show, in *Twelfth Night* Shakespeare considers once again the fact that "what great ones do the less will prattle of" (1.2.33).[10] Notably, the baiting metaphors that structure this witty comedy about the dogging of a matrimonially-minded upstart also shaped the "snarling" contests of wit that characterized turn-of-the-century theatrical culture.[11] While recent critics have viewed *Twelfth Night*'s allusions to bearbaiting from the perspective afforded by the "nearly identical cultural situations" of the theatre and the blood sport, I argue that these reflect a concern with the effect that the ad hominem attacks of satiric "substractors" (1.3.34–35) have on public life and collective memory.[12]

Bearbaitings continued to be tied to Leicester well into the 1590s, as Harington's *Ajax* demonstrates. This controversial pamphlet, which retails court gossip while detailing methods for the disposal of human waste, went through four editions, spawning numerous sequels and responses (thirteen imprints altogether) in the year it appeared.[13] If the reading public enjoyed learning about the court's privy doings, court figures were less enthusiastic about the chatter that *Ajax* provoked. Elizabeth I was especially enraged that the author "had aimed a shafte at Leicester"; after observing her reaction, Robert Markham found he "would not be in [the author's] beste jerkin for a thousand markes."[14] In the offending passage, the narrator touts his invention of the flush toilet, opining that he "may one day be put into the Chronicles, as good members of our countrey, more worthily then the great Beare that carried eight dogges on him when Monsieur was here."[15] Leicester's opposition to the French match, which D. C. Peck describes as "the central political event behind *Leicester's Commonwealth*," had first caused the dogs to "bark at the Bear that is so well britched" well over a decade before *Ajax* was published.[16] Yet Harington assumes his readers will still laugh at the allusion. Given that Harington elsewhere advocates using Holinshed's *Chronicles* as toilet paper, there can be little doubt regarding what he made of the "great Beare's" innovative attempts to go down in history as a "good member" of his country.[17] No wonder Elizabeth took offense and Shakespeare took note.

Leaving the *Chronicles* behind, Shakespeare began to experiment in different generic registers with the perdurable materials out of which he had fashioned his own "lugg'd bear" (*1 Henry IV*, 1.2.74). Leslie Fiedler notes that low comedy or satire is "the proper mode for rendering the foredoomed defeat of Old Age in love."[18] Lyly had pushed against these expectations by celebrating Endymion's "foredoomed defeat" as a Neoplatonic success, while his portrayals of Sir Tophas and Corsites struck the more conventional satiric note. As we saw in previous chapters, Shakespeare's initial approach to these materials was synthetic. Royal favorites who dream of becoming made men but who turn into asses instead, Bottom and Falstaff recall all three of Lyly's aging lovers. While Shakespeare invests them with the aspiring thoughts of an Endymion, "stitched to the stars ... much higher ... than [they] can reach," Bottom's "rare vision" of the Fairy Queen (*A Midsummer Night's Dream*, 4.1.205) exceeds his ability to describe or inhabit it, and Falstaff remains weighed down by the mercenary nature of his ambitions.[19] Uniquely memorable, both characters are also figures of ridicule.

Twelfth Night follows its predecessors in situating the unsettling convergence of erotic desire and social ambition in aging males, and in provoking derisive laughter at their "certain deformity," a word identified throughout the early modern period with the targets of social ridicule.[20] The treatment reserved for the amorous Malvolio reproduces key aspects of that inflicted on the lecherous Falstaff (or the Falstaffian Leicester, for that matter).[21] But *Twelfth Night* also deploys the bearbaiting trope to new effect, privileging its empathetic potential over its evaluative one, and ultimately insisting that "none can be call'd deform'd but the unkind" (3.4.368). Like the twins, whom C. L. Barber describes as forming a "composite," the play's two bears function as two halves of a whole, with Orsino assuming the positive and Malvolio absorbing the negative aspects of the age-in-love figure.[22] The "main difference" between these characters is thus not "one of class," or not of class only, but of generic emphasis and orientation.[23] It is as if Shakespeare decided to offer rival portraits of the great favorites: one reflecting the perceptions of others, and drawing on the materials of anticourt writers like Allen and satirists like Jonson; the other reflecting the way they might have seen themselves, and drawing on the materials of court writers like Lyly or Sir Walter Ralegh. The "lunatic" Malvolio (4.2.22) recalls the conventional butts of Elizabethan satire, channeling the anger that a false etymology associated with the genre, and triggering derisive laughter on- and offstage.[24] In contrast, the elegant Orsino hearkens back to Lyly's moon-lover, triggering responses of a different sort.

Until Sebastian and Viola arrive, all Illyrians suffer to some extent from Endymion's condition of having "waxed old" without "knowing it" (*Endymion*, 5.1.76). Orsino and Malvolio come to embody a more general condition in this play, endemic in late Elizabethan culture, of waking up from "such a dream that when the image of it leaves" all must "run mad" (2.5.193–94). This disenchantment, far from purging the "dream" in the manner of Jonsonian satires, testifies to its enduring allure by resituating it as an object of reflective nostalgia—a fantasy not about the future but about a rapidly receding past, when such dreams had more purchase on reality.[25] According to Svetlana Boym, this form of nostalgia has utopian dimensions, and privileges "longing and loss, the imperfect process of remembrance," lingering on "the patina of time and history, in the dreams of another place and another time." When Boym defines the object of reflective nostalgia as located "somewhere in the twilight of the past or on the island of utopia where time has happily stopped, as on an antique clock," she might as well be writing about Illyria, before the antique clock strikes in the third act.[26] Shakespeare's generic experimentation accounts for the "elegiac," "melancholy," or "autumnal" tone of *Twelfth Night*, which it shares with the sonnets.[27] At the turn of the seventeenth century, just a few years before Elizabeth's death, the playwright turned to a form of longing that mediates between individual and collective memory to counter the reductive fictions about the Elizabethan regime that he had helped disseminate in earlier plays.[28]

Although no single male character carries the full burden of his legacy, Falstaff haunts *Twelfth Night* in a variety of shapes. Various critics note that Shakespeare pursues a strategy of twinning in this play, epitomized by the young shipwrecks who share "One face, one voice, one habit," yet are "two persons" (5.1.216). So Cristina Malcolmson argues that "Viola and Maria are twinned" usurpers of privileged status: one performs the part of the man, the other of her mistress. Viola and Malvolio are "twinned" servants intent on marrying their superiors. And Malvolio and Orsino are "twinned" in their failure to secure Olivia's hand in marriage.[29] These shared qualities establish the inhabitants of Illyria as analogues of one another, in ways that raise concerns familiar to readers of this book. Characters are grouped together in structures of favoritism (Viola, Malvolio), in practices of theatrical usurpation (Viola, Maria), in eroticized forms of social mobility (Viola, Sebastian, Malvolio), and in bearbaiting plots (Malvolio, Orsino).[30] The upstart twins who function as catalysts for the plot are meritorious candidates for election by an imperious lady. And the older male characters who surround these twins, and whose unruly energies the twins absorb and redirect, share a common ancestry in the materials that Shakespeare drew on to fashion his "whoreson round man" (*1 Henry IV*, 2.4.140).

This comparative arrangement of characters is advertised through the play's multiple signifying names, which invite audiences to collaborate in the construal of meaning. The forged document that incites Malvolio to act on his sociosexual fantasies contains a notorious "fustian riddle" involving the initials "M. O. A. I." (2.5.107–8). The steward interprets these as a reference to himself, since "every one of these letters are in [his] name" (2.5.141). As a number of readers have noticed, most of those letters are also in Viola's and Olivia's names. The three names are near-anagrams, implying an unequal division of material held in common.[31] Given that the same "characters crush[ed] . . . a little" (2.5.140) produce different names, the most basic units of dramatic personhood, we are invited to "work . . . out" what else these scrambled "alphabetical position[s]" might "portend" (2.5.127, 119). Malcolmson finds that the missing letters in "Viola" stand for the distinctive trait that she lacks of Malvolio, the "ill will" spelled out in the steward's name. Orsino's servant, of gentle status like Olivia's servant, has the ambition to make an upwardly mobile marriage but not the self-interest that satirists assumed accompanied such ambition.[32] In other words, Cesario is a "servingman" worthy of Olivia's "favors" (3.2.6), one who lacks the traits—including advancing age—that in Malvolio invite ridicule.

As this example suggests, the characters in *Twelfth Night* emerge from processes of division and subtraction. "How have you made division of yourself?" a stunned Antonio asks Sebastian and Viola/Cesario; "An apple, cleft in two, is not more twin / Than these two creatures" (5.1.222–24). This metaphor borrows from a famous passage in Plato's *Symposium*, in which the Greek gods, having made "primeval man . . . round, his back and sides forming a circle," with "four hands and four feet" and "two privy members," grow fearful of their own creatures:

> Terrible was their might and strength, and the thoughts of their hearts were great, and they made an attack upon the gods. . . . Doubt reigned in the celestial councils. Should they kill them and annihilate the race with thunderbolts . . . then there would be an end of the sacrifices and worship which men offered to them. . . . At last, after a good deal of

reflection, Zeus discovered a way. He said: "Methinks I have a plan which will humble their pride and improve their manners.... I will cut them in two and then they will be diminished in strength and increased in numbers... and if they continue to be insolent and will not be quiet, I will split them again."... He spoke and cut men in two, like a sorb apple which is halved for pickling, or as you might divide an egg with a hair.... Apollo was bidden to heal their wounds and compose their forms.[33]

The image of Viola and Sebastian as a cleft apple recalls the moment Zeus splits his "round" creatures like a "sorb apple" or an "egg." New creatures forged out of an original "man-woman," the twins are distinguishable by the "little thing" that Viola lacks "of a man" (3.4.303), an anatomical area to which *Twelfth Night; or What You Will* returns obsessively.

That *Twelfth Night*'s "master's mistress" (5.1.326) is half of a formerly round whole makes her creator an analogue of Plato's Zeus, whose strained relationship to his creations becomes an allegory of authorial regret. Zeus charges Apollo—the god Shakespeare elsewhere associates with keeping his own poetic "invention" from becoming "deformed"—with refashioning his original work.[34] After the originary moment, in other words, creation becomes a form of re-creation or revision. As if to emphasize such aesthetic applications, Plato assigns his myth to Aristophanes, the playwright renowned for cutting personal satire and revered by Jonson for the "dignity of his spirit and judgement" (*Every Man Out*, induction, 245). Shakespeare often likens his artistry to the forces that produce life; in Sonnet 20, which relies on the same creation myth, the poet and Nature parallel one another in the creation of a "master mistress" (1–2). Where Nature produces the original by adding ("one thing to my purpose nothing," 20.12), the poet produces his version by subtracting ("a woman's face, but not acquainted," 20.3). The same judicious redaction shapes *Twelfth Night*'s characters, defined more by what they lack than what they have. Contra Jonson, Shakespeare insists that his "creatures," apparent borrowings from Plautus's *Menaechme*, result from artistic processes described by Aristophanes.

Insofar as these processes include the cutting and remastering of the Falstaff materials, Shakespeare also, and perhaps ironically, expresses discomfort with the strain of dramaturgy that produced his "whoreson round man" and inspired Jonson's comical satires. *Twelfth Night* pushes against the conventions of satire, which depends on stable demarcations, by giving us a surfeit or excess of these licentious old men. "Increased in number," the characters deriving from Falstaff are also "diminished in strength," like Apollo's redacted creatures. While several critics identify Sir Toby Belch as a version of Falstaff, for example, they "all agree" that "Sir Toby lacks Falstaff's imaginative brilliance."[35] An old knight much given to "quaffing and drinking," who cannot "confine" himself to "the modest limits of order" (1.3.9–14), Toby inherits Falstaff's carnivalesque elements. Jensen suggests that Shakespeare may have derived the idea of splitting Falstaff from *The First Part of Sir John Oldcastle* (1600), which features "two new Sir Johns with very different devotional identifications." Interested in confessional conflicts over festivity, she takes Sir Toby, Malvolio, and Feste to be the relevant fragments.[36] But other characters, including Malvolio and Orsino, qualify as well. Introducing a signature note of escalation, Shakespeare offers us five or six versions of his old knight, with the meager *miles gloriosus* Sir Andrew Aguecheek serving as a surplus shard. That cowardly "carpet" knight (3.4.236) receives the unkindest cut of all—the anti-Leicestrian material on erectile dysfunction. An ambulatory castration joke, Sir Andrew has hair that "hangs like flax on a distaff" so that "a huswife" could take him "between her legs and spin it off" (1.3.102–4). Yet another old man reduced to a "feminine suppository," he illustrates Shakespeare's strategy of "spending again what is already spent" (*Sonnets*, 76.13) in *Twelfth Night*.[37]

Following theatrical precedent, Shakespeare places a "fair princess" at the center of an erotic meritocracy.[38] Olivia is the stationary planet around which the cleft characters orbit, the round "O" or "nought" (1.1.11) targeted by their various wills. Cesario, Sebastian, Orsino, Malvolio, and Sir Andrew all pursue this "cruell'st she alive," who seems determined to lead her "graces to the grave, / And leave the world no copy" (1.5.241–43). Their language about their "marble-breasted tyrant" (5.1.124) hearkens back to an earlier era, when the queen's marriage was the most pressing issue confronting the English political nation. Orsino imagines that Olivia's "sweet perfections" can only be fitted "with one self king" (1.1.38), for example, and Cesario thinks that Olivia's refusal to give herself in marriage means that she does "usurp" herself, for "what is [hers] to bestow is not [hers] to reserve" (1.5.188–89). Stephen Greenblatt remarks that only Elizabeth I "provided a model" for a "career" like Olivia's. Shakespeare fosters the parallel at every turn, making Orsino address Olivia in the court's Petrarchan discourses, figuring Viola/Cesario as "a rare courtier" (3.1.86) and as "Orsino's embassy" (1.5.166), and having Olivia distribute rings and miniatures, "favors" commonly awarded by Elizabeth I.[39] Provided with an "allow'd fool" (1.5.94) who recalls Richard Tarleton, Olivia takes fierce exception to the mistreatment of her favorites, as Elizabeth did (echoing Markham, Feste warns Sir Toby, Sir Andrew, and Fabian that he "would not be in some of your coats for twopence" [4.1.30–31]). Olivia conducts herself as a queen might, moreover, advertising her powers of life and death over her household and relying on the royal "we" when negotiating with other characters.[40] These reimagine Olivia, the "daughter of a count" (1.2.36), as a regal figure, whose tyrannical decision to abjure "the company / and sight of men" (1.2.40–41) has plunged Illyria into a paralytic state of deferred desire.[41] Viola's surmise that Sebastian must be in "Elizium" (as the 1623 Folio spells it, 1.2.4) confounds Illyria not just with the happy fields of Greek mythological lore but also with England, the land of Eliza. Like many things in this retrospective play, the pun is an old one, dating to George Peele's *Arraygnment of Paris* (1584), and refurbished by Jonson in *Every Man Out of His Humour* (2.1.22).[42]

The parallel between Olivia and Elizabeth may not be an "exact one," as Carole Levin observes, but it is an evocative one, which sets the tone for the play as a whole and shades all relations within it.[43] Orsino announces his intention to emulate Endymion by reclining on "sweet beds of flow'rs" (1.1.39) in the play's first scene. When he compares his love to the sea, he channels Ralegh's Ocean, in helpless thrall to a chaste moon. Orsino's "high fantastical" constructions introduce Olivia as a type of Cynthia or Diana, with some notable consequences for himself:

> O, when mine eyes did see Olivia first,
> Methought she purg'd the air of pestilence!
> That instant was I turn'd into a hart,
> And my desires, like fell and cruel hounds,
> E'er since pursue me. (1.1.15, 18–22)

In a few brief lines Orsino assigns himself the roles of Actaeon and of Endymion, the classical figures closely identified in the period with the perils and pleasures of royal favoritism.[44] To cite the most pertinent example, Jonson had combined these myths to target courtiers seeking to become "eternally engallanted" in *The Fountaine of Selfe-Love or Cynthia's Revels* (4.3.3). A parody of *Endymion*, this play satirizes a whole host of behaviors associated with court favoritism, including the "painting, slicking, glazing, and renewing old rivelled faces" (Palinodia 21), and the staging of "scene[s] of courtship" with recycled "play-particles" (3.4.40, 3.5.96). Jonson illustrates the reciprocal relationship between court and theater when he borrows the "play-particle" Philautia or Self-Love from a disastrous 1595 Accession Day entertainment that Francis Bacon wrote at the Earl of Essex's behest. According to the political wisdom of the time, "self love" was a "false believe" avoided by good "Counslers."[45] Although the earl had meant to persuade Elizabeth I that he loved her more than himself in the Accession Day entertainment, she came away unconvinced.[46] Like Essex or Leicester, also allegedly given over to "selfe love of him selfe," Jonson's courtiers drink from the Fountain of Self-Love, where "young Actaeon fell, pursued and torn / By Cynthia's wrath, more eager than his hounds" (1.2.82–83).[47] When Shakespeare recycles Jonson's lines at the beginning of *Twelfth Night*, he avails himself of the same technique to place Orsino's courtship of Olivia in comparative relation to "scene[s] of courtship" from the past. These include his own, since *Merry Wives* had also fused the Actaeon and Endymion myths to show the horned Falstaff, whose lusty "flames aspire" too high, "wink[ing]" and "couch[ing]" on stage before his Fairy Queen (5.5.97–98, 48), in imitation of the moon's lovers. Orsino's opening performance comprises the same elements as Falstaff's concluding turn, even if this noble "hart" appears far more decorous than that "brib'd buck" (*Merry Wives*, 5.5.24).

Olivia casts such a powerful spell that all her suitors conjure past performances in this manner. The enthralled Sebastian agrees to be ruled moments after they meet; he too hopes to perform an elegant version of the lapse into bestiality by letting "fancy still [his] sense in Lethe steep / If it be thus to dream, still let me sleep!" (4.1.60–63). Like Circe's island, which according to Boym signifies the paradoxical pleasures of nostalgic longing, "the seduction of non-return home," Illyria is "an ultimate utopia of regressive pleasure and divine bestiality," an "Elyzium" constituted of the "reliques" and "memorials" (3.3.18–23) of an earlier time.[48] When the captain claims that Sebastian stood "like Arion on the dolphin's back" (1.2.15) in emulation of the "Arion . . . ryding aloft upon his old friend the Dolphin" at Kenilworth, he identifies Illyria more with the rarefied world of the old Elizabethan court entertainments.[49] In this fantastical world—the world of Leicester's Kenilworth, of Peele's *Arraygment*, of Lyly's *Endymion*, of Ralegh's poetry—time is held in suspense, while mature men abandon themselves to the adoration of a queen whose "summer ever lastethe."[50] Like the courtiers described by Cardinal Allen, who committed to the "single lyfe to the danger of their soules, and decay of their families, to attend [Elizabeth I's] pleasure," Olivia's suitors appear destined to forgo marriage and the begetting of lawful children.[51] Into this somnolent state of affairs, the young twins arrive like time-keepers, ominous reminders that the older characters are wasting "the treasure of [their] time" (2.5.77).

By drawing on the competing languages of nostalgia and satire, *Twelfth Night* stages rival evaluations of its central characters, putting into conflict the discourses of praise and blame that shaped Elizabethan conversations about "what great ones do." Elizabeth's admirers lauded her management of "houshold affaires," for example, noting she "kept the like equall hands balancing the sloth or sumptuousnesse of her great Stewards, and white staves, with the providence, and reservednesse of a Lord Treasurer."[52] In much the same way, Shakespeare invites us to admire Olivia's ability to "sway her house, command her followers, / Take and give back affairs, and their dispatch, / With such a smooth, discreet, and stable bearing" (4.3.16–20). But he also puts this regal woman in humiliatingly compromising positions. The business with Malvolio enacts a grotesque parody of the Actaeon myth.[53] Claiming unauthorized knowledge of Olivia's "c's, her u's, and her t's" (2.5.88), Malvolio wants to trade "services" with his mistress, hoping thereby to become "Count Malvolio" (2.5.158, 35). As Dympna Callaghan points out, the numerous puns on "Count" and "cunt" and "cut" help put Olivia's "private parts . . . on display for everyone's amusement."[54] Orsino (an actual count) and Sebastian (a future count, since the play endows Olivia with the power to encount her husband) participate in this public exposure, even if they claim no special knowledge of Olivia's "great Ps" (2.5.87). For all her "smooth, discreet, and stable bearing" poor Olivia fares at times little better than Sir Andrew's huswife, Falstaff's Mistress Quickly, or the "naked feind in the forme of a lady" who exposes "her bettelbroude urchin" to Leicester's "gase of . . . retoricke speculation" in *News*.[55]

Indeed, the "sport royal" (2.3.173) of *Twelfth Night* borrows broadly from satiric representations of "Cynthia's sports" (*Cynthia's Revels*, 4.6.37). "Swagger[ing] it in black and yellow" and kissing "away [his] hand in kindness" (*Cynthia's Revels*, 3.5.99, 3.4.41), Malvolio epitomizes the Jonsonian courtier "sick of self-love" who tastes "with a distemp'red appetite" (*Twelfth Night*, 1.5.90–91).[56] When one of Jonson's courtiers seeks preferment with the ladies by "dancing" (*Cynthia's Revels*, 4.5.48), he chooses men like Ralegh or Christopher Hatton as aspirational models, taking the malicious gossip about their theatricality seriously.[57] Likewise, Malvolio feels that he need only deliver the right performance, aimed at satisfying his lady's eccentric erotic tastes, to become a "made" man (2.5.155). Numerous in-jokes confirm Malvolio's status as a vehicle for such "pastime" (3.4.138) by encouraging audiences to remember past times. Disguised as the provocatively named Sir Topas, Feste serenades Malvolio with "Hey, Robin, jolly Robin, / Tell me how thy lady does" (4.2.72–73), an old song about a provocatively named courtier's currying favor with a lady.[58] Topas's questions about "th'opinion of Pythagoras" (4.2.57) point back, meanwhile, through *Cynthia's Revels* (4.3.110–18) to *Endymion*, where Cynthia mocks "the ridiculous opinions" that Pythagoras holds (4.3.46–47). Of course, the idea that a man's soul might inhabit an animal's body is relevant to those undergoing "suche a metamorphosis" at a lady's hand "as poetes do seyn was made of the companyons of Ulisses."[59] Predictably enough, Malvolio follows Sir Tophas, Bottom, and Falstaff in being made an "ass" (2.3.168).[60]

Designed to provoke the "scornful" laughter that Sir Philip Sidney says we reserve for "deformed creatures," Malvolio is "ridiculous" (3.4.38) in part because he deviates from age-related ideals of comportment.[61] Sir Toby first directs our attention to Malvolio's age when he sings "There dwelt a man in Babylon" (2.3.78–79), an old ballad about the "filthy lust" of the town "Elders" for the chaste Susanna.[62] Shakespeare resorts to the disciplinary discourses that policed male sexuality to shape audience reactions to Malvolio throughout the play. Where Sebastian is in the bloom of what Cicero calls "unadvised adolescencye," when men are subject to "the fervent heate" of sexual passion, Malvolio occupies the position of an advisor who has "lead his prince to virtue by his worth and authority," a role that requires being "old (because knowledge rarely comes before a certain age)."[63] Olivia relies on her steward's counsel, valuing him for his age-appropriate "sad and civil" (3.4.5) affect. Unfortunately, Malvolio himself fails to appreciate that "love is not a good thing in old men, and those things which in young men are the delights, courtesies, and elegances so pleasing to women, in old men amount to madness and ridiculous ineptitude, and whoever indulges in them will cause some women to despise him and others to deride him."[64] Behind on his reading of "politic authors" (2.5.161), Olivia's steward ignores learned advice on aging, lapses into "midsummer madness" (3.4.56), and becomes "a common recreation" (2.3.135) to all.

Like the costume change that marks Bottom's translation, Malvolio's cross-gartered stockings signal his conclusive transformation into an ass. That the steward finds his new outfit challenging to wear—"this does make some obstruction in the blood, this cross-gartering" (3.4.20–21), he fusses—indicates a bad fit not between costume and class, as is often thought, but between costume and bodily composition.[65] Doctors, who believed that "obstruction" resulted from the cooling effects of aging, advised "olde men" to "beware" of making "obstructions," which "with clammy matter stoppe the places where the natural humours are wrought and digested."[66] While a youth like Sebastian might wear tight garments without injury to his health, this was not the case for older men. Judging by Sir Toby's reference to "Peg a Ramsey," another old ballad, about a married man who yearns for the yellow stockings he wore in his bachelorhood, Malvolio compounds the problem by wearing clothes that had been fashionable in his youth. Not only is he too old for his clothes, but these are also old-fashioned.[67]

The ladies' horrified reaction to Malvolio's turn as a youthful gallant confirms that the "delights" which are "pleasing to women" in "young men" appear as "madness" in older ones. Maria, "a beagle, true bred" (2.3.179) complains that the steward "does smile his face into more lines than is in the new map, with the augmentation of the Indies; you have not seen such a thing as 'tis." She can "hardly forbear hurling things" at Malvolio, and she feels confident that Olivia "will strike him" (3.2.75–82), as indeed Olivia does in some productions. Taking their cue from the fairies in *Endymion* and *Merry Wives*, Maria and her accomplices bind Malvolio up—possibly to a stake or pillar—so as to "fool him black and blue" (2.5.10).[68] Malvolio thus endures what amounts to a "bear-baiting" (2.5.8) for his violations of generational decorum. Fabian claims that if the gulling of Malvolio "were play'd upon a stage now, I would condemn it as an improbable fiction" (3.4.127–28). The metatheatrical joke is all the more delicious for the fact that these "play-particles" had been played on all manner of public stages before. Shakespeare insists on the familiarity of this satiric pattern, reproduced here for "our pleasure and [Malvolio's] penance" (3.4.137–38).

As an aging steward pursued by dogs for violating his "due tyme and season," Malvolio would have raised familiar historical ghosts as well as theatrical ones.[69] The staff of office that he brandishes (5.1.284), like the steward's chain that he fingers, evoke not just actual bears, but also Elizabeth's former Lord Steward, the Earl of Leicester, whose staff had become a lightning rod for age-related ridicule.[70] Like that allegedly hypocritical nobleman, Shakespeare's "kind of Puritan" (2.3.140) dreams about marrying his noble mistress, wishing to cast "nets and chains and invisible bands about that person whom most of all he pretendeth to serve."[71] Olivia's steward looks to "the Lady of the Strachy" who married "the yeoman of the wardrobe" (2.5.39–40) for a historical precedent. Although they do not always know what to make of this glancing allusion, or numerous others like it, even modern critics feel prompted by it to consider real life models for Malvolio.[72] Original audiences might have recalled another "example" of a "time-pleaser" or "affection'd ass, that cons state without book ... the best persuaded of himself, so cramm'd (as he thinks) with excellencies, that it is his grounds of faith that all look on him love him" (2.3.147–52). Like the "great Beare" who schemed to obtain a crown he could not claim by "right, title" or "descent of blood," Malvolio imagines himself a prince. He fantasizes about "sitting in his *state*" and, Leslie Hotson points out, "a *state* is no count's chair, but a canopied royal throne."[73] Here, then, is Shakespeare's most explicit rendering of the familiar scenario by which an aging favorite who is not born great attempts an erotically appealing performance to "achieve greatness" or "have greatness thrust upon 'em" (2.5.145–46).

By giving this undignified scenario a scatological bent, *Twelfth Night* enhances the leveling effect of its satire. Peter Smith argues that the riddling "M.O.A.I." in Maria's letter form "a deliberate echo of the title of *The Metamorphosis of A Iax*." And indeed, there is a logic to having Malvolio spell out "the abbreviated title" of this obscene work, since it intimates that Elizabeth's steward was as well-informed about his lady's "great Ps" as Olivia's steward claims to be.[74] In discussing "close vault" privies in *Ajax*, "my Lord of Leicester" objects to the contraption on the grounds that in "a Princes house where so many mouthes be fed, a close vault wil fil quickly."[75] The earl's concern about the vast quantity of waste produced at court spoofs the "exquisite combination of intimacy, degradation, and privilege" Gail Kern Paster identifies in her discussion of Malvolio as "belonging to the body servants of the great."[76] Improving on an old pun, *Ajax* collapses serving Elizabeth with servicing her privies. The narrator is "so wholly addicted to her highnesse service" that he "would be glad, yea even proud, if the highest straine of my witte, could but reach, to any note of true harmony in the full consort of her Majesties service, though it were the basest key that it could be tuned to.... If men of judgement thinke it may breed a publike benefite, the conceit thereof shall expell all private bashfulnesse."[77] His tongue-in-cheek "publike" discussion of the queen's great P's, meant specifically to appeal to "men of judgement," is among the numerous precedents for the Malvolio plot in *Twelfth Night*.

Twelfth Night was probably written or rewritten with an eye to pleasing these same "men of judgement," since it was performed at the Middle Temple on February 2, 1602.[78] Its more salacious moments recall the verse satires popular at the Inns of Court, like Thomas Nashe's *The Choice of Valentines; or Nashe, his Dildo* (1592–93?) or John Marston's *The Metamorphosis of Pygmalions Image* (1598), both of which elaborated with pornographic panache on the contradictions inherent in a cult of virginity that employed tropes of sexual service. Like Jonson's comical satires, or Harington's *Ajax*, these verse satires catered to and cultivated a "simultaneous enthrallment with and distaste of court culture."[79] Government authorities evidently regarded this development as a threat, since they censored key works by Marston, Middleton, Nashe, and others through the Bishop's Ban of 1599.[80] Significantly for my purposes, the average age of those banned was thirty and the average age of those doing the banning was sixty-three.[81] The period's pornographic satire was especially appealing to younger Elizabethan men-about-town, in other words, who used it to indulge their negative perceptions of the aging court.

Twelfth Night's outré material, its legal terminology, its shafts aimed at Jonson, and its reference to the "bay windows transparent as barricadoes" of the Middle Temple Hall (4.2.36–37)—all appear designed with these disgruntled young men in mind.[82] Anthony Arlidge proposes that in "laughing at Malvolio's social pretensions," the Middle Templars "would also have been laughing at themselves, for there were few better places than the Inns of Court to climb the greasy pole of social advancement."[83] I think it even more likely that they were laughing at their elders. Harington's pamphlet and Jonson's comedies show that jokes about Elizabeth's favorite men—even those who were long dead—were de rigueur at the

Inns of Court, and for good reason. All three of the queen's "upstart" favorites had launched their storied careers from the Inns of Court. Chosen Revels Prince by the Inner Temple in 1561–62, Robert Dudley brought *Gorboduc*—a play meant to advance his courtship of the queen—to the Twelfth Night feast of 1562. Christopher Hatton's handsome personage had attracted Elizabeth's attention on the same or a similar occasion.[84] The last of the queen's carpet knights, the Middle Templar Walter Ralegh, who had been knighted on Twelfth Night in 1585, had probably attended the 1597/98 Twelfth Night festivities, "play-particles" of which found their way into both *Every Man Out* and *Twelfth Night*.[85] When Feste alludes to "King Gorboduc" (4.2.14) in a play called *Twelfth Night* performed at Middle Temple, the joke invokes this institutional history, reminding audiences of the men who had greatness thrust on them by the queen. The fantasy of election by a powerful woman may have retained its allure for this younger generation, since John Webster, a likely attendant at the Middle Temple performance of *Twelfth Night*, would go on to write *The Duchess of Malfi* (1612–13), which grants the steward Antonio the aristocratic marriage denied the steward Malvolio.[86] After Essex's rebellion, however, Elizabeth for all intents and purposes isolated herself, and none in attendance that night could hope to follow the great favorites' path to promotion. This state of affairs seems to have generated a good deal of resentment, which the Malvolio plot exploits.

That resentment extended to ladies who vainly make men dream of advancement. Indeed, the bearbaiting "device" (3.4.140) in *Twelfth Night* operates like the "straw-devices" of slanderers mentioned by Jonson (*Cynthia's Revels*, 3.3.6) or the "slanderous devices" that the Privy Council had objected to in the 1580s.[87] It implicates Olivia in a public shaming; "you wrong me," Malvolio snarls at her "and the world shall know it" (5.1.302–303). Earlier in the play, when speaking to Cesario about the favors she has granted him, Olivia compares her honor to a baited bear:

Under your hard construction must I sit,
To force that on you in shameful cunning
Which you knew none of yours. What might you think?

Have you not set mine honor at the stake,
And baited it with all th'unmuzzled thoughts
That tyrannous heart can think? (3.1.115–20)

Olivia's keen sense of being on a stage, vulnerable because of her gender and sexuality, subject to "hard construction" and "baited . . . with all th'unmuzzled thoughts / that tyrannous heart can think" expresses something of the shock that court figures must have felt when they found themselves objects of public speculation by satirists. Olivia openly calls bluff on Jonson's disingenuous claim that only a "hard construction" would find topical reference in the scenarios of satire, like the one in which "a countess" who has "graced" men "beyond all aim of affection" is humiliated (*Every Man Out*, 2.3.328, 228–32).[88] Branding those who set her sexual "honor at the stake" as tyrants, Olivia casts the satiric processes that result in popular judgments as a usurpation of royal authority.

Viewed in the context of the performance at Middle Temple, *Twelfth Night* stages the revenge of a "whole pack" (5.1.378) on a domineering woman and the men "so wholly addicted to her service" that they are willing to strike the "basest key." Olivia is punished not just because she pretends to "social" and "bodily autonomy," as Paster and others argue, but also because she presides over an erotic meritocracy.[89] Audience members who laugh at the Malvolio plot become participants in this baiting, which Sir Toby likens to a form of legal judgment when he considers that "we may carry it thus . . . till our very pastime, tir'd out of breath, prompt us to have mercy on [Malvolio]; at which time we will bring the device to the bar" (3.4.137–39). As we saw in previous chapters, anticourt polemicists promoted the idea that public figures could be brought to trial in the court of public opinion. Toby imagines tiring of this familiar "pastime," which *Twelfth Night* plays out to the point of exhaustion. The taste of surfeit that attends the baiting of Malvolio reflects a sense that "the joke . . . goes too far," to quote Ralph Berry, and that it goes on for "too long."[90] By indulging the satiric impulse to the point of surfeit, *Twelfth Night* generates the feelings of remorse and regret that darken its mood. Even Feste's fooling "grows old" (1.5.110–11), although the weary clown is the only one attuned to what Anne Barton calls the "realities of death and time." His melancholy final song underlines that aging, the bodily process by which time hastens us toward death, is among the play's principal concerns.[91]

Twelfth Night is not just a satire—it is also a romantic comedy, which hews to its own time by depicting "the follies" of the age (*Every Man Out*, induction, 15) as the folly of age. And the ridiculed Malvolio is not the only character who violates generational decorum. Until that antique clock upbraids Olivia for wasting time, most Illyrians ignore the fact that "youth's a stuff will not endure" (2.3.52). Sir Andrew, who prides himself on how his leg looks dancing a galliard, prefers not to "compare" himself to "an old man" (1.4.118–119). But a "dry hand" signals "age and impotence;" in Sir Toby's felicitous locution, Andrew is an "old boy" (3.2.8).[92] This oxymoron, which recalls the boys who cross-dressed like old men to depict old men behaving like boys in *Endymion*, indicates that misrule in Illyria does not result from gender or class reversal only. The play's adult males are all old boys, aging usurpers of youthful privileges, generation-bending counterparts of the gender-bending twins. In its focus on these elderly "boys quarrelling over worthless things and . . . engrossed in childish preoccupations," *Twelfth Night* evokes Petrarch's "ninety-year-old little boys," whose "most notable folly . . . was his desire to continue to have love affairs."[93] Barber argued long ago that "madness" is the play's operative word.[94] In the particular sense of a disrespect for the limits set by time, madness is a condition affecting not just Malvolio, but all Illyrians, including Olivia, who acknowledges being "as mad" as her steward (3.4.14).[95]

If literary critics rarely comment on *Twelfth Night*'s preoccupation with aging, theatre practitioners have long been alert to it. *Twelfth Night* is often staged as a fin-de-siècle affair, in which an old order exhausts itself, an interpretation that involves the use of aging actors. So John Barton's influential production (1969/70), which highlighted the "elegiac" elements in the play, cast Maria as an elderly woman desperately eager to secure a marriage.[96] Trevor Nunn's melancholy 1996 film featured several aging males in the cast, including Nigel Hawthorne (Malvolio), Mel Smith (Sir Toby), and Ben Kingsley (Feste). And in Tim Carroll's recent production for the Globe (2012–13), all major parts, with the exception of the twins, were performed by actors well beyond the third age, the period that Ralegh identifies as appropriate for indulging in "days of love, desire, and vanity."[97] Orsino (Liam Brennan) was in his early fifties, Malvolio (Stephen Frye) in his mid-fifties, and Sir Andrew (Roger Lloyd Pack) in his late sixties—all "old boys" in hot pursuit of Mark Rylance's Olivia. Crowned, heavily made-up, and dripping with pearls, this regal lady conjured up images of aging and raging queens appropriate to the play's subject matter. According to the *New York Times* reviewer, even modern-day American spectators found themselves "thinking of . . . Elizabeth I."[98]

While the all-male cast of the Globe production showcased the play's gender-bending effects, the advanced median age of the actors highlighted generational transgressions, contrasting the dignified behavior of the twins to the undignified behavior of their elders. Besides unleashing the satiric potential of the play, this production made visible the unusual configuration of the generational conflict in *Twelfth Night*, in which two youthful outsiders struggle to integrate into an alluring social elite constituted of aging celibates. Even without the difficult business of Malvolio's disruptive final line, this represents a substantial revision of the argument of new comedy as explained by Northrop Frye, in which the younger generation endeavors to replace the older generation, not to mate with it. *Twelfth Night*'s odd swerves from convention follow its preoccupation with the Elizabethan past, albeit in an unexpected way. Like Jonson's comical satires, *Twelfth Night* caters to a desire to see old men beaten "before [their] whore" (*2 Henry IV*, 2.4.257). But this punitive spectacle, satisfying to theatergoers eager for a specific kind of satiric fare, is amended by the twin youths who embrace Olivia and Orsino, redeeming them—and the court figures they evoke—from the general curse of resentment.

Expanding on ambiguities already present in his portrayal of Falstaff, Shakespeare splits this source material in *Twelfth Night*, refashioning the age-in-love trope by calling attention to its reproducibility and to its generic malleability. Multiple allusions establish a dizzying number of precedents for the aging lovers of *Twelfth Night*, ranging from the historical Leicester to Lyly's devoted lover to Shakespeare's own lecherous old knight to Jonson's benighted courtiers. This wealth of models shows the innovative performances of Elizabeth's favorites to be radical not just because they prompt public debate or provoke judgments but also because they serve as "example[s]" and inspire imitations, including those of the satirist and of the comic dramatist. Ralegh, who knew a thing or two about the process by which "greatnesse" might be achieved, explains in "Of Favorites" that if "one man acted ill his part / Lett an other mend the play."[99] The emulation of former favorites can lead to refinement; where Malvolio acts "ill his part," Orsino is the "other" who "mend[s] the play." Orsino lacks the social ambition and mercenary motives that deform most Elizabethan iterations of the aging lover, since his "love, more noble than the world, / Prizes not quantity of dirty lands" (2.4.81–82). Mocked by other characters, he is spared by the play itself, which displaces his less attractive traits, like "self-love" or "narcissism and potential effeminacy," onto Malvolio.[100] By providing these mirrors more than one of the queen's favorites, Shakespeare counters one-sided accounts of the court's impact on English culture and underlines the logical glitch in Jonson's attack on the probability of romantic comedies, showing that these could reflect the dreams which structured Elizabethan political reality.

Olivia describes her suitor as "of great estate, of fresh and stainless youth" (1.5.259), which may appear to disqualify Orsino for the role that I am here proposing. Yet Orsino's views on marriage show that he is older than Olivia. A proponent of letting "still the woman take / An elder than herself" (2.4.29–30), he is "elder" than Olivia, who in turn is "elder" than Viola. We are encouraged to think Olivia "cannot love" Orsino (1.5.262) because of his age when Toby explains that "She'll not match above her degree, neither in estate, years, nor wit; I have heard her swear't" (1.3.109–11). Orsino sends Cesario to Olivia because he thinks she would reject "a nuntio's of more grave aspects" (1.4.28), a fear shown to be warranted when Olivia decides to "show favor" to Cesario because he is a "youth" (3.2.19). Shakespeare endows Orsino with a substantial past, which links him not just to the seasoned Antonio but also to Viola's deceased father, who reported to his young daughter that Orsino "was a bachelor then" (1.2.29). Olivia's suitor is uncle to a daring "young nephew Titus," old enough to have been injured in the naval skirmish with Antonio (5.1.63). All this backstory dates Orsino, identifying him with an older generation of men, including Malvolio and Sir Andrew. That Orsino has remained a bachelor indicates an unwarranted delay and even a breach of marital norms; "he might have took his answer long ago," Olivia shrewishly observes (1.5.263).

Through a verbal demotion of his duke, Shakespeare strengthens the parallels between this aging "Count Orsino" (1.5.101) and the "overweening rogue" who dreams of being made "Count Malvolio" (2.5.29, 35). The captain in 1.2 first identifies Orsino as "a noble duke" who governs Illyria (1.2.25), a man whose "favors" causes others to be "advanc'd" (1.4.1–2), not one who need beg favors for himself. Yet Orsino speaks like "an aspiring courtier," Leonard Tennenhouse observes, and negotiates "sexual relations which completely overturn his position of political superiority in relation to Olivia."[101] If Orsino's Petrarchan rhetoric is hard to reconcile with that of a "Duke... in love with a Countess," perhaps he is not a duke after all, just as Olivia is not really a countess. Only the captain refers to Orsino by this title. Other characters refer to Orsino as "the Count" who "woos" Olivia (1.3.107–8). Sir Toby assures Sir Andrew that "she'll none o' th' Count" (1.3.109–11), for example, and Olivia consistently calls her unwanted suitor "Count Orsino"—"if it be a suit from the Count, I am sick, or not at home" (1.5.107–8). Cesario is identified as "the County's man" by Olivia (1.5.301; 3.1.100), Olivia's servant (3.4.57–58), Maria (2.3.132), and Sir Toby (3.2.34). And Antonio remembers having fought "'gainst the Count his galleys" (3.3.26) when he is arrested "at the suit of Count Orsino" (3.4.326–27).[102] A preponderance of evidence thus reframes Orsino's relationship to Olivia as one in which a "Count Orsino" courts a maiden "princess" (5.1.299).

This scenario is more in keeping with *Twelfth Night's* retrospective elements, especially when we consider that "Count Orsino" translates to "Earl Little Bear."[103] Baited by his "desires, like fell and cruel hounds,"

Orsino raises the same familiar ghosts as Malvolio does. Although he was sometimes referred to as a "great Beare," Leicester deferred to his older brother, the Earl of Warwick, describing himself and Ambrose to Elizabeth as "your Ursus Major and Minor, tied to your stake."[104] Satirists followed suit when they called the earl a "Bearwhelp."[105] With his telltale name, his dashing nephew, and his Petrarchan posturing, Orsino evokes the more romantic aspects of the elegant earl who had courted Elizabeth in the guise of "Deep Desire" and whom "dogges" had wanted to see "fast chained to a stake, with muzzle-cord, collar, and ring, and all other things necessary" for his amorous efforts.[106] Unlike this bear-like target of Elizabethan satire, and unlike his counterpart Malvolio, *Twelfth Night*'s "little bear" avoids the humiliation of a protracted public baiting. He deviates further still from historical and satiric precedent when he secures the marriage conventional to the ending of romantic comedy. If the Malvolio plot caters to "men of judgment," the Orsino plot helps Shakespeare mount a defense of the "autumn judgments" that Jonson had mocked.

All those references to bearbaiting signal Shakespeare's interest in engaging the same audiences about the same subjects as Jonson, although with different ends, and arguably greater success. By the turn of the century, bearbaiting, like the related words "device" and "sport" used in *Twelfth Night*, had become linked with the genre for which Jonson professes a "*caninum appetitum*" (*Every Man Out*, induction, 305).[107] Thomas Middleton's *Microcynicon: Six Snarling Satires* (1599) and William Goddard's *A Mastif Whelp with Other Ruff-Island-lik Currs Fetcht from Amongts the Antipedes. which Bite and Barke at the Fantasticall Humorists and Abusers of the Time* (1615) show that satirists habitually figured attacks on actual persons as a form of dogging.[108] When Thomas Dekker accused Jonson of being "a Ban-dog" that bites after collaborating with Nashe on the tantalizingly titled *Isle of Dogs* (1597), Dekker hinted at the reason that this play ran afoul of authorities, namely its satiric treatment of real people.[109] Although homonymically Jonson may have "loved dogs," the Elizabethan authorities did not share his enthusiasm. Jonson later acknowledged that *Isle of Dogs* was censored for glancing at "particular persons."[110] We may never know why the play raised the government's hackles or whom it targeted, but Jonson was instrumental in furthering the association of personal satire with "dogs [that] do bark" (*Cynthia's Revels*, 3.3.29).

Jonson is a particular target of *Twelfth Night* for other reasons, including the fact that he arrogates unprecedented powers to satirists. His "public, scurrilous, and profane jester" Carlo Buffone is a "bandog" who specializes in "absurd similes" that "swifter than Circe . . . transform any person into deformity," for example (*Every Man Out*, "Characters," 19–20; 1.2.185–86). The comparative allusion to Circe invokes the public debate about the queen's transformative powers to insist on the satirist's superior abilities. Through their "absurd similes" satirists can degrade even the men elevated by the queen, a point Buffone makes and illustrates. According to a credible anecdote, Jonson based the character on Charles Chester or Jester, an "impertenent fellow" who had provoked Ralegh into sealing his "mouth . . . with hard wax."[111] In *Every Man Out*, Puntarvolo plays Ralegh to Carlo's Charles. The Petrarchan, Ovidian, and Arthurian affectations of this "vainglorious" courtier—back from hunting deer, the self-identified "knight errant" finds himself "planet-struck" by his wife, a "brighter star than Venus" ("Characters," 11; 2.2.120, 105–6)—are "tedious" (2.2.135) because they borrow from the stale discourses of the Elizabethan court.[112] Constituted of the same "play-particles" as Puntarvolo, Orsino mitigates such satiric depictions of the queen's courtiers.

Although Jonson avers himself greedy "to catch at any occasion that might express his affections to his sovereign," his mockery of the aging court undermines his praise of the "Blessèd, divine, unblemished, sacred, pure / Glorious, immortal, and indeed immense" Elizabeth (*Every Man Out*, 5.6.79–80).[113] And at every turn Jonson identifies Shakespearean forms of theatricality with the "old stale" (4.3.237) targets of his political satire. His attempts to usurp Elizabeth's royal authority are thus also attempts to establish artistic supremacy over Shakespeare. Eager to revise old models of subject and sovereign relations, Jonson proposes an alliance of sovereign and satirist, in which the (young) satirist's masculine judgment compensates for the (aged) sovereign's feminine lack of judgment. While the comical satires appeal to virile rational faculties, the "old" new comedy caters only to effete pleasures, "servilely" fawning on the audience's "applause" (*Every Man Out,* induction, 55).[114] By his personification, Jonson links old-style romantic comedies with old-style courtiers. When Macilente likens the ladies' shallow preferment of well-clad revelers over men of sober judgment to their worship of "my lord chancellor's tomb" (3.3.22), he also equates effeminate theatricality with bygone royal favorites, acknowledging Christopher Hatton's "gravity, his wisdom, and his faith / to my dread sovereign" only in passing (3.3.23–24). The female "comet" at which Jonson's court gallants "wonder," meanwhile, recycles Shakespearean comic repartee "of the stamp March was fifteen years ago" (3.3.119–21). And Captain Shift, the Falstaff clone, prides himself on having "seen Flushing, Brill, and the Hague with this rapier, sir, in my Lord of Leicester's time" (3.1.299).

Despite their rejection of the tired tropes of new comedies, Jonson's comical satires rely on that most old-fashioned of mechanisms, election by a queen, for closure. Indeed, Jonson defended the controversial 1599 ending to *Every Man Out* by explaining "there hath been precedent of the like presentation in divers plays" before.[115] While this may be true, Jonson's comedies substantially revise the relationship between the queen-figure and her elect man. Like Macilente, Criticus becomes Cynthia's chosen "minion" (*Cynthia's Revels,* 4.5.26) by play's end, deputed to pass judgment and impose punishment on other courtiers. In contrast to Lyly's sovereign goddess, this much weaker Cynthia needs help to "distinguish times / And sort her censures" (5.5.186–87). Criticus is better equipped to decide who is fit and "Unfit to be in Cynthia's court" (4.6.33) than she is. The goddess accepts his advice, acknowledging that "Princes that would their people should do well / Must at themselves begin, as at the heads" (5.5.257–58). In proposing that the queen's judgment needs masculine correction, Jonson aligns himself with the polemicists who justified their attacks on the queen's men as invitations to commit "the noble act of justice." These arguments were grounded, as Jonson's satires are, on the misogynist assumption that Elizabeth's feminine passion distorted her judgment. *Leicester's Commonwealth* warns against "the general grudge and grief of mind, with great mislike" generated on account of the "excessive favor showed to" Leicester "so many years without desert or reason," noting that "the grief and resentment thereof doth redound commonly in such cases not only upon the person delinquent alone, but also upon the sovereign by whose favor and authority he offereth such injuries."[116] For all its startling insinuations, the passage reflects the common view, shared by Jonson, that "the Prince is a publique person, and therefore ought to be without private affection and respect, or partialitie."[117] By combatting the effects of regal partiality, Criticus enacts a "fantasy of wish-fulfillment" in which advancement at court reflects "learning and moral probity" rather than personal charisma—values that Leah Marcus argues Jonson saw himself as embodying and that he hoped would "earn him the place of royal favorite."[118]

Insofar as satire renders up private matters for public discussion, it is a perverse reenactment of the favorite's desire for intimacy with "great ones." Although Jonson does not seem attuned to this irony, Shakespeare is. The Falstaff plays endorse the idea that the critical detachment of theatrical audiences enables them to compete with their monarch in the exercise of "right wits" and political "good judgments" (*Henry V*, 4.7.47–48). But in *Twelfth Night* "private affection" and "excessive" emotion define all participants in the bearbaiting scenario, including the dogs who become interchangeable with the bears they pursue. From Valentine to Feste to Orsino, characters react to the perception of favoritism by the bitter show of "grief and resentment," passions that turn out to be as distorting as "excessive favor." Sir Toby, Sir Andrew, and Feste all loathe Malvolio because he is Olivia's favorite, and their own good fortunes depend on securing or maintaining her favor for themselves. Like Orsino, they are motivated by the desire to act out against the "instrument / That screws" them from what they take to be their "true place" in Olivia's "favor" (5.1.122–23). The rancorous resentment of Olivia's "minion" (5.1.125), far from distinguishing the other men from the ambitious steward or the upwardly mobile twins, implicates them in their own judgments. When Orsino suspects Viola of having usurped Olivia's affections, he calls her a "dissembling cub"—that is, a younger, craftier, smaller bear: "what wilt thou be," he asks, "when time hath sow'd a grizzle on thy case? (5.1.164–65). As a "cub" Viola is quite literally the "Count's youth" (3.2.34). The "whirligig of time" (5.1.377), which raises Viola and Sebastian aloft, ensures Orsino's demotion to a snarling dog, who threatens to "tear" Viola to pieces (5.1.127). The proliferation of "coxcomb[s]" and "assehead[s]" (5.1.205–6) at play's end further attest to the ready transformation of baiters into baited.[119]

In emphasizing the masculine competition for a place in Olivia's affection, *Twelfth Night* presents the resentment of favorites as a distempered form of self-love. Since this resentment is the product of thwarted desire, the play's ban-dogs are invested in the same structures of desire as the bears they bait. Malvolio is "dogg'd" (3.2.76) for acting on a fantasy held in common—not just "the dream of acting the part of a gentleman," of "laying claim to higher status," as Greenblatt would have it, but the much more specific Elizabethan dream of being preferred by a powerful woman.[120] Like Jonson's Criticus, the participants in Malvolio's baiting believe that their "sport" enacts a form of justice, that it enforces civilized constraints of behavior, that it protects class and generational hierarchies. Shakespeare reframes it as a violent revenge instead, "a savage jealousy" that "savors nobly" only to those who give in to it (5.1.119–20). Fabian defends the "device against Malvolio" by claiming that it "may rather pluck on laughter than revenge" (5.1.360–66). But Fabian's defense would have rung hollow to Sidney, whose presence also haunts this play, and who saw laughter "at deformed creatures" as "most disproportioned to ourselves and nature."[121] On one end of the spectrum, comedy resembles a scapegoating mechanism in which social revenge is exacted from individuals charged with breaking decorum.[122] Pushed far enough it approaches what Frye calls "a lower limit," "the condition of savagery, the world in which comedy consists of inflicting pain on a helpless victim," and shades into something altogether different, like the revenge tragedies that haunt the final moments of *Twelfth Night*.[123] When the unregenerate Malvolio threatens all assembled, the medicinal qualities that Jonson claims for satire are shown to work like the poisons of revenge tragedies instead.[124] If the bearbaiting "device" has a self-perpetuating power in *Twelfth Night*, its ability to reproduce itself involves the spread of complicity and guilt, a contaminating process that leaves some audience members "ashamed" of themselves, as Ralph Berry is.[125] Unlike Fabian, or Jonson for that matter, Shakespeare had second thoughts about the ethics of engaging in such "sportful malice" (5.1.365).

Twelfth Night gives the satiric impulse free reign but in a way that undermines the satirist's normative claim to moral and intellectual superiority.[126] Since characters are versions of one another, efforts to draw lines, arrive at distinctions, or establish standards founder. In the Falstaff plays the old knight's isolation renders judgment possible; Hal and Poins, or Mistress Ford and Mistress Page, can bait Falstaff without finding themselves implicated in this baiting. Because Falstaff only is guilty of the generational and gendered transgressions associated with the court, his baiting results in the reassertion of commonly held norms and values. But the elaborate system of similitudes linking the characters of *Twelfth Night* challenges attempts at stable judgments. As Berry points out, "the movement upwards is caricatured in Malvolio, but the others demonstrate it too. There is a general blurring of social frontiers in Olivia's household, and this contributes to the frictions and resentments of the play."[127] If Falstaff stands for judgment, Malvolio stands for the limits of judgment. According to satiric norms, Malvolio deserves punishment for thinking he can convert sexual appeal into sociopolitical advantage. But what about Maria, Sebastian, or Viola, then? Or any Elizabethan intent on advancing himself by serving a powerful woman in some base function, as Leicester, Hatton, Harington, Jonson, Shakespeare, and the lawyers of Middle Temple did? How, under such circumstances, can anyone claim with certainty to tell the dog from the bear? In provoking these questions, *Twelfth Night* performs a metatheatrical version of what Sidney claims is the highest function of comedy: opening the satirist's "eyes" by having "his own actions contemptibly set forth." Taking his cue from Leicester's brilliant nephew, who had ample reasons to distrust "people who seek a praise by dispraising others," Shakespeare proposes that "instead of laughing at the jest" we "laugh at the jester."[128]

Although it reproduces the patterns of the Falstaff plays, *Twelfth*

Night thus comes to a more skeptical evaluation about the discourses of embodiment that marked the advent of the public sphere. The slanderous "pastimes" associated with this phenomenon assume an uncontrollable life of their own in this play. Like the sea described by Orsino in the first scene, "nought enters there, of what validity or pitch so'ever, / But falls into abatement and low price / Even in a minute" (1.1.11–13). The play's maritime images of ravenous, indiscriminate hunger combine with its multiple references to dogs to evoke yet another myth, that of Scylla, the monstrous creature furnished with a ring of baying dogs' heads for a waist. The licentious, satiric, and pornographic works of disgruntled Elizabethan subjects sought redress for the perception that serving a queen was an emasculating condition. Like Malvolio, the queen's great favorites became scapegoats for the regime itself because they epitomized this condition, which was common to all Elizabethans. The barking authors of satires sought to distinguish themselves from these submissive men by placing limits on their monarch's sovereignty. When they unmuzzled their "tyrannous" thoughts, these "substractors" may well have gone about bringing to light a worse alternative. As Olivia points out in one of the play's many oblique allusions, "If one should be a prey, how much the better / To fall before the lion than the wolf!" (3.1.128–29). In these days of media-fueled resentment and toxic masculinity, Shakespeare's old-fashioned comedy can seem oddly prescient in expressing reservations about the new forms of "sportful malice" transforming Elizabethan society.

Not that *Twelfth Night* concludes on the violent notes that haunt it. The characters who are able to recognize and acknowledge their similarities to one another manage to escape with their dignity partially restored. When Olivia movingly identifies herself with a baited bear, she inspires Viola to "pity" (3.1.123). Olivia claims "that's a degree to love," a claim that Viola denies because "very oft we pity enemies" (3.1.123–25). Olivia confirms the wisdom of Viola's observation, when she in turn finds it in her heart to pity Malvolio, who has publicly accused her of having wronged him, exposing her to "much shame" (5.1.308). Olivia's "Alas, poor fool, how they have baffled thee" shows her recognition that he has been "notoriously abus'd" (5.1.369, 379), as she herself is. The structures of kinship among the characters encourage moments of kindness that unsettle satiric judgment. If *Twelfth Night* gives us in Malvolio a courtly servant become communal enemy, it also asks us to feel an adulterating compassion for this troubled and troubling butt of ridicule. Readers from Charles I to Charles Lamb to Ralph Berry have modeled their responses to Malvolio on Olivia's, finding that something about the play's "design" forces us into "reversing" the satirical "judgments" it initially provokes.[129] The claim that "none can be call'd deform'd but the unkind" (3.4.368) gets at this aspect of the play, and conveys an abiding skepticism regarding the satirist's task as Jonson defined it: to use the stage as a "mirror" where the audience might see "the time's deformity / Anatomized in every nerve and sinew" (*Every Man Out*, induction, 116–19). *Twelfth Night* undermines the credibility of the satiric tradition it draws on, offering a critique of the "whole pack" of writers dogging the Elizabethan government, and urging us to temper our judgments of public figures with compassion.

It also generates a revised version of satiric materials, which values the aging lover for his longstanding and controversial association with the performative arts. Shakespeare does not seek to persuade, correct, or provoke rational judgment in his portrait of Orsino. The traits he ridicules in Malvolio he aestheticizes in Orsino, who is a poet and a lover, rather than a lunatic.[130] While all of Olivia's suitors think about courtship in theatrical terms, Orsino is interested in this performance as an end in itself. A playwright of sorts, he unclasps "the book even" of his "secret soul" to the boy actor Cesario, giving him tips on how not to be "denied access," and appreciatively noting that "it shall become thee well to act my woes" (1.4.14–16, 26). The pleasure that Orsino takes in refining this performance helps shield him from the ridicule endured by Malvolio, as does the fact that we never see Orsino courting Olivia in person. This omission allows audiences to respond to the lyrical count on grounds other than the ones proposed by satirists. If Orsino fails as Olivia's lover, he succeeds as an artist, since his intended "audience" (1.4.18) proves receptive to his "book," albeit not in the way he had hoped. His actual audience is even more susceptible. Like the "little western flower, / Before milk-white, now purple with love's wound" (2.1.166–67) in *A*

Midsummer Night's Dream, Viola is transformed by the erotic energies Orsino misdirects at a fair vestal. Insofar as her enraptured response serves as model for our own, Orsino "seduces rather than convinces," as all nostalgic creations do.[131] His desire for Olivia may be vain, in that it produces no biological issue, but it inspires Viola's affection and engenders the play's strange, melancholic beauty.

Orsino's continuance in the "old tune" has made his courtship "fat and fulsome" (5.1.108–9) to Olivia, a metaphor that links his failed suit with the past, and with the music that he claims, in his famous first line, as "food for love" (1.1.1). The count never enters without a retinue of musicians, to a soundtrack designed to generate feelings of loss, longing, and melancholy by contrasting an "inadequate present" to an "idealized past."[132] Orsino prefers these "old and antique song[s]" over the "light airs" of "these most brisk and giddy-paced times" (2.4.3–6) because they dally "with the innocence of love / like the old age" (2.4.47–48). Orsino's songs feed a love for an "old age" that he both represents and recreates on stage. As Boym points out, music "is the permanent accompaniment of nostalgia—its ineffable charm ... makes the nostalgic teary-eyed and tongue-tied and often clouds critical reflection on the subject."[133] Shakespeare's musical refashioning of his "whoreson round man" suspends "critical reflection" in this manner, encouraging audiences to indulge affective and aesthetic responses instead. The conjunction of "innocence" with "the old age" revises the trope of the "old boy" along nostalgic lines, making the aging lover a figure for a desire shared by all those past the first age. Hearing and recalling the "antique" tunes played at the count's request, an audience member may even revisit the time when he himself was "a little tine boy" (epilogue, 1), bringing these individual memories to bear on the play's representation of a collective past. Orsino makes a utopia out of this past, imagined longingly as a refuge from the present, a place where "free maids ... weave their thread with bone," sit " in the sun," and "chaunt" all day long (2.4.43–49). In love of old, with a love for old songs, Orsino acquires the patina of an antique, consistent with his self-identification as Endymion, the aging hero of an old play about an aging court.

A glamorous version of the *senex amans*, Orsino embodies a powerful longing for an earlier Elizabethan moment, when artists collaborated with aristocrats in generating the rich court culture that haunted Shakespeare throughout his career. As we saw in previous chapters, Leicester had been the premier patron in this former age, his generosity the munificent force that drove the flowering of the arts and letters in Elizabethan England. A great innovator, he also had a reputation for loving antiquities, and patronized both antiquarians and historians. Eager to secure an afterlife for his efforts, Leicester had tried to keep Kenilworth "exactly as it had been in July 1575.... the deliberate fossilization of the castle and its picture collection suggests a desire to create a lasting memorial to the revels of 1575."[134] Goran Stanivuković proposes that the chivalric Orsino represents a lost "masculine ideal," of the sort popularized by the medieval romances alluded to in the retrospective Kenilworth entertainments.[135] We might glimpse in Orsino's interactions with Cesario and Feste a "memorial" to another lost ideal, especially relevant to the theatrical artists who brought *Twelfth Night* to the stage. Orsino behaves like a gracious patron, recalling aspects of Leicester's legacy not remembered in the satiric tradition, including his generous support of musicians, artists, actors, and fools, or his attempts to conserve the "reliques" of earlier times. Viola honors Orsino's reputation as a discerning patron by presenting herself as a performer who can "sing / And speak to him in many sorts of music" (1.2.57–58). It's hard not see in her trajectory a reflection of the now aging playwright's youthful dreams and hopes, which needs must have involved establishing a level of intimacy with the great. If Leicester exerted an uncommon pull on Shakespeare's memory, it was not only because the earl was ridiculous, as satirists proposed. "One remembers best what is colored by emotion," Boym explains, and that emotion can be either negative or positive.[136] Where anger and resentment fueled most contemporary representations of the queen's dead favorites, *Twelfth Night* draws on other emotions as well, including pity, loss, longing, and affection.

A decade after *Endymion* appeared in print Shakespeare revisits the aging Elizabethan court to find that its revels have now ended. He returns home to "the unrealized dreams of the past and visions of the future that became obsolete," acknowledging his artistic dependency on the fantasies fostered by the court in its heyday.[137] Not only does the autumnal *Twelfth Night* embrace the fantastical elements of the new comedy derided by Jonson, but it embraces them as "old," identifying itself, and by extension its writer, with the aging court that Jonson targeted.

Perhaps the best evidence that Shakespeare found pity in his heart for the faded and fading stars of the old regime is the final treatment he reserves for Olivia and Orsino. Neither of them achieves the rejuvenation of an Endymion. But if Orsino and Olivia are not restored to their youths, Shakespeare restores them, by the artificial means of his twin youths, to versions of themselves. In their loving union with Orsino and Olivia, Viola and Sebastian set about redeeming the Elizabethan past. The elevation of the meritorious twins in *Twelfth Night* balances the failure of Malvolio's fantasy, reendowing the dream of eroticized social mobility with a utopian resonance. The humbled Olivia is able to partner without diluting her sovereignty, since she secures Sebastian's compliance to her rule before she marries him (4.1.63–64).[138] And the castigated Orsino is allowed a marriage with his "fancy's queen" (5.1.388) which is founded on male amity and thus bypasses the problem of his indecorous, age-defying erotic desire.[139] By these magical means, Illyria attains the renewal that eluded Elizium. Orsino's retreat into a compensatory fantasy fulfills the promise made in the epilogue of *1 Henry IV*. And Shakespeare conclusively shows Jonson that comedies about "a Duke . . . in love with a Countess" could be "near and familiarly allied to the time."

Twelfth Night finds in the experience of lost enchantment an aesthetic magic of its own. The *Sonnets* take up where this play leaves off, embracing the impulse to identify with the aging lover. The fate from which Viola saves Orsino haunts the sonnet speaker, who is also in love with "antique" forms and whose "besetting sin" is also "self-love" (62.1).[140] In *Endymion*, Lyly identified sonnet-writing as an activity likely to induce age-inappropriate behavior. His hero, after devoting the "prime of his youth" to "devising sonnets" ends up "having waxed old and not knowing it": "how could my curled hairs . . . be turned to grey and my strong body to a dying weakness?" (1.2.64–65, 5.1.74–76). It might be said of Shakespeare's sonnet speaker that he has waxed old, and knows it, but devises sonnets nonetheless—devises sonnets, in fact, about the "dying weakness" of aging bodies. The nostalgic atmosphere of the sequence, its famous sense of generic and cultural belatedness, owes much to its invocation of an aging court. By the time Shakespeare picked up his "antique pen" (19.10), the fashion for sonnets had, along with the queen's two eldest favorites, died away. In their evocation of "the rich proud cost of outworn buried age" (64.2), the sonnets betray an ongoing imaginative engagement with these bygone "great princes' favorites" (25.5). The aging speaker posits a homology between himself and the favorites, grounded in what the sequence describes as a vain form of sexuality—at once futile and arrogant, biologically sterile but imaginatively reproductive.

In a sequence initially committed to persuading "fairest creatures" (1.1) to adopt the reproductive habits of the rose, Shakespeare offers royal favorites at first by way of contrast, since they are "But as the marigold at the sun's eye, / And in themselves their pride lies buried, / For at a frown they in their glory die" (25.5–9). "Those who are in favor with their stars" can, as Leicester and Hatton did, boast of "public honour and proud titles" (25.1–2), but they die childless. The sequence's frequent antitheses of youth and age trade in the *Endymion* effect, associated with the queen's men, by reproducing in the space of a line or two the deep devastation of having waxed old without knowing it. Struck by how quickly "Sap" is "check'd with frost and lusty leaves quite gone" (5.7), the speaker pleads with the young man to reproduce before "forty winters shall besiege thy brow, / And dig deep trenches in thy beauty's field" (2.1–2). The anxiety about procreation is linked to the court through military and heraldic metaphors, which construe aging as the attenuation of aristocratic identity, the gradual reduction of "youth's proud livery" to "a tott'red weed of small worth" (2.4–5). A few sonnets hold the "mortal moon" who "hath her eclipse endured" (107.5) to account. Sonnet 7, for example, uses an epic simile to compare the young man to a monarchical sun, to whom all pay "homage" (3) at first,

> But when from highmost pitch, with weary car
> Like feeble age he reeleth from the day,
> The eyes ('fore duteous) now converted are
> From his low tract and look another way:
> So thou, thyself outgoing in thy noon,
> Unlook'd on diest unless thou get a son. (7.8–14)

The pun on son links the young man's failure to reproduce to the decline of the sun's "sacred majesty" (7.4). Shakespeare was struck by this aspect of the Elizabethan court. "The Phoenix and the Turtle," a poem about the relationship between Elizabeth and an unidentified courtier, also characterizes the love between the "Turtle and his queen" as beautiful but sterile, "leaving no posterity" because of their "married chastity" (31, 62).

The sonnet sequence retains a conventional emphasis on the waste, vanity, and futility of the age-in-love trope throughout, an apparent indictment of the court this figure evokes. But the advice so liberally bestowed on the young man in the procreation sonnets comes from a failure, for, like the queen's favorites or the old boys in *Twelfth Night*, the speaker has been a poor manager of his own "youthful sap"(15.7). And if in Sonnet 138 he initially experiences the persistence of sexual desire into old age as a form of categorical degradation, the speaker embraces by the sonnet's end the deviant idea that faults can be flattering. By adopting the adulterating viewpoint of this "decrepit" speaker (37.1), Shakespeare returns the category of age to the central place it occupies in Castiglione's account of the distinction between lust and love. Because the sonnet speaker is "no longer youthful," his struggles to leave "sensual desire behind" take on a desperate cast. And yet few readers find this aging lover to be a "senseless fool" like Malvolio.[141] The conventions of the sonnet work toward the unconventional end of empathy with the figure of "age in love," charged now with the poetic search for nonbiological modes of perpetuation and immortality.

As he ceases to advocate for conventional forms of procreation, the speaker's "barren rhyme" (16.4) begins to transform into "pow'rful rhyme" that outlives "the gilded monuments of princes" (55.2). In the process, the "wrackful siege of batt'ring days" (65.6) becomes less an obstacle to than a source of beauty. Time itself is an artist who etches faces, a rival of and therefore also a figure for, the sonneteer. As indelible as "the lines and wrinkles" (63.4), or the "parallels" that Time sets in "beauty's brow" (60.10), the speaker's "black lines" (63.13) paint his age far more memorably than the young man's youth. In Sonnet 73, he turns the gaze on himself and discovers there the fairest creature of them all. The sonnet evokes the lingering beauty of "the twilight of such day / As after sunset fadeth in the west," arguing that it makes "love more strong" to love that which one "must leave ere long" (73.5–6; 13–14). Like the "great favorites'" who have "spread" their "fair leaves" to the sun, the speaker admits to "yellow leaves, or none, or few" that appear at first to signal his barrenness (73.2). By reminding the readers of the "quires" of "yellow leaves" in their hand, however, where the sonnets still sing, the first quatrain testifies to the speaker's successful transcendence of his own mortality—a transcendence secured not despite his aging but because of it. Christopher Martin argues that Shakespeare's sequence celebrates youth at the expense of age by opposing beauty to age.[142] But the speaker's sense of aesthetics, preoccupied at first with salvaging beauty from the ravages inflicted by time, shifts over time to accommodate the idea of beauty worn—even enhanced—by those ravages. The "bare ruin'd choirs, where late the sweet birds sang" (73.4) are more, not less, lovely for being "rn'wd" (to use the original spelling) and for thus containing the promise of both death and renewal. In its concluding phoenix-like image of the loving speaker as a "glowing . . . fire," who "on the ashes of his youth doth lie . . . Consumed with that which it was nourished by" (73.8–12), Sonnet 73 represents "age in love" not as a figure of ridicule, but as a figure of tragic beauty.

As he grew old along with his monarch, Shakespeare returned compulsively and with ever greater complexity to the topic of aging male sexuality. An extended meditation on the subject, the sonnets follow the great favorites in exploiting the speaker's unorthodox erotic experiences to secure his unparalleled status. The phoenix is the epitome of beauty because it is immortal and unique, the reason Elizabeth I chose it as an emblem. The sequence's search for timeless beauty paradoxically ends in the elevation of timeworn beauty; what we remember, finally, is not the "fair," "kind," "true," and anodyne young man, but the magnificent and highly individual ruin he occasions. "Beauty spent and done" ("A Lover's Complaint," 11) is beauty still. In making "age in love" a vessel for his peculiar aesthetics of ruin, the Virgin Queen's most observant male subject showed he had learned a thing or two about how to convert limitations into greatness, transgression into transcendence. These are lessons that he carried into *Antony and Cleopatra* (1608), a play about an aging queen and the "noble ruin of her magic" (3.10.18).

CHAPTER 4

Antony

Early seventeenth-century tragedies that express their concern with personal monarchy in gendered terms—those that insist on Elizabeth I's reign as a context—often include virulent representations of sexually active and lubricious older men. The two plays that Steven Mullaney claims address the conundrum of Elizabeth's aging body are cases in point. Both *Hamlet* (1600–1601) and *The Revenger's Tragedy* (1607) feature young men who vie with despised elders for the favors of a regal woman.[1] That both premiered at the Globe would have underscored this shared pattern of cross-generational triangulation. In a repertory situation, an actor's past roles shape reception of new ones, a phenomenon enhanced by the association of actors with certain types, like that of the aging lover or the revenger.[2] Richard Burbage, who pioneered the role of Hamlet, likely appeared as Vindice, while Middleton's "royal villain" (3.5.146) may have been played by John Lowin, the actor who had played *Hamlet*'s "treacherous, lecherous, kindless villain" (2.2.581) in 1603. Claudius poisons his older brother to gain access to Gertrude's bed and to the throne of Denmark. By translating his sexual service to Gertrude into a crown, he lives out the darkest fantasies of Elizabethan England, succeeding where the Leicester of anticourt polemic had failed. Claudius's analogue in *The Revenger's Tragedy* is also a "royal lecher" of "silver years" with a penchant for poisoning, who presides over a court given over to "Dutch lust, fulsome lust" and "Drunken procreation" (1.1.1, 1.2.11, 1.3.56–57). Given that his topic is "the transgression of aging sexuality," Mullaney's focus on the female characters to the exclusion of these male representatives of "marrowless age" (*Revenger's Tragedy*, 1.1.5) is a little strange.[3] Neither *Hamlet* nor *The Revenger's Tragedy* construes generational violations as the exclusive purview of female characters.[4]

On the contrary, Middleton premises his play on a savage contempt for superannuated male sexuality. If *Hamlet* sometimes shifts "contaminating agency from Claudius to the female body" of his queen, as Janet Adelman argues, *The Revenger's Tragedy* identifies the aging male body as a primary source of cultural contamination.[5] Middleton borrows from medical discourses that condemned "intemperate and riotous living" in older men, inviting us to share in a pervasive disgust with his "old, cool duke" who is "as slack in tongue as in performance" (1.2.74–75).[6] Clutching the skull of his dead lover, Vindice vents in his opening soliloquy a murderous rage against this "dry" figure of "grey-haired adultery," a "parched and juiceless luxur" with "spendthrift veins," who has "scarce blood enough to live upon" but who nonetheless "riot[s] it like a son and heir" (1.1.8–11). One of several "exc'llent characters" drawn from court satire (1.1.5), the Duke indulges the excesses that medical authorities argued hastened aging. Immersed in "sensuall lustes and voluptuous appetites," neither he nor Claudius manages "the pageaunte . . . of their age" according to socially approved protocols.[7] Such "old men lustful," Vindice maintains, relying on the conventional theatrical metaphor, "do show like young men, angry, eager, violent, / Outbid like their limited performances. / Oh, 'ware an old man hot and vicious: / 'Age, as in gold, in lust is covetous'" (1.1.34–37). From his abstract personification of "Age . . . in lust" to his biting references to role-playing and generational cross-dressing, the terms of Vindice's denunciation are familiar: he confounds dramatic and sexual "performance" to express outrage with the categorical violations that the Duke commits. The Duke helpfully endorses Vindice's judgment, describing himself as being in his "old days . . . a youth in lust," and acknowledging "Age hot" to be "like a monster" (2.3.126–129).

By the simple expedient of naming the object of all that monstrous senescent lust Gloriana, after Elizabeth I's public *persona*, Middleton teases out *Hamlet*'s latent political implications. According to Adelman, "the subjection of male to female" is "the buried fantasy of *Hamlet*."[8] While she reads this submerged fantasy in psychoanalytic terms, Middleton's brilliant coup de théâtre emphasizes its historical, political, and cultural dimensions instead. The skull that Vindice brandishes functions simultaneously as a *memento* of Shakespeare's haunted play and of the deceased queen, identifying one with the other. Historicist scholars have long linked Shakespeare's masterpiece to the Elizabethan succession crisis, but *Hamlet's* particular investments are sometimes hard to discern, because analogies between the Danish and the English court are woefully imprecise.[9] Emboldened by Elizabeth's death, Middleton evokes her court more directly than Shakespeare does. Where the sexually active Gertrude is an imperfect match for the Virgin Queen, for example, Gloriana's "purer part" resisted the "palsy lust" of the Duke (1.1.33–34), like Lyly's Cynthia stayed Endymion's passion, or Elizabeth Leicester's. By withholding Gloriana's name until the climactic third act, Middleton makes the connection between memories of the queen and memories of *Hamlet* a retroactive one, inviting audiences to participate in a historically informed revision of the opening soliloquy and the old play it recalls. No wonder critics have found *The Revenger's Tragedy* to be a "dramatized interpretation" of Hamlet's "Elizabethan undertones."[10]

The villainous old man in lust who plays a starring role in this interpretation epitomizes the deceased Gloriana's troubling powers over her men. Blazoning his beloved in the Petrarchan tropes of the court, Vindice claims that even the "uprightest man" would break "custom" under the influence of her "two heaven-pointed diamonds" (1.1.19–24). Vindice also repurposes Hamlet's favorite metaphor to describe how Gloriana made even "a usurer's son / Melt all his patrimony in a kiss" (1.1.26–27). In keeping with such themes, *The Revenger's Tragedy* depicts a world in which "place is governed by ambition" and sexual charisma "rather than the proprieties of due succession," a world of "carnality and licentiousness" familiar from Elizabethan anticourt polemics.[11] Like Cardinal Allen's Elizabeth I, who reduced English noblemen to "effeminate dastardie," Gloriana casts such a powerful spell over the nation's sons that they lose masculine rigor and forgo patriarchal duty.[12] Vindice acknowledges his complicity in this state of affairs, chiding himself "for doting on [Gloriana's] beauty"

(3.5.69–70). It takes him fully nine years to recover from the one he refers to ambiguously as his "poisoned love" (1.1.14).

By blending motifs of *Hamlet* with the topoi of anticourt polemics, *The Revenger's Tragedy* exhumes the earlier play's "buried" engagement with the Elizabethan court. True to the genre after which he is named, Middleton's tainted protagonist struggles with putting that past behind him but ends up repeating it instead. Vindice's revenge outdoes Hamlet's in both the sharpness of its allegory and "the quaintness of [its] malice" (3.4.109). Where Gertrude is collateral damage in the earlier play's finale, the "form that living shone so bright" (3.5.67) becomes the favored means of punishment in the later one, showcasing Vindice's posthumous control over Gloriana's maidenhead, and, by extension, Middleton's over the queen's.[13] A potent Petrarchan relic, Gloriana's "quaint piece of beauty" (3.5.54) retains enough charisma to lure the "slobbering Dutchman" (3.5.164) to his death. *The Revenger's Tragedy* stages a macabre parody of Elizabethan courtship, in which the poisonous skull, dressed like "an old gentlewoman in a periwig," puts the "old surfeiter" (3.5.113, 53–54) to sleep, permanently, with a kiss. For good measure, Vindice and his brother Hippolyto then assault this latter-day Endymion, while forcing him to watch his illegitimate son replace him in the arms of his duchess. Three different young men contribute to the extended "hell" endured by the "old Duke" (3.5.184, 208). Modern police procedurals would call this overkill. *The Revenger's Tragedy*'s infernal scene of punishment—with its emphasis on cross-generational violations, its violent contempt for the "poor lecher" (3.5.158) at its center, and its grotesquely material caricature of Neoplatonic claims about the spirituality of kisses—clarifies that, like the anonymous writers of *Leicester's Commonwealth*, Middleton was no fan of Gloriana's aging court.

Although Vindice dies at the end of *The Revenger's Tragedy*, Richard Burbage returned shortly thereafter to the Globe in yet another play about a judgmental young man and a dissipated older man. This time, however, Burbage played the "amorous surfeiter" (*Antony and Cleopatra*, 2.1.33) who fills his "vacancy with his voluptuousness" even though "the dryness of his bones / Call on him for't" (1.4.26–28). Regular theatergoers must have wondered at the migration of the age-in-love role from the clown Will Kempe, who first played Bottom and Falstaff, to the burly player John Lowin, who had recently played Claudius and Falstaff, to the lead actor Richard Burbage, who played Antony (and had probably played Orsino).[14] Burbage, who turned forty in 1607, was just entering the stage of life known as green old age. While he may have forfeited the role of Octavius because he gained weight as he aged, the casting of the company's lead player in the role of Antony also signals a radical shift in perspective and values.[15] As Simon Palfrey and Tiffany Stern note, the "heroic 'type'" for which Burbage was known constitutes "an invitation to command the stage, and more often than not the audience's sympathies."[16] *Antony and Cleopatra* pits generational opposites against one another, as *Hamlet* and *The Revenger's Tragedy* do. Deviating from established pattern, however, Shakespeare assigns the central male role to the aging lover, not the eager "young man" (3.11.62) who orchestrates this surfeiting elder's "declining day" (5.1.38).

While historicist critics have long identified in Cleopatra a distorted reflection of Elizabeth I, they have little to say about Antony. Theodora Jankowski examines the political uses that Cleopatra makes of her sexuality and her theatricality, for example, but dismisses Antony as having "no talent for regal spectacle."[17] Arguing for "a perceived shift from Elizabethan magnificence to Jacobean 'measure,'" Paul Yachnin reconstructs a seventeenth-century *Antony and Cleopatra* rich in topical meanings—all deriving from the confrontation between Cleopatra, a version of Elizabeth, and Octavius, a version of James.[18] Katherine Eggert, too, finds a play constituted of "Cleopatran displays" and "Roman reactions," in which Antony plays the passive role of a privileged "playgoer."[19] Like Claudius or Middleton's old Duke, Antony is near invisible to critics interested in reconstructing the historical context of the play.[20] Yet he shares top billing with Cleopatra, and the other characters speculate and gossip about him as much as they do about her. If we accept that the political resonances of *Antony and Cleopatra* "must *mean* something" in context, then Antony must have a part in this meaning-making process.[21] Reading Antony in light of the Elizabethan tradition on lecherous old men, I show that his connection to the dead queen's court is more encompassing than previously suspected. The "greatest soldier in the world," Antony is also its "greatest liar" (1.3.38–39) and its greatest lover, a composite made out of Shakespeare's favorite materials, and designed to recall other "scene[s] of courtship," actual and theatrical.[22] Through its male protagonist, *Antony and Cleopatra* puts into play a whole range of memories about Elizabeth and her favorite men, including the oft-repeated allegations that these provided her with sexual services.

As we have seen, the Elizabethan *senex amans* shared his affinity for the theater with Elizabeth's courtiers, who, according to Ben Jonson, borrowed "play-particles" to woo the queen.[23] Shakespeare makes this theatrical approach to courtship, evident also in Falstaff or Malvolio, a defining feature of Antony. Cleopatra highlights her lover's theatrical agency, by directing him both seriously and mockingly in his scenes of "excellent dissembling" (1.3.78–79). Although she exerts control over these ad hoc performances, she also acknowledges her deep dependence on Antony's sexual, military, and theatrical virtuosity—she needs his "inches" to show "there were a heart in Egypt" (1.3.39–40). Like Elizabeth I at Tilbury, whose legendary speech she here echoes, Cleopatra recognizes the gendered constraints that require her to use a male proxy, who can act in her stead. She wishes "as the president of [her] kingdom" to "appear there for a man" (3.7.16–17), but cannot do so without the "soldier, servant" who "makes peace or war" as she affects (1.3.70–71). Most scholars nowadays agree that Elizabeth assumed "the heart and stomach of a king" so as to outrank her men and that Cleopatra's desire for a male body politic reflects this rhetorical strategy.[24] Read in its entirety, the Tilbury speech also compensates for the perceived failings of the queen's body natural by proposing a male substitute, Elizabeth's "lieutenant general," the Earl of Leicester. "Never" has a "prince commanded a more noble or worthy subject," Elizabeth asserts, identifying their collaboration as an essential feature of her rule.[25] Under patriarchal conditions, the "heart" of female rule can only manifest through such "noble" performances, although these may take the individuals involved to the "heart of loss" (4.12.29), because they violate normative standards of masculine behavior. While *Antony and Cleopatra*'s Roman characters sound like the antigovernment pamphleteers of the 1580s and 1590s in their strident denunciations of the protagonists, the play itself wonders if defect might not generate perfection, in the form of new and more expansive notions of masculine excellence.

The rest of this chapter focuses on Shakespeare's remarkable final contribution to the theatrical "fashion" for "old man's venery," the great general who loves a queen whom "no other of nature can match or of art imitate," like the Earl of Essex's Elizabeth.[26] During the Jacobean vogue for elegies of Elizabeth, Shakespeare was berated for offering no public comment on her death.[27] A few years later, he wrote *Antony and Cleopatra*, a play that Eggert and Leonard Tennenhouse describe as an "elegy" in dramatic form.[28] While *Antony and Cleopatra* does indeed celebrate "queenship with the full weight of nostalgia," it distinguishes itself from other elegies by emphasizing the prospective aspects of this longing.[29] A generic hybrid, which blends elegy and other modes, *Antony and Cleopatra* situates the utopian possibilities of queenship not just in the past, as I have argued *Twelfth Night* does, but also in the "new earth, new heaven" (1.1.17) of the future. It achieves this turn to the future by revising the overdetermined figure of the aging lover, normally used to satirize the "limited performances" of Elizabeth's courtiers, into an unlikely model for masculine mimesis. Rather than being merely elegiac, Shakespeare's approach to his male protagonist has the immediate force of a eulogy, a rhetorical genre with deep associations to Antony and his classical forebear, who both use Caesar's funeral oration to reshape Rome's political future. *Antony and Cleopatra* is characteristically Shakespearean in its interrogation of its own generic impulses; a play about a man famous for giving a eulogy, in which characters obsessively eulogize one another, it cautions against the emotions that make people "good, being gone" (1.2.126), even as it summons these emotions to redefine key historical figures from the recent and the classical past.

Plutarch's Elizabethan translator, Sir Thomas North (yet another client of Leicester's) urged his readers to turn to the *Parallel Lives* for the analogues that might help them achieve sound political judgments about the past.[30] As its title indicates, this work pairs descriptions of Greek and Roman worthies to clarify their individual contributions and achievements. In his dedicatory letter to Elizabeth I, North extends these comparisons to contemporary English persons, asking the queen "who is fitter to revive the dead memorie of their fame, than she who beareth the lively image of their vertues?"[31] While not specifying whose "dead memorie" and ancient virtues the "lively image" of Elizabeth revives, the prefatory materials present Plutarch's biographies as a rich trove of political knowledge. The "Scholemistresse of Princes," ancient "historie" is relevant to all those interested in "publike ... affairs" and eager to achieve "judgement and knowledge," regardless of rank. Inviting his readers to play the role of the prince, North emphasizes civic and political applications; in contrast to the "private" knowledge generated at "Universities," the *Parallel Lives* produce the more "profitable" knowledge fit for "cities." Plutarch's "stories" should be valued for what we might anachronistically call their public-making potential—they "reach to all persons, serve for all tymes, teache the living, revive the dead." Because they promote the ability to forge connections over time while imparting political competency, these "examples past" teach readers "to judge of things present & to foresee things to come."[32] Like the "fantasies of the past" that Svetlana Boym describes, North's translation, "determined by needs of the present," aims for "a direct impact on realities of the future."[33]

Shakespeare took the invitation to profit from the *Parallel Lives* to heart. Plutarch's *Lives* was one of the playwright's favorite books, and "The Life of Marcus Antonius" was his favorite part of that book, providing source material for three different plays and numerous allusions. James Shapiro speculates that Shakespeare returned to Antonius late in his career "because he was discovering in it connections to new cultural preoccupations, or because he found himself identifying with the character of Antony."[34] At this stage in his life, the forty-four-year-old Shakespeare may indeed have identified with the aging Roman general rather than with his youthful opponent, the "scarce-bearded Caesar" (1.1.21), especially given Antonius's proclivity for all things theatrical. Caesar's favorite "passed away the time in hearing of foolish plays" (Plutarch, 183), surrounding himself with "tumblers, antic dancers, jugglers, players, jesters and drunkards" (195).[35] Plutarch describes his subject as a real-life braggart soldier, moreover, famous for his "Asiatic" eloquence and "full of ostentation, foolish bravery, and vain ambition" (175). Like Antony, the mature Antonius played "many pretty youthful parts" to entertain the women in his life (185). Shakespeare presents Antony in more positive light than Plutarch does, by glossing over some unsavory aspects of Antonius's career, like his responsibility in Pompey's murder.[36] Given this tendency to idealize the male protagonist, we might expect him to downplay Antonius's histrionic tendencies, which consistently arouse Plutarch's condemnation. Instead, Shakespeare magnifies them, making theatricality a defining feature of his Antony.

That Antonius sacrificed his reputation to this love of theater had become a commonplace by the time the playwright first took up the topic. Stephen Gosson illustrates the pitfalls awaiting playgoers by describing how "Antonius . . . gave him selfe daily to beholding Playes, for which he grewe into contempte among all his friendes," for example.[37] In *Julius Caesar* Brutus evinces the conventional contempt toward Antony, regarding his rival as no threat because he is "given / To sports, to wildness, and much company" (2.1.189–90). Brutus's judgment is famously shortsighted, however, and the funeral scene shows Antony's embrace of theater to have been neither vain nor foolish. Most critics would agree with Palfrey and Stern when they describe Antony's eulogy of Caesar as "*about* the power of the theatre to move great assemblies." Where Brutus appeals to reason in his funeral oration, Antony channels his audience's grief to political purpose, in a superb display of Ciceronian eloquence. Although we might find in Antony's "demonic Shakespearean charm" evidence of troubling demagoguery, Caesar casts a positive light on his favorite's theatrics, basing his preference for Antony over Cassius on the fact that the latter "loves no plays / As thou dost, Antony" (1.2.203–4).[38] Mocked by some, feared by others, Antony's love of the theater is valued by his Roman superior, as it is later by the Egyptian queen, and by his English creator. To Shakespeare, Antonius was first a lover of plays, a man who patronizes theater by sponsoring it, attending it, performing in it, and applying its lessons to politics.

As he grew older, Shakespeare glimpsed in Antonius's biography other resemblances that had escaped him at an earlier age. Plutarch presents

Antonius's love of Cleopatra, "the last and extremest mischief of all" (199), as an extension of the general's lifelong enthusiasm for the theater; together, they fashion the queen's identity as "a new Isis" (243) and indulge in "foolish sports" and "fond and childish pastimes," including amorous role-play (206–7). Antonius is at once a theatrical artist and the lover of a queen, which explains why he and Cleopatra became identified with Elizabeth I and her men by the turn of the seventeenth century. The general's willingness to play the lover to a self-styled moon goddess conformed to a pattern that Shakespeare had used throughout his career to think about the court. When he returned to "The Life of Marcus Antonius" life near the end of his own, this pattern came to dominate his presentation of the ancient Roman and his love for a mercurial queen.

While she was still alive, the Virgin Queen had welcomed the turn to the classics for a parallel that might bring into perspective her unorthodox reign. Besides assuming the guise of various classical goddesses, including Venus and Diana, the English queen also promoted an association with the historical Cleopatra, renowned as Elizabeth was for her "voice and words," which "were marvelous pleasant; for her tongue was an instrument . . . which she easily turned to any language" (Plutarch 203).[39] *The Blessedness of Brytaine or a Celebration of the Queen's Holyday* (1588), a panegyric poem dedicated to the Earl of Essex and "published with Authoritie," celebrates this quality in Elizabeth, praising her as

> The Starre of Women Sex, Grave Wisdoms store:
> Sententious, speaking Tongs in filed phraze,
> Profoundly learnd, and perfect in eche Lore,
> Her Fame, no Rav'ning Time shall ever Raze
> . . . .
> What should Nymphs, or Goddesses Recount?
> Or Ægypt Queenes, or Roman Ladies name?
> Sith as Supreme, our Sov'raigne dooth surmount.
> In choise of Good, the cheefe of all those same?
> For to compare the Great, with simple small,
> Is thereby not to praise the Best at all.

All those "nymphs," "Goddesses," "Roman ladies" and "Ægypt Queenes" are citations, which help the author establish Elizabeth as comparatively "Supreme." She "dooth surmount" previous embodiments of feminine excellence, just as Enobarbus claims Cleopatra overpictures "that Venus where we see / The fancy outwork nature" (2.2.200–201).[40] Marguerite Tassi argues that Enobarbus's famous description "directs his onstage and offstage auditors to imagine... a particular painting of Venus in association with Cleopatra"; like other comparisons in *Antony and Cleopatra*, this one also directs offstage audiences to remember Elizabeth, who cultivated a resemblance to both Venus and Cleopatra.[41] In the wake of the Spanish Armada, *The Blessedness of Brytayne* proposes a specific way in which the English "Starre" eclipses her Egyptian forebear, namely through successful resistance to "cursed Circes" and "Fell Raging Rome."[42] There would be no defeat at Actium for Elizabeth.

The queen encouraged these flattering classical comparisons in other venues as well. At Greenwich, she displayed a bust of Julius Caesar, for example. The royal garden there also included a "tower," located on "the Venus Hill," containing tapestries on classical themes and inscribed with a Latin motto, translated by Thomas Platter as "'When Antonius the eloquent was compelled by war to seek help of the queen, this inscription was made.'" The allusion is to the battle of Actium, but the inscription followed by the dates 1581 and 1585, suggesting a more proximate reference, when another general (Leicester?) had made a similar request for help to another queen.[43] Like Cleopatra's, Elizabeth's iconography featured snakes, including the embroidered specimen displayed on the sleeve of her magnificent gown in the Rainbow Portrait (ca. 1600–1602), where she appears as Cynthia, the "Queen of Love and Beauty." Roy Strong argues that the snake, which holds a jeweled heart in its mouth, signifies judgment's successful conquest of passion, another way perhaps that Elizabeth had bested her Egyptian analogue.[44] Symbols of wisdom and immortality, snakes had long been associated with the moon goddess Isis, whose persona the historical Cleopatra had adopted, as her Shakespearean counterpart does, and as Elizabeth adopted that of the moon goddess Cynthia.[45] Cleopatra's suicide by asp, which cemented her claims

FIG. 6. Rainbow Portrait of Elizabeth I, attributed to Marcus Gheeraerts the Younger (1600–1602). By permission of Hatfield House Library and Archives, Hatfield, Hertfordshire, England.

to immortality and her identification with Isis, became a favorite topos of Western literary and historiographical descriptions after Plutarch. Another portrait of Elizabeth dating from the 1580s or 1590s and now housed at the National Portrait Gallery evokes this iconographic tradition more forcefully, by showing the queen grasping a snake with her hand. Although someone eventually painted flowers over the snake, the original recalls Plutarch's description of "Cleopatra's image, with an aspic biting of her arm" carried in Octavius Caesar's triumph, the source for Shakespeare's tableau of the dying Cleopatra (Plutarch, 293).

In both royal portraits, the snake conveys Elizabeth's mastery over emblematic animals, a reading substantiated by a piece of fabric still in existence today, which once belonged to Elizabeth and may have come from the Rainbow Portrait's gown.[46] Embroidered with flowers and smaller animals, including birds, a frog, and a bear, the fabric evokes bowers "over-canopied with luscious woodbine, / with sweet musk-roses and with eglantine," places where "the snake throws her enamell'd skin" and Circean queens do favors to men transformed into "bear or wolf or bull" (*A Midsummer Night's Dream*, 2.1.251–55, 180). The snake portraits offer a visual equivalent for the queen's metamorphic powers over men, another quality Elizabeth shares with Plutarch's queen of Egypt, and with Shakespeare's "serpent of old Nile" (1.5.25). Indeed, those who compared Elizabeth to Circe borrowed a tactic of Octavian propaganda; Plutarch, too, makes his Cleopatra a Circe-like enchantress, who uses "charms and amorous poisons" to subject the "effeminate" Antonius to her every whim and plunge him in a "deep sleep" (249, 241, 208). If both queens were ranked among "the daughters of Circe," it was because both were considered "charming and enchanting," but not always "safe company" for men.[47]

Under such circumstances, Plutarch's Antonius, "subject to a woman's will" and no longer "master of himself" (248–50), became one of North's examples from the past that "teacheth us to judge of things present." Antonius's character and the contours of his career lent themselves to parallels with a number of Elizabethan courtiers. Although nowadays we may not think about the great Roman general as a favorite, for example, Plutarch presents him as one, claiming Antonius became the "chiefest" man in Rome because he secured Caesar's favor (182). His position as Caesar's General of the Horsemen paralleled that of Leicester and Essex, who had both served as Master of the Horse before becoming Elizabeth's generals.[48] The Roman general's vaunted eloquence, his status as an upstart, and his patronage of plays and players—all aligned him with specific Elizabethan favorites, including Leicester, who was scorned for surrounding himself with players, and Sir Walter Ralegh, who had seduced Elizabeth by the sole means of "a bold and plausible tongue."[49] Like Cleopatra, who had been romantically tied to three great soldiers, Elizabeth I "loved a soldier," and "her prime favorites" all had "a touch or tincture of Mars in their inclination."[50] That Antonius was the "valiantest man and skillfullest soldier of all those that" Caesar "had about him" (Plutarch, 182) made him a natural point of comparison for Essex, whose biographer describes him as pathologically anxious to "preserve his own status as the indisputable colossus in English military affairs," and for Leicester, Elizabeth's general at Tilbury.[51] Leicester's detractors often associated him with classical figures noted for ambition, in fact, explaining that the earl did "tread upon his equales, thinkeinge with Pompie to have no equals nor yet with Cesar to have no rivals."[52] Like the ambitious Leicester, Antonius had inspired love and condemnation in equal measure, and became a favorite subject of gossip because he had devoted himself so absolutely to his queen that others believed "he was not his own man" (Plutarch, 258).

These numerous parallels go a long way in explaining the popularity enjoyed by the classical lovers in late sixteenth- and early seventeenth-century England. Before Shakespeare took up their cause, Marcus Antonius and Cleopatra had already been the subject of several closet dramas, including Samuel Daniel's *Cleopatra* (1594), revised early in James's reign to emphasize the resemblance between Elizabeth and Cleopatra.[53] Notably, Daniel dedicated the first edition of his play to Leicester's niece, Mary Sidney, Countess of Pembroke.[54] In the aftermath of Leicester's death in 1588, the classical lovers appear to have held special appeal for members of the earl's immediate circle. Mary Sidney translated the companion piece to Daniel's play, Robert Garnier's *Marc Antoine* (1578), in 1590, and Philip Sidney's friend Fulke Greville wrote a play on the same topic between 1595 and 1600. The Countess of Pembroke's *Antonie* focuses on the plight of its hero, whose wife "movd'e [his] queen (ay me!) to jealousie," who sacrificed his life and "honor" for that queen's love, and who as a result became "scarse maister" of himself. A "slave" to Cleopatra, Antony describes himself in his final moments as breaking "from the enchanter that him strongly held," and denounces his beloved in familiar terms, as a "Sorceres," complete with "poisned cuppes."[55] The popularity of Mary Sidney's translation—it was printed in 1592 and again in 1595—attests to a robust public appetite for her depiction of extreme masculine subjection. Shakespeare turned to it for help with fleshing out his Antony, who worries about the "poisoned hours" that "had bound me up / From mine own knowledge" (2.2.90–91), and finds that "These strong Egyptian fetters I must break" (1.2.117). When Shakespeare transforms Antonius's story "into a narrative of male masochism" that challenges "conventional notions of heroism and masculinity inherent in the Classical tradition," he was working with literary and historical precedent.[56]

Although we no longer have a copy of Greville's *Antonie and Cleopatra*, Sidney's friend left us the best evidence that the classical lovers functioned as an "example" of the queen's transformative powers over men. A member of Leicester's and Essex's factions at court, Greville consigned his *Antonie* to the fire around the time of Essex's fall, fearing that the "irregular passions" and "childish wantonesse" on display were "apt enough to be construed, or strained to a personating of vices in the present Governors, and government."[57] While scholars assume *Antonie* posed a problem because it predicted Essex's disgrace, Greville describes his self-censoring act in a biographical sketch of Elizabeth I, which defends the queen more generally against the charge of favoritism, contrasting her practices in these matters to "the latitudes which some moderne Princes allow to their Favorites."[58] Echoing John Knox on the emasculating effect of female rulers, Greville absolves Elizabeth of the "tyranny" associated with favoritism, the "metamorphosing prospect" of which would "transforme her people into divers shapes of beasts, wherin they must lose freedome, goods, fortune, language, kinde all at once," making them resemble "*Circes* guests."[59] More was at stake for Greville than the deceased queen's reputation. His apotheosis of Sidney as a "true modell of Worth"—a "man fit for Conquest . . . or what Action soever is greatest, and hardest amongst men"—hinges on denying Elizabeth I's "metamorphosing" powers over men.[60] In addition, Greville had himself been a royal favorite, the one who had "the longest lease and the smoothest time without any rubs."[61] Like Hatton and, for most of his adulthood, Leicester, this self-proclaimed "Robin Goodfellow" had deviated from aristocratic norms by choosing the single life to serve the queen.[62] Greville's denials of tyrannous wrongdoing are thus on par with his suppression of his manuscript. By consigning his "Aegyptian, and Roman Tragedy" to a fiery "sepulture," Greville obscured his own participation in the "irregular passions" at court, laying the groundwork for his revisionist history of an "unmatchable Queen and woman," who, in contrast to Circe and Cleopatra, allowed her men to remain their own man.[63]

As we saw already in previous chapters, men in Greville's circle had in fact granted Elizabeth the rhetorical power to "transforme" them into "into divers shapes of beasts" while she was alive. In one poem, she addresses Walter Ralegh as a "silly Pug," a diminutive term of endearment "often applied to a plaything, as a doll or pet."[64] Elizabeth had similarly described Leicester as her "lapdog."[65] And she reportedly called the rebellious Essex an "ungovernable beast" who "must be stinted of his provender."[66] The queen's men echoed her figurative language by combining animal and bondage metaphors to convey their submission; according to Hatton, Elizabeth I "did fishe for men's souls, and had so sweet a baite, that no one coude escape hir network."[67] When Shakespeare's Cleopatra contemplates baiting her "bended hook" and drawing up "tawny-finn'd fishes," imagining each one "an Antony" (2.5.12–14), she recalls a court in which all men agreed to be the queen's "fishes." Even Sidney, Greville's epitome of immutable manhood, reproduces equivalencies between successful courtiers and domesticated animals; in one self-referential sonnet, Stella's "ambitious" bird, "brother Philip," creeps into her "favour" by singing "love ditties," while in another sonnet Astrophil imagines himself competing with a dog for Stella's favors.[68] Rather than being aberrant, the production of what Catherine Bates calls, in reference to Sidney's lyrics, a "masculinity... not masterly but mastered" was a pervasive feature of court culture.[69] Men displayed their submission to the queen frequently, publicly, and visibly. A shocked Platter reports that the great aristocrats at court even "play[ed] cards with the queen in kneeling posture."[70] The English treated Elizabeth "not only as their queen, but as their God," according to Platter, and England seemed a veritable "woman's paradise" where "the women have more liberty than in other lands, and know just how to make good use of it."[71]

If Elizabethans felt compelled to retell Marcus Antonius's story, it was because the Roman general provided a classical referent for extremes of masculine subjection, as did the gods Mars and Hercules with whom Plutarch associates Antonius. When the star-dazzled Astrophil compares himself to a "prancing" Mars (53.6), inspired by Stella to perform, he draws on a long tradition likening Elizabeth's powers over her courtiers to Venus's power over Mars. This tradition dates back at least as far as the 1575 entertainments at Kenilworth, where the metamorphosed Deep Desire, a figure for Leicester, assured the queen that "Mars would be your man," thereby inviting her to take the role of Venus.[72] In *Endymion*, Cynthia mocks the doting Corsites, who "having lived so long in Mars his camp" is now "rocked in Venus's cradle" (4.3.126–28). According to Adelman, "any woman who managed to disarm any man could be seen as reenacting" Venus's "victory over the war god."[73] At the Elizabethan court, however, "what Venus did with Mars" (*Antony and Cleopatra*, 1.5.18) became a shorthand for a male courtier's metamorphosis by a queen, just as had been the case for Plutarch's Antonius, and is the case for Shakespeare's Antony.

Elizabeth I knew her rule hinged on her ability to elicit submissive performances from her powerful male courtiers. The Armada years had taught the queen "just how difficult it was for a woman ruler to assert control over the execution of policy in wartime," for one thing.[74] Isolated in her palaces, far from the scenes of military conflict, Elizabeth operated through male proxies, like Leicester or Ralegh, who fought the Spanish "in [her] stead" in 1588.[75] Mary Nyquist finds in Shakespeare's representation of Cleopatra as "an epistolary heroine" an attempt to relegate the Egyptian queen to the domestic sphere.[76] Anyone who has read a biography of Elizabeth I knows, however, that in crises the queen resorted to a barrage of letters to ensure that her men enacted her will. According to Simon Adams, Leicester's "'often sending' to her when away was expected."[77] Not all of her men responded well to such directives; Essex ignored Elizabeth's letters, questioned her judgment, and sought to impose his own. When he developed a reputation for being "not rulable," Francis Bacon advised Essex that instead of flying "the resemblance or imitation of my Lord of Leicester and my Lord Chancellor Hatton," he should take them as "authors and patterns." Although Bacon shared Essex's misgivings about the elder favorites, he knew "no readier mean to make her Majesty think you are in your right way."[78] Years after Leicester and Hatton had died, the queen still considered them "patterns," and still pressured younger men to act like them.

Elizabeth's point of view may have more merit than Bacon acknowledges. Leicester, "a lover of stage plays and a notable patron of the theatre," had orchestrated the speech to the troops at Tilbury, thus engendering the legend of "the Warrior Queen [Elizabeth] had never really been," as John Guy puts it.[79] Few acts of political theater have been more successful in earning a woman a place in history than that one. Although Leicester's gamble paid off, it was a risky move; and a recurring question in late Elizabethan versions of the "Life of Marcus Antonius" is whether Antony "should . . . then to warre have ledd a Queene?"[80] Nothing Leicester did was uncontroversial, of course, so his contemporaries often refused to allow that Elizabeth favored him with "desert or reason."[81] Male biographers have followed suit, categorizing the earl along with Hatton as "creatures entirely of her private preference rather than her political judgment."[82] In fact, Elizabeth's preference for her elder favorites shows a canny sense of what constitutes masculine "desert" in a gynocracy. For several decades, Leicester and Hatton had helped Elizabeth appear as "president" of her kingdom. Leicester also helped her defeat "Fell Raging Rome," as manifested in the Spanish Armada's attempted invasion of England. When Enobarbus tells Cleopatra that only Antony is at fault for the defeat at

Actium, he may be crediting another general with victory for another battle at sea. In these matters, at least, the comparison to Antonius redounds to the Elizabethan general's credit.

Shakespeare draws on all the theatrical resources at his disposal to strengthen the resemblances between long-dead classical figures and recently deceased Elizabethan ones in *Antony and Cleopatra*. Other scholars have detailed the ways in which Cleopatra's behavior appears modeled on Elizabeth's, from her bouts of bad temper to her treatment of rivals to her preference for transportation by barge.[83] Cleopatra also shares Elizabeth's "pose of sexual availability," even if she delivers on that pose as Elizabeth never did; watching "Cleopatra sitting on her throne and decked in her royal robes and crown," Eggert argues, "Shakespeare's audience might recall their magnificent, if sexually ambiguous, former queen."[84] The gestures that Shakespeare assigns to his boy actor would have abetted this process of remembrance. The Virgin Queen was famously proud of her hands, telling the French Ambassador that "her hands were very long by nature and might, *an nescis longas Regibus esse manus*." In a well-rehearsed bid for politically productive intimacy, Elizabeth removed her glove and showed de Maisse her hand, which "was formerly very beautiful, but it is now very thin, although the skin is still most fair."[85] When Cleopatra theatrically proffers her hand for Caesar's messenger to kiss the "bluest veins," specifying that this "a hand that kings / Have lipp'd, and trembled kissing" (2.5.29–30), she recalls another queen given to showing her hands as a sign of ancient sovereignty. Hands were associated in the period with agency and judgment, and, in such moments, Cleopatra insists on the primacy of her political identity. Her royal status is briefly eclipsed by Antony's death, which makes her "No more than e'en a woman, and commanded / By such poor passion as the maid that milks / And does the meanest chares" (4.15.73–75). But even here Shakespeare ensures that we do not forget Cleopatra's majesty by having her borrow a favorite analogy from Elizabeth, who repeatedly likened herself to a milkmaid to highlight the constraints that she operated under by virtue of her political role. A widely circulated anecdote held that when the queen was imprisoned by her sister, for example, she "often declared that nothing would give her greater happiness than to be a milkmaid like those whom she saw out on the field."[86]

The visual, verbal, behavioral, and gestural correspondences between Elizabeth I and Cleopatra matter because, among other things, they attest to Shakespeare's investment in his female protagonist as a ruler-figure. For most adults in the original audiences, who had been born during Elizabeth's long reign, the queen had defined what it meant to be a monarch. Cleopatra's performance prompts these spectators to remember that they have seen some majesty, and that they, like Antony, should know it again. Nearly fifty years ago, Kenneth Muir proposed that the resemblances between Cleopatra and Elizabeth I give the lie to Roman readings of *Antony and Cleopatra*, which value public duty over private desire, and treat the Egyptian queen as the unworthy and apolitical object of the Roman general's lust.[87] L. T. Fitz cautioned soon thereafter that this interpretative tradition, along with its counterpart celebrating the lovers' "transcendental love," was the product of sexist assumptions about the nature of women that made a "reasonable assessment of the character of Cleopatra" impossible.[88] Yet modern readers persist in finding that "neither Romans nor Egyptians regard [Cleopatra] as a political figure, and she doesn't take herself seriously either," and that "Shakespeare is assuredly less interested in the politics that envelop Antony and Cleopatra than in their love."[89] These views are hard to reconcile with the evidence described above, and with the facts of the play, in which Cleopatra insists on her role as "Egypt," and other characters, including Antony, consistently address her as queen.[90] The modern interpretative traditions on *Antony and Cleopatra* may reflect the fact that, unlike Shakespeare's original audience, we have no recent memories of female rule to draw on. When actors "play something like" the Elizabethan past for us (*Hamlet*, 2.2.595), we do not always recognize what Shakespeare asks us to recognize. Reading Shakespeare's plays against other works from the period, like *The Revenger's Tragedy*, can help in this regard. If Middleton's Vindice poses the dead Gloriana in the posture of a whore, Shakespeare shows his "great fairy" like a political artist of infinite variety—immortal because she is not only changeable in herself but also the cause of enduring change in others.

Because *Antony and Cleopatra* so persistently evokes the Elizabethan past, I think it safe to assume, with Yachnin, that it must have meant something different to its original audiences. And I think that difference must have affected perceptions not just of the female protagonist, but also of the male protagonist, and of the relationship between the two. Trying to reconstruct those perceptions is valuable for a number of reasons, including the fact that it sheds light on our own prejudices. Notably, even those critics who view Cleopatra as a political operator tend to relegate her love for Antony to the private realm. So Jankowski finds that Cleopatra's relationship with Antony causes her to "abandon her previous successful strategies for rule."[91] This tendency to separate the private and public aspects of the relationship imposes modern norms on a classical setting and an Elizabethan context. As they were for Elizabeth, collaborative relationships with men (including Caesar and Pompey) are among Cleopatra's most "successful strategies for rule." She rules *through* Antony. Cleopatra explicitly values her lover's military prowess; "the demi-Atlas of the world," he is to her "the arm / And burgonet of men" (1.5.23–24). His departure upsets her because it restricts her ability to enact her political will: "That Herod's head / I'll have," she complains, "but how, when Antony is gone, / Through whom I might command it?" (3.3.4–6). And she reacts violently to criticism of Antony because it calls into question her "judgment" about his merits, an intolerable thing for a monarch (1.5.72–74). When this "wrangling queen" chooses to "to chide, to laugh, / To weep" (1.1.48–50) in an effort to control her lover's behavior, she is not abdicating political authority. She is enacting it. That Cleopatra loves Antony, in addition to finding him useful, is arguably the source of her tragedy.

Although *Antony and Cleopatra* concerns the intersections of love and politics, private desire and public duty, it does not treat these as opposites. Rather, in its "mutual pair" (1.1.37), it recreates a queenly mode of publicity that blends the two, at considerable cost to the individuals involved. Egypt is as much a political realm as Rome, and the dramatic conflict involves two distinctive approaches to politics—one that is associated with the past, and makes room for individual emotion, and therefore women; and one that is associated with the present, and insists on relegating individual emotion, and therefore women, to the private realm. Writing about Cleopatra, Irene Dash suggests that women in power have "the unusual opportunity of combining sexual and political selves."[92] I would say, though, that female rulers in premodern societies were forced take this synthetic approach because of the misogynist assumption that women naturally privileged "will before reason."[93] The political is always personal for queens, to invert the old feminist saw, and any man who serves a queen perforce risks the accusation that he "make[s] his will / Lord of his reason" (3.13.3–4). Elizabeth had sound reasons for preferring men like Leicester and Hatton, who agreed to serve her faithfully to the detriment of their families and their reputations. Essex never could resign himself to those conditions. Yet, even though his resemblance to Antony consists of being "a great general in decline," Essex is the royal favorite most frequently identified with Shakespeare's hero.[94] History and literary history alike have been far kinder to that troubled nobleman than they have been to his predecessors, a fact that I suspect Elizabeth would find infuriating, and that reflects continuing discomfort with men like Leicester or Antonius, whose subjection to a woman makes them no longer master of themselves. At least some of Elizabeth's contemporaries recognized that the queen had "wisely judged of [Leicester's] vertues, and worthily rewarded his loialtie and paines."[95] When we fail to recognize what is at stake in Elizabeth's preferences for such men, we allow ourselves to be blinded by rationalist biases inherent in the bourgeois public sphere, which requires that private emotion be bracketed off, and which has therefore problematized all forms of feminine participation in politics since the seventeenth century.[96] It is no coincidence that these criteria for political participation were first developed in response to the particulars of Elizabeth I's reign, by men "anxious to control and prime popular opinion and report" on matters like their ruler's marriage and succession.[97]

Near the end of his career, Shakespeare set about revising Plutarch's "Life of Marcus Antonius" to alter negative perceptions of female rule that he had helped to perpetuate, with increasing qualms and misgivings, in earlier plays. Strategically, he counters impressions of queenship generated by "the common liar" (1.1.60) not by rejecting the old patterns associated with the age-in-love trope, but by staging them again, shifting the generic register this time to the tragic mode. *Antony and Cleopatra* forces audiences to reexperience old "play-particles" by endowing them with new emotional resonance. Using his actors as "medium[s] for raising the dead," Shakespeare engages in a layered act of "surrogation," replacing unsatisfactory substitutes for historical figures, like Bottom and Titania, or Falstaff and Hal, with alternatives in the form of Antony and Cleopatra.[98] As we have seen, although Shakespeare's earlier age-in-love figures provoke judgments that enforce patriarchal norms of behavior, many also elicit affective responses that temper those judgments. Even Claudius gets the opportunity to court audience sympathies in his soliloquy (Middleton never grants his Duke the same privilege). As a group, these lecherous old men attest to Shakespeare's desire for a "public life" that blends "strong feelings with rational debate and collective judgment."[99] With Falstaff or Malvolio, the need for "collective judgment," in the form of a baiting or a banishment, eventually subordinates those strong feelings. Such is not the case with Antony, whose ability to arouse passion and affection in others unsettles all attempts at stable judgment.

If Antony's "great fairy" channels the historical Elizabeth I, she also recalls the many fairy queens who had stood in for Elizabeth over the years, including Lyly's moon goddess, Middleton's Gloriana (the name "Cleopatra" means "glory of the fatherland"), and Shakespeare's own Titania. Like these precursors, Cleopatra takes the "fleeting moon" as her planet (5.2.240), and exerts a powerful spell over the men in her vicinity. Shakespeare highlights her advanced age, moreover, thereby forging tight connections with previous works critical of the Elizabethan court. While the historical Cleopatra was thirty-eight at the time of her death, just at the cusp of green old age, Shakespeare's wrinkled queen often appears much older. The frequent mentions of her ancient lineage endow Cleopatra with an "aura of age," according to Adelman, and in the two protagonists—as in the subplots of *Endymion*, *A Midsummer Night's Dream*, or *Twelfth Night*—"the folly of love is explicitly associated with the folly of old age."[100] Onstage observers are often disturbed by the ways in which the "charms of love" survive Cleopatra's "wan'd lip," taking this as evidence that in the Queen of Egypt "witchcraft" has joined "with beauty" (2.1.21–23). As it did for the Catholic polemicists who raged against Elizabeth, that age cannot wither Cleopatra confirms her unnatural powers over men.

In Plutarch's Marcus Antonius, Shakespeare found rich material for his revision of the aging lover. Antonius was at the time of his death around fifty-six years of age, roughly of an age with Falstaff, and equally given over to "riot and excess." The Roman general spent a lifetime indulging in the "banquets and drunken feasts" that physicians thought would cause some to "become old men" at "fortie."[101] Shakespeare's Antony calls attention to his advanced age on a number occasions, as when he sarcastically proposes that Cleopatra "To the boy Caesar send this grizzled head" (3.13.17). He shares with his historical counterpart and other senescent stage surfeiters a taste for wine, a tendency to play the lover, and a desire to hear the chimes at midnight.[102] Like Falstaff, Claudius and Middleton's Duke, Antony is subject to the onstage judgments of abstemious youths because he "drinks, and wastes / The lamps of night in revels" (1.4.4–5). That last metaphor, recalling as it does Cicero's injunctions against carnal "surfette," in which he compares the aging body to "a Lampe, if to muche oyle bee infused into it, burnethe not brightly," shows just how significant age is to a consideration of Antony's character.[103] In love with a queen who is "wrinkled deep in time" (1.5.29), this monumental Roman—"Here's sport indeed! how heavy weighs my lord" (4.15.32), Cleopatra complains—is rooted so deeply in Elizabethan stage satire that he at times recalls Lyly's preposterous Sir Tophas, the fat knight who loves old wines and old matrons. Both are characteristically Elizabethan hybrids of the *miles gloriosus* and the *senex amans*, the two types evoked at the opening of the play, when Philo describes his captain bursting out of Roman armor to be "transform'd / Into a strumpet's fool" (1.1.12–13). Taking his cue from his precursors, Antony ends the play as Endymion, Tophas, Bottom, Falstaff, and Middleton's Duke do, yet one more superannuated lover laid out prone on stage before his queen.

The multiple patterns that link Antony to his stage predecessors may have eluded critics thus far because *Antony and Cleopatra* takes a fundamentally different attitude than earlier plays toward older men who break rules and have not "kept [the] square" (2.3.5–6). A generic hybrid, "shap'd" only "like itself" (2.7.42), it transforms comic and satiric tropes to show a figure normally painted as a gorgon who comes to resemble a god instead.[104] Omissions can be as telling as repetitions in this regard; although Antony seems like a "doting mallard" (3.10.19) at times, he is never called an ass (Caesar is). The bearbaiting trope, a device for courting contempt in previous plays, appears only as a ghostly trace, in the lovely image of Antony surrounded by "hearts / that spannell'd [him] at heels" (4.12.20–21). Antony's claims to being like Mars register differently than Tophas's claims to being "all Mars and Ars" (*Endymion*, 1.3.96), because Shakespeare avails himself of the historical Antonius's identification with Hercules to remind us that some braggarts make good their claims. As Janet Adelman puts it in what is still the best reading of the play, the "*miles gloriosus* and hero are two sides of the same coin."[105] Shakespeare also elevates the derided figure of the old man in lust by endowing Antony with select touches of Endymion. The lover of Egypt's "eastern star" has his thoughts "stitched to the stars" and "higher" (*Endymion*, 1.1.5–7), like Lyly's moon-lover. Far from requiring the Neoplatonic sublimation celebrated in *Endymion*, however, Antony's transcendence has carnal and even Bacchanalian dimensions. I argued in the previous chapter that *Twelfth Night* gives us fragments of the age-in-love figure to counter the attacks of the satiric "substractors" who hounded the Elizabethan court. *Antony and Cleopatra* goes further still, reassembling these fragments "by Isis" to arrive at the "well-divided disposition" of its paragonal "man of men" (1.5.53, 71–73), a new Osiris.[106]

The changes that Shakespeare makes to his source encourage audiences to help in this process of reassembly by remembering certain key figures. Shapiro, who acknowledges that *Antony and Cleopatra* is a political play, nonetheless holds to the position that it contains no "reductive and dangerous one-to-one correspondences between ancient and modern figures."[107] Although there is nothing reductive about him, Antony is nonetheless a composite designed to produce a series of connections between "ancient and modern," real and virtual figures. Plutarch's virile Antonius had "seven children by three wives" (294), but Antony claims that he has "forborne the getting of a lawful race" for Cleopatra (3.13.107), for example. When he rates his love for Cleopatra over the generative obligations of the aristocratic male, Antony evokes not just his classical forebear, but also courtiers like Greville or Hatton who chose the single life to serve Elizabeth, and characters like Endymion, who chooses the "solitary life" to devote himself to Cynthia.[108] As might be expected, *Antony and Cleopatra* reproduces the transfiguration metaphors that characterized critical and panegyric discourses about Elizabeth's relationship to her men. Yet another "old ruffian" (4.2.4), Antony has all the traditional traits of Circe's victims: effeminacy, beastliness, drunkenness, and sleepiness.[109] From the first, the Romans portray Cleopatra as a witchlike figure whose charms have brought this "triple pillar of the world" (1.1.12) down. The pillar was a commonplace of Elizabethan political discourses; Leicester was at once "the chef[est] pillar" on which Elizabeth "wholy relies and puts all hir truste," for example, and "the only handsaw that shall hew the maine p[illars]and postes. . . . a sunder and ruinate all of this noble land."[110] One need not be a Freudian critic to see that this vision of fallen "pillars" and "postes" trades in anxieties about national castration, made explicit in works like Allen's pamphlet, *News from Heaven and Hell*, or *Leicester's Commonwealth*, and manifest also in the way Shakespeare's Romans react to Antony. Without the hard pillar-like property that defines him, Antony becomes in Caesar's estimation "not more manlike / Than Cleopatra; nor the queen of Ptolemy / More womanly than he" (1.4.5–7). Such sentiments echo those who condemned men like Leicester for serving Elizabeth's "filthy lust."[111]

Although Antony inspires the contempt reserved for surfeiting older men, he also excels at undermining the contempt he inspires, and transforming it into a paradoxical form of admiration. Like *The Revenger's Tragedy*, *Antony and Cleopatra* opens on the spectacle of an aristocratic older man who has succumbed to erotic impulses. When Philo complains about his general's "dotage" (1.1.1), he chooses a word that conflates senility and infatuation, used in the period to condemn amorous old men.[112] Cicero's English translator explained, for example, that "libidinous volupte" is a quality "founde in younge men" but when "this folishnes ... entangleth and captivateth the senses of old men," and these "keep not them selves within the limittes of reason" it "is commonly called Dotage."[113] As we have seen, Elizabethan playwrights relied on such views of superannuated sexuality to provoke the "wonderfull laughter" of the "commen people."[114] Following conventional wisdom on senescent sexuality, Philo argues that Antony's passion "O'erflows the measure" (1.1.2). His indictment borrows from the same vocabulary and the same assumptions as Vindice's indictment of the Duke (or Maria's indictment of Malvolio, or Hamlet's indictment of Claudius, for that matter); as always, the recourse to generational criteria of judgment has a leveling effect, enabling an inferior's critical attack on a superior guilty of breaching social decorum. Convinced that his view is rational and therefore accurate, Philo instructs all present to "take but good note" and "see" for themselves (1.1.11–13), inducting the audience into the processes of evaluation thus initiated.[115]

But here the similarities between Middleton's opening scene and Shakespeare's end. Vindice delivers his assessment of "grey-haired adultery" in a soliloquy, an appropriate choice for a play that solicits agreement for age-related behavioral norms, in which even the elderly lover finds "age hot" to be "monstrous." In contrast, Philo responds to Demetrius, who must have offered a more positive reading of Antony's behavior, since it prompts Philo's contradiction ("Nay, but" [1.1.1]). Demetrius's disagreement haunts the conversation, undermining the views Philo expresses, and destabilizing a set reaction to Antony's spectacular shattering of norms. Although Antony may be under the "wonderfull thralldom" of a Circean sorceress, I doubt Philo's monologue provokes "wonderfull laughter" in audiences. For one thing, Philo feels more conflicted than he acknowledges, since his speech borrows not just from the discourses that condemned aging sexuality, as Vindice's soliloquy does, but also from the heroic conventions of the epic, as Vindice's does not. The image of Antony's "great captain's heart" bursting out of his buckled armor (1.1.8) is especially ambiguous, since the heart connotes both passion and courage, qualities Antony has in spades, and the Roman armor comes then to stand for rigid, perhaps undesirable, and certainly ineffective constraints on these qualities. It is hard to know which of the two qualities makes Antony more godlike: his capacity for passion or his superhuman courage. The difficulty is compounded by Philo's allusion to Mars, by Mars's dual status as god of war and Venus's lover, and by the licentious behavior of these classical gods. This confusion is prologue to the play that follows, in which Shakespeare takes materials with a long history of eliciting contempt and magically transforms them into a character who eludes categorization and judgment. Although Shakespeare assembles his Protean hero out of a familiar "mixture and shreds of forms," Antony never becomes "truly deformed," as Ben Jonson's Amorphus does.[116] His "dotage" may overflow the measure, but it makes him something other than a monster.

An emasculating passion that disregards social, political, and cultural prohibitions at great personal cost might even require a superhuman form of courage. Antony is vulnerable to the Roman discourses that seek to regulate his sexual behavior; at times, he reproves his own "white hairs" for "doting" (3.11.13–15), and becomes "unqualitied with very shame" (3.11.44) because of his relationship to Cleopatra. He repeatedly overcomes these mechanisms of sociocultural control, however, including his sexless marriage with Octavia, to return again to his "Egyptian dish" (2.6.126). Although Antony knows he should "from this enchanting queen break off," he elects to lose himself "in dotage" (1.2.128, 114), embracing the behavior rejected by Lyly's Endymion, who avoids "a dotage no less miserable than monstrous" (*Endymion*, 1.1.30). According to Ovid, a major influence in this play as in the others I have examined, passions like Antony's have the power to turns lovers into beasts *or* gods. Where *Endymion*, *Hamlet*, or *The Revenger's Tragedy* consider only the former possibility, *Antony and Cleopatra* considers the latter, too. When Antony comes on stage promising to exceed all limits in his search for "new heaven, new earth" (1.1.17), we see something more than the familiar "strumpet's fool" (1.1.13)—we see Burbage and not Kempe, for one thing—and the expectations that we brought into the theater about "age in love" are shattered accordingly.[117]

The explosive combination of traits contained in Burbage-playing-Antony troubles conventional thinking about masculine merit throughout the play, in a way that engages onstage audiences in debate. As we have seen already in the case of Falstaff, elderly rule-breakers have a stimulating effect on other people's evaluative powers. The "desire to judge... correctly"—the same desire that North attributes to his readers—is among the "dominant passions" of *Antony and Cleopatra*, and it is one endowed with distinctly political and historiographical dimensions.[118] In their efforts to come to terms with Antony, other characters habitually compare him to past or mythic figures; although Cleopatra threatens Charmian with "bloody teeth" for contrasting her "man of men" to Caesar (1.5.70–73), she finds later that "In praising Antony I have disprais'd Caesar" (2.5.107). Octavius, careful not to compare his rival with other worthies, measures Antony against a past version of himself. The young Antony was the very pattern of immutable manhood—his "cheek / So much as lank'd not" (1.4.70–71) under the most severe hardship. Through such comparisons, characters model the retrospective behaviors that North assured his readers "teacheth us to judge of things present." While these frequent comparisons imply that Antony is exemplary, onstage observers disagree about what to make of that example, a situation exacerbated by the opacity of the protagonists' motivations and their common status as the subject of incessant rumors.

In the endless chatter about the titular characters, *Antony and Cleopatra* dramatizes the specific desire to judge those who are "in the public eye" (3.6.12). Shapiro points out that Antony is "so habituated to being observed"—and talked about—"that he expects this will hold true even in the afterlife."[119] Much of this talk testifies to the "aspiring minde" of the talkers, as one defense of Leicester put it.[120] Inferiors by virtue of class, age, or military ability, the other male characters spread the "perception of [Antony's] sexual subjection" in an effort to attain "parity" with the famous general, who, as the sole survivor of Rome's heroic past, is "the pine... that overtopp'd them all" (4.12.24–25).[121] All this amplifies a pattern found in Plutarch, whose Herculean Antonius also violates expectation, and is therefore also the subject of malicious report and gossip, including the "rumour in the people's mouths that the goddess

Venus was come to play with the god Bacchus, for the general good of all Asia" (201–2). The numerous messengers charged with bringing "good news" (1.3.19), "bad news" (2.5.86), "strange news" (3.5.2), and even "stiff news" (1.2.100) report on Antony's Egyptian behavior to the Romans and his Roman behavior to Cleopatra.[122] Even Enobarbus, Antony's closest companion, sounds like a reporter, offering a play-by-play analysis of his master's behavior—"He will to his Egyptian dish again" (2.6.126); "'Tis better playing with a lion's whelp / Than with an old one dying" (3.13.93–94); "Yes, like enough! high-battled Caesar will / Unstate his happiness, and be stag'd to th' show, / Against a sworder!" (3.13.29–31). Through frequent metatheatrical devices, like Enobarbus's asides, or Philo's opening instructions, Shakespeare "deliberately" draws his audiences "into the act of judging," turning us into "the characters who stand aside and comment."[123] As we formulate comparative judgments about the male protagonist, we become conscious of our own participation in retrospective processes of evaluation.

Designed to encourage comparisons with the past, Antony's character raises problems of assessment specifically for those who think in conventional ways about surfeiting older men. Pompey, who recognizes that Antony's "soldiership / Is twice" that of Octavius and Lepidus, nonetheless dismisses the "ne'er lust-wearied Antony" as an "amorous surfeiter" (1.5.32–38), deeming him incapable of quick action. Antony's efficient military campaign shows Pompey's judgment of his great rival to be as faulty as Brutus's was in the earlier play. Jacobean audiences must have shared in Pompey's surprise, since they shared in his prejudices about the effects of lust on older men, having long feasted on contemptuous depictions of old lechers. Sir Tophas, Falstaff, Claudius, Middleton's Duke—all provoke derisive laughter, on- or offstage, for abandoning themselves to "surfette."[124] But "almost nothing" in *Antony and Cleopatra* is "easy to judge," the hero least of all.[125] Plutarch is baffled that Antonius, having "committed the greatest faults," manages to secure such "wonderful love" from others (178–81). Shakespeare presents these apparently contradictory traits as integral to one another, allowing his actor to arouse the tragic emotions of empathy and admiration that help audiences overcome preexisting judgments. Antony commands allegiance and affection not despite his sensual surfeit or his love of the theater (which the audience presumably shares), but because of them. These are consistent features of his allegedly inconsistent character, fully realized in his love for a shape-shifting queen. A man willing to give himself up to "sport," "soft hours," and constant "pleasures" (1.1.45–47) at the risk of his reputation must needs register differently to theatrical artists, themselves purveyors of lowly pleasures, than to a classical historian. By the same token, those playgoers who respond with pleasure to the actor's performance of Antony can only condemn the character's embrace of "soft hours" and "sport" by condemning it in themselves.[126]

Antony is most vital when indulging the behaviors that hasten aging and death; to paraphrase Eugene Waith, he is most himself when giving himself away.[127] This paradox enables Shakespeare to retain Antonius's well-established reputation for surfeit, while changing perceptions of such behavior. Consider 2.7, a scene in which all the major characters are thoroughly inebriated. This state of general intoxication has the odd effect of bracketing off moralistic and rational judgments about drunkenness, "that beggarly damnation," deemed the "worst of all the deadly sins" by Middleton's vengeful brethren (4.2.182–83). Left without the crutch of conventional thinking, we have to adjudicate a contest that I, for one, think Antony handily wins. Where Lepidus slurs his words, and Octavius's slippery "tongue / Spleets what it speaks" (2.7.123–24), Antony becomes more articulate and expansive under the influence. The reluctant Caesar finds drunkenness "monstrous labor" (2.7.99); in contrast, Antony's embrace of "the conquering wine" that "hath steep'd our sense / In soft and delicate Lethe" has positively ecstatic dimensions. In Caesar's telling phrase, "the wild disguise hath almost / Antick'd" all, with the ironic exception of the oldest man on stage, whose bounty is replenished rather than depleted by wine. Although we might laugh with Antony in this scene, we never laugh at him, as we do at the other drunken men onstage, or at all the other lubricious old men who haunt this play. Indeed, Antony's ability to surpass others in "Egyptian bacchanals" compares favorably to that of the "monarch of the vine," "Plumpy Bacchus" (2.7.104–25). According to

Leonard Barkan, this "quintessentially metamorphic divinity," associated with "extremes of emotion," "half-prophetic and half-destructive madness," and "the ascendancy of the female principle," is a god of "a nonrational and ecstatic sort"—an appropriate counterpart to a man who makes his "will / Lord of his reason."[128] In contrast to his precursors, whose emasculation by Circean queens made them like the unfortunate Actaeon (see previous chapters), Antony appears here like a god, the one celebrated for his fertility, his ability to regenerate, his love of women, and his affinity with the theater (according to Gosson, "Playes were consecrated unto Bacchus for the firste findinges out of wine").[129] Cleopatra's lover shares a propensity for "belly cheer" and a tendency to drink "like the god Backus out of his cuppes" with all the old men described in this book, including Falstaff and the Leicester of anticourt polemic.[130] Strikingly, however, in Antony such behavior strives to make itself "fair and admired" (1.1.51).

Characters in *Antony and Cleopatra* agree on very few things. One of them is that Antony is notable: "note him, / Note him, good Charmian, 'tis the man, but note him" (1.5.54). A constellation of linked words—"news," "report," "reporter," "fame," "note"—make Antony a celebrity, the embodiment of "the character traits most revered" and most feared by his community.[131] Like his classical forebear, or Hercules and Mars, Antony signifies supreme masculine prowess—"there appeared such a manly look in his countenance as is commonly seen in Hercules' pictures," Plutarch writes about Antonius (177)—and the willing subjugation of that prowess to a woman's pleasure. Patriarchal societies legitimate themselves by reference to men's physical superiority to women, a principle that Antony, as the "the pine ... that overtopp'd them all" embodies and should enforce. When this self-proclaimed "man of steel" (4.4.33) bends and kneels to a queen instead, he relinquishes his place of privilege, affirming her power at the expense of normative gender structures. The oldest and the highest-ranking man in Rome now "comes too short of that great property / Which still should go with Antony" (1.1.58–59). Like the complaints about his desertion, the fallen pillar imagery indicates how profoundly Antony's surrender to Cleopatra shakes the structural foundation of his society. By turning his broad back on gerontocratic Rome, and electing to let "the wide arch / Of the rang'd empire fall" (1.1.33–34), Antony threatens to undo the ideological basis of Western patriarchy. Predictably enough, he becomes, like the Elizabethan Earl of Leicester, "the subject of all pleasant discourses at this day throughout the realm."[132]

Antony's ability to unsettle norms and set tongues a-wagging worries Caesar, who finds his rival dangerous precisely because he is "th'abstract of all faults / That all men follow" (1.4.9–10). While Caesar could mean that Antony concentrates in himself all men's faults, according to the OED, "abstract" here also means "a perfect embodiment of a particularly quality or type."[133] A perfect embodiment of faults makes those faults perfect, causing "all men to follow" him. The phrase captures Shakespeare's strategy in *Antony and Cleopatra*, which is to endow Antony with the most derided faults only to make these faults overwhelmingly attractive. Lepidus confirms the subversive effect of Antony's charm when he describes his rival's faults as like "the spots of heaven," made "more fiery by night's blackness" (1.4.12–13). The "night's blackness" stands for the ostensible subject of his praise, Antony's "goodness" (1.4.11). But the image reverses representational norms by stellifying Antony for his faults. Intentionally or not, Lepidus revises Ovid's *Metamorphoses*, where the "Romane Capteynes wyfe, the Queen of Aegypt" and her lover are dismissed in favor of the traditional male heroes Aeneas and Caesar, who are lifted "among the starres that glister bright."[134] The early modern tendency to describe political, heroic, or erotic ideals as stars derives from this passage, and conveys the power that some individuals have to guide and inspire others, as the English "Starre" guides the English, and Stella inspires Astrophil. An amplification of Plutarch's Antonius, Shakespeare's fallen "star" (4.14.106) is "even more astonishing in his ability to inspire others to outdo themselves." Not only does Shakespeare "exalt" Antony for this "talent," so do rival characters, who cannot criticize Antony without also paying tribute to him.[135] What is so worrisome about Antony from the Roman point of view, then, is not just that he commits faults but that his commitment of those faults makes them attractive and exemplary, confounding conventional wisdom and setting new "patterns" for others to emulate, to borrow Bacon's locution. Antony is an "example" from the past that "we may knowe what to like of, & what to follow, what to mislike, and what to eschew," all at once. No wonder the Caesars of this world feel threatened.

The idea of Antony as an "abstract... that all men follow" recalls Hamlet's description of players as the "abstract and brief chronicles of the time" (2.2.524–26), while endowing Antony's performances with an idealizing force. Antony does not just represent certain past behaviors—like that of Antonius or of Elizabeth's favorites—but he also models future behaviors (including that of the actors who will play him in years to come). After Antony dies, Caesar's henchmen recognize that a "rarer spirit never / Did steer humanity" (5.1.31–32). In another echo of Hamlet's concern with theatrical personation, Agrippa then likens the deceased Antony to a "spacious mirror" in which a diminished Caesar "must needs see himself" (5.1.34). Raised again for each performance, the fallen Antony continues even now to reduce Octavius Caesar to a mere "boy," a trick that Shakespeare manages by deploying generational against gendered categories. Men who violate generational decorum lose their privileged gender status in earlier plays, becoming foolish asses, or impotent "old boys." In contrast, Antony is never anything other than a fully-grown man, an old lion who retains the ability to transform other men into whelps, even after he is dead.[136] The phallic puns that attend Antony's demise absolve him of impotence, promising a rich harvest of virtuoso performances. When Cleopatra bids Antony "O, come, come, come" and "welcome, welcome" (4.15.37–38), we are left in little doubt about his renewable talent for dying. "Age in love" comes to be associated as a result not with diminished but with enhanced masculine capacity; at play's end, the fallen pillar becomes the "soldier's pole," making all other men appear like boys and girls. "Though grey / Do sometimes mingle with our younger brown," an undaunted Antony tells Cleopatra, rejecting all conventional wisdom on the subject, "yet ha' we / A brain that nourishes our nerves, and can / Get goal for goal of youth" (4.8.19–22). Under such conditions, achieving masculine excellence involves becoming more like Antony.

Seizing on Marcus Antonius's uncanny ability to render "things that seem intolerable in other men" attractive (Plutarch, 177), Shakespeare makes Antony simultaneously a subjected male and aspirational model, thus upending the values that the Circe myth normally enforces. Like all the other aging male characters who populated the Renaissance stage, Antony endures "a metamorphosis and change" under female rule like "the companyons of Ulisses."[137] But where the myth endows the female enchantress with agency, representing the men who fall victim to her sexual allure as entrapped animals, Antony emphasizes his agency in embracing Cleopatra. He claims that "our dungy earth alike / Feeds beast as men," acknowledging the common charge that old men who give into lust are like animals only to assert "the nobleness" of his choice by kissing Cleopatra (1.1. 35–38). Over the course of the play, his choice to return to her again and again enacts "the relocation and reconstruction of heroic masculinity."[138] Odysseus subjects Circe with his sword, thereby reestablishing the normative distinctions between men and beasts, and men and women. Antony voluntarily blurs these lines, ceding his sword to Cleopatra who wears it in their sexual play, while he dons her tires and mantles (2.5.25). This moment restages the cross-dressed Falstaff's scene of courtship in a different key, releasing the protagonists into a gender convergence facilitated by age. Although he struggles with his Roman thoughts, Antony ultimately celebrates his union with Cleopatra as defiant of Rome's repressive values and the male heroes who embody them: "We'll hand in hand / And with our sprightly port make the ghosts gaze. / Dido, and her Aeneas, shall want troops / And all the haunt be ours" (4.14.51–54).[139] Insofar as we accept the play's claims about the exemplary nature of Antony's transformative passion—and a number of critics, including A. C. Bradley, have—we learn to look at the much-maligned figure of "age in love" in an entirely new way.[140]

Rather than embodying defect, Antony might even represent a new kind of perfection, a possibility most ardently articulated by the lovers themselves in the final few acts. Invoking familiar Neoplatonic tropes of transcendence, Antony and Cleopatra from the first present themselves as capturing "Eternity in our lips, and our eyes" (1.3.35). Antony affirms this initial vision repeatedly, until he lays "of many thousand kisses the poor last" on Cleopatra's lips (4.15.20–21). According to Anne Barton, each kiss "asks to be read as an attempt to regain the kind of wholeness, that primal sexual unity" found in the creation myth of Plato's *Symposium*— the same creation myth Shakespeare drew on to fragment his age-in-love figure in *Twelfth Night*.[141] Shackled by his Roman thoughts, Antony worries about dissolving into shards at times, but Cleopatra works hard to reassemble her lover into a new whole during his death scene. Begging Antony to "die when thou hast liv'd / Quicken with kissing" (4.15.38–39), the Egyptian queen evokes both Lyly's Cynthia, whose kisses quicken, and Middleton's Gloriana, whose kisses kill. When she doubts that her "lips" have "that power" (4.15.39), she even recalls Ovid's Aurora, who lacks the power to rejuvenate her lover. Cleopatra evokes all these precursors to overcome them, first elevating the fallen Antony visually, by hoisting him up, and then verbally, by immortalizing him as "the crown o'th'earth" (4.15.64). Nor does his elevation imply a rejection of carnal desires, as Endymion's does. "Give me some wine," Antony calls out as Cleopatra labors to lift him up, in a heavenly bit of "sport" (4.15.32) calculated to eclipse all previous instances of "sportful malice" involving lusty old men (*Twelfth Night*, 5.1.365).[142] Drinking, dying, and rising, Antony invokes Endymion and Falstaff at the same time, canceling out the rote responses that they provoke, and challenging the patriarchal worldview they uphold. Even the critics who insist Antony's suicide is "botched" must contend with the optics and poetics of the death scene, which, along with Cleopatra, strain conventional thinking, and which endorse Antony's triumphant claim that he is "a Roman by a Roman / Valiantly vanquish'd" (4.15.56–57).[143] Among the things that Antony vanquishes in this coming together with Cleopatra are prejudices about his dotage. Shakespeare, meanwhile, vanquishes decades of rumor, gossip, slander, and satire about the queen's men. The sexual innuendoes in Antony's death scene glance at punitive accounts of royal favorites at their ladies' feet, like Middleton's Duke, or Falstaff in *Merry Wives*, or the "bere whelp" in *News from Heaven and Hell*, whose "pricke of desire" is turned "into a pillor of fier" by the "lady with the supported nose."[144] While these precursors are all destined for hell (the "bere whelp" is there already),

Shakespeare secures a different afterlife for Antony, who ascends to "the golden world" of poetry, and haunts a transformed Elizium with his Cleopatra.[145] This fallen star is no mere Fallstaff. Shakespeare finds it sweating work to assign new meanings to all these old patterns; by sheer dint of theatrical labor and sublime poetry, however, his queen succeeds in "draw[ing]" her "amorous surfeiter" high enough to "set" him "by Jove's side" (4.15.30–36).

Antony and Cleopatra's divided catastrophe, which isolates Cleopatra among boys and women and thus reinforces her resemblance to the aging Elizabeth I, imbues this new masculine ideal with the persuasive force of felt emotion. Indeed, when it comes to the circumstances that inspired Shakespeare's revision of old materials, we need look no further than the death of his queen, which prompted a series of public reevaluations echoed in *Antony and Cleopatra*. As Catherine Loomis points out, while the Privy Council prepared for a smooth transition to James's reign, the "literary response taught the country how to mourn and remember the Queen, and how to welcome and accept the new King." Pamphlets like *Englands Caesar* (1603) and *Ave Caesar* (1603) likened James's accession to that of Augustus Caesar, cementing Elizabeth's association with Cleopatra and heralding the new king's identification with the Roman emperor—a cornerstone of Shakespeare's portrayal of the victorious Octavius.[146] Elizabeth's public mourners imagined her showing like a queen in death, surrounded by the material signs of her sovereignty, "Tryumphant drawne in robes so richly wrought / Crowne on her head, in hand her Scepter," which is how Shakespeare shows his Egyptian queen.[147] Anticipating Charmian's final tribute to her "eastern star" (5.2.308), one poem hailed Elizabeth as a "celestiall starre, / Earthes ornament, whom heaven smiles to see," describing her grave as a "great monument," containing a "farre more pretious shade" than any Egyptian "Piramis."[148] The English queen lay "like a sweet beauty in a harmlesse slumber" in her grave; Shakespeare, meanwhile, has his Egyptian queen look "like sleep" in her monument (5.2.346).[149] And just as Cleopatra takes "the stroke of death" as "a lover's pinch" (5.2.295), Elizabeth's mourners found that

> Death now has ceaz'd her in his ycie armes,
> That sometime was the Sun of our delight:
> And pittilesse of any after-harmes,
> Hath veyld her glory in the cloude of night.[150]

Because planetary tropes had featured prominently in Elizabeth's cult, eclipse imagery now conveyed grief at her death. In what is thought Shakespeare's sole comment on Elizabeth's death, the sonnet speaker mourns "Our mortal moon" who "hath her eclipse endured" (107.5). Antony thinks about a different queen when he fears that "our terrene moon / Is now eclips'd" (3.13.153–54). But he chooses the same metaphor, which came burdened with communal mourning for Elizabeth. We might well ask, with Cleopatra, "what does he mean?" (4.2.23). And we can take Enobarbus's answer for our own: "to make his followers weep" (4.2.24).[151] Like Antony, Shakespeare knows of old that tearful "passion ... is catching" (*Julius Caesar*, 3.1.283). If *Antony and Cleopatra* meant something different to the original audiences, it also did something different to them. Using "odd tricks which sorrow shoots / Out of the mind" (4.2.14–15), Shakespeare embraces his hero's rhetorical prowess as his own, making his audience reexperience powerful feelings of grief, loss, guilt, and regret associated with Elizabeth's death.

A common refrain among those mourning Elizabeth concerned the lack of adequate comparison by which to measure their loss, which some blamed on those who had remained silent, even as "Cynthia," the "fayrest Rose, the sweetest Princely Flower" was "with'red now by Death's coold nipping power."[152] Like Greville, who labeled Elizabeth "unmatcheable," Henry Chettle found that "no Princesse ever-living in the earth can be remembered to exceede her. Her wisedome was without question ... unequalled.... So expert in Languages that she answered most Embassadors in their Native tongues."[153] While some did allow that she was "*preteritis melior*, better than those which went before hir," and thus left open the possibility that she might function as "a precedent to those that shall followe hir," the idea that Elizabeth was sui generis gained traction around the time of her death.[154] The Earl of Northumberland assured

James that the English wished for "noe more queens, fearing we shall never enyoy an wther lyke to this."[155] A friend of John Manningham's similarly recalled "Wee worshipt noe saintes, but wee prayd to ladyes in the Q[ueenes] tyme," and wished that the practice might be "abolished... in our kinges raigne."[156] Even those men who had found with Astrophil that there was pleasure "in the manage" by a queen seemed eager to forget the unorthodox arrangements to which they had consented.[157] Cast as a form of praise, superlative representations of Elizabeth I as a "peerelesse Princesse" contained the disturbing implications of her reign.[158] These comments isolated Elizabeth and rendered her unique and inimitable—not a "modell of true worth" but an aberration of history. "No grave upon the earth shall clip in it / A pair so famous," Caesar claims, as he attempts to consign Antony and Cleopatra to a similar fate (5.2.359–60).

In this context, we might see Shakespeare's "lass unparalleled" (5.2.316) as supplying the missing parallel for the "unmatcheable" Elizabeth. Among the old servants Chettle berates for omitting to honor the English queen is Shakespeare, that "the silver-tongued *Melicert*," who should "mourne her death that graced his desert."[159] The passage is a stinging one; Shakespeare stands accused of betrayal and ingratitude, behaviors he condemns in play after play, including *Antony and Cleopatra*. They stop their nose "Against the blown rose" that "kneel'd unto the buds" (3.13.39–40), Cleopatra observes bitterly, using language Elizabeth might have used. Enobarbus deserts soon thereafter, even though his tendency to become "onion-ey'd" around his master shows that he loves Antony. The old soldier fears, as so many Elizabethan men did, that his powerful emotions might transform him into "an ass" or a woman (4.2.35–36). He quickly comes to regret his decision, however, which registers as a self-betrayal: "I am alone the villain of the earth / And feel I am most so" (4.6.29–30). In turning his countenance from Antony, Enobarbus has turned away from his own feelings, and thus from a version of himself. Calling as witness his "sovereign mistress," "the blessed moon"—Cleopatra's planet and Elizabeth's—he begs for forgiveness, proposing "the world rank" him "a master-leaver and a fugitive" (4.9.11–20). An "inveterate judge of men" and perennial skeptic, Enobarbus is sometimes seen as a spokesperson for

Shakespeare.[160] He utters some of the play's most emotionally wrenching lines, becoming an unlikely conduit for overwhelming shame and regret. That Enobarbus's epiphany is precipitated by a reminder of his patron's generosity matters; "how would thou have paid, / My better service," he wonders, "when my turpitude / Thou dost so crown with gold!" (4.6.31–33). Through his pathetic death, which "blows" our "heart" as much as his (4.6.33), *Antony and Cleopatra* disowns the view that emotion "preys on reason" and that what restores the "heart" must needs diminish "the brain" (3.13.197–98), arguing instead that we should let emotions guide our judgments of other people.

Like all the other likenesses and comparisons discussed in this book, the one between Enobarbus and Shakespeare invites us to think not just about similarities, but also about differences. After a career-long struggle with the complex feelings that the Elizabethan court had inspired in him, Shakespeare elects in *Antony and Cleopatra* "to follow with allegiance a fall'n lord," thus conquering "him that did his master conquer" (3.13.44–45). That means securing a better "place i'th'story" (3.13.46) for those who had "graced his desert." According to Loomis, "the literary response to the death of Queen Elizabeth reveals not only a terrible sense of loss, but also a concerted effort, made mostly by male authors, to reconstruct a new and improved version of the Queen, one that refuses to grow old, make demands, or die."[161] Shakespeare chose a different approach than his contemporaries, giving us a queen who does grow old, make demands, and die. Living, Elizabeth I revived the dead Cleopatra's "memorie" and "vertues," including her ability to answer "Embassadors in their native tongues." Shakespeare's Cleopatra in turn revives aspects of the dead Elizabeth, including her ability to elicit stunning performances from her male subjects, an attribute that many survivors of the reign appeared eager to forget. By reminding his audience that Elizabeth had a precedent (the historical Cleopatra) and by giving her a successor (the theatrical Cleopatra), Shakespeare implied that Elizabeth might serve as a model (she serves as his model) and thus paid tribute to the transformative potentialities glimpsed in her reign. No one was better suited to this task of rememorialization than the poet who had spent a career thinking about Elizabeth I's effect on men, and whose imagination was, like Antony's, stirred by this extraordinary woman to create great art.

In *Antony and Cleopatra*, the spirited debate about the protagonists culminates in series of eulogies of Antony, which underline the idea that "what our contempts doth often hurl from us / We wish it ours again" (1.2.123–24). The idea that people are "good, being gone" (1.2.126) resonated in Jacobean England, Loomis argues, because the recently deceased Elizabeth was "appreciated more after her death."[162] The same is true of the men who served the queen. Implicitly comparing himself to Antonius and Endymion, the eponymous narrator of *Leicester's Ghost* complains about being forgotten:

> Who consecrats Colosses to my prayse?
> Who studies to immortalize my name?
> Who doth a stately *Pyramid* upraise
> T'entoombe my corps, that slept in *Cynthias* days?[163]

But some writers did seek to "immortalize" the deceased earl, whom all the world admir'd," depicting him "Not as a man, though he in shape exceld / But as a God, whose heavenlie wit inspir'd, / Wrought hie effects."[164] Indeed, those who honored Elizabeth after she died often praised the men associated with her. Celebrating "that more glorious time," William Herbert reviews the contributions of these male courtiers, presenting "Much honor'd *Dudley*," as "valiant," "wise," and

> Patient in perill, prone to every good,
> Belov'd of men, and graced by soveraigne eyes,
> Cleere was thy thought, as cleere as cristall flood,
> Loyall thy love, and royall was thy blood:
> Fain'd rumour shuns all trueth, beleeve not fame,
> She staines the white as snowe, the purest name.[165]

Antony and Cleopatra shares Herbert's anxiety about how "fame" and "fain'd rumour" might distort accounts of the "Loyall" men who had served a celebrated queen. This anxiety informs "the complex longing" that surrounds Antony, whose "heroic grandeur is always constructed retrospectively, in his—and its—absence." Through her dream of an "Emperor Antony" (5.2.76), Cleopatra performs what Janet Adelman describes as "an impassioned act of memory," which aims in part to prevent "quick comedians" from bringing Antony "drunken forth" and boying her "greatness / I'th'posture of a whore" (5.2.216–21).[166] In a play where the retrospective and the prospective are confounded, the future revels preempted by the classical queen sound like the past revels that her off-stage audiences remember. All come together in an instant.

Eulogies, like other forms of history, can help transform retrospective judgments into future potentialities by creating the desire for a return to the past. Such nostalgia forges a "relationship between individual biography and the biography of groups or nations, between personal and collective memory," and thus transforms the past for future use.[167] Plutarch's Elizabethan translators believed in their obligation to pass "the remembrance of things past to their successors." They thought history served as "instruction of them to come," and valued it because "There is nether picture, nor image of marble, nor arche of triumph, nor piller, nor sumptuous sepulcher, that can match the durableness of an eloquent history."[168] Plays may be better suited still to assuring the survival of "things past" than histories, because they stage the past as something that happens again and will happen again.[169] Their superior eloquence conjures the present emotions that forge the necessary connections between "personal and collective memory." According to Francis Bacon, "the minds of men" watching a play "are more open to affections and impressions than when alone."[170] Seizing on this aspect of playgoing, *Antony and Cleopatra* pushes auditors to mourn the dead again by making them weep, as Antony makes Eros, Enobarbus, and Cleopatra weep. Every time Burbage succeeded in eliciting tears for Antony, the actor altered perceptions of those "graced by soveraigne eyes," a group of men that had been widely mocked and that, according to Herbert, included Shakespeare. By such means, *Antony and Cleopatra* aims to transform all spectators into women with a "private affection and respect, or partialitie" for the dead.[171] It may have had some success in doing so; in 1616 the satirist

Robert Anton complained of Bacchanalian women "growne ... mad" and "impudent" by "irregular motion" at "base Playes" featuring "Cleopatres crimes."[172] To be sure, not all spectators of Shakespeare's play are thus moved (George Bernard Shaw was not). But those who are learn to take on a queen's perspective, which does not bracket off emotion or affection in judging merit. Insofar as Cleopatra moves "slippery people / Whose love is never link'd to the deserver / Till his deserts are past" (1.2.185–87) to love Antony, she calls the abstemious Caesar, and all those misogynistic young men that populated Elizabethan plays, "ass / Unpolicied" (5.2.307–8). The ability to inspire such emotion may well be worth "all that is won and lost" (3.11.70) after all.

Shakespeare identifies in the unorthodox relationships of the recent and the classical past possibilities of mutuality and collaboration that seemed threatening at the time, but that now are "good being gone." According to Adelman, he "exploits the conflicts of opinion which are built into the traditional accounts of the lovers"—and, I would add, of the Elizabethan figures they shadow—to show that tradition is "the common liar."[173] Not only does Shakespeare force a reevaluation of his two sets of historical lovers, but he also uses his lovers to force a reevaluation of the theater, intimately bound to them throughout. Antony plays Osiris to Cleopatra's Isis, Mars to her Venus, her lover, her soldier, her servant, her general, and, finally, her husband. Their collaboration, which has erotic, aesthetic, political, and affective dimensions, defies decorum to generate unconventional definitions of masculine merit.[174] To accept Antony as a "man of men" means learning to prize men for their capacity to arouse and experience passion, rather than for their ability to control or repress it. Steven Mullaney, defining theater as an "affective technology," describes emotions as "boundary phenomena ... hard to contain in rigid or exclusive categories because they are, by their very nature, things that happen betwixt-and-between."[175] They overflow the measure, taking us beyond the limits of rational discourse. Shakespeare, who shares his hero's gift for summoning and cultivating adulterating emotions in others, personifies this affective aspect of the theater in his hybrid colossus, whose legs bestride oceans, and whose capacious heart bursts out of all constraints. In elevating Antony, the playwright exalts his own craft, while acknowledging its deep dependence on female rule. Among other things, Antony's love for Cleopatra models the relationship between a loyal audience and the theater, which generates emotions that are at once degrading and elevating, depending on one's perspective. The central pair evoke not just the relationship between play and playgoer, but also the relationship between two players, "stirr'd" by the one another into performing "Excellent falsehood" (1.1.40–44). Between the two lovers, between the lover of plays and the play, and between the two players, passion proves transformative and ennobling, leading to a "new heaven, new earth" inaccessible to judgmental young men like Vindice or Hamlet, puritan naysayers like Gosson, anticourt satirists like Jonson, or rationalist politicians like Octavius Caesar.

Through his divided catastrophe, Shakespeare also allows Cleopatra the last word on "age in love," ceding the stage to the queenly perspective on such matters for the first time. Ever since Bottom first dreamt of his fairy queen, the playwright had allowed rational considerations to overcome the seductive appeal of his deviant old lovers. Like Hal, Titania turns her countenance from her monstrous minion, after a painful disillusionment, in which her "visions" are punctured, and she recognizes that she was "enamor'd of an ass" (4.1.76–77). Once her "eyes . . . loathe his visage" (4.1.79), she resumes her submissive position in patriarchal culture, which means deferring to male judgment about the differences between a proper man and a "hateful fool" (4.1.49). *A Midsummer Night's Dream* toys with the idea that masculine merit might look quite different from a feminine perspective—Hermia does not look with the same eyes as Egeus, either— but it works hard to contain the subversive implications of that idea. *Antony and Cleopatra* makes no such efforts. Cleopatra remains faithful to her vision of Antony to the end, offering us "Nature's piece 'gainst / fancy, condemning shadows quite" (5.2.99–100). Here, she recalls the epilogue of *A Midsummer Night's Dream*, as if making amends for all those old shadows that have now come to offend.

Harnessing the emotions released by the play's echoes and resemblances, Cleopatra makes us wish Antony ours again in the fifth act. Twenty years after Leicester's death, and four years after Elizabeth's, another old adulterer devoted to a "terrene moon" becomes a figure of mythic "bounty" and generosity, an "autumn" that paradoxically grows "the more by reaping" (5.2.86–87). Besides endowing him with the power to confound all manner of convention, Antony's Bacchanalian properties have kept the possibility of a resuscitation alive all along, "if only as desire," in Barbara Bono's haunting phrase.[176] It is a desire that Cleopatra's final tribute expertly fans. Co-opting the Circe myth to feminocentric ends, her "eyes . . . so royal" (5.2.318) render Antony's immersion in delight "dolphin-like," showing his "back above / The element they liv'd in" (5.2.88–89). His face "like the heavens," his voice like "rattling thunder," his "bounty" without winter in it, all testify to the outsize feelings of wonder, admiration, and gratitude that Antony (through Burbage) inspires in others (5.2.78–92). Like Dolabella, those of us who are susceptible to Cleopatra's eulogy apprehend far more than we can comprehend in this description. That our feelings may be out of proportion to the youthful body of the boy playing Cleopatra or to the aging body of the actor playing Antony matters little—indeed, this contradiction may even be an asset. As Elizabeth I had demonstrated, performances that overcome bodily weaknesses associated with age generate the impression of virtuosity and greatness. Those of us who have felt Antony's power to overcome misogynistic prejudices must therefore needs approve Cleopatra's claim that "t'imagine / An Antony were nature's piece 'gainst fancy."[177] There have been such men—we have seen them, onstage if not in life—and Cleopatra's dream urges us to believe there "might be such" men again (5.2.93). Even Caesar thinks that Cleopatra looks "like sleep / As if she would catch another Antony / In her strong toil of grace" (5.2.346–48). By calling attention to the performer who only looks like death, the medium who has just so successfully revived the dead, he reminds us that Cleopatra will rise again, and again, and again. In a utopian future, every man may learn through such repeat performances to think himself another Antony.

EPILOGUE

The baffled Hamlet, holding two miniatures before his mother, demanding to know how she could have stooped to Claudius, expresses a whole generation's resentment about the vagaries of queenly judgment. In Margaret Atwood's "Gertrude Talks Back," the unrepentant Queen of Denmark confronts her miniature-wielding son, summarily dismissing his claims about his father's superiority to Claudius. Gertrude tells Hamlet that every time she wanted to "warm up" her "aging bones," Old Hamlet would react as if she had "suggested murder." The queen prefers Claudius, whose more generous approach to aging, female sexuality, and the pleasures of the flesh allows her to stop "tiptoeing around."[1] With characteristic insight, Atwood identifies the idea that women might have different criteria for determining masculine excellence as a significant source of *Hamlet*'s trouble. Gertrude had eyes and she chose Claudius.

The works discussed in this book all concern themselves with women like Gertrude, who elect unorthodox men to high places, including their beds and their thrones. When Puck finds his "mistress with a monster is in love" (*A Midsummer Night's Dream*, 3.2.6), he gives comic expression to pervasive reservations about this scenario, shared by the common people who gossiped about Leicester's sexual proclivities, the exiled courtiers who complained about them, and the three generations of playwrights who restaged them. And yet, *A Midsummer Night's Dream*, *Twelfth Night*, and *Antony and Cleopatra* show that the dream of election by a powerful woman could also be enthralling, a "most rare vision" to which theatrical audiences succumbed time and again (*A Midsummer Night's Dream*, 4.2.204–5).

EPILOGUE

Shakespeare kept offering new and improved versions of the age-in-love figure associated with that dream, attesting to its enduring popularity and commercial viability. Only when women are in power does their perspective on masculine excellence become such a source of widespread hope, anxiety, and fascination. The possibility that feminine ideas regarding masculine merit might alter the basis of society took root in the Elizabethan imagination, I have argued, because of Elizabeth I's alleged preference for "subtile, fine, and fox-like" men like Claudius, who defied patriarchal norms and who enjoyed a bit of theatrical sport while doing so.[2] On the one hand, Elizabeth's less favored subjects felt with Hamlet that her favorites usurped proper men, without having "merited . . . to be so highly favored of [her Majes]tie."[3] On the other hand, male subjects hoped that they, too, would have their deserts graced one day, as Shakespeare did.

After *Antony and Cleopatra* purged the age-in-love trope of its negative associations, the dream of election by a powerful woman continued to haunt English culture (as indeed did the ghost of the woman who had inspired that dream).[4] Not all newer versions embrace the transformational possibilities glimpsed in Antony's relation to Cleopatra, but some do. Webster's Duchess "stains time past, lights time to come" when she chooses the steward Antonio purely for what she takes to be his merits.[5] And in *Cymbeline*, Imogen surrounds herself with tapestries celebrating "Proud Cleopatra, when she met her Roman, / And Cydnus swell'd above the banks" (2.4.70–71). Emulating this example, she chooses Posthumous against her father's wishes, lighting the time to come in her own way. When a choric gentleman approves Imogen's choice of a husband, arguing that "By her election may be truly read / What kind of man" Posthumous is (1.1.53–54), he shows himself far more tolerant of "men of this kind" than Bacon was.[6] Like Imogen, women from Margaret Cavendish to Willa Cather to Janet Adelman have loved *Antony and Cleopatra* for keeping alive alternative ways of thinking about men and women. One "would think that [Shakespeare] had been Metamorphosed from a Man to a Woman," Cavendish wrote with wonder, "for who could Describe *Cleopatra* Better than he hath done?"[7] It helped that Shakespeare had known a "wonderful piece of work" (1.2.154–55), who was a cause of change and inspiration to him throughout her long reign.

One measure of how little attitudes toward female rule have progressed over the last four hundred years is the account given by some biographers of Elizabeth's elder favorites, which hews closer to Elizabethan anticourt polemics than to Shakespeare's late plays. For example, John Guy, Elizabeth's most recent biographer, proposes that "dashing" men were the queen's "main weakness," and that "these could, and sometimes did, cloud her judgment." When Guy describes the capable Sir Christopher Hatton as "an unctuous flatterer" for declaring "himself to be Elizabeth's 'everlasting bondman,' seemingly without a hint of hypocrisy," he sounds nearly as outraged as a Vindice or a Hamlet.[8] Notably, what Guy finds intolerable is not the possibility that Hatton was a hypocrite, but the possibility that he was not. Hatton loved the queen he served and believed in her superiority. This apparently is harder for Guy to accept than it was for Shakespeare, who embraced alternative ideals of masculinity in *Antony and Cleopatra*. To some extent, antimonarchical biases explain the contempt with which scholars often treat Hatton and Leicester, and the correspondent enthusiasm they feel for the Earl of Essex, who showed this "ageing spinster" a thing or two about masculine indomitability.[9] If the Elizabethan period teaches us anything, however, it is that progressive sentiments expressed in relation to female leaders can mask deeply misogynistic impulses. Years ago, Peter Erickson warned against the elevation of Essex as a "proto-democratic" figure because his "resistance to Elizabeth has a strong masculinist and misogynist aura that should not recommend it as a model and inspiration for our own ideal of subversion."[10] And Carole Levin denounced attacks on Hatton and Leicester as attacks on Elizabeth's judgment.[11] Yet we continue to privilege Essex's career over those of his elders when trying to understand how Elizabethan men felt about their queen.

Although the queen's elder favorites were uniquely memorable to their contemporaries, we have all but forgotten them. This is evident in the lack of political value that historicist readings of Shakespeare assign to a Claudius or an Antony. I have focused in this book on contemporary perceptions of the elder favorites, many of which were unflattering. I would like to conclude by remembering the debt we owe to Leicester, who patronized, employed, and inspired artists like Kempe, Burbage, Sidney, Spenser, and Shakespeare. English Renaissance culture was made immensely richer by men of his kind, in ways hard either to describe or to overestimate. According to Erickson, "Instead of making more of Essex's, or Shakespeare's, radical potential, we must... look elsewhere to more contemporary literature for possible images of subversion."[12] I can understand this impulse, but I think it misguided. This book started as an investigation of dated material but it ended up feeling strangely timely. The 2016 American election showed our democracy to be stubbornly hostile to female politicians, for all too familiar reasons. I cannot be the only student of Elizabeth's reign who found the vitriolic attacks on Secretary Clinton's judgment uncannily reminiscent of those on Elizabeth I's. We might do worse than turn to the Elizabethan past for ideas on how to overcome this present hostility and make our future more hospitable to female rule.

NOTES

INTRODUCTION

1. All quotations from Shakespeare are from *Riverside Shakespeare*.
2. Vaughan, *Approved Directions*, 113. Bartholomaeus Anglicus defines the "striplyng age" as between 14 and 28 years of age, although he notes that some "phisitions" extend it to "the end of thirtie or five and thirtie," the time in life "to get children." The characters I examine in this book would have fallen in the age known as "Senecta"—"old men" who not yet reached the state of "Senium," or extreme old age (*Batman upon Bartholome*, 70v). The division into stages was commonplace, although there was disagreement about the chronological age signaling the advent of a new stage. Functionality played as much of a role as chronology in staging life; see, e.g., Shahar, *Growing Old*, 12–18; and Alexandra Shephard, *Meanings of Manhood*, 54–55, 215–17. The disagreements derived partly from the different paradigms for staging life—Aristotelian, Galenic, Ptolemaic, and Christian; see Burrow, *Ages of Man*; and Bruce Smith, *Shakespeare and Masculinity*, 71–82. Shephard argues for "the use of 50 as the milestone from which to approach ageing in the early modern past" (216). Beam agrees that the individual lifespan "was divided into three to twelve stages, with the first stage of old age "beginning anywhere from 40 to 65, but typically located around age 50" ("Female Old Age," 99). Men in the "green" old age were especially suited to governance and public service; see Thomas, "Age and Authority," 211; and Shephard, 41–42, 231–32.
3. Ralegh, *History*, 127–28. This task confronts men in the sixth stage, with the seventh stage reserved for extreme old age. Ralegh also identifies the "third age," which follows infancy and school years, as the time for amorous pursuits.
4. The sonnet speaker's sense that his age exposes him to judgment is shared by other aging males in the lyric tradition; see, e.g., Donne, "Canonization," where the lover feels others "flout" his "five grey hairs" (3).
5. Klause, "Shakespeare's *Sonnets*," 306. Other critics who consider the issue are Hallet Smith, "Bare Ruined Choirs," 233–49; and Martin, *Constituting Old Age*, 113–25.

209

6. Fiedler, "Eros and Thanatos," 235, 238. Anthony Ellis concurs "that the laughter this figure provokes has a timeless quality," although his own analysis is "grounded in the distinct social and political contexts" (*Old Age, Masculinity*, 3, 9).
7. Adams, *Leicester and the Court*, 28.
8. Thomas, "Age and Authority," 211. In 1597, the thirty-four-year-old Robert Sidney was too young for a position in the queen's entourage.
9. Roser, "Life Expectancy"; Oeppen et al., "Measurements of Late Medieval Mortality," 162.
10. Quoted in Klein, "Tim Kaine's Feminism."
11. For the "debilitating" effect of erotic desire on rational masculinity see Breitenberg, *Anxious Masculinity*, 9.
12. *Leicester's Commonwealth*, 73; Rosenberg, *Leicester*, 26. The earl's regal aspirations were much discussed; if he was "little inferyor to a kynge in atoritye and superioritye," he conducted himself as the "emperor in [his] owen desiers" (*News*, 144).
13. Castiglione, *Courtier*, 340.
14. Levin, *Heart and Stomach*, 45–47, 66–90. See also Robert Shephard, "Sexual Rumours," 101–22; and Cressy, *Dangerous Talk*, 69–75.
15. Adams notes that scholars underestimate Leicester's importance as favorite because Essex has eclipsed his stepfather in the historiographical imagination (*Leicester and the Court*, 46–67). One exception is Perry, who examines the Jacobean tradition on Leicester (*Literature and Favoritism*). For theatrical allusions to Leicester, see Jones and White, "*Gorboduc*," 3–16; Lake, "From *Leicester His Commonwealth*," 128–61; and Tricomi, "Philip, Earl of Pembroke," 332–45.
16. Quinn, "Celebrity," 156, 159.
17. Levin observes, "Rumors about Elizabeth's sexual misconduct . . . centered on her relationship with Dudley" (*Heart and Stomach*, 45).
18. Cressy, *Dangerous Talk*, 62–67.
19. Adams, "Dudley, Robert."
20. Middleton, *Revenger's Tragedy*, 1.1.34–36. All references to Middleton are to *Works*.
21. Middleton, *Mad World, My Masters*, 4.2.18–21, 31. The fashion extended to poetry; see Achileos, "Youth, Old Age," 39; and Martin, *Constituting Old Age*, 100–136.
22. See, e.g., Guy, "The 1590s," 1–19.
23. Middleton, *Mad World, My Masters*, 4.4.51–52.
24. Bruster, *Question of Culture*, 64.
25. Essex's claims about his intentions are a famous instance of this ploy, used also by the Wyatt rebels against Mary Tudor in 1554 and by the participants of the Northern Rebellion against Elizabeth in 1570. For the queen as the victim of a conspiracy of "evil counsels," see Lake and Pincus, "Rethinking the Public Sphere," 6–7. Indirect means were favored because treason and sedition laws made speaking openly against the queen a crime; see Levin, *Heart and Stomach*, 68–69; and Lacey

Baldwin Smith, *Treason*, 137. Like Perry, I am skeptical of the idea that "attacking the king's servants provides a way to voice dissent while maintaining" loyalty to the monarch (*Literature and Favoritism*, 10).

26. Goldring, "Portraiture, Patronage," 170–74.
27. Doty, *Shakespeare, Popularity*, 4–18.
28. See, e.g., the portrait included in Ralph Lever's *The Philosophers Game* (1563).
29. Habermas, *Structural Transformation*, 8.
30. Golding, "To . . . Lord Robert Dudley," 4v. Like Golding's Ovid (see chapter 2), his translation of Bullinger's *A Confutation of the Popes Bull . . . against Elizabeth* (1572) reproduces the Dudley bear badge.
31. Blundeville, *Profitable Treatise*, D3r; "To the Ryght Noble Erle of Leycester," A2. The final quote comes from a poem printed on the title page, which also reproduces the Dudley bear badge. On Leicester's clients presenting him as an exemplar, see Rosenberg, *Leicester*, 51–52; and Vanhoutte, "*Itinerarium*."
32. Francis Bacon to the Earl of Essex, October 4, 1596, in *Letters and Life of Francis Bacon*, 2:44.
33. Lake, *Bad Queen Bess?*, 11.
34. "Letter of Estate," 25, 27, 30.
35. *Briefe Discoverie*, 49–50.
36. Doty, *Shakespeare, Popularity*, 47–49. As subsequent chapters show, these patterns explain why "personalized satire" came to be represented as "animal-baiting" (Scott-Warren, "Bear-Gardens," 80n50). Notably, Vincentio's complaint refers to Lucio's slander that the "old fantastical duke of dark corners" is an expert "woodman" (*Measure for Measure*, 4.3.156–62).
37. On Shakespeare's tendency to invite audiences to scrutinize political phenomena, see also Kastan, *Shakespeare after Theory*, 109–27.
38. Gosson, *Plays Confuted*, C8v–D1r.
39. *Briefe Discoverie*, 110.
40. *Leicester's Commonwealth*, 186; Lake and Pincus, "Rethinking the Public Sphere," 6.
41. Wittek makes the case for "the formative function of Shakespeare's theater in the news culture" (*Media Players*, 1); on political competence, see Kisery, *Hamlet's Moment*.
42. Wittek, *Media Players*, 3. The Jacobean "discourse of favoritism"—a major strain of which looked back on Leicester—prepared the ground for the transformations described by Habermas by giving "symbolic expression to deep and recurring political tensions inherent in the ongoing centralization of the state" (Perry, *Literature and Favoritism*, 4, 33).
43. Habermas, *Structural Transformation*, 27. Others have found Habermas's emphasis on the "critical reasoning of private persons on political issues" (29) overly restrictive; e.g., Wilson and Yachnin take a "post-Habermasian" approach to the topic,

which "focuses on a plurality of publics rather than on a single public sphere" and "is interested in accidental and unintended outcomes as much as intended ones" (introduction, 7). See also Yachnin, "Performing Publicity"; and Doty, who argues that what matters is not "the quality and depth of the arguments" but the fact that "private people . . . are talking about the political sphere on a significant scale at all" (*Shakespeare, Popularity*, 137).

44. Castiglione, *Courtier*, 146, 204, 106.
45. Wotton to Sir Edmund Bacon, July 2, 1613, *Letters and Life of Sir Henry Wotton*, 2:32–33.
46. Blundeville, *Profitable Treatise*, N2r, Q3r.
47. Shannon, *Sovereign Amity*, 151–53.
48. Blundeville, *Profitable Treatise*, O1r, Q3r. For the commonplace that women are natural tyrants, see, e.g., Knox, *The First Blast of the Trumpet*.
49. Sidney, "Defense of Leicester," 252.
50. Perry, *Literature and Favoritism*, 9. Perry identifies Shakespeare's *Henry V* with this "dream" but thinks Falstaff "an attempt, perhaps, to exorcise the specter of Richard II's wanton favorites" (7). For Falstaff as reflection of Elizabeth's minions instead, see chapter 3.
51. Warner, *Publics and Counterpublics*, 40, 62.
52. See, e.g., Baldwin, *Organization and Personnel*, 290–92; Duncan-Jones, *Shakespeare*, 31–61; and Streitberger, "Personnel and Professionalization," 346.
53. Greenblatt, *Will in the World*, 48–51.
54. Duncan-Jones, *Shakespeare*, 14.
55. Naunton, *Fragmenta Regalia*, 67.
56. A supporter of the Duke of Norfolk, quoted in Levin, *Heart and Stomach*, 78; Naunton, *Fragmenta Regalia*, 68, 50–51. Shannon claims favors bestowed on men like Leicester and Hatton bypassed "the evolving system of Tudor 'meritocracy'" (*Sovereign Amity*, 146). Arguably, however, promotions of favorites represent a refinement of this system, in which alternate ideas of merit might be glimpsed; see chapter 4.
57. Platter, *Travels*, 194.
58. E.g., MacCaffrey, who claims "Leicester and Hatton were advanced to high office . . . because of their private attraction for the Queen" (*Elizabeth I*, 457). Later in the same passage, he anachronistically characterizes Burghley and Walsingham as "professionals" and Leicester and Hatton as "amateurs." Guy emphasizes Leicester's "flashy good looks," which Elizabeth found "irresistible" (*Elizabeth*, 44). Peck also describes Leicester as "the Queen's creation, above his intrinsic merits" (introduction to *Leicester's Commonwealth*, 49). These stereotypes are misogynistic, in that they cast a "powerful woman" as easily "dazzled by a man's dancing" (Levin, *Heart and Stomach*, 79). See also Collinson, who argues the stereotype "ignores Hatton's

long political apprenticeship and underestimates his considerable ability; while Leicester, thanks to his many enemies, has been unfairly dismissed and vilified" ("Elizabeth I").
59. Montrose, "Shaping Fantasies," 35.
60. MacFaul, "Kingdom with my Friend," 52.
61. Thomas, "Age and Authority," 205. See also Taunton, *Fictions of Old Age*, 127–32.
62. See, e.g., Thomas, "Age and Authority"; and Shepard, *Meanings of Manhood*, 70.
63. Cicero, *Booke of Old Age,* 11r-v. According to Thane, this treatise was "widely read in Europe," shaping "feelings about old age from the ancient world onwards" (*Old Age*, 40). See also Taunton, *Fictions of Old Age*, 1–9; Martin, *Constituting Old Age*, 10–11, 19–25; and Shephard, *Meanings of Manhood*, 23.
64. A prosperous old age was the reward for a virtuous life, and "that old age which had no noble deedes to defende it selfe withal … was wretched and miserable" (Cicero, *Booke of Old Age*, 46r). "Flourishing old age" was considered "a continuation … of patriarchal manhood"; however, only the righteous might expect to reap its rewards (Shephard, *Meanings of Manhood*, 41–42).
65. Thomas, "Age and Authority," 238–39; Shephard, *Meanings of Manhood*, 44–45, 231–45. Extreme old age often produced less enviable social conditions; see, e.g., Taunton, *Fictions of Old Age*, 38–39, 48–72; Martin, *Constituting Old Age*, 137–75; Ellis, *Old Age, Masculinity*, 15–39; and Collington, "Sans Wife," 185–207.
66. Shahar, *Growing Old*, 5–6.
67. Taunton, *Fictions of Old Age*, 5; Martin, *Constituting Old Age*, 18. See also Ellis, *Old Age, Masculinity*, 15–16; and Shepard, *Meanings of Manhood*, 45.
68. The premodern bias against senescent sexuality is gerontophobic only if we privilege the (modern) view that human beings "largely ground" their "identities" upon "sexuality" (Martin, *Constituting Old Age*, 107).
69. Shephard, *Meanings of Manhood*, 3. According to Shephard, "Apart from gender, age was the most directly acknowledged difference to inform constructions of normative manhood" (9).
70. Shephard, *Meanings of Manhood*, 21, 1.
71. Cicero, *Booke of Old Age*, 21v-22r.
72. Young men were compared to animals because of their alleged failure to control passions (Thomas, "Age and Authority," 218).
73. Shahar, *Growing Old*, 38.
74. Joubert, *Popular Errors*, 117.
75. Castiglione, *Courtier*, 338–40.
76. In advanced senescence, "the physiological changes occurring in the body … cause the old man to become childlike" (Shahar, *Growing Old*, 39). Very old men were likened to women and children—all three groups lacked the heat associated with courage, for example; see Vaughan, *Approved Directions*, 107, 214; Shahar, *Growing*

Old, 71; and Ellis, *Old Age, Masculinity*, 17. This amounts to a privileging of men we would consider middle-aged. The "gender convergence" brought about by extreme age "may have been positive for women but was negative for men" (Shephard, *Meanings of Manhood*, 221).

77. Cicero, *Booke of Old Age*, 23v-r.
78. See *King Lear*, where the forty-eight-year-old Kent describes himself as "not so young . . . to love a woman for singing, nor so old to dote on her for anything" (1.4.37–38); Cicero, *Booke of Old Age*, 24v; Boorde, *Breviarie*, 31; and Stubs, *Anatomie of Abuses*, which attributes the beheading of John the Baptist to Herod's "foolish dotage" (76).
79. Stubs, *Anatomie of Abuses*, 64.
80. Vaughan, *Approved Directions*, 70; Boorde, *Breviarie*, 31. For the regimen that old men were advised to follow, see Shahar, *Growing Old*, 38–40, who also notes that only men were urged to refrain from sexual intercourse (78); and Ellis, *Old Age, Masculinity*, 1–3.
81. Cicero, *Booke of Old Age*, 3r, 43r.
82. Cicero, *Booke of Old Age*, 51v.
83. See also Collington, "Sans Wife," 192.
84. Thomas, "Age and Authority," 243.
85. Bartholomaeus, *Batman upon Bartholome*, 70; Shahar, *Growing Old*, 64.
86. Collington discusses cuckoldry as the plight of older men ("Sans Wife," 188).
87. Joubert, *Popular Errors*, 117. Citing Joubert, Martin argues that the individual "constitution" enabled resistance to social protocols regarding aging (*Constituting Old Age*, 8).
88. Breitenberg, *Anxious Masculinity*, 20.
89. Shahar describes the charivari as a punishment for transgressive sexuality (*Growing Old*, 80–81). For Sonnet 138 as an instance of "the May-December topos that informs the cuckoldry plots" of Shakespeare's plays, see Fineman, *Shakespeare's Perjured Eye*, 165.
90. *Othello* is the exception. It does follow the May-December plot—one reason that I use this play only to illustrate general points about age and sexuality.
91. Cicero, *Booke of Old Age*, 46v, 33v; conduct manuals reveal "misgivings that, far from being self-contained exemplars, many men constantly worked against the patriarchal goals of order and control" (Shephard, *Meanings of Manhood*, 10).
92. Hatton to the Earl of Leicester, July 21, 1584, in Harris, *Life and Times of Sir Christopher Hatton*, 382.
93. Dyer to Christopher Hatton, October 9, 1572, in Harris, *Life and Times of Sir Christopher Hatton*, 17. Dyer's letter gives the lie to Guy, who claims "none of Elizabeth's contemporaries . . . believed that a woman's high rank could trump her gender" (*Elizabeth*, 11).

94. Taylor, "Social Imaginaries," 106.
95. Peck, introduction to *Leicester's Commonwealth*, 48. On the peculiar "intensity of personal vilification" directed at Leicester, see also Adams, *Leicester and the Court*, 50.
96. Lord Burleigh to Christopher Hatton, July 13, 1581, in Harris, *Life and Times of Sir Christopher Hatton*, 177; Frye, *Elizabeth I*, 9.
97. Montrose, "Shaping Fantasies," 32.
98. Eggert, *Showing Like a Queen*, 2.
99. Smith, *Shakespeare and Masculinity*, 104.
100. Bates, *Masculinity, Gender*, 1.
101. Montrose, *Subject of Elizabeth*, 171.
102. Grady, "Impure Aesthetics," 276, 285.
103. Dutton, *Mastering the Revels*, 61.
104. Hunt, *Shakespeare's Speculative Art*, 3.
105. The most detailed account of Lyly's influence on Shakespeare is Hunter's *John Lyly*, 298–349. Although Shakespeare refers only once directly to Lyly (in *1 Henry IV*), his influence is "evident throughout Shakespeare's comedy" (298). Philippa Berry shows how "the lunar image" of Elizabeth I popularized by *Endymion* shaped *A Midsummer Night's Dream* (*Chastity and Power*, 134, 144–46). Others have argued for *Gallathea*'s influence on Shakespeare's romantic comedies; see, e.g., Rackin, "Androgyny, Mimesis," 29–41; and Scragg, "Shakespeare, Lyly, and Ovid," 125–34.
106. Prologue, *Endymion*, 7. Lyly urges his audience not to indulge in "pastimes"; however, as Patterson (*Censorship*, 28–29) and Dutton (*Licensing*, xi) argue, disclaimers like this are invitations to analogic reading. On Lyly's fusing of real and fictional figures, see also Bruster, *Question of Culture*, 65–93.
107. Gurr, *Playgoing*, 151.
108. Doty, *Shakespeare, Popularity*, 23.
109. Jonson, *Bartholomew Fair*, in vol. 4 of *Works*, induction, 64–65, 103.
110. Dutton, *Licensing*, xi.
111. Privy Council Minutes, August 15, 1597, in Chambers, *Elizabethan Stage*, 4:323. On the significance of this title, see chapter 3.
112. Privy Council Minutes, July 28, 1597, in Chambers, *Elizabethan Stage*, 4:322.
113. Dutton, *Mastering the Revels*, 113. Dutton sees the measures taken by the Privy Council, like the 1598 measure restricting the acting companies to two, as responsive to the commercial interests of these theatrical troupes (*Licensing*, 24).
114. In *Every Man Out of His Humour*, probably censored for including a player who performed the part of Elizabeth (see chapter 3); *Endymion* and *Cynthia's Revels*; *The Revenger's Tragedy*; *Antony and Cleopatra*; and *The Merry Wives of Windsor*, respectively.
115. Bevington, *Tudor Drama*, 1.

116. See also Dutton, *Licensing*, xi; and Patterson, who calls attention to the prohibitive function of the intentional fallacy associated with formalist criticism (*Censorship*, 31–33).
117. Bevington, 25. As McDonald observes, "it has become axiomatic that satire was foreign to Shakespeare's natural temper" (*Shakespeare and Jonson*, 77).
118. Bevington resists the idea that Titania refers to Elizabeth because it implies "outrageous treatment" of the queen (*Tudor Drama*, 10). This prejudice persists. Grady proposes that one function of the "western vestal" speech is to "immunize the play from an undesired infernal interpretation of Titania—the Fairy Queen of this play—who might easily be seen, thanks to Spenser, as an allusion to Elizabeth" ("Impure Aesthetics," 285). I doubt a play can "immunize" itself against well-established associations in this manner. The bias against political readings seems peculiar to Shakespeareans.
119. Steggle, *Wars of the Theatres*, 18.
120. Jonson, *Every Man Out*, in vol. 1 of *Works*, 3.1.410–1; "To the Memory of My Beloved, the Author, Mr. William Shakespeare," in *Riverside Shakespeare*, 97.
121. Essex to Elizabeth I, May 12, 1600, quoted in Chambers, 1:324–25.
122. Privy Council minutes, May 10, 1601, Chambers, 4:332. According to Chambers, Richard Tarleton was reprimanded for targeting Leicester and Ralegh in a play (1:324).
123. Jonson, *Every Man Out*, 2.3.348–49.
124. Dutton, *Licensing*, xvii.
125. "glance, v.1," OED online, http://www.oed.com/view/Entry/78698 (accessed November 3, 2017).
126. On *The Murder of Gonzago*, see also Dutton, *Licensing*, 7; and Yachnin, "Performing Publicity," 205–8.
127. Patterson, 11, 18. As long as playwrights veiled matters, the censors applied what Dutton calls the "court standard in their licenses" (*Licensing*, 6). See also Bednarz, who argues that Shakespeare represents the layering "of an oblique topical subtext" as "a powerful mode of covert communication" (*Shakespeare and the Poets' War*, 193).
128. Patterson emphasizes the reader's role in determining meaning in this process, since "authors who build ambiguity into their works have no control over what happens to them later" (*Censorship*, 18). As Dutton notes, in reference to *A Game at Chess*, "The audience was apparently expected to be able to make sense of composite or multi-faceted allusions which may have no literal or one-to-one relation to person or events, but imaginatively merge disparate materials" (*Mastering the Revels*, 241).
129. Carlson, *Haunted Stage*, 39.
130. Warner, *Publics and Counterpublics*, 11.
131. In an age given to political applications, Leicester's preeminence made him a favorite point of reference for decades after his death. One of the few documents offering

hard evidence of early modern reading habits, the Earl of Pembroke's edition of George Chapman's *The Conspiracy and Tragedy of Charles Duke of Byron* (1607–8), contains a marginal note identifying the titular character, a royal favorite, with Pembroke's great-uncle, Leicester; see Tricomi, "Philip, Earl of Pembroke," 342. Perry argues that "successive favorites" were "pigeonholed... into the same ethically charged stereotypes" devised for Leicester (*Literature and Favoritism*, 2), although the aging sexuality motif seems not to have transferred over to Jacobean favorites.

132. Naunton, *Fragmenta Regalia*, 51.
133. Middleton, *Revenger's Tragedy*, 1.1.34–35.

1. *ENDYMION* AT THE AGING COURT

1. Bevington reviews the evidence for dating, concluding that the play was performed at court on February 2, 1588 (introduction to *Endymion*, 8–9).
2. Lyly, *Endymion*, 5.1.73–76. Further references appear parenthetically.
3. Betts, "Image of this Queene," 155.
4. Gascoigne et al., *Princely Pleasures*, c 6r. For the performative aspects of the relationship between Elizabeth and Leicester in the entertainments, see Susan Frye, *Elizabeth I*, 56–96.
5. "prick, n.," OED online, http://www.oed.com/view/Entry/151146 (accessed November 3, 2017).
6. The other would be William Cecil, Lord Burghley. The queen came close to marrying Dudley in the early 1560s (Doran, *Monarchy and Matrimony*, 40–72). Although he gave up hope after 1575 (Levin, *Heart and Stomach*, 47, 73), Leicester functioned as Elizabeth's "surrogate husband" for the remainder of his life (Adams, "Dudley, Robert"). Leicester became Master of the Horse in 1558, member of the Order of the Garter in 1559, member of the Privy Council in 1562, Constable of Windsor Castle in 1562, Earl of Leicester in 1564, and Lord Steward in 1587.
7. Cicero, *Booke of Old Age*, 12v–13r, 30r, 26v.
8. Knox, *First Blast of the Trumpet*, 11.
9. Shephard, *Meanings of Manhood*, 29.
10. Ovid, *Metamorphoses*, 7.377. Circe represents effeminizing sensuality in early modern works; see, e.g. Britland, "Circe's Cup"; and Kermode, *Shakespeare, Spenser*, 84–115. Sullivan examines the association of Circe and sleep, which signals the descent into brutishness, in *Sleep, Romance*.
11. On Golding and Leicester, see Rosenberg, *Leicester*, 156–60.
12. Allen, *Admonition*, viii.
13. See Lake and Pincus for the regime's attempts at mobilizing various publics, "Rethinking the Public Sphere." Dutton points out that it is hard to "distinguish sexual discourse from that of religion and politics" in this period (*Licensing*, 52).
14. Allen, *Admonition*, xix, vii.

15. *Leicester's Commonwealth*, 87.
16. *Briefe Discoverie*, 14. On this pamphlet, see also introduction and chapter 2.
17. *Leicester's Commonwealth*, 75.
18. For censorship "flash-points," see Dutton, *Licensing*, xviii. Perry identifies the tract as a source for the emergent "cultural fantasy" of the "all-powerful royal favorite" (*Literature and Favoritism*, 2).
19. Deats, "Disarming of the Knight," 289. Pincombe describes Endymion as a "ludicrously impotent courtly lover" (*Plays of John Lyly*, 94).
20. Castiglione, *Courtier*, 145.
21. Halpin first proposed that Endymion refers to the Earl of Leicester in his much maligned *Oberon's Vision*, 77–78. He cast Lady Douglas Sheffield as Tellus. While many of Halpin's identifications are dubious, an aging royal favorite must needs have called Leicester to mind in the 1580s. Leicester occupied the position of leading favorite for thirty years; see Adams, *Leicester and the Court*, 46–67.
22. Traditionally, Lyly's plays were read as flattering to Elizabeth I, but recent scholars argue "apparent allusions" to the queen "are often remarkably unflattering" (Alwes, "'I Would Faine Serve,'" 213). Maurice Hunt, for example, sees *Endymion* as a critical "glass" reflecting the queen's "problematic removed virginity" (*Shakespeare's Speculative Art*, 116). Lyly does consistently represent Elizabeth I as attractive, regardless of her age.
23. Castiglione, *Courtier*, 335.
24. *Leicester's Commonwealth*, 114. Like Scragg, I think Lyly "remained embedded in the literary consciousness" of the 1590s and early 1600s ("Victim of Fashion," 214).
25. Mullaney, "Mourning and Misogyny," 151.
26. Montrose, *Subject of Elizabeth*, 213, 241.
27. Allen, *Admonition*, llvii, xv–xvi, xix, xx. His portrait of Elizabeth is consistent with premodern views about sexually active older women "as possessing some secret knowledge which enabled [them] to bend others to [their] will" (Shahar, *Growing Old*, 80).
28. Elizabeth thought Leicester's conduct in the Netherlands gave "the world just cause to think that we are had in contempt by him that ought most to respect and reverence us"; "Letter to the Earl of Leicester," April 1586, in *Elizabeth I: Collected Works*, 277.
29. Berry, *Chastity and Power*, 135.
30. Martin, *Constituting Old Age*, 112. On the origins of the moon cult as a "private" form of adulation practiced by Sir Walter Ralegh in the 1580s, which spread to become "public" in the 1590s, see Strong, *Cult of Elizabeth*, 48. Berry attributes the prevalence of lunar images in part to *Endymion*'s influence (*Chastity and Power*, 134).
31. Both Mullaney and Montrose cite Anthony Rivers, a Jesuit priest, who claimed that at the Christmas celebrations in 1600, the queen was "painted in some places near

half an inch thick" (quoted in Montrose, *Subject of Elizabeth*, 243). Basing himself on this same evidence, Mullaney argues that the queen was "a painted image no less than the Rainbow portrait was" ("Mourning and Misogyny," 147). As Riehl observes, however, "this story is hardly unbiased, nor is it eyewitness testimony" (*Face of Queenship*, 60).

32. Montrose, *Subject of Elizabeth*, 230, 213.
33. Ralegh, "Ralegh to Elizabeth," in *Elizabeth I: Collected Works*, 307.
34. See Marotti's "Love is Not Love" for an influential statement of this position; for a critique informing my comments, see Minogue, "Woman's Touch," 559–61.
35. Montrose, *Subject of Elizabeth*, 244; MacCaffrey, *Elizabeth I*, 396. Hammer reminds us that while "Elizabeth's ageing was effectively overlooked . . . the same was not true" for the men around her; nonetheless, he attributes the continued wooing of the queen to her "splendid royal ego," and labels the whole process "grotesque" ("Absolute and Sovereign Mistress," 39–42). See also Guy, *Elizabeth*, 147.
36. Minogue, "Woman's Touch," 561. Martin notes that "the abrasive judgments" of critics in this regard "betray an implicit repugnance for the aged physique" of the queen (*Constituting Old Age*, 52).
37. Vaughan, *Approved Directions*, 29.
38. Aging had been characterized as a cooling process since the translation of Aristotle's *Parva Naturalia* in 1240 (Thane, *Old Age*, 52–53).
39. Taunton, "Time's Whirligig," 32.
40. De Villanova, *Defence of Age*, B 2v, A 2r, B 3r. As Shahar notes, writers who discussed the problems of aging limited themselves to men, since "the emphasis was always on the physical powers, the power of doing, the power to command and to think" (*Growing Old*, 19).
41. Castiglione, *Courtier*, 430, 346, 358. Dust notes that *Endymion* and *The Courtier* share a concern with "whether an old man can be a good lover" ("Kiss," 88). On aging in *The Courtier*, see also Ricci, "Old Age," 57–73.
42. Strong, *Cult of Elizabeth*, 15, 47. Not all contemporary portraits of Elizabeth follow this pattern of rejuvenation; see, e.g., Arnold, *Queen Elizabeth's Wardrobe*, 40–41; and Riehl, *Face of Queenship*, 151–70.
43. Martin, *Constituting Old Age*, 33.
44. The charges of vanity occur in the earliest scholarship on Elizabethan literature; see, e.g., Halpin, *Oberon's Vision*, 60. Recent historians and new historicists, eager to separate themselves from their predecessors, nevertheless depict the queen as vain. Adams finds that "Elizabeth's notorious vanity permeated all aspects of Court life" (*Leicester and the Court*, 37). Guy, who aims to convey "the truth about the ageing Elizabeth," faults William Camden for drawing "a veil over her vanity and temper tantrums" (*Elizabeth*, 6, 1). Montrose agrees that vanity was her salient characteristic (*Subject of Elizabeth*, 232). The word "vanity," which bears distinctly feminine and

derogatory connotations, casts the queen's efforts as failures. Montrose describes de Maisse's "perceptions of the vanity and melancholy of this personage" which in "no way negate his numerous observations of her grace, vitality, and political cunning" (233). However, de Maisse never describes the efforts of the queen as vain; instead, he bears ample testimony to their success; see below.

45. Arnold, *Queen Elizabeth's Wardrobe*, 3. Arnold's findings substantiate the 1593 claim of Sir John Fortescue (the Chancellor of the Exchequer) that "'as for her apparel, it is royal and princely, beseeming her calling, but not sumptuous nor excessive'" (1). Elizabeth's average expenses during the last four years of her reign were a mere fraction of James's expenses for the first five years of his: £9535 to James's £36377 annually.

46. Strong's expression, cited by Montrose, *Subject of Elizabeth*, 222.

47. "Queen Elizabeth's First Reply to the Parliamentary Petitions," November 12, 1586, in *Elizabeth I: The Collected Works*, 186.

48. Elizabeth I, "Queen Elizabeth to Monsieur, May 14, 1582"; "Queen Elizabeth to James VI of Scotland, circa June or July 1585"; and "Queen Elizabeth to Robert Devereux, Earl of Essex, July 1597," in *Elizabeth I: The Collected Works*, 251, 262, 386.

49. Montrose, *Subject of Elizabeth*, 244. He takes the quotation from Devereux, *Lives and Letters of the Devereux*, 2:131, who cites Ralegh's *History of the World* (1614) as the source. The anecdote is reproduced in Hyde, "Difference and Disparity." Both sources were written after the occurrence of the incident they describe.

50. "Letter Exchange between Sir Robert Cecil and Robert Devereux, Earl of Essex," in *Elizabeth I: The Collected Works*, 335.

51. I phrase myself cautiously because immediate reactions are irretrievable. What I am talking about are eyewitness accounts, as provided by letters, journals, and other documents, written in the aftermath of an actual encounter with the queen (like the journal of de Maisse, discussed below).

52. Harington, *Nugae Antique*, 2:215–17.

53. Rowland Whyte to Sir Robert Sidney, August 30, 1600, in *Letters*, 529–30.

54. Montrose acknowledges the highly "subjective" nature of his collection of "slanderous, flattering, or merely curious anecdotes," which he justifies by reference to his interest in "perceptions and ideological appropriations of the Queen" (*Subject of Elizabeth*, 247). Fair enough, except that most works he cites in support of his claim that Elizabeth had become an object of contempt during her own lifetime were written after she died. Compare Bishop Goodman's sense in the 1650s that in the latter part of Elizabeth's reign "the people were very generally weary of an old woman's government" (quoted in *Court of King James I*, 1.97) to the French Ambassador's sense in 1597 that "her government is fairly pleasing to the people, who show that they love her, but it is little pleasing to the great men and nobles; and if by chance she should die, it is certain that the English would never again

NOTES TO PAGES 42–47

submit to the rule of a woman" (De Maisse, *Journal*, 11–12). De Maisse mentions the queen's gender as a source of resentment but not her age (although he does discuss her age in other contexts; see below).

55. Harington, *Nugae Antique*, 1:317.
56. Platter, *Travels*, 192. See also Arnold, *Queen Elizabeth's Wardrobe*, 11–12; and Guy, *Elizabeth*, 363, for other such testimonials from foreign visitors.
57. Richards, "Love and a Female Monarch," 158.
58. Harington, *Nugae Antique*, 1:362, 1:360, 1:167.
59. Simon Forman's dream testifies in similar fashion to the lasting allure of this "little elderly woman" capable of "talking and reasoning of many matters" (quoted in Montrose, "Shaping Fantasies," 32). Levin points out that the queen's attractiveness stems from her power in the Forman dream; clearly, the aphrodisiacal aspects of power need not benefit men only (*Dreaming*, 151). See also Hackett, "Dream-Visions," 45–66.
60. Montrose, *Subject of Elizabeth*, 232.
61. Martin, *Constituting Old Age*, 48–49.
62. De Maisse, *Journal*, 37.
63. Riehl, *Face of Queenship*, 46–47, 75–77.
64. De Maisse, *Journal*, 110, 38, 60–61, 82.
65. Machiavelli, *Prince*, 71.
66. De Maisse, *Journal*, 27.
67. Marlowe, "Elegia XIII," *Poems*, 59–60, ll.42–43.
68. "An Epilogue by Shakespeare?," in *Riverside Shakespeare*, ll.8–15.
69. Davison, *Davison's Poems*, 254. The queen's "agelessness" became a "persistent theme of late panegyric" (Hackett, "Dream-Visions," 64).
70. Ralegh, "Nature that Washt Her Hands in Milke," *Poems*, 112, ll.32–34. The concern with aging in Ralegh's poetry may respond to "the spectacle of an aging monarch" (Martin, *Constituting Old Age*, 107).
71. Spenser, *Amoretti*, 67.5; *Poetry*, 614. See also Ralegh's "Ocean to Cynthia," which dwells on its speaker's "vain thought" (129). The lover who loves in vain derives from the Petrarchan tradition. George Gascoigne was another poet who assumed the pose of the aging lover; see Laam, "Aging the Lover."
72. For these rumors, see Levin, *Heart and Stomach*, 71–90; and Robert Shephard, "Sexual Rumours," 101–22.
73. Allen, *Admonition*, xviii–xix.
74. Adams, "Dudley, Robert."
75. *Leicester's Commonwealth*, 193; Haynes and Murdin, "Confession of Arthur Guntor," 365. On Leicester vs. Hatton and Ralegh, see, e.g., Montrose, *Subject of Elizabeth*, 203; and Perry, *Literature and Favoritism*, 31. According to Perry, a distinctive contribution of *Leicester's Commonwealth* is the representation of Leicester as

221

an upstart. In fact, the charge haunted Leicester from the onset of his career; see Vanhoutte, "*Itinerarium*."
76. *Leicester's Commonwealth,* 80. The Duke of Norfolk made a similar observation earlier in the reign (MacCaffrey, *Elizabeth I,* 92).
77. Elizabeth to the Earl of Leicester, April 1586, in *Elizabeth I: The Collected Works,* 277.
78. Hatton's correspondence routinely refers to these nicknames. For example, Walsingham wrote to Hatton that the queen "feareth greatly her Mutton, lest he should take some harm amongst those disordered people" (April 23, 1579, in Harris, *Life and Times of Sir Christopher Hatton,* 115).
79. Notably, Burghley's personal relationship with the queen "was based upon trustworthiness and length of service" rather than "elaborate romantic courtesies" (Hammer, "Absolute and Sovereign Mistress," 42).
80. Elizabeth I to Lord Burghley, received May 8, 1583, in Wright, *Queen Elizabeth and Her Times,* 2:201.
81. Castiglione, *Courtier,* 165.
82. Quoted in Shephard, "Sexual Rumours," 104.
83. Naunton, *Fragmenta Regalia,* 51.
84. L'Aubespine-Chateauneuf, "Ambassade," 79. Translation mine.
85. Peck, introduction to *News,* 142. See also chapter 3.
86. One sympathetic contemporary describes Leicester's "aged bodie" at this time ("Dead Mans Right," A3r).
87. Holinshed, *Chronicles,* 1426. The work's pro-Leicestrian tendencies are evident in its inclusion of a long treatise "of the earles of Leicester by succession" (1419). See also *News.*
88. "Epitaphium," *Leicester's Commonwealth,* 292.
89. Naunton, *Fragmenta Regalia,* 51–52. The Latin phrase translates as "I came, I saw, I went back."
90. On this tract's depiction of Leicester as "some sort of sex addict or monster," see also Lake, "From *Leicester his Commonwealth,*" 143; and Perry, *Literature and Favoritism,* 27.
91. Sidney, "Defense of Leicester," 262.
92. *Leicester's Commonwealth,* 89.
93. Doran, *Monarchy and Matrimony,* 58.
94. Leicester to Elizabeth I, January 16, 1570, *Calendar of State Papers,* 198–99. On the badge's ubiquity, see also the introduction. The badge featured prominently in various entries into Dutch cities; see, e.g., *Delineatio Pompae Triumphalis* (1586).
95. Nichols, *Progresses,* 1:527.
96. In the *Letter* purportedly written by Robert Laneham describing the entertainments, initially suppressed but reprinted in 1585. See also Stephen Dickey, "Shakespeare's Mastiff Comedy," 278.

97. *Leicester's Commonwealth*, 72–73, 193.
98. Warner, *Publics and Counterpublics*, 25.
99. *Leicester's Commonwealth*, 100, 193.
100. On the tract's popularity, see Peck, introduction to *Leicester's Commonwealth*, 46–51.
101. Lake, *Bad Queen Bess?*, 127.
102. *Leicester's Commonwealth*, 187.
103. Harington, *Tract on the Succession*, 44.
104. Sidney, "Defense of Leicester," 256.
105. "Letter of Estate," 24.
106. *Discours de la Vie Abominable*, front matter. The accompanying poem identifies Leicester as the infamous bear, noted for his ferocity, his tyranny, and his luxury.
107. Camden, *Annales*, 3.288. According to Adams, Camden derived these materials from *Leicester's Commonwealth* (*Leicester and the Court*, 53–56).
108. Dickey discusses the hierarchical nature of bearbaitings as well as their noisiness ("Shakespeare's Mastiff Comedy," 263).
109. Quoted in "Dudley Bear and Ragged Staff," 68; entry dated September 7, 1588 (Galloway, *Records of Early English Drama*, 90).
110. Walsingham to the Earl of Leicester, September 29, 1584, in *Leicester's Commonwealth*, 285.
111. Proclamation 672, in Hughes and Larkin, *Tudor Royal Proclamations*, 2:506–8, 507.
112. *Leicester's Commonwealth*, 192; Sidney, "Defense of Leicester," 252–53.
113. Peck, introduction to *Leicester's Commonwealth*, 9.
114. *Leicester's Commonwealth*, 186; Warner, 69.
115. Peck, introduction to *Leicester's Commonwealth*, 7–8.
116. Privy Council to the Mayor of London, "in defense of the Earl of Leicester," June 1585, in *Leicester's Commonwealth*, 283–84.
117. Bevington, *Endymion*, 195–96n1–9. The barking wolves are mentioned repeatedly; e.g., Endymion denies being a wolf who barks at Cynthia (2.1.34). According to Pincombe, the expression "He barks at the moon that endeavours to disparage truth" was proverbial (*Plays of John Lyly*, 83).
118. See also Shakespeare, *Venus and Adonis*, 799–800.
119. Efforts to connect the play to Leicester's marriage to Lettice Knollys or Oxford's affair with Anne Vavasour are unpersuasive because these events predate the play by many years; see Bond, *Works of John Lyly*, 198; Hunter, *John Lyly*, 187; and Bevington, introduction to *Endymion*, 27. By 1588, Elizabeth had forgiven both noblemen for their amorous trespasses. Bevington proposes instead that the play refers to suspicions surrounding the Earl of Oxford's loyalties (27–35).
120. Perhaps Lyly intended *Endymion* to distance Oxford from his fellow Catholics Henry Howard and Charles Arundell, suspected of having coauthored *Leicester's Commonwealth*. Peck makes a persuasive case for Arundell's coauthorship; see his

introduction to *Leicester's Commonwealth*, 13–26. Oxford accused Howard and Arundell of treason at Leicester's behest (Peck, 19–20). On Oxford's complicated relationships with these noblemen, perhaps referenced in Endymion's dream, see also Bevington, introduction to *Endymion*, 30–32.

121. *Leicester's Commonwealth*, 75.
122. The epilogue accounts for the fact that some critics have identified Endymion with Lyly; see, e.g., Hunt, *Shakespeare's Speculative Art*, 125; or Pincombe, *Plays of John Lyly*, 77–87.
123. Sir Walter Ralegh, in his ascendancy at the time, was thirty-four in 1588. Essex was twenty-three. Leicester died later that same year.
124. The number depends on whether all the characters age along with Endymion, a subject on which there is critical disagreement.
125. Berry characterizes as "fairly comical" scholarly attempts to "fit real names to characters" (*Chastity and Power*, 116). Bevington reviews the most important arguments in his introduction to *Endymion*; examples identifying Endymion as Leicester include Halpin, *Oberon's Vision*, 49–77; and Bond, *Works of John Lyly*, 9–10 and 81–103. Although these interpretations are often excessive, it is clear to me, as it has been to most recent commentators, that Lyly invites what Dutton calls "analogic" readings (*Licensing*, xi).
126. For the old man as Burghley, see, e.g., Bennett, "Oxford and Endimion," 354–69.
127. Bond and Halpin agree on Shrewsbury; Halpin argues for Sussex and Bond for Sidney.
128. For Gabriel Harvey, see Bond, *Works of John Lyly*, 10; for Philip II, see Bevington, introduction to *Endymion*, 43.
129. For Corsites as Sir Henry Lee, see Bennett, "Oxford and Endimion," 367. Paulet was notoriously unsympathetic to his charge; for Corsites as Paulet, see Bond, *Works of John Lyly*, 10.
130. For Endymion as James IV, attempting to distance himself from Mary, Queen of Scots (Tellus), see Feuillerat, *John Lyly*, 141–90. For Endymion as Oxford, see Bennet, "Oxford and Endimion"; and Bevington, who complains about "the unsatisfactoriness of such topical readings" (introduction to *Endymion*, 27) but nonetheless proceeds to make the case for Oxford, on different grounds than Bennet's.
131. *Leicester's Commonwealth*, 89.
132. As Le Comte notes, "anyone of Elizabeth's leading courtiers might be called Endymion." He cites a passage in William Browne's *Brittania's Pastorals* (1613–16), which identifies Endymion with Ralegh, Leicester, and Essex (*Endymion in England*, 70–71). On the play's applicability to Elizabeth's courtiers, see also Dutton, *Mastering the Revels*, 65; and Hackett, "Dream-Visions," 50–51.
133. Sallie Bond, "John Lyly's *Endimion*," 189–90. This perceptive essay emphasizes aging, even though it also argues that Lyly's "approach to the drama . . . tends to remove *Endimion* from any pointed comparison with the English realm" (191).

134. Bartholomeaus, *Batman upon Bartholome*, 71.
135. Cicero, *Booke of Old Age*, 24v.
136. Castiglione, *Courtier*, 335. *Endymion*'s general debt to Castiglione is widely recognized; see Bevington, introduction to *Endymion*, 12, 15–21; Hunter, *John Lyly*, 128; and Dust, "Kiss."
137. On the various strains of the myth, see Le Comte, 1–39; Bevington, introduction to *Endymion*, 10–14; and Thomas, "Endimion and Its Sources," 35–52. My comments about Lyly's use of his sources reflect information made available by these scholars.
138. *Arden of Faversham*, 14.150–54. Tantalizingly, this passage suggests that Elizabeth I's taking of favorites might provide a model for emulation.
139. Allen, *Admonition*, xv; see also *Leicester's Commonwealth*, which repeatedly accuses Leicester of having "rise[n] and mount[ed] aloft from base lineage" (174).
140. On Lee as Endymion, see Hackett, "Dream-Visions," 64; Spenser, *Epithalamion*, 21.378–382; *Poetry*, 636.
141. On these rumors, see Levin, *Heart and Stomach*, 77–90. Although Le Comte does not mention the connection to contemporary rumors, he notes that Spenser's "apostrophe [to Cynthia] is perfectly in tune with the occasion, except for the esoteric reminder that Cynthia had been seduced with a fleece of wool" (*Endymion in England*, 42).
142. Bacon, "Endymion, or the Favourite," in *Wisdom of the Ancients*, 717–18.
143. Sullivan, *Sleep, Romance*, 74.
144. Although Adams describes Leicester as "practically" Elizabeth's "surrogate husband" ("Robert Dudley"), it might be more accurate to say that the earl functioned as a surrogate wife.
145. Shephard, *Meanings of Manhood*, 74.
146. Allen, *Admonition*, xxi.
147. Hatton to Elizabeth I, undated, in Harris, *Life and Times of Sir Christopher Hatton*, 21.
148. "A Letter from Robert, Earl of Leicester," 25. The editor, Conyers Read, argues that the letter was written to Lady Sheffield, around 1573.
149. Hatton to Leicester, July 21, 1584, in Harris, *Life and Times of Sir Christopher Hatton*, 381.
150. Leicester to Hatton, July 23, 1584, in Harris, *Life and Times of Sir Christopher Hatton*, 383.
151. This correspondence substantiates Adams's claim that faction did not play as great of a role as is sometimes assumed at the Elizabethan court (*Leicester and the Court*, 60). See also Hammer, "Absolute and Sovereign Mistress," 40–42.
152. I am grateful to Jo Carney Eldridge, whose paper "Elizabeth's Courtships and the Great Chain of Being" at the 2009 Queen Elizabeth I Society meeting first alerted me to the relevance of the queen's nicknames.
153. Sir Thomas Heneage to Hatton, December 29, 1582, in Harris, *Life and Times of Sir Christopher Hatton*, 297–98.

154. See, in contrast, Bond, who claims the "overall effect" of Lyly's style "would be to take the audience far away from the frustrations of everyday life in Elizabeth's court" ("John Lyly's *Endimion*," 192).
155. Hatton to Elizabeth I, September 19, 1580, in Harris, *Life and Times of Sir Christopher Hatton*, 158; Hatton to Elizabeth I, undated letter, in Harris, *Life and Times of Sir Christopher Hatton*, 28.
156. Dutton, *Licensing*, xi.
157. Other court writers likened the power that monarchs wield over subjects to the power that humans wield over animals. For Sidney, "the dog" who "was in his collar taught his kind" emblematized the reluctant monarchical subject (*Old Arcadia*, in *Major Works*, 42–138, ll.137–38).
158. A famous anecdote recounts that Elizabeth referred to Leicester as her lapdog, "as soon as he is seen anywhere, the people say that I am coming" (quoted in Kendall, *Robert Dudley*, 87). For the bridling metaphor, see her 1566 speech to a joint delegation of Lords and Commons, where she refers to members as "bridleless colts" who "do not know their rider's hand" (*Elizabeth I: Collected Works*, 93).
159. Ovid, *Metamorphoses*, 14.297.
160. In a related move, "*Endymion* intentionally conjures the witch" Dipsas (Neufeld, "Lyly's Chimerical Vision," 193). Audience members versed in mythology would know that Hecate, the goddess of witchcraft, invoked by Ovid's Circe and his Medea, "was identified as the third, waning face of the moon" (Berry, *Chastity and Power*, 131). Cynthia is also implicated in Endymion's enchanted sleep because "the moonwort covering the bank on which he reclines links it to the moon goddess" (Hunt, *Shakespeare's Speculative Art*, 111). On the three faces of the moon, see also Pincombe, *Plays of John Lyly*, 97–98; Purkiss, *Witch*, 186; and Hackett, *Virgin Mother*, 182–86. Although Neufeld mentions Circe, she follows Purkiss and Pincombe in identifying Medea as the classical figure most relevant to the play's depiction of its major female characters.
161. Betts, "Image of this Queene," 176.
162. Chapman, "Hymnus in Cynthiam" (1594), *Poems*, 31–45, ll.10, 494, 516–18; Hackett, "Dream-Visions," 49.
163. Gascoigne et al., *Princely Pleasures*, C5r.
164. Harington, *Nugae Antique*, 1:358–59.
165. Gascoigne et al., *Princely Pleasures*, C6r.
166. Another line that recalls Leicester's appearance as Deep Desire is Tellus's description of Endymion as a plant that "pricks" (3.1.37).
167. Neufeld, 195, 204.
168. Castiglione, *Courtier*, 339. Ralegh, "The Sheepheards Praise of his Sacred Diana," 17–18, in *Poems*, 4–5.
169. Vickers, "Diana Described," 273.

170. Ovid, *Metamorphoses*, 3.302; Golding, "Prefatory Epistle," 99. Actaeon is a recurring figure in court literature and in anticourt propaganda. *Leicester's Commonwealth* puts an interesting spin on the Actaeon myth by claiming that those who know of Leicester's perfidies cannot reveal them, since "it would have been as dangerous unto them as it was to Actaeon to have seen Diana and her maidens naked" (100). A picture of this scene was among Leicester's substantial collection displayed at Leicester House (Goldring, *Robert Dudley*, 225, 302).

171. Verstegan, *Declaration*, 30.

172. Platter, *Travels*, 195–96.

173. Bevington, introduction to *Endymion*, 18.

174. Bevington, introduction to *Endymion*, 55. Dares, in a conversation with Samias about what Eumenides has just said, refers to Geron as "the other old man" (5.1.3). Although the implication is that Eumenides is old, Bevington argues that the reference is to "Geron, the other man besides Eumenides, and who is old (as Eumenides is not; the play employs a double sense of time)" (*Endymion*, 163n3). This seems an attempt to make the evidence square with the theory. Bond suggests sensibly that having the characters age would reinforce "visually the theme of Cynthia's immutability" ("John Lyly's *Endimion*," 196). Bond is unique in pointing out that fifty-five-year-old women can be worthy objects of amorous desire (196n7).

175. Bevington, introduction to *Endymion*, 11.

176. Sullivan, *Sleep, Romance*, 17.

177. For Lettice Knollys, see Bond, *Works of John Lyly*; for Lady Sheffield, see Halpin, *Oberon's Vision*, 61; for Anne Vavasour, see Bennet, "Oxford and Endimion"; for Mary, Queen of Scots, see Berry, *Chastity and Power*, 129. Bevington takes Tellus to be an embodiment of the Catholic Church (introduction to *Endymion*, 32–33).

178. Lyly's other plays testify to his familiarity with this distinction. Allegorical readings of *Endymion* echo discussions of the queen's two bodies; see, e.g., Saccio, who writes that "Cynthia and Tellus clearly offer to Endimion higher and lower kinds of love, rapt adoration of a goddess or pursuit of ordinary earthly beauty" (*Court Comedies*, 173); or Purkiss, who writes that "Cynthia is goddess and a queen" where Tellus "is seductress and figure of the world" (*Witch*, 188).

179. Perry, *Literature and Favoritism*, 54.

180. Although Sullivan never discusses *Endymion*, the pattern here is consistent with the one he describes, where the "male hero is lulled asleep by the blandishments of a female enchantress (or her nymph)" (*Sleep, Romance*, 11).

181. Allen, *Admonition*, xxi.

182. Hackett, "Dream-Visions," 45.

183. A possibility sometimes posited by readers who identify Tellus with Anne Vavasour, who bore Oxford an illegitimate child; or with Lady Sheffield, who bore Leicester

184. an illegitimate child. Tellus discusses the picture she has made of Endymion in 4.1.1–31; see Bevington, introduction to *Endymion*, 19–20.
184. Quoted in Cressy, *Dangerous Talk*, 70–71.
185. Castiglione, *Courtier*, 350.
186. Cicero, *Booke of Old Age*, 23v-r; Purkiss, "Medea," 41. Hackett characterizes this as an "audacious" eroticized moment, "Dream-Visions," 50; however, the Neoplatonic valence of the kiss here trumps its erotic one.
187. De Villanova, *Defence of Age*, B 2v.
188. See, e.g., Grigsby, *Pestilence*, 35–44.
189. Edward Blount added the song in the 1628 edition. Whether the songs are Lyly's own or "is a matter of debate, but prevailing opinion" is that "the songs, written by Lyly himself, were copied out separately for the boy choristers and were then held back from original publication as part of the boy actors' repertory" (Bevington, introduction to *Endymion*, 2).
190. Chaucer, *Canterbury Tales*, VII.718–19. On Tophas's ancestry, see Bevington, introduction to *Endymion*, 14; and Deats, "Disarming of the Knight," 284. On Tophas, Thopas, and Spenser's *Faerie Queene*, see Pincombe, *Plays of John Lyly*, 101–105; and Hackett, "Dream-Visions," 51, 55.
191. Wyatt, "Mine Own John Poyntz," in *Complete Poems*, 186–89, ll.50–51.
192. *Leicester's Commonwealth*, 92.
193. Bevington, Introduction to *Endymion*, 14; on Lyly as a satirist, see also Berry, *Chastity and Power*, 113, 116, 130–31.
194. Fleetwood, *Itinerarium*, 31; *Endymion*, 5.2.34.
195. Hunter, *John Lyly*, 316.
196. Oddly enough, Pincombe finds Tophas "not at all a parody of Endymion" since the former is "emasculated" while the latter a "supervirile warrior" (*Plays of John Lyly*, 104).
197. "bandog, n." OED online, http://www.oed.com/view/Entry/15158 (accessed November 3, 2017).
198. Purkiss, *Witch*, 187. That Dipsas provides a reflection of Elizabeth was first put forward by Berry, who notes that the "misogynistic representations" of Dipsas and Bagoa "contaminate by their proximity the icon of Elizabeth" (*Chastity and Power*, 133). Tophas is rarely seen as a vehicle for such allegory, although Deats does note that his "descent into absurdity" lampoons Endymion's deterioration ("Disarming of the Knight," 288).
199. *Leicester's Commonwealth*, 89.
200. Cicero, *Booke of Old Age*, 51v.
201. Bevington, introduction to *Endymion*, 13.
202. Hunter, *John Lyly*, 94.
203. Bevington, introduction to *Endymion*, 58.

204. Hunter, *John Lyly*, 97. Hunter thinks Tophas was played by a boy (237) but some critics, taking references to Sir Tophas's age and stature literally, argue that an adult actor may have been used in the part (Bevington, introduction to *Endymion*, 57).
205. Halpin suggests that the epilogue, by begging for the queen's protection from "the malicious that seek to overthrow us with threats," recognizes that the powerful men at court might take exception to the play (*Oberon's Vision*, 51).
206. As Hunter memorably put it, Lyly remained in his "posture of painful supplication for the rest of his life," without obtaining the preferment that he claimed the queen had promised him (*John Lyly*, 78).While Hunter and others have cast Lyly as a "victim of fashion," Scragg proposes that he may have fallen afoul of the queen instead ("Victim of Fashion," 221).
207. Parker, *Shakespeare from the Margins*, 21, 25–26.

2. FALSTAFF AMONG THE MINIONS OF THE MOON

1. Hackett, *Shakespeare and Elizabeth*, 23–30.
2. Rowe, *Life of Mr. William Shakspear*, ix. Dennis has an earlier version of the anecdote in *Comical Gallant*, A2r.
3. Bradley, "Rejection of Falstaff," 77–78.
4. All quotations from Shakespeare are from the *Riverside Shakespeare*. There are two major exceptions to my generalization about the critical tradition: the Oldcastle controversy raises the possibility that Falstaff satirized Lord Cobham (see below), while *Merry Wives* has been linked to the Order of the Garter (e.g., Erickson, "Order of the Garter").
5. "minion, n.1 and adj.," OED online, http://www.oed.com/view/Entry/118859 (accessed March 18, 2018). The word derives from the French "mignon." It gained prominence in relation to the young men around Henry VIII (Walker, *Plays of Persuasion*, 66–72) and acquired sexual connotations in the Elizabethan period; see, e.g., Cardinal Allen's use of it, below. Shannon surveys the meanings of this word, arguing that the more negative connotations it accrued "emerge within the same time frame in which the absolutist theory of kingship underwent such expansion" (*Sovereign Amity*, 144).
6. Kastan, *Shakespeare after Theory*, 136.
7. Lyly, *Endymion*, 1.1.40; Ralegh, "Ocean to Cynthia," ll.271–73. For the moon as a symbol of constancy-in-change, see e.g., Bevington, introduction to *Endymion*, 16. The moon became the image "most closely associated" with Elizabeth during the final decade of her reign (Berry, *Chastity and Power*, 135). See also Strong, *Cult of Elizabeth*, 48.
8. *Leicester's Commonwealth*, 190–91.
9. Allen, *Copie of a Letter*, 10, 27; *Admonition*, XVIII. On the latter passage, see also Levin, *Heart and Stomach*, 80–81; and Perry, *Literature and Favoritism*, 33.

10. Machiavelli, *Prince*, 77; Blundeville, *Profitable Treatise*, D 2r-v.
11. Camden, *History*, 53.
12. Shannon, *Sovereign Amity*, 147.
13. *Briefe Discoverie*, 110.
14. *Briefe Discoverie*, 14; Perry, *Literature and Favoritism*, 4.
15. Habermas, *Structural Transformation*, 25–27.
16. De Certeau, *Writing of History*, 8.
17. "Letter of Estate," 29.
18. "Letter of Estate," 26.
19. *Leicester's Commonwealth*, 193.
20. According to Shannon, "Hal's dissimulation of *mignonnerie* raises the banner of impropriety from his very first appearance with Falstaff" (*Sovereign Amity*, 174). First-time spectators do not realize that Hal *is* dissimulating until the scene ends and a solid basis for comparison is established. Only then does Shakespeare distinguish Hal from those genuinely in the grips of favoritism.
21. *Leicester's Commonwealth*, 72–73.
22. Carlson, *Haunted Stage*, 7, 49, 46.
23. Castiglione, *Courtier*, 147.
24. *Briefe Discoverie*, 46; *Leicester's Commonwealth*, 188.
25. Berger, *Waking Trifles*, 144.
26. "Letter of Estate," 29. For Falstaff as Hal's collaborator, see Berger, *Waking Trifles*, 144–45; and "Prince's Dog," 40–73. For rumors about Leicester, see Levin, *Heart and Stomach*, 47, 71–90, and previous chapters.
27. *Leicester's Commonwealth*, 193; Warner, *Publics and Counterpublics*, 90.
28. Peck repeatedly refers to the materials about Leicester as constituting his "black legend" (introduction to *Leicester's Commonwealth*).
29. Yachnin, "Populuxe Theatre," 38–68. Levin, *Heart and Stomach*, demonstrates that gender shaped perceptions of the queen; as McLaren shows, queenship encouraged "men—and not women: the exclusion is important—to image themselves as both citizens and subjects" (*Political Culture*, 8). Feminist critiques of Jürgen Habermas's work show the bourgeois public sphere to be similarly premised on the exclusion of women; see, e.g., the essays by Fraser and Eley in Calhoun, *Habermas and the Public Sphere*. I think it no coincidence, therefore, that the gardener in *Richard II* stages "a type of politically engaged subjects" talking to a queen (Doty, *Shakespeare, Popularity*, 51); or that the "dream of the impersonal monarch" emerged during Elizabeth's reign (Perry, *Literature and Favoritism*, 9).
30. Whitney, *Early Responses*, 92. On Cleopatra, Elizabeth I, and theatricality, see Eggert, *Showing Like a Queen*, 138–39.
31. Habermas defines the public as a collection of "private persons" who participate in the "public sphere" through discussion of political issues (*Structural Transformation*,

28). Early modern scholars have tweaked this to offer a "historically grounded conception of the public sphere" (Lake and Pincus, "Rethinking the Public Sphere," 2). For how this idea pertains to early modern literature, see Perry, *Literature and Favoritism*, 3–4; Doty, *Shakespeare, Popularity*, 186–87; and Wilson and Yachnin, introduction to *Making Publics*, 5.

32. Kastan, *Shakespeare after Theory*, 123. See also Helgerson, *Forms of Nationhood*, 222–28; and Grady, *Shakespeare, Machiavelli*, 143–54. In their eagerness to find in Falstaff a "plebeian, subaltern" resistance (Grady, 151), critics often disregard evidence of Falstaff's social rank (including his fat, which marks him out as a man of leisure), or his appalling behavior as military commander. As Knowles notes, however, Falstaff clearly "belongs to the elite chivalric class" ("*1 Henry IV*," 418).

33. See, e.g., Fraser, who writes that "deliberation" is associated with men and "can serve as a mask for domination" ("Rethinking the Public Sphere," 119).

34. Camden, *Annales*, 3.287. Both descriptions suggest syphilis; however, Kendall suspects the fever resulted from malarial infection (*Robert Dudley*, 232), as does Adams ("Dudley, Robert").

35. For synchronic and diachronic forms of celebrity, see Quinn, "Celebrity," 159.

36. Perry, *Literature and Favoritism*, 24.

37. Castiglione, *Courtier*, 340.

38. On this, see also introduction and chapter 1.

39. Jonson, *Cynthia's Revels*, vol. 1 of *Works*, 4.3.94–96. The character who speaks these lines, Philautia or Self-Love, is closely associated with the queen's favorites. For more, see next chapter.

40. See Rosenberg, *Leicester*, for books; and Goldring, *Robert Dudley*, for the arts.

41. Doty, *Shakespeare, Popularity*, 189.

42. Because few play-texts survive, scholars have been unable to ascertain whether the earl used the traveling troupe to promote specific positions; "there is a strong possibility that on the one hand Leicester himself, or on the other the players and their writers, chose to present plays which supported the patron's public activities" (Gurr, "Privy Councilors," 230).

43. Maclean, "Tracking Leicester's Men," 259.

44. Jones and Stallybras, *Renaissance Clothing*, 8.

45. Entry dated September 7, 1588, Galloway, *Records of Early English Drama*, 90.

46. "Within any theatrical culture audience members typically see many of the same actors in many different productions, and they will inevitably carry some memory of those actors from production to production" (Carlson, *Haunted Stage*, 53)—and from troupe to troupe.

47. Susan Frye, *Elizabeth I*, 78. For the earl as a theatrical patron, see Maclean, "Tracking Leicester's Men," and Gurr, "Privy Councilors." For the earl's patronage and his courtship of the queen, see my "*Itinerarium*." Two descriptions of the 1575

entertainments at Kenilworth appeared in print: *The Princely Pleasures at Kenilworth* (1576), reprinted in *The Pleasauntest Workes of George Gascoigne Esquyre* (1587); and *A Letter, Whearin Part of the Entertainment unto the Queenz Maiesty, at Killingworth Castl . . . is signified* (1575), purportedly written by Robert Laneham (which contains a description of a bearbaiting). Shakespeare's *A Midsummer Night's Dream* (1595–96) and his *Twelfth Night* (1601–2) allude to the Kenilworth entertainments. On the speculations of biographical critics who place an impressionable eleven-year-old Shakespeare of prodigious memory at Kenilworth in 1575, see Belsey, *A Future for Criticism*, 47. On Gascoigne's relationship to Leicester, see Rosenberg, 166–72.

48. Gascoigne, *Noble Arte of Venerie*, 133.

49. The *Riverside* editors conjecture that Mistress Quickly makes an error in consigning Falstaff to Arthur's bosom, when she must have meant Abraham, but Falstaff is associated with Arthur elsewhere; see *2 Henry IV*, where he enters singing about "When Arthur was first in court" (2.4.33). Leicester's bear badge was an attempt to establish descent from Arthur through etymology (Arthur was thought to derive from the Welsh "Arth," meaning bear, or from the Latin Arcturus, a star in the constellation of Ursa Major). After the chance of marrying Elizabeth evaporated, Leicester continued to use Arthurian iconography; in The Hague, for example, he entered through an arch decorated with the ragged staff, which included a representation of Arthur, and which announced that "we hope he proves a second Arthur" (*Delineatio Pompae*). Holinshed includes descriptions of this entry and of the banquets with "wine in abundance" attended by Leicester (*Chronicles*, 1426). Leicester's recourse to Arthurian themes explains why the person posing as Elizabeth's illegitimate son in 1588 identified himself as Arthur Dudley; see Cressy, *Dangerous Talk*, 72.

50. Quoted in Cressy, *Dangerous Talk*, 73.

51. Nashe, *Pierce Penniless*, 69. Nashe's beast fable reproduces many features of anti-Leicestrian discourse; e.g., he endows the bear, a "hungrie usurper," with insatiable appetites, a tendency to poison enemies, and the power to "blinde" the lion "as he liste" (69–74).

52. Charnes, *Notorious Identity*, 3.

53. "Dead Mans Right," A3v.

54. The more than sixty surviving manuscripts indicate that *Leicester's Commonwealth* remained in wide circulation throughout the early modern period. Most extant copies date to the seventeenth century. Although few Elizabethan copies of this proscribed book survive, it nevertheless must have spawned an underground tradition, making "the retailing of scandalous stories about" Leicester "a national pastime" (Peck, introduction to *News*, 141).

NOTES TO PAGES 89–93

55. Perry, who examines the Jacobean tradition on Leicester, notes that these allusions form part of "mountain of evidence for the ongoing popularity of the libel" (*Literature and Favoritism*, 36). Dutton gives a persuasive account of the tendency to read analogically in *Licensing*; see also introduction.
56. "Epithaphium," *Leicester's Commonwealth*, 292, ll.5–6. This poem is sometimes attributed to Sir Walter Ralegh; see *Poems*, 120.
57. Bruster, *Question of Culture*, 81.
58. Untitled poem, in *Leicester's Commonwealth*, 293, ll.13–22.
59. According to Scott-Warren, bearbaitings may have been popular because of local pride in the breed, for which the English had long been famous ("Bear Gardens," 73–74).
60. Untitled poem, *Leicester's Commonwealth*, 293, ll.29–30.
61. *News*, 145. Further references to this treatise are included parenthetically.
62. *Briefe Discoverie*, 46, 61.
63. Warner, *Publics and Counterpublics*, 94.
64. Habermas, *Structural Transformation*, 16.
65. *Leicester's Commonwealth*, 129. *News* was inspired by this passage, which goes on to note that the earl will not be able to avoid being called to account in the next life.
66. Cicero, *Booke of Old Age*, 21v.
67. Castiglione, *Courtier*, 338.
68. Jonson, *Every Man Out*, in vol. 1 of *Works*, 3.1.410–11; Lake and Pincus, "Rethinking the Public Sphere," 6.
69. Gascoigne et al., *Princely Pleasures*, C 6r.
70. The author coyly refuses to name Leicester's paramours who "are yet liveing and may amend" (*News*, 154). The references to a gaping gulf allude to John Stubbs's notorious 1579 pamphlet of that name. Based on an earlier reference, which describes Leicester as having as great a difficulty "to winde him selfe out of the Duke of Norfolk's business as" he "had afterward to untwist [him] selfe from a lady of his name and blud" (151), Peck identifies the lady as Lady Sheffield, née Douglas Howard, cousin to Norfolk and mother to Leicester's illegitimate son Robert Dudley. Peck suggests that the reference to her nose may reflect a failed treatment for syphilis but no other sources mention Lady Sheffield's nose (*News*, 151n26). Although she was not of Norfolk's name, Elizabeth was of his "blud" (they were cousins), and she was famously "high-nosed" (Naunton, *Fragmenta Regalia*, 38). It is likely that the author wishes to call Elizabeth to mind as well as Lady Sheffield; according to the conjectures of Elizabeth's more imaginative subjects, these two ladies had literally occupied the same position vis-à-vis Leicester. Other scholars who see the fiend as a stand-in for the queen include Betts, "Image of this Queene," 155; and Montrose, *Subject of Elizabeth*, 203.
71. Privy Council to the Mayor of London, June 1585, in *Leicester's Commonwealth*, 282–84, 283.

72. Warner, *Publics and Counterpublics*, 79.
73. Verstegan, *Declaration*, 30.
74. "Dead Mans Right," A3v–A4r.
75. *Leicester's Ghost*, 25. Its modern editor reviews the evidence for dating, arguing that parts of the poem were written while Elizabeth was still alive (Williams, introduction, xiv). The charge shows up in *Leicester's Commonwealth*; see previous chapter, and "Letter of Estate," 30.
76. On the gendered aspects of the "bourgeois model of 'rational-critical debate,'" see also Warner, *Publics and Counterpublics*, 51.
77. *Leicester's Ghost*, 10.
78. Yachnin, "Populuxe Theatre," 49.
79. See Bevington, introduction to *Endymion*, 1–7. For Lyly's influence on Shakespeare, see Hunter, *John Lyly*, 298–349; and Montrose, *Purpose of Playing*, 162–68. 5.5 of *Merry Wives* riffs on scenes in *Endymion*, including the pinching of Corsites by fairies; see below.
80. See Montrose, *Purpose of Playing*, 151–78, on Titania; Levin, *Heart and Stomach*, on Olivia, 136–37; Eggert, *Showing Like a Queen*, on Gertrude and Cleopatra, 100–168; and Erickson, "Order of the Garter," on the wives of Windsor.
81. Tophas is "an important Janus-faced figure" who "looks back to Chaucer's Sir Thopas, Roister Doister, and Gascoigne's Pasiphilo and forward to Falstaff, another braggart warrior" (Deats, "Disarming of the Knight," 284).
82. Barkan, *Gods Made Flesh*, 262.
83. The name Titania was used by Ovid in reference to Diana and Circe; by the 1590s "the figure of the Fairy Queen was firmly associated with Elizabeth I" (Hackett, "Dream-Visions," 59). On the play's "bestialized eroticism," see Boehrer, "Economies of Desire," 100. Boehrer thinks about the bestiality in terms of same-sex desire, where my argument relates it to transgressive heterosexual desire instead.
84. Leicester accused Simier of relying on magic potions to sway Elizabeth; by way of retaliation, Simier informed Elizabeth of Leicester's secret marriage to Lettice Knollys; see Levin, *Heart and Stomach*, 60–61. The episode was a favorite source of gossip. The addition to the French translation of *Leicester's Commonwealth*, for example, accuses Leicester of attempting to murder Simier ("Appendix B," *Leicester's Commonwealth*, 238).
85. See Woodcock, "Fairy Queen Figure." Woodcock argues that the Lady of the Lake in the Kenilworth entertainment is a fairy queen (100). The fairy queen continued to be a favorite at court entertainments after Leicester's suit had failed, and the association with Elizabeth proved perdurable. Thomas Dekker's *The Whore of Babylon* (1607) identifies *"Titania the Fairie Queene"* as "our late Queen *Elizabeth*," for example (Hopkins, *Drama and the Succession*, 53–54).
86. Greenblatt, *Will in the World*, 46–47.

87. On this aspect of the play, see Montrose, "Shaping Fantasies," 52. For more recent takes on the play's relation to Elizabeth, see Clement, "Imperial Vot'ress"; and Hackett, "Dream-Visions," 59–61.
88. "Letter of Estate," 31.
89. Golding, "Prefatory Epistle," in Ovid, *Metamorphoses*, 405, l. 4. On the possible homage to Leicester as patron, see also my "*Itinerarium*," 99.
90. Barkan, *Gods Made Flesh*, 262.
91. Hackett, "Dream-Visions," 60. Hackett goes on to argue that while Bottom as a commoner is elevated, Titania is degraded by the experience—an accurate assessment, which points to the play's ambivalence regarding female rulers.
92. As Wilder puts it, "While parodying the player's trade socially and affectively, Bottom nonetheless comes to embody many of these traits without parody" ("Changeling Bottom," 46).
93. Dutton, *Licensing*, 34.
94. Although Grady identifies Bottom as the "privileged vessel" of the aesthetic because of his relationship with Titania, he subordinates Titania's political associations to her status as a "personification of natural fertility and its associated properties of sexuality and maternity" ("Impure Aesthetics," 287).
95. Parker, *Shakespeare from the Margins*, 22, 42.
96. Montrose, "Shaping Fantasies," 32.
97. Barkan, *Gods Made Flesh*, 261.
98. Bacon, "Endymion, or the Favourite," *Wisdom of the Ancients*, 717. See also chapter 1.
99. *Leicester's Commonwealth*, 191; Verstegan, *Declaration*, 53.
100. Worden asserts that, with the exception of Wolsey in *Henry VIII*, "there are no favourites with major parts in Shakespeare" ("Favourites," 171). Perry briefly discusses Falstaff, but without noting specific allusions (*Literature and Favoritism*, 7–8). MacFaul includes a longer discussion of Falstaff, in which he casts Falstaff as a "scapegoat for the prince's sins" ("Kingdom with my Friend," 63).
101. John Pole, describing Leicester, quoted in Robert Shephard, "Sexual Rumours," 104; see previous chapter.
102. Carlson, citing Herbert Blau, *Haunted Stage*, 1.
103. According to an old tale, the queen intervened on Cobham's behalf. See Richard James, "Epistle-Dedicatory," 143; and Rowe, *Life of Mr. William Shakspear*, ix. Taylor's reconstruction of the circumstances "lend[s] . . . plausibility" to this tradition ("William Shakespeare," 352); see also Kastan, *Shakespeare after Theory*, 93–94. As Dutton points out, however, "it is possible that the Cobhams intervened as and when they did, not simply out of family pique, but because the fat knight had immediate and uncomfortable political connotations" (*Mastering the Revels*, 10).
104. Prologue to *Sir John Oldcastle* (1600), A2r.

105. Traub points out the name could also refer to castration, an equally apt association (*Desire and Anxiety*, 57).
106. *Briefe Discoverie*, 49.
107. For accusations of treason see, e.g., *Leicester's Commonwealth*, 73; and "Letter of Estate," 25. Both men served as generals.
108. The 1587 edition of Holinshed's *Chronicles* parallels the Cobhams and the Dudleys; a genealogical treatise on the Earls of Leicester is followed by a similar treatise on the Lords Cobham, which includes a Latin poem on Sir John Oldcastle, 1424–1505. The material on Leicester was cut from later editions. The woodcut appears in Foxe, *Actes and Monuments*, 592.
109. Poole, "Saints Alive!" 54, 64; Verstegan, *Declaration*, 53; "Letter of Estate," 31. There's substantial overlap between the Marprelate controversy and the earlier controversy about Leicester (Lyly contributed works to both). "Letter of Estate" reproduces the association with Bacchus, 31. *News* claims that Leicester was "so greate a student of *Baccus*" that he thought there would be "quaffing in heaven as there is in Flanders" (148). For a recent account of Falstaff's connection to Oldcastle and to the Marprelate controversy, see Jensen, *Religion and Revelry*, 153–56.
110. Sidney, "Defense of Leicester," 256; see also previous chapter.
111. Nashe picks up the infernal themes in his description of Leicester as "a right earthly divell" (*Pierce Penniless*, 81).
112. *Leicester's Commonwealth*, 89.
113. Sidney to Sir Francis Walsingham, March 24, 1586, *Prose Works*, 3:167.
114. See Baldwin, *Organization and Personnel*, 241–43, on Kempe as Bottom. Although earlier scholars proposed other actors, including Thomas Pope, for the part of Falstaff (Baldwin, 229–32), Wiles's argument that "Falstaff was written for Kemp" is now broadly accepted (*Shakespeare's Clown*, 120). The similarities between Bottom and Falstaff lend weight to Wiles's argument, since "playwrights . . . specifically created and designated parts suited to the particular range and talents of individual actors" (Stern and Palfrey, *Shakespeare in Parts*, 41). We do not have a birthdate for Kempe, who began his theatrical career in the early 1580s (Butler, "Kemp, William").
115. The earl's alleged fondness for drink was linked to his residency in the Netherlands—unfairly so, according to Adams ("Dudley, Robert"). For Kempe's biography, see Butler, "Kemp, William"; and Wiles, *Shakespeare's Clown*, 24–42.
116. Hornback, *English Clown*, 5, 132–34.
117. Jones and Stallybras, *Renaissance Clothing*, 2–3.
118. Wotton to Sir Edmund Bacon, July 6, 1613, *Life and Letters of Sir Henry Wotton*, 2:32–33. Roland Whyte describes a now lost play, *The Overthrow of Turnhout*, which depicted several living gentlemen and in which the actor who played Sir Francis Vere "got a beard resembling his, and a watchet satin doublet with hose trimmed with silver lace" (Whyte to Robert Sidney, October 26, 1599, *Letters*,

362–63). Jones and Stallybras discuss Middleton's *Game of Chess*, in which the actor playing Gondomar had obtained the Spanish Ambassador's cast-off clothing (*Renaissance Clothing*, 196).

119. So many lines refer to Falstaff's sweat staining his shirt that Shakespeare may have meant for it to become stained (Wiles, *Shakespeare's Clown*, 124).
120. Kempe may have had other garments associated with Leicester in his possession; according to Platter, English actors were "most expensively and elaborately costumed" because "eminent lords or Knights at their decease" bequeathed clothes to servants, who sold them to actors (*Travels*, 167).
121. See also, e.g., *Leicester's Commonwealth*, which describes the earl as among the "cunning practitioners in the art of dissimulation" (132).
122. Chambers and Greg, *Dramatic Records*, 2:262–63.
123. Allen, *Admonition*, xviii.
124. On Tarleton's connection to Leicester, see Wiles, *Shakespeare's Clown*, 12; and Billington, *Social History*, 35.
125. See, e.g., Whitney, *Early Responses*, 81; and Bevington, introduction to *Henry IV, Part I*, 32.
126. My argument thus explains why Falstaff is so eager to prove that "being old and fat is no natural bar" to his desires, and why Shakespeare collapses "the characteristics of the clown with those of the courtly wit" (Ellis, *Shakespeare's Practical Jokes*, 86–89).
127. Entry dated September 7, 1588, Galloway, *Records of Early English Drama*, 90. See also previous chapter.
128. Roach, *Cities of the Dead*, 78.
129. Berger, *Waking Trifles*, 134–35.
130. As Wilson and Yachnin note, "the idea of 'the public' or 'the world' motivates public making" by promising "boundlessness or even immortality" (introduction to *Making Publics*, 5). On the leveling effects of "embodied writing," see Bruster, *Question of Culture*, 80–81.
131. Hobbes, *On Human Nature*, IX.13, 46; Gosson, *Plays Confuted*, C8v–D1r.
132. Warner, *Publics and Counterpublics*, 69.
133. Freedman, "Falstaff's Punishment," 165.
134. Dutton, *Licensing*, 30–38.
135. See also Rackin, *Stages of History*, who describes this moment in terms of the players deferring to "the present realities of female power and authority that hovered at the margins of their historical stages" (147).
136. Whitney, *Early Responses*, 71–111.
137. Rackin gives the classic account of Wales as a place of "female enchantment" (*Stages of History*, 171–76).
138. Sullivan, *Sleep, Romance*, 82. Sullivan describes the Welsh lady and Lady Hotspur as a Circean figures (72–80). Berger reviews the reasons that Falstaff's lines here

might refer to Hal ("Prince's Dog," 43–44). Falstaff, not Hal, "has a passion for friendship, a tendency to be 'bewitched'" (Shannon, *Sovereign Amity*, 171).

139. On idleness, effeminacy, and bestiality as characteristic of Circe's victims, see Brodwin, "Milton and the Renaissance Circe." The dispersal and regendering of the Circe myth in *1 Henry IV* helps account for the ambivalent sexuality and gendering of Falstaff (and, I would argue, Hal) noted by critics like Parker, *Shakespeare from the Margins*, 21–23; and Traub, *Desire and Anxiety*, 50–70.

140. Cicero, *Booke of Old Age*, 21v-22r.

141. According to Bradley, "all competent estimates" involve separating "the real Falstaff" from the "degraded" one "befooled" by women ("Rejection of Falstaff," 78). Even critics skeptical of Bradley's assumptions have confirmed his judgment by ignoring *Merry Wives*. As Rackin demonstrates, "From Maurice Morgan to Harold Bloom, male critics have fallen in love with the Falstaff of the history plays and identified with him," while they have rejected *Merry Wives*, because "Falstaff's humiliations are devised by women" (*Shakespeare and Women*, 67–68). The result, Rackin shows, has been a critical tradition that labels the Falstaff from *Merry Wives* an "impostor" (68), a position against which my argument advocates.

142. Erickson, "Order of the Garter," 119, 130. I do not believe, as Erickson does, that *Merry Wives* is a court play that "favors aristocratic interests" (124); rather, I agree (albeit for different reasons) with Freedman that it was written for the public stage ("Shakespearean Chronology"). The quote from Auden is from "Prince's Dog," 157–58. Falstaff's age situates him as a contemporary of Elizabeth and Leicester, both born in 1533.

143. Ralegh had gone in person. Leicester sponsored others to go in his place. The *Galleon Leicester* participated in the ill-fated Fenton expedition in 1582, for example (Adams, "Robert Dudley"). Fenton is the name of Ann Page's courtly suitor in *Merry Wives*.

144. The licenses and monopolies that the queen awarded her favorites were a source of incessant grumbling; see *Leicester's Commonwealth*, 96; and "Letter of Estate," 31.

145. Falstaff's association with animals is well established; see, e.g., Sullivan, *Sleep, Romance*, 85; and Traub, *Desire and Anxiety*, 56–57. In the space of one scene Hal refers to Falstaff as a "dog," an "old boar," and a "town bull" (*2 Henry IV*, 2.2.107, 146, 158).

146. Kegl argues the "'abominable terms' promote collective identities" in this play ("Adoption," 254).

147. Golding, "Prefatory Epistle," 405, 408. On Actaeon and Elizabeth, see, e.g., Berry, *Chastity and Power*, 28–29, 99, 137–38; Dutton, *Mastering the Revels*, 133–34; and previous chapter. On Falstaff and Actaeon, see Steadman, "Falstaff as Actaeon," and Barkan, *Gods Made Flesh*, 281–82.

148. Privy Council Letter to the Mayor of London, June 1585, in *Leicester's Commonwealth*, 282–84.
149. On the Garter and its origins see, e.g., Platter, *Travels*, 207.
150. Holinshed immortalized Leicester's ostentatious celebration of the Garter Feast during his stay in the Netherlands (*Chronicles*, 1433). Hunt describes the associations of the Order in relation to the motto's retributive properties ("The Garter Motto," 383–406).
151. Jonson, "To the Memory of my Beloved, the Author Mr. William Shakespeare," in *Riverside Shakespeare*, 97, l.29.
152. According to Camden and others, this is what Leicester did in the Netherlands (*Annales*, 214).
153. *Leicester's Commonwealth*, 73.
154. "Letter of Estate," 24.
155. Sullivan, *Sleep, Romance*, 82. Sullivan's language recalls Traub's argument about Falstaff as a fantasized mother figure rejected by Hal in his bid for male subjectivity. Where Traub sees Hal as a "'prototypical' male subject" (*Desire and Anxiety*, 51), I think his political status as a prince dominates Shakespeare's representation. Traub's argument leads her to liken Falstaff to Elizabeth I (69–70), where I think we are supposed to compare the queen to Hal.
156. Doty, *Shakespeare, Popularity*, 83.
157. For Fluellen's comparatives as a parodic reflection of humanist historiography, see Rackin, *Stages of History*, 239–40. Fluellen does not seem to remember Falstaff's name, a fact that Rackin attributes to Falstaff having "acquired the impotence (fall-staff) of fiction" along with its "license" (240).
158. De Certeau, *Writing of History*, 8.
159. The indeterminacy about who plays the Fairy Queen, or the incongruity of Mistress Quickly playing the Fairy Queen, highlight this act of usurpation. We are meant to think of Elizabeth but the relation is one of likeness rather than of identity, as critics like Helgerson assume (*Adulterous Alliances*, 72).
160. Rackin, *Stages of History*, 138.
161. Prologue to *Sir John Oldcastle*, A2r.
162. Quoted in Whitney, *Early Responses*, 74. Whitney cites Hotson in supposing the reference is to Henry Brooke, Lord Cobham (74–75).
163. Rowe, *Life of Mr. William Shakspear*, XVIII.
164. Whitney notes that a central question raised by the early reception of this character is "how a satiric butt came to release so many positive reactions and sympathetic applications" (*Early Responses*, 73). For every reader who applauds the wisdom of Hal's decision, another derides its callowness; see, e.g., Bradley, "Rejection of Falstaff"; Kastan, *Shakespeare after Theory*, 145; and Helgerson, *Forms of Nationhood*,

227. Hunter reviews arguments on either side ("Shakespeare's Politics"), as does Crewe ("*2 Henry IV*: A Critical History," 433–50).

165. The "inexhaustible" qualities of Falstaff, his "resistance to closure," are key to "the character's enduring popularity" (Whitney, *Early Responses*, 70–71).

3. REMEMBERING OLD BOYS IN *TWELFTH NIGHT*

1. Shaw, "Better than Shakespeare?," xxviii.
2. Whitney, *Early Responses*, 71–111.
3. Jonson, *Every Man Out*, 3.1.23. Further parenthetic references to Jonson's plays are to vol. 1 of *Works*. Falstaff describes himself as an "apple-john" (*1 Henry IV*, 3.3.4). There are continuities as well between *Merry Wives* and *Every Man in His Humour* (1598); see McDonald, *Shakespeare and Jonson*, 31–55.
4. The Cambridge editors point out that *Every Man Out* obsessively refers to the Falstaff plays, especially *Merry Wives* (1:240); on the *Henriad*, see also Gras, "*Twelfth Night*," 547. Shift further resembles Falstaff in having a "shift of names," in plying his trade at Paul's, and in being associated with dirty shirts (3.1.7–10). On the censoring, see Clare, "Comical Satires," 34; and Dutton, *Mastering the Revels*, 136–37. Jonson erred in identifying the actor as Elizabeth rather than featuring a substitute as Lyly and Shakespeare had; "to represent the Queen theatrically could only draw attention to the discrepancies between images of immortality and perpetual youth and the reality of the Queen's old age" (Clare, 35).
5. Carlson, *Haunted Stage*, 26.
6. The connection between this passage in *Every Man Out* and the plot of *Twelfth Night* is often noted; see Clare, "Comical Satires," 33; and Bednarz, *Poets' War*, 180. Although little consensus exists about what the connection signifies (Gras, "*Twelfth Night*," 545), most critics agree that *Twelfth Night* has an oppositional relation to Jonson's comedies (Bednarz, 180–81; Leonard, "Shakespeare and Jonson Again," 45–69).
7. McDonald, *Shakespeare and Jonson*, 1–16. McDonald proposes Shakespeare's and Jonson's plays exist on a "sliding scale," with Jonson's "most satiric" and Shakespeare's "most romantic" comedy at either end (55).
8. Hunter, "English Folly," 85. Bednarz's claim that Shakespeare's "most radical closural variation before 1599" on comic form is in *Love's Labor's Lost* (*Poets' War*, 63) disregards the ending of *Merry Wives*, in which Falstaff is exposed and his romantic plots foiled. On the "nearly satirical" effect of *Merry Wives*, see also Bevington, "Shakespeare vs. Jonson," 114.
9. Jensen, *Religion and Revelry*, 20.
10. Kerrigan discusses the relation between gossip and social structure, "Secrecy and Gossip in *Twelfth Night*."
11. Middleton, *Microcynicon*, in *Works*, 1974. For the "violent literary fantasies" that characterized the wars of the theatres, see Bruster, *Question of Culture*, 65–93.

12. Dickey, "Shakespeare's Mastiff Comedy," 262. On *Twelfth Night*'s bearbaiting references, see also Berry, "*Twelfth Night*," who argues that the "subliminal metaphor" figures the audience as spectators and Malvolio as the bear (118); and Scott-Warren, who finds that "the sports of baiting and playing occupied homologous social positions" ("Bear Gardens," 64).
13. Bruster, *Question of Culture*, 80–82.
14. Markham to Harington, in Harington, *Nugae Antique*, 1:240.
15. Harington, *Ajax*, 171.
16. *Leicester's Commonwealth*, 192; Peck, introduction to *Leicester's Commonwealth*, 19.
17. Harington, *Ajax*, 70. According to Donno, Harington's satire is so obscure as to make identifications difficult (introduction to *Ajax*, 21). The scandal caused by the pamphlet indicates that contemporaries were able to identify Harington's targets, however, and Scott-Warren persuasively takes this reference to Leicester as the "Beare" to be the source of the queen's disfavor ("Harington, Sir John"). Harington refers to "Sarcotheos" (72) when describing Ajax's pedigree—Donno attributes this name to Harington's coinage but Sarcotheos is also Leicester's companion in the anonymous satire *News from Heaven and Hell* (see chapter 2). In a section decrying courtly pride Harington also takes a jab at "close stools" dressed in "fugered satin and velvet" (111). Leicester was a fan of these luxurious conveniences; see Donno, 111n5; and Adlard, *Amye Robsart*, 243.
18. Fiedler, "Eros and Thanatos," 238.
19. Lyly, *Endymion*, 1.1.5–7. All references are to this edition.
20. Castiglione, *Courtier*, 145. See below for some examples of "deformity" used in this manner.
21. According to Jensen, "Falstaff's siege on the marital, sexual, and economic values of Windsor ... are punished in the same way [as] Malvolio's attack on 'cakes and ale'" (*Religion and Revelry*, 158). Given the similarities, however, these characters may suffer for the same crime.
22. Barber, *Shakespeare's Festive Comedy*, 247.
23. On Malvolio's madness and class, see Kamps, "Madness and Social Mobility."
24. According to this false etymology, the word "satire" derives from *sat irae*, meaning "full of anger" (Gurr, *Playgoing*, 159).
25. On Jonson's medicinal views of satire, see, e.g., Craik and Pollard, "Imagining Audiences," 13.

Bruster identifies this phenomenon with the Martin Marprelate controversy but, as I argued in the previous chapter, the kerfuffle about Leicester created the same "abusive, flyting atmosphere" (68). Scott-Warren notes that "although nobody has ever proved that Malvolio or Morose represented real individuals, they are clearly embedded in the satirical culture" that Bruster describes ("Bear-Gardens," 80n50).

26. Boym, *Future of Nostalgia*, 41, 13. Boym sees nostalgia as a modern phenomenon; however, she also explores its roots in Renaissance melancholy, and cites *Hamlet* and Robert Burton's *Anatomy of Melancholy* (5). Although the word "nostalgia" was not coined until later in the seventeenth century, "the feeling of nostalgia was voiced" in many early modern texts (Karremann, "Passion for the Past," 152). Mullaney identifies a "sadness" closely related to nostalgia, "a kind of homesickness in reverse," as one of the unintended consequences of the Protestant Reformation (*Reformation*, 31).
27. Critics apply these adjectives repeatedly to the play; see Schiffer, "Taking the Long View."
28. Boym, *Future of Nostalgia*, 54.
29. Malcolmson, "What You Will," 166. See also Jensen, who argues that Feste and Toby are "complementary" (*Religion and Revelry*, 177); and Hollander, who sees Viola and Sir Andrew as analogues ("Morality of Indulgence," 233).
30. On Malvolio and Orsino as baited bears, see Dickey, "Shakespeare's Mastiff Comedy"; and Scott-Warren, "Bear-Gardens," 66. That *Twelfth Night* focuses on eroticized forms of social mobility is a commonplace; see, e.g., Malcolmson, "What You Will"; and Schalkwyck, "Love and Service."
31. In this context, Peter Smith describes the "linguistic essentialism" that informed early modern attitudes towards names and anagrams ("Alphabetical Position," 1211).
32. Malcolmson, "What You Will," 171. On the significance of names, see also Arlidge, *Prince of Love*, 85–95.
33. Plato, *Symposium*, 30–31.
34. See the epigraph and dedication of Shakespeare's *Venus and Adonis*, 1799.
35. Schiffer, "Taking the Long View," 9. Critics who link Sir Toby to Falstaff include Jensen, *Religion and Revelry*; Barber, *Shakespeare's Festive Comedy*, 249–50; Barton, "Sense of an Ending," 107–8; and Arlidge, *Prince of Love*, 89.
36. Jensen, *Religion and Revelry*, 160.
37. *News*, 157.
38. See, e.g., *Endymion, Cynthia's Revels*, or *Every Man Out*, where the courtier Fastidious Brisk dreams of being "graced" by court ladies (2.3.231).
39. Greenblatt contends "this was a career that Elizabeth herself, let alone her male subjects, could not tolerate in any woman of lesser station" (*Shakespearean Negotiations*, 69). On Olivia's use of miniatures, see Levin, *Heart and Stomach*, 134. Hotson, who speculates that Elizabeth I commissioned *Twelfth Night* to entertain Duke Bracciano in 1601, claims that Orsino represents the Italian duke, while Olivia is "a romanticized and youthful shadow" of the queen (*First Night*, 121). The portrait of Olivia is not an entirely flattering one, however; see below. Other critics have noted the analogy with the queen (e.g., Suzuki, "Gender," 141).

40. Hotson, *First Night*, 126. Notably, in Emanuel Forde's *The First Part of Parismus the Renowmed Prince of Bohemia*, one possible source for *Twelfth Night*, the character named Olivia is a middle-aged queen; see Staniyuković, "Masculine Plots," 116.
41. Tennenhouse, "Power on Display," argues that "the absence of desire in Olivia is tantamount to political disruption" (85), with evident topical applications in late Elizabethan England.
42. In Peele's *Arraygnment of Paris*, Diana describes England and Elizabeth: "The place Elyzium hight, and of the place / Her name that governs there Eliza is" (5.1.67–68). The pun was still current at the time of Elizabeth's death; see Petowe, who finds that "sweet Eliza in Elizium lives, / In joy beyond all thought" (*Elizabetha quasi vivens*, A 4r).
43. Levin, *Heart and Stomach*, 136.
44. On Orsino and the Actaeon myth, see also Smith, "Alphabetical Position," 214–15, and Dickey, "Shakespeare's Mastiff Comedy," 274. Hotson points out the parallels between Orsino's rhetoric and Ralegh's *First Night* (125).
45. Blundeville, *Profitable Treatise*, title page.
46. According to one witness, the entertainment caused all manner of analogic readings, and the disgruntled queen "said that if she had thought there had been so much said of her, she would not have been there that night" (Rowland Whyte to Robert Sidney, November 22, 1595, *Letters*, 88). A marginal note Bacon wrote explains to Essex that it was "the Queen's unkind dealing, which may persuade you to self-love" (Guy, *Elizabeth*, 255).
47. "Letter of Estate," 31. *Cynthia's Revels* extends a pattern also evident in *Every Man Out*; indeed, Jonson's appropriation of Lyly's allegory might have been a consequence of the negative reactions to the earlier play (Dutton, *Mastering the Revels*, 132). "Actaeon" is usually read as Essex; see, e.g., Clare, "Comical Satires," 39; and Dutton, 133. The fountain may refer to the one at Nonesuch palace, which depicted Actaeon's fate as a warning against "the fruits of an evil mind and an evil spirit" (Platter, *Travels*, 196). See also chapter 1.
48. Boym, *Future of Nostalgia*, 8.
49. Laneham, *Letter*, 42. Since the nineteenth century, the captain's line has been identified as an allusion to Kenilworth. Belsey disputes the allusion, chiefly because Greenblatt and other biographical critics have speculated that the eleven-year-old Shakespeare attended the entertainments in 1575 (*Future for Criticism*, 47). As I note in the previous chapter, however, Shakespeare need not have a prodigious memory to refer to the Kenilworth dolphin, since the accounts of the Kenilworth entertainments were reprinted in the mid-80s.
50. Ralegh, "Cynthia," 23.10, in *Poems*, 46.
51. Allen, *Admonition*, xxi.
52. Greville, *Sir Philip Sidney*, 183.

53. Paster, *Body Embarrassed*, 33.
54. Callaghan, "Body Politics," 140. On Olivia's humiliation, see also Paster, *Body Embarrassed*, 30–34.
55. *News*, 155.
56. Malvolio is frequently identified with Jonson's satires; see Hollander, "Morality of Indulgence"; Malcolmson, "What You Will," 182; and Bevington, "Shakespeare vs. Jonson."
57. "This was how . . . Hatton had first attracted the Queen's attention" (Clare, "Comical Satires," 40).
58. The song "Ah, Robin" is attributed to Sir Thomas Wyatt; see *Poems*, CXXXIX, 175–76. Others have connected Feste's alias to Lyly's play but without being able to make much of it. So Arlidge notes only that both *Twelfth Night* and *Endymion* link "love and misrule" (*Prince of Love*, 14). Jensen argues that "Maister Parson," the title given "Sir Topas," alludes to the "bad" Sir John in *Sir John Oldcastle* and "should be seen as a theatrical in-joke that signals this scene's return to the earlier Oldcastle controversy" (*Religion and Revelry*, 164).
59. Knox, *First Blast of the Trumpet*, 11.
60. Smith notes Malvolio's resemblance to Bottom but not to the other two characters ("Alphabetical Position," 1213).
61. Sidney, *Defence of Poesy*, 245.
62. "The Ballad of Constant Susanna" (1624); see also Hotson, the only critic to have noted that Malvolio is repeatedly teased about his age (*First Night*, 100–111). Hotson proposes that Shakespeare satirizes the elderly Sir William Knollys, the Controller of the Royal Household—one of five royal offices that came with a staff—for having made a fool of himself over a maid of honor (103–8). I think another surfeiting old man the better candidate. Notably Sir Toby sings snatches from the ballad "Three Merry Men We Be," in which Robin and Arthur—two names associated with Leicester—beat one another with "a Staff of another Oakgraff." Knollys had a pattern of falling for much younger women; however, the young women who captured his interests had no power to advance his career. He could and did rely for that purpose on his blood-ties to Elizabeth. As Leicester's brother-in-law and Essex's uncle, Knollys might well have been associated with the phenomenon of royal favoritism. Leicester married Knollys's sister Lettice in 1578. Knollys and Leicester were friends and allies; Leicester had knighted his brother-in-law in 1586 during the ill-fated campaign in the Netherlands. See Stater, "Knollys, William." Hotson's argument about Knollys rests in part on his belief that the play was commissioned for a court performance, a position few other critics or editors have accepted.
63. Cicero, *Booke of Old Age*, 43r; Castiglione, *Courtier*, 334. Cicero writes about such old men that their "service" is better than young men's, since "matters of great

waight, are not done wyth bodily strength, nimbleness, celeritie . . . but wythe counsaile, wisedome, authoritie and pollicie" (11r).

64. Castiglione, *Courtier*, 334. Petrarch subscribed to similar beliefs (*Secret*, 130–31).
65. See, e.g., Callaghan, who deems that stockings are "incongruous" because Malvolio is a servant wearing the costume of a gentleman ("Body Politics," 136). While the saffron used for yellow dye was indeed a luxury associated with court fashions (Jonson's courtiers wear yellow garments), Malvolio is a "gentleman" in his own right (4.2.82, 5.1.280). Jonson's Philautia wears yellow, so it may have been associated with self-love more specifically. Jones and Stallybras demonstrate attacks on yellow clothes featured prominently in anticourt polemics later in the seventeenth century (*Renaissance Clothing*, 67). On the associations of Malvolio's stockings, see also Linthicum, "Cross-gartered Yelllow Stockings." Schalkwyck argues persuasively that Malvolio and Cesario may be "of equal rank," and that stewards, who "occupied critical positions of authority and trust" could "be drawn from the yeomanry, the lesser gentry, and in some case the upper gentry" ("Love and Service," 87). For Malvolio as a gentleman, see also Berry, who notes that there are "twenty-two references to 'gentleman', more than any other play in the canon. . . . And all sixteen of the references that precede Malvolio's are to Cesario" ("*Twelfth Night*," 116n10). Some critics think Orsino's reference to Sebastian's "right noble" blood suggest a higher rank (5.1.264); see Kamps, "Madness and Social Mobility," 240; and Greenblatt, *Shakespearean Negotiations*, 71–72. This ambiguous reference cannot much alter an impression created over the four previous acts, however, nor are Viola, Sebastian, or their father ever identified by title.
66. Elyot, *Castel of Helthe*, 41. The medical definition of "obstruction" was dominant in the sixteenth century; see "obstruction, n.," OED online, http://www.oed.com/view/Entry/129985 (accessed March 24, 2018), where all examples prior to this one are drawn from discussions of health or diet.
67. An equivalent comic effect might be obtained in a modern-dress production by having Olivia's steward dressed in tight bell-bottoms.
68. A director "who elects, as Bill Alexander did in the 1987–88 RSC staging of the play, to chain Malvolio (Anthony Sher) to a stake during the dark-house scene is likely to be chided" even though "the connection is powerfully supported by the evidence of one early 'reading' of *Twelfth Night*," Ben Jonson's *Epicene* (Scott-Warren, "Bear-Gardens," 66). Notably, the baiting metaphors in *Epicene* involve Mrs. Otter and her husband, and reproduce the gendered pattern that I have identified. Insofar as Mrs. Otter insists on treating her husband as her subject, and on being herself called a princess, she is modeling her relationship on that of Elizabeth I and her favorites.
69. Cicero, *Booke of Old Age*, 22r.

70. Dickey notes the association with bears, "Shakespeare's Mastiff Comedy," 268. For works that made comic capital of Leicester's position as Lord Steward, see previous chapter.
71. *Leicester's Commonwealth*, 93.
72. As Kamps observes, "The Lady of the Strachy has never been successfully linked to a historical person, but it is clear in the context of the play she is supposed to be a real person, suggesting that Malvolio's mad desire is already a historical reality" ("Madness and Social Mobility," 237). Although no direct source has been found for the Malvolio plot, critics often speculate that he is "modeled on a real person" (Schiffer, "Taking the Long View," 9). Hopkins finds that "*Twelfth Night* has a number of references" to Elizabeth's court, which "despite many attempts to elucidate them, remain entirely opaque to us" (*Drama and the Succession*, 102). She includes the possible allusion to the ring given by the queen to Essex and the famous anecdote about the queen's desire for a dog (5.1.6–8). Hopkins thinks that Malvolio's being a steward refers to the Stuart succesion (105). Interestingly, Malvolio has also been seen both as a representation of Shakespeare himself (Greenblatt, *Will in the World*, 82–83), and as Shakespeare's representation of Jonson (Riggs, *Ben Jonson*, 84).
73. *Leicester's Commonwealth*, 131; Hotson, *First Night*, 126.
74. Smith, "Alphabetical Position," 1220.
75. Harington, *Ajax*, 162. This passage, too, might have occasioned the queen's displeasure.
76. Paster, *Body Embarrassed*, 32. Paster cites Harington in her analysis of this scene, but without noting the possible allusions to the pamphlet in the play.
77. Harington, *Ajax*, 61–62.
78. Arlidge and Gras argue the play was commissioned for the Middle Temple performance, a proposition that Harbage had previously rejected because we have no evidence of professional companies being commissioned in this manner (*Rival Traditions*, 116). As Gras points out, though, to say that "that *Twelfth Night* was written for performance at Middle Temple is not to say that the play was written only for that purpose" ("*Twelfth Night*," 546). That the Templars' taste for satire extended to plays is attested to by Jonson's dedication of *Every Man Out* to the "Noblest Nurseries of Humanity and Liberty in the Kingdom, The Inns of Court" (appendix D to *Every Man Out*, *Works*, 1:427). Jonson adapted aspects of verse satire to the stage in the wake of the Bishop's ban (Dutton, "Jonson's Satiric Styles," 59).
79. Betts, "Image of this Queene," 162. According to Hunt, all early modern pornography contained elements of political satire (*Invention of Pornography*, 11).
80. There has been some debate about whether the ban aimed to suppress satire or pornography, with McCabe making an argument for the former ("Elizabethan Satire"), and Boose arguing the latter position ("Bishops' Ban"). Boose makes a compelling case that the censorship of Gascoigne's *A Hundreth Sundrie Flowers* (1573) set a precedent for the 1599 ban; what the authorities objected to was the

dissemination "to a mass readership" of a book that "sexualized" the "politics of courtly discourse" (191).
81. Bruster, *Question of Culture*, 92.
82. On *Twelfth Night*'s use of legal terminology and the reference to the windows, see Akrigg, "Middle Temple"; and Arlidge, *Prince of Love*, 26–27, 37–40.
83. Arlidge, *Prince of Love*, 47.
84. On Dudley and *Gorboduc*, see, e.g., Axton, *Queen's Two Bodies*, 39–45; Jones and White, "Gorboduc,"; Vanhoutte, *Strange Communion*, 111–34; and Astington, *Actors and Acting*, 70–71. The Revels Prince at the Inner Temple was the "Prince of Sophie," which helps make sense of Fabian's comment that "I will not give up my part of this sport for a pension of thousands to be paid from the Sophy" (2.5.179–80; Arlidge, *Prince of Love*, 58–61). On Hatton, see MacCaffrey, "Hatton, Sir Christopher." Hatton participated in several festivities for the queen put on at the Inner Temple, and may have coauthored another tragedy put on for the queen (*Tancred and Gismund* [1568]).
85. *Every Man Out* may have been performed at the Middle Temple in 1598–99; like *Twelfth Night*, it makes use of material—including the device of the fake letter—from the Middle Temple revels of 1597–98 (Gras, "*Twelfth Night*," 552–54). On Ralegh, see Nicholls and Williams, "Ralegh, Sir Walter"; Guy, *Elizabeth*, 74; and Arlidge, *Prince of Love*, 71, 83–84. According to Guy, traditionally Elizabeth had first Leicester and then Essex sit next to her at Twelfth Night festivities (268).
86. Arlidge, *Prince of Love*, 6.
87. Privy Council to the Mayor of London, June 1585, in *Leicester's Commonwealth*, 283.
88. As Clare notes, Jonson's disclaimer "contradicts the initial boast of Asper that he would expose the follies of the time" ("Comical Satires," 32).
89. Paster, *Body Embarrassed*, 34. On Olivia as the "real threat to the hierarchical gender system," see also Howard, "Crossdressing," 43.
90. Berry, "*Twelfth Night*," 111–12. See also Hollander, "Morality of Indulgence," 222.
91. Barton, "Sense of an Ending," 110.
92. *Riverside Shakespeare*, 444n73.
93. Petrarch, *Secret*, 131; Shahar, *Growing Old*, 64.
94. Barber, *Shakespeare's Festive Comedy*, 242.
95. Kamps thinks Malvolio fails to perform his class identity, and goes so far as to classify Malvolio as a "commoner and Toby's subordinate" ("Madness and Social Mobility," 235). As the careers of Elizabeth's favorites show, in a complex and multitiered hierarchical society not every upstart is a commoner, however.
96. Schiffer, "Taking the Long View," 30, 19.
97. Ralegh, *History*, 127.
98. Brantley, "Boys Will Be Boys (and Sometimes Girls)," *New York Times*, November 10, 2013. Brantley specifies that the images conjured are of a "young Elizabeth" but

the fifty-something Rylance looks middle-aged even by our standards. I can only think that the usual blindness to male aging in our culture accounts for Brantley's comment.
99. Ralegh, "Of Favorites," *Poems*, 49.9, 19–20, 122.
100. Howard, "Crossdressing," 432. She identifies the treatment of Orsino as "much less satirical" than the treatment of Olivia.
101. Tennenhouse, "Power on Display," 84.
102. The ambiguity regarding Orsino's rank is usually treated as a textual problem (Schiffer, "Taking the Long View," 4). My argument implies it might instead be a "functional ambiguity" (Patterson, *Censorship*, 18). On Orsino's "equivocal title," see also Suzuki, "Gender," 154.
103. As Dickey notes, "The real bear of the play, etymologically speaking, is Olivia's other main suitor, the Duke of Illyria, named Orsino from the Latin ursus, and more immediately from the Italian orsino" ("Shakespeare's Mastiff Comedy," 273). On Orsino as "little bear," see also Schleiner, "Orsino and Viola." Arlidge, *Prince of Love*, endorses Hotson's theory that the allusion is to the visiting Duke of Bracciano (*First Night*, 15). Arlidge and Hotson cite Webster's *The White Devil* (1612), which deals with the scandalous lives of members of the Orsini family, in support of this theory. But Webster's play also compares its Duke of Bracciano to Leicester, suggesting a complex network of connections at work (5.3.153–54). Like Malvolio, Orsino has been identified with a number of historical figures (Gras, "*Twelfth Night*," 555).
104. Leicester to Elizabeth I, January 16, 1570, *Calendar of State Papers*, 198.
105. *Leicester's Commonwealth*, 73. See also *News*, 155.
106. Gascoigne et al., *Princely Pleasures*, C6r; *Leicester's Commonwealth*, 193.
107. Bevington, "Shakespeare vs. Jonson," 120.
108. Harington is fond of the trope as well; see his section on hunting, where he segues from a discussion of dogs to a description of "this captious time" when so many are "readie to backbite every mans worke" (*Ajax*, 110).
109. Dekker, *Satiromastix*, 4.1.133–34. The quip implies that the eponymous isle might have been Gran Canaria, renowned for its mastiffs. It may also have been the island where Elizabeth I kenneled her dogs; as Marcus points out, the play may have explored "likenesses between the Queen's canines and her courtiers" ("Jonson and the Court," 31).
110. Jonson to Cecil, 1605, *Works*, 2:646.
111. Aubrey, "Sir Walter Raleigh," 255. Steggle argues for the legitimacy of Aubrey's anecdote, concluding that, despite Jonson's protestations to the contrary, personification played an important role in *Every Man Out* ("Charles Chester," 319). Chester was widely associated with the Canaries, lending further credence to the identification not just because Buffone is fond of canary wine (Steggle, 314–16,

322), as Falstaff is, but also because these islands were renowned for the breeding of "bandogs."
112. Gras argues that the "derisive treatment" Jonson reserves for Puntarvolo shows his contempt for "stock romantic plots" ("*Twelfth Night*," 547). Puntarvolo has been identified with Ralegh, Harington, and Anthony Munday; see Steggle, *War of the Theatres*, 12.
113. Jonson, "Appendix A" to *Every Man Out*, *Works*, 1:422. Bednarz offers a contrasting reading, in which *Every Man Out* furnishes a "counter-ideal for what it condemns" (*Poets' War*, 64).
114. The generic designation "Comicall Satyre," Jonson's own, appears on the title page of *Every Man Out* (1600); *Works*, 1:249.
115. Jonson, "Appendix A," *Works*, 1:421.
116. *Leicester's Commonwealth*, 186–87.
117. Blundeville, *Profitable Treatise*, o1.
118. Marcus, "Jonson and the Court," 32.
119. Baiting all the characters, "the play ... reproduces the arbitrary and inconclusive nature of a baiting contest" (Dickey, "Shakespeare's Mastiff Comedy," 272).
120. Greenblatt, *Will in the World*, 83–84.
121. Sidney, *Defence of Poesy*, 245.
122. McDonald speculates that "the rise of dramatic satire probably aided Shakespeare in making the transition from comedy to tragedy" (*Shakespeare and Jonson*, 72), a transition heralded by the bifurcated portrayal of Orsino and Malvolio.
123. Frye, *Anatomy of Criticism*, 45.
124. On Malvolio's threat as a rebuttal of Jonson's theories, see Bednarz, *Poets' War*, 192.
125. Berry, "*Twelfth Night*," 119.
126. See also Bednarz, who argues that Shakespeare "followed Jonson's example" in order to "contradict him" (*Poets' War*, 179).
127. Berry, "*Twelfth Night*," 114.
128. Sidney, *Defence of Poesy*, 230, 233.
129. Berry, "*Twelfth Night*," 4. Not all readers are so moved by Malvolio; Barber derides Lamb's response as a "romantic and bourgeois distortion" (*Shakespeare's Festive Comedy*, 255–56). On the conflicted critical responses to Malvolio, see Schiffer, "Taking the Long View," 10.
130. As Gras notes, "The Orsino plot line is implicitly connected with poetry and the theater by imagery concerning theatrical role-playing" ("*Twelfth Night*," 559).
131. Boym, *Future of Nostalgia*, 13.
132. Karreman, "Passion for the Past," 153.
133. Boym, *Future of Nostalgia*, 4.
134. Goldring, "Portraiture, Patronage," 183.
135. Stanivuković, "Masculine Plots," 126.

136. Boym, *Future of Nostalgia*, 52.
137. Boym, *Future of Nostalgia*, xvi.
138. Callaghan, Paster, and Howard argue that Olivia is punished; however, she is also rewarded, Levin observes, with the nontraditional marriage that she has sought all along (*Heart and Stomach*, 137). Sir Toby does not say that Olivia wishes never to marry—just that she does not wish to marry someone who can claim superior status.
139. On amity between Orsino and Viola, see Osborne, "Marriage of True Minds," 100.
140. Greenblatt, *Will in the World*, 83.
141. Castiglione, *Courtier*, 340.
142. Martin, *Constituting Old Age*, 113–25.

4. ANTONY

1. All references to Shakespeare are from the *Riverside Shakespeare*. All references to Middleton are from the *Works*.
2. Carlson, *Haunted Stage*, 8. The strongest evidence for typecasting practices in early modern theater involves comic roles (Bentley, *Profession*, 206–33).
3. Mullaney, "Mourning and Misogyny," 152.
4. See also Neill, who argues that Vindice's anger is focused on the "illegitimate son and the transgressive mother" ("Bastardy, Counterfeiting," 398).
5. Adelman, *Suffocating Mothers*, 24.
6. Cuff, *Differences of the Ages*, 115.
7. Cicero, *Booke of Old Age*, 48r.
8. Adelman, *Suffocating Mothers*, 24.
9. Among those who do make connections are Mullaney, who finds it "tempting" to identify Hamlet's mother and Elizabeth ("Mourning and Misogyny," 148); and Erickson, who argues that "Queen Gertrude functions as a degraded figure of Queen Elizabeth," with Hamlet reflecting Essex (*Rewriting Shakespeare*, 86). For Essex, see also Patterson, *Popular Voice*, 11, 27, 93–94. Leicester is rarely mentioned in this context, even though he was Essex's stepfather, and thus provides a point of comparison for Claudius. Recent critics have generally emphasized that *Hamlet* is acutely "aware of its late Elizabethan status" (Mullaney, 149).
10. Mullaney, "Mourning and Misogyny," 158. See also Neill, "Bastardy, Counterfeiting," 413.
11. Neill, "Bastardy, Counterfeiting," 410; *Leicester's Commonwealth*, 87.
12. Allen, *Admonition*, xix. On the tendency of anticourt polemicists to ascribe Circean powers to Elizabeth, see previous chapters.
13. Mullaney, "Mourning and Misogyny," 162.
14. While Orsino seems the most likely part for Burbage to have played in *Twelfth Night* (Baldwin, *Organization and Personnel*, 240), Astington suggests he may have played Malvolio instead (*Actors and Acting*, 37). Both are age-in-love parts

NOTES TO PAGES 163–167

(see previous chapter). Lowin was young to play Claudius and Falstaff; however, he had the right physique. See Butler, "Lowin, John."

15. Baldwin, *Organization and Personnel*, 238.
16. Palfrey and Stern, *Shakespeare in Parts*, 45.
17. Jankowski, "Egypt's Queen," 98.
18. Yachnin, "Courtiers," 4.
19. Eggert, *Showing Like a Queen*, 140, 145.
20. In contrast, ahistorical readings often put Antony at the center of the play; on this critical tendency, see Fitz, "Egyptian Queens."
21. Yachnin, "Courtiers," 7.
22. Jonson, *Cynthia's Revels*, in vol. 1 of *Works*, 3.4.40.
23. Jonson, *Cynthia's Revels*, in vol. 1 of *Works*, 3.5.96.
24. Marcus, *Puzzling Shakespeare*, 56. On the implication of this male rhetoric, see also Levin, *Heart and Stomach*, 121. Morris first noted that Cleopatra, in her desire to figure as "president" of her kingdom, recalls Elizabeth I at Tilbury ("Queen Elizabeth I 'Shadowed,'" 276). Based in part on this evidence, Jankowski argues that Cleopatra emulates Elizabeth in manipulating the fiction of the king's two bodies, although "unlike Elizabeth, she does this by making her political adversaries . . . her lovers" ("Egypt's Queen," 96). Guy is one exception to the consensus that a woman could outrank men by such means (*Elizabeth*, 11).
25. Elizabeth I, "Armada Speech," August 9, 1588, in *Elizabeth I: Collected Works*, 325–26.
26. Middleton, *Mad World My Masters*, 4.2.19, 31; "Letter Exchange Between Sir Robert Cecil and Robert Devereux," in *Elizabeth I: Collected Works*, 335.
27. Loomis, *Death of Elizabeth*, 79–81.
28. Tennenhouse, *Power on Display*, 146; Eggert, *Showing Like a Queen*, 162.
29. Eggert, *Showing Like a Queen*, 160. Shapiro, too, sees *Antony and Cleopatra* as a "tragedy of nostalgia" (*Year of Lear*, 266).
30. Rosenberg, *Leicester*, 160.
31. North, "To . . . Princess Elizabeth," in Plutarch, *Lives* (1579), 2r.
32. North, prefatory materials, in Plutarch, *Lives*, 3–6r. Besides the letter to Elizabeth, these include Norton's "To the Reader" and his translation of "Amiot to the Readers."
33. Boym, *Future of Nostalgia*, xvi.
34. Shapiro, *Year of Lear*, 229.
35. Plutarch, "Marcus Antonius," in *Shakespeare's Plutarch*, 183, 195. Unless noted otherwise, all references are to this edition.
36. Logan, "High Events," 156.
37. Gosson, *Plays Confuted*, E8r.
38. Palfrey and Stern, *Shakespeare in Parts*, 170. For Ciceronian rhetoric's use of passions as "critical tools to civil persuasion," see Rowe, "Minds in Company," 55.

39. According to Platter, Elizabeth spoke Latin, French, Italian, and Spanish, in addition to English (*Travels*, 165).
40. For the citational function of such references, see Belsey, "Myth of Venus."
41. Tassi, "O'erpicturing Apelles," 299.
42. Kyffin, *Blessedness of Brytaine*, A3v, B2r. That the Armada made English people think of Actium is further corroborated by Stow, who wrote that the Spanish ships exceed in "number" those "at command of Egyptian Cleopatra" (*Annales*, 46).
43. Platter, *Travels*, 226.
44. Strong, *Cult of Elizabeth*, 50.
45. Adelman, *Common Liar*, 81.
46. "Elizabeth I Dress," http://www.bbc.com/news/uk-england-hereford-worcester-36301188 (accessed April 4, 2018).
47. Adelman, *Common Liar*, 65.
48. Leicester was made Master of the Horse in 1558. He retained the position until 1587, when he was instrumental in securing it for his stepson; see Hammer, "Absolute and Sovereign Mistress," 45.
49. Leicester was a prominent patron of players, a feature of his character linked to his rise to power and to his influence over Elizabeth; see previous chapters, as well as, e.g., *News*, 156, 144; and *Leicester's Commonwealth*, 128. The description of Ralegh is Naunton's (*Fragmenta Regalia*, 72).
50. Naunton, *Fragmenta Regalia*, 56.
51. Hammer, "Devereux, Robert." Leicester fashioned a military identity long before his assignments in the Netherlands and at Tilbury; in a portrait that Federico Zuccaro painted for the Kenilworth entertainments (1575), he appears "the heroic Captain who vanquishes Spain and liberates the Protestant Netherlands" (Goldring, "Portraiture, Patronage," 180).
52. "Letter of Estate," 29. Like so much of the chatter about the earl, this bit reflects an image he sought to project. Many of the pictures in his possession had classical themes; at Leicester House, he kept eleven marble busts, one of himself, one of Elizabeth, and nine of Roman emperors; see Goldring, *Robert Dudley*, 218.
53. Yachnin, "Courtiers," 8–9.
54. Luce, introduction to *Antonie*, 40.
55. Mary Sidney, *Antonie*, ll.10–11, 129, 15, 80–82.
56. Starks, "Immortal Longings," 244.
57. Greville, *Sir Philip Sidney*, 155–56. On Greville's biography, see Gouws, "Greville, Fulke."
58. Greville, *Sir Philip Sidney*, 176. See, e.g., Hunter, who argues that the Essex rebellion "turned" Greville's "general observations into what seemed like particular references" (*John Lyly*, 149); Bullough, *Sources*, 216; and Yachnin, "Courtiers," 9.
59. Greville, *Sir Philip Sidney*, 194.

60. Greville, *Sir Philip Sidney*, 33.
61. Naunton, 74; see also Nowell Smith, introduction, x.
62. Francis Bacon, quoted in Nowell Smith, introduction, ix.
63. Greville, *Sir Philip Sidney*, 215.
64. "Elizabeth to Ralegh," *Elizabeth I: Collected Works*, 308; "pug, n.2," OED online, http://www.oed.com/view/Entry/154210 (accessed November 3, 2017). For the queen's pet names, see also previous chapters, especially chapter 1.
65. Kendall, *Robert Dudley*, 87; see also Susan Frye, *Elizabeth I*, 67.
66. Quoted in Guy, *Elizabeth*, 328.
67. Harington, *Nugae Antique*, 1:358. Lyly likens Endymion to a fish; see chapter 1.
68. Sidney, *Astrophil and Stella*, 83.1–9; in *Major Works*, 59.
69. Bates, *Masculinity, Gender*, 14.
70. Platter, *Travels*, 193.
71. Platter, *Travels*, 228, 182.
72. Gascoigne et al., *Princely Pleasures*, C7r.
73. Adelman, *Common Liar*, 83. See also Bono, *Literary Transvaluation*, 167–86.
74. Guy, *Elizabeth*, 132.
75. Elizabeth I, "Armada Speech," 326.
76. Nyquist, "Profuse, Proud Cleopatra," 98.
77. Adams, *Leicester and the Court*, 138.
78. Francis Bacon to the Earl of Essex, October 4, 1996, in *Letters and Life of Francis Bacon*, 2:42.
79. Guy, 106.
80. Mary Sidney, 72, ll.451. Cleopatra echoes this passage when she asks Enobarbus, "Is Antony or we in fault for this?" (3.13.3).
81. *Leicester's Commonwealth*, 187.
82. MacCaffrey, *Elizabeth I*, 457.
83. Morris, "Queen Elizabeth I 'Shadowed'"; Muir, "Elizabeth I"; and Rinehart, "Shakespeare's Cleopatra."
84. Eggert, *Showing Like a Queen*, 134–36.
85. De Maisse, *Journal*, 59. Other dignitaries were treated to the same ceremony; see Arnold, *Queen Elizabeth's Wardrobe*, 11–12. Elizabeth appears to have used such tactics since the beginning of her reign; her 1559 speech in response to a parliamentary request that she marry has her "stretching out" and showing her audience her hand, with the ring signifying her marriage to England. She reprised this gesture in her conversations with the Scottish Ambassador, William Maitland, in 1561 (*Elizabeth I: Collected Works*, 59, 65).
86. Platter, *Travels*, 221. The queen relied on the analogy in her speeches; e.g., "If I were a milkmaid with a pail on mine arm, whereby my private person might be little set by, I would not forsake that single state to match myself with the greatest monarch"

("Speech at the Close of the Parliamentary Session," March 15, 1576, in *Elizabeth I: Collected Works*, 170). For more examples, see Mueller, "Virtue and Virtuality," 229–31, 243n31. On Cleopatra's use of the analogy, see also Muir, "Elizabeth I," 199–200.

87. Muir, "Elizabeth I," 199; see also Dash, *Wooing, Wedding*, 277. Frye even claims Cleopatra is "a counter-historical figure" (*Fools of Time*, 71). For a useful overview of the deeply divided critical tradition on *Antony and Cleopatra*, see Deats, "Shakespeare's Anamorphic Drama." On the tendency of readings to reflect either the Roman or Egyptian perspectives embedded in the play, see Hirsh, "Rome and Egypt."
88. Fitz, "Egyptian Queens," 297. As Fitz points out, Cleopatra's first line aligns her with Lear, another ruler for whom love is a form of politics (303).
89. Nyquist, "Profuse, Proud Cleopatra," 97–98; Logan, "High Events," 162.
90. On Cleopatra as a political figure, see also Dash, *Wooing, Wedding*, 209–47.
91. Jankowski, "Egypt's Queen," 105.
92. Dash, *Wooing, Wedding*, 209.
93. Blundeville, *Profitable Treatise*, Q3r.
94. Bullough, *Sources*, 216.
95. "Dead Mans Right," A4r.
96. The ability to bracket off one's subject position is granted primarily to (white) males and an "exacerbation of sexism" is "characteristic of the liberal public sphere" (Fraser, "Rethinking the Public Sphere," 114). Eley argues that the "category of the 'public man' and his 'virtue' was constructed via a series of oppositions to 'femininity,'" so that the "*natural* identification of sexuality and desire with the feminine allowed the *social* and *political* construction of masculinity," and "women were to be silenced, to allow masculine speech, in the language of reason, full rein" ("Nations, Publics," 309). See also Warner, *Publics and Counterpublics*, 65–124.
97. Lake, "Politics of 'Popularity,'" 68.
98. Roach, *Cities of the Dead*, 80.
99. Yachnin, "Performing Publicity," 209.
100. Adelman, *Common Liar*, 138.
101. Plutarch, "Marcus Antonius," 294–95, 183; Du Laurens, *Preservation of Sight*, 177.
102. Like Falstaff, Antony wants to "mock the midnight bell" (3.13.184).
103. Cicero, *Booke of Old Age*, 23v.
104. On the play's generic hybridity, see Neely, *Broken Nuptials*, 136–65.
105. Adelman, *Common Liar*, 135. On Antony as a Herculean figure, see also Waith, *Herculean Hero*, 113–21; and Bono, *Literary Transvaluation*, 153–67.
106. On the Isis and Osiris myth, see Bono, *Literary Transvaluation*, 150–51, 191–213; Adelman, *Common Liar*, 81, and *Suffocating Mothers*, 183–84; and Starks, "Immortal Longings," 246–47.
107. Shapiro, *Year of Lear*, 266.
108. Lyly, *Endymion*, 2.1.16.

109. Sullivan, "Sleep, Epic," 266. For Cleopatra and Circe, see also Britland, "Circe's Cup," 116–19.
110. "Letter of Estate," 35. For other examples of this language, see chapter 2.
111. Allen, *Admonition*, xviii.
112. "dotage, n.," OED online, http://www.oed.com/view/Entry/56966 (accessed November 3, 2017).
113. Cicero, *Booke of Old Age*, 24v.
114. Gosson, *Plays Confuted*, C8v-Dr.
115. My reading of this scene, and indeed of the play, is indebted to Rackin, "Shakespeare's Boy Cleopatra."
116. Jonson, *Cynthia's Revels*, in vol. 1 of *Works*, 2.3.66–67.
117. On the ways in which an audience's reception depends on the manipulation of expectations derived from previous performances, see Carlson, *Haunted Stage*, 5.
118. Adelman, *Common Liar*, 24.
119. Shapiro, *Year of Lear*, 236. On the other characters' tendency to discuss Antony, see also Logan, "High Events," 161.
120. "Dead Mans Right," A4r.
121. Charnes, *Notorious Identity*, 122.
122. No other Shakespearean play has this many messengers (Charnes, *Notorious Identity*, 106).
123. Adelman, *Common Liar*, 24–31.
124. Cicero, *Booke of Old Age*, 23r.
125. Barton, "Nature's Piece," 6.
126. Hirsh notes that "Shakespeare makes it difficult for a playgoer to root against Antony and Cleopatra even if outside the theater the same individual would be inclined to condemn behavior resembling that of the lovers" ("Rome and Egypt," 187).
127. Waith, *Herculean Hero*, 115.
128. Barkan, *Gods Made Flesh*, 38–39.
129. Gosson, *Plays Confuted*, C1r; Starks, "Immortal Longings," 249. Osiris and Bacchus are often identified with one another; see Bono, *Literary Transvaluation*, 200.
130. "Letter of Estate," 31. *News* claimed Leicester was "so greate a student of *Baccus*" that there would be "quaffing in heaven" (148).
131. Quinn, "Celebrity," 156, 159.
132. *Leicester's Commonwealth*, 72.
133. "abstract, adj. and n.," B3b, OED online, http://www.oed.com/view/Entry/758 (accessed November 3, 2017).
134. Ovid, *Metamorphoses*, 15.929, 950.
135. Logan, "High Events," 159. On Antony as an "exemplary antihero," see Starks, "Immortal Longings," 244.

136. See also Starks, who writes that although Antony's "role is based on a rejection of traditional masculinity and heroism, it is, nevertheless, a *male* rather than a female role" ("Immortal Longings," 244); and Neely, who finds that "heroic activity" in Antony is never "feminized" (*Broken Nuptials*, 146).
137. Knox, *First Blast of the Trumpet*, 11.
138. Adelman, *Suffocating Mothers*, 177. See also Sullivan, "Sleep, Epic," 270.
139. According to Bono, Antony here "decisively reverses Roman values" (*Literary Transvaluation*, 187).
140. Bradley writes, "the passion that ruins Antony also exalts him, he touches the infinite in it" (*Shakespearean Tragedy*, 87). Many have agreed; see, e.g., Waith, *Herculean Hero*; or Brower, *Hero and Saint*, 316–43.
141. Barton, "Nature's Piece," 6.
142. As Neely notes, it also recalls the earlier reference to Antony as Cleopatra's fish (*Broken Nuptials*, 157).
143. See, e.g., Barton, "Nature's Piece," 7; and Rackin, "Shakespeare's Boy Cleopatra," 208. For more on critical attitudes towards Antony's suicide, see my "Antony's 'Secret House of Death.'"
144. *News*, 155–58; see also chapter 2.
145. Rackin, "Shakespeare's Boy Cleopatra," 209–10.
146. Loomis, *Death of Elizabeth*, 1, 47–82. On James and Octavius, see also Yachnin, "Courtiers."
147. Petowe, *Elizabetha quasi vivens*, B3r.
148. Herbert, *Englands Sorrowe*, C3r.
149. Petowe, *Elizabetha quasi vivens*, B3r.
150. Chettle, *Englandes Mourning Garment*, D2v. See also Loomis, *Death of Elizabeth*, 67.
151. On the relationship between onstage and offstage weeping, see Steggle, *Laughing and Weeping*. Laughter and tears were considered "contagious" in the period (5).
152. Rowlands, *Ave Caesar*, A5r.
153. Chettle, *Englandes Mourning Garment*, C3v.
154. Manningham, *Diary*, March 27, 1603, 216.
155. "Henry, Earl of Northumberland, to King James," in *Correspondence of King James VI*, 55.
156. Manningham, *Diary*, April 1, 1603, 221.
157. Sidney, *Astrophil to Stella*, 49.14, in *Major Works*, 172.
158. Herbert, *Englands Sorrowe*, C4v.
159. Chettle, *Englandes Mourning Garment*, D2v-r. See also Eggert, *Showing Like a Queen*, 131.
160. Adelman, *Common Liar*, 25. See also Brower, 328–29.
161. Loomis, *Death of Elizabeth*, 6.

162. Loomis, *Death of Elizabeth*, 44. Antony delivers these lines about the deceased Fulvia, concluding "The hand could pluck her back that shov'd her on" (1.2.127). At the risk of sounding like Ben Jonson's picklocks, I would say that this glances at the rumors concerning the death of Leicester's first wife, Amy Robsart.
163. *Leicester's Ghost*, 81.
164. "Dead Mans Right," A4v.
165. Herbert, *Englands Sorrowe*, D1r.
166. Adelman, *Suffocating Mothers*, 177, 186.
167. Boym, *Future of Nostalgia*, xvi.
168. Norton, prefatory materials to Plutarch's *Lives*, 3v.
169. Carlson, *Haunted Stage*, 3.
170. Bacon, quoted in Rowe, "Minds in Company," 47.
171. Blundeville, *Profitable Treatise*, O1r.
172. Anton, *Philosophers Satyrs*, 46–47.
173. Adelman, *Common Liar*, 53.
174. Although I argue from different grounds and towards different ends, I agree that *Antony and Cleopatra* "reaches toward a new kind of masculinity" (Adelman, *Suffocating Mothers*, 190).
175. Mullaney, *Reformation*, 19.
176. Bono, *Literary Transvaluation*, 209. On Antony as the "primary" object of desire in the play, see also Adelman, *Suffocating Mothers*, 177.
177. Barton finds that Cleopatra "here bestows upon Antony an heroic identity so colossal, but also in a sense so true" ("Nature's Piece," 20).

EPILOGUE

1. Atwood, "Gertrude Talks Back," 16–19, 17.
2. *Leicester's Commonwealth*, 75.
3. "Letter of Estate," 29.
4. For Elizabeth's influence on the strong female characters of Jacobean drama, see Loomis, *Death of Elizabeth*, 119–61.
5. Webster, *Duchess of Malfi*, 1.1.209.
6. Bacon, "Endymion, or the Favourite," *Wisdom of the Ancients*, 717–18.
7. Cavendish, "CXXIII," *CCXI Sociable Letters*, 244–45.
8. Guy, *Elizabeth*, 397, 61.
9. Guy, *Elizabeth*, 147.
10. Erickson, *Rewriting Shakespeare*, 91.
11. Levin, *Heart and Stomach*, 79.
12. Erickson, *Rewriting Shakespeare*, 91.

BIBLIOGRAPHY

Achileos, Stella. "Youth, Old Age, and Male Self-Fashioning: The Appropriation of the Anacreontic Figure of the Old Man by Jonson and his 'Sons.'" In *Growing Old in Early Modern Europe*, edited by Erin Campbell, 39–53. Aldershot: Ashgate, 2006.

Adams, Simon. *Leicester and the Court*. Manchester: Manchester University Press, 2002.

———. "Dudley, Robert, Earl of Leicester (1532/3–1588)." In *Oxford Dictionary of National Biography*. Accessed November 3, 2017. http://www.oxforddnb.com.

Adelman, Janet. *The Common Liar: An Essay on Antony and Cleopatra*. New Haven: Yale University Press, 1972.

———. *Suffocating Mothers: Fantasies of Maternal Origin in Shakespeare's Plays, "Hamlet" to "The Tempest."* New York: Routledge, 1992.

Adlard, George. *Amye Robsart and the Earl of Leycester*. London, 1870.

Akrigg, G. P. V. "*Twelfth Night* at the Middle Temple." *Shakespeare Quarterly* 9, no. 3 (Summer 1958): 422–24.

Allen, William. *An Admonition to the Nobility and People of England and Ireland*. 1588.

———. *The Copie of a Letter Written by M. Doctor Allen Concerning the Yeelding up of the Citie of Daventrie....* Antwerp, 1587.

Alwes, Derek B. "'I Would Faine Serve': John Lyly's Career at Court." In *John Lyly*, edited by Ruth Lunney, 213–35. Aldershot: Ashgate, 2011.

Anton, Robert. *The Philosophers Satyrs*. 1616.

Arden of Faversham (1592). In *English Renaissance Drama*, edited by David Bevington, Lars Engle, Katharine Eisaman Maus, and Eric Rasmussen, 421–81. New York: Norton, 2002.

Arlidge, Anthony. *Shakespeare and the Prince of Love: The Feast of Misrule in the Middle Temple*. London: Giles de la Mare, 2000.

Arnold, Janet. *Queen Elizabeth's Wardrobe Unlock'd*. Leeds: Maney & Son, 1988.

Astington, John. *Actors and Acting in Shakespeare's Time*. Cambridge: Cambridge University Press, 2010.

Atwood, Margaret. "Gertrude Talks Back." In Atwood, *Good Bones and Simple Murders*, 6–19. New York: Bantam, 1994.

Aubrey, John. "Sir Walter Raleigh." In *Aubrey's Brief Lives*, edited by Oliver Lawson Dick, 23–35. Jaffrey NH: David Godine, 1999.

Auden, W. H. "The Prince's Dog." In *Henry the Fourth Parts I and II: Critical Essays*, edited by David Bevington, 157–80. New York: Garland, 1986.

Axton, Marie. *The Queen's Two Bodies: Drama and the Elizabethan Succession*. London: Royal Historical Society, 1977.

Baldwin, Thomas Whitfield. *The Organization and Personnel of the Shakespearean Company*. Princeton: Princeton University Press, 1961.

Bacon, Francis. *The Letters and Life of Francis Bacon*. Edited by James Spedding. 7 vols. London, 1861–74.

——. *Of the Wisdom of the Ancients (1858)*. In vol. 6 of *The Works of Francis Bacon*, edited and translated by James Spedding, Robert Leslie Ellis, and Douglas Denon Heath, 693–764. Cambridge: Cambridge University Press, 2011.

"The Ballad of Constant Susanna" (1624). In *English Broadside Ballad Archive*. University of California, Santa Barbara. Accessed November 3, 2017. https://ebba.english.ucsb.edu.

Barber, C. L. *Shakespeare's Festive Comedy: A Study of Dramatic Form and its Relation to Social Custom*. Princeton: Princeton University Press, 1972.

Barkan, Leonard. *The Gods Made Flesh: Metamorphosis and the Pursuit of Paganism*. New Haven: Yale University Press, 1986.

Bartholomaeus Anglicus, and Stephen Batman. *Batman upon Bartholome, His Book De Proprietatibus Rerum*. London, 1582.

Barton, Anne. "*As You Like It* and *Twelfth Night*: Shakespeare's 'Sense of an Ending'" (1972). In Barton, *Essays, Mainly Shakespearean*, 91–112. Cambridge: Cambridge University Press, 2007.

——. "Nature's Piece 'gainst Fancy: The Divided Catastrophe in *Antony and Cleopatra*." London: Bedford College, 1973.

Bates, Catherine. *Masculinity, Gender, and Identity in the English Renaissance Lyric*. New York: Cambridge University Press, 2007.

Beam, Aki C. L. "'Should I as Yet Call You Old?': Testing the Boundaries of Female Old Age in Early Modern England." In *Growing Old in Early Modern Europe*, edited by Erin Campbell, 95–116. Aldershot: Ashgate, 2006.

Bednarz, James. *Shakespeare and the Poets' War*. New York: Columbia University Press, 2001.

Belsey, Catherine. *A Future for Criticism*. Chichester: Wiley-Blackwell, 2011.

——. "The Myth of Venus in Early Modern Culture." *English Literary Renaissance* 42, no. 2 (Spring 2012): 179–202.

Bennett, Josephine Waters. "Oxford and Endimion." *PMLA: Publications of the Modern Language Association of America* 57, no. 2 (June 1942): 354–69.

Bentley, G. E. *The Profession of Player in Shakespeare's Time, 1590–1642*. Princeton: Princeton University Press, 1984.

Berger, Harry, Jr. "The Prince's Dog: Falstaff and the Perils of Speech-Prefixity." *Shakespeare Quarterly* 49, no. 1 (Spring 1998): 40–73.

———. *Waking Trifles of Terrors: Redistributing Complicities in Shakespeare*. Stanford: Stanford University Press, 1997.

Berry, Philippa. *Of Chastity and Power: Elizabethan Literature and the Unmarried Queen*. New York: Routledge, 1989.

Berry, Ralph. "*Twelfth Night*: The Experience of the Audience." *Shakespeare Survey* 34 (1981): 111–20.

Betts, Hannah. "'The Image of this Queene so Quaint': The Pornographic Blazon, 1588–1603." In *Dissing Elizabeth: Negative Representations of Gloriana*, edited by Julia M. Walker, 153–84. Durham: Duke University Press, 1998.

Bevington, David. Introduction. In John Lyly, *Endymion*, edited by David Bevington, 1–72. Manchester: Manchester University Press, 1996.

———. Introduction. In *Henry the Fourth*, edited by Bevington, xi–xxii.

———. "Shakespeare vs. Jonson on Satire." In *Shakespeare 1971: Proceedings of the Shakespeare Congress, Vancouver, 1971*, edited by Clifford Leech and J. M. R. Margeson, 107–22. Toronto: University of Toronto Press, 1972.

———. *Tudor Drama and Politics*. Cambridge MA: Harvard University Press, 1968.

———, ed. *Henry the Fourth Parts I and II: Critical Essays*. New York: Garland, 1986.

Billington, Sandra. *A Social History of the Fool*. New York: Faber & Faber, 1984.

Blundeville, Thomas, trans. *A Very Briefe and Profitable Treatise Declaring Howe Many Counsells and What Maner of Counselers a Prince Ought to Have*. London, 1570.

Boehrer, Bruce. "Economies of Desire in *A Midsummer Night's Dream*." *Shakespeare Studies* 32 (2004): 99–117.

Bond, R. Warwick, ed. *The Complete Works of John Lyly*. Oxford: Oxford University Press, 1902.

Bond, Sallie. "John Lyly's *Endimion*." *SEL: Studies in English Literature, 1500–1900* 14, no. 2 (Spring 1974): 189–99.

Bono, Barbara. *Literary Transvaluation: From Vergilian Epic to Shakespearean Comedy*. Berkeley: University of California Press, 1984.

Boose, Lynda E. "The 1599 Bishop's Ban, Elizabethan Pornography, and the Sexualization of the Jacobean Stage." In *Enclosure Acts: Sexuality, Property, and Culture in Early Modern England*, edited by Richard Burt and John Michael Archer, 185–202. Ithaca: Cornell University Press, 1994.

Boym, Svetlana. *The Future of Nostalgia*. New York: Basic, 2001.

BIBLIOGRAPHY

Bradley, A. C. "The Rejection of Falstaff" (1902). In David Bevington, *Henry the Fourth Parts I and II: Critical Essays*, 77–98. New York: Garland, 1986.

——— . *Shakespearean Tragedy* (1904). New York: Penguin, 1991.

Breitenberg, Mark. *Anxious Masculinity in Early Modern England*. Cambridge: Cambridge University Press, 1996.

Britland, Karen. "Circe's Cup: Wine and Women in Early Modern Drama." In *A Pleasing Sinne: Drink and Conviviality in Seventeenth-Century England*, edited by Adam Smyth, 109–26. Cambridge: D. S. Brewer, 2004.

Boorde, Andrew. *The Breviarie of Health*. Second edition. London, 1575.

A Briefe Discoverie of Doctor Allens Seditious Drifts. . . . London, 1588.

Brodwin, Leonora Leet. "Milton and the Renaissance Circe." *Milton Studies* 6 (1974): 21–83.

Brower, Reuben A. *Hero and Saint: Shakespeare and the Graeco-Roman Tradition*. Oxford: Oxford University Press, 1971.

Bruster, Douglas. *Shakespeare and the Question of Culture*. New York: Palgrave Macmillan, 2003.

Burrow, J. A. *The Ages of Man: A Study in Medieval Writing and Thought*. Oxford: Oxford University Press, 1986.

Butler, Martin, "Kemp, William (d. in or after 1610?)." In *Oxford Dictionary of National Biography*. Accessed November 3, 2017. http://www.oxforddnb.com.

——— . "Lowin, John (d. in or after 1610?)." In *Oxford Dictionary of National Biography*. Accessed November 3, 2017. http://www.oxforddnb.com.

Bullough, Geoffrey. *Narrative and Dramatic Sources of Shakespeare*. Vol. 5. New York: Columbia University Press, 1964.

Calhoun, Craig, ed. *Habermas and the Public Sphere*. Cambridge MA: MIT Press, 1992.

Callaghan, Dympna. "'And All is Semblative a Woman's Part': Body Politics and *Twelfth Night*." In *Twelfth Night: Contemporary Critical Essays*, edited by R. S. White, 129–59. New York: St. Martin's, 1996.

Calendar of State Papers, Domestic Series, of the Reign of Elizabeth, Addenda, 1566–1579. Edited by Mary Anne Everett Green. London: Longmans, 1871.

Camden, William. *Annales, the True and Royal History of the Famous Empresse Elizabeth, Queene of England, France and Ireland*. London, 1625.

——— . *The History of the Most Renowned and Victorious Princess Elizabeth, Late Queen of England: Selected Chapters* (1630). Edited and translated by Wallace T. MacCaffrey. Chicago: University of Chicago Press, 1970.

Campbell, Erin, ed. *Growing Old in Early Modern Europe*. Aldershot: Ashgate, 2006.

Carlson, Marvin. *The Haunted Stage: Theater as Memory Machine*. Ann Arbor: University of Michigan Press, 2004.

Castiglione, Baldesar. *The Book of the Courtier* (1528). Translated by Charles S. Singleton. New York: Doubleday, 1959.

BIBLIOGRAPHY

Cavendish, Margaret. *CCXI Sociable Letters Written by the Thrice Noble, Illustrious, and Excellent Princess, the Lady Marchioness of Newcastle*. 1664.

Certeau, Michel de. *The Writing of History*. Translated by Tom Conley. New York: Columbia University Press, 1988.

Chambers, E. K. *The Elizabethan Stage*. 4 vols. Oxford: Clarendon, 1923.

Chambers, E. K., and W. W. Greg, eds. *Dramatic Records of the City of London*. Oxford: Malone Society, 1907.

Chapman, George. *The Poems of George Chapman*. Edited by Phyllis Brooks Bartlett. New York: Modern Language Association, 1941.

Charnes, Linda. *Notorious Identity: Materializing the Subject in Shakespeare*. Cambridge MA: Harvard University Press, 1993.

Chaucer, Geoffrey. *The Canterbury Tales*. In *The Riverside Chaucer*, edited by Larry D. Benson, 212–16. Boston: Houghton Mifflin, 1987.

Chettle, Henry. *Englandes Mourning Garment . . . in Memorie of their Sacred Mistresse, Elizabeth, Queen of Vertue*. London, 1603.

Cicero, Marcus Tullius. *The Worthye Booke of Old Age*. BC 44. Translated by Thomas Newton. London, 1569.

Clare, Janet. "Jonson's 'Comical Satires' and the Art of Courtly Compliment." In *Refashioning Ben Jonson: Gender, Politic, and the Jonsonian Canon*, edited by Julie Sanders, Kate Chedgzoy, and Susan Wiseman, 28–47. New York: St. Martin's, 1998.

Clement, Jennifer. "'The Imperial Vot'ress': Divinity, Femininity, and Elizabeth I in *A Midsummer's Night's Dream*." *Explorations in Renaissance Culture* 34, no. 2 (2008): 163–84.

Collington, Philip. "Sans Wife: Sexual Anxiety and the Old Man in Shakespeare." In *Growing Old in Early Modern Europe*, edited by Erin Campbell, 185–207. Aldershot: Ashgate, 2006.

Collinson, Patrick. "Elizabeth I (1533–1603)." In *Oxford Dictionary of National Biography*. Accessed November 3, 2017. http://www.oxforddnb.com.

Craik, Katharine A., and Tanya Pollard. "Imagining Audiences." In *Shakespearean Sensations: Experiencing Literature in Early Modern England*, edited by Craik and Pollard, 1–25. Cambridge: Cambridge University Press, 2013.

Cressy, David. *Dangerous Talk; Scandalous, Seditious, and Treasonable Speech in Pre-Modern England*. Oxford: Oxford University Press, 2010.

Crewe, Jonathan. "*2 Henry IV*: A Critical History." In vol. 2 of *A Companion to Shakespeare's Works*, 4 vols, edited by Richard Dutton and Jean E. Howard. Malden MA: Blackwell, 2006.

Cuff, Henry. *The Differences of the Ages of a Mans Life, Together with the Originall Causes, Progresse, and End Thereof*. London, 1607.

Davison, Francis. *Davison's Poems, or a Poeticall Rapsodie*. London, 1602.

Dash, Irene. *Wooing, Wedding, and Power: Women in Shakespeare's Plays*. New York: Columbia University Press, 1981.

"The Dead Mans Right." In *The Phoenix Nest*. London, 1593. A2r-A3v.

Deats, Sara, ed. *Antony and Cleopatra: New Critical Essays*. New York: Routledge, 2005.

———. "The Disarming of the Knight: Comic Parody in Lyly's 'Endimion.'" In *John Lyly*, edited by Ruth Lunney, 284–91. Aldershot: Ashgate, 2011.

———. "Shakespeare's Anamorphic Drama: A Survey of *Antony and Cleopatra* in Criticism, on Stage, and on Screen." In Deats, *Antony and Cleopatra: New Critical Essays*, 1–93.

Delineatio Pompae Triumphalis qua Robertus Dudlaeus Comes Leicenstrensis Hagae Comitis fuit Exceptus. The Hague (?), 1586.

Dennis, John. *The Comical Gallant: or, The Amours of Sir John Falstaffe*. London, 1702.

Dekker, Thomas. *Satiromastix* (1602). In *The Dramatic Works of Thomas Dekker*, edited by Fredson Bowers, 299–385. Cambridge: Cambridge University Press, 1953.

Devereux, Walter Bourchier. *Lives and Letters of the Devereux, Earls of Essex, in the Reign of Elizabeth I, James I, and Charles I*. London, 1853.

Dickey, Stephen. "Shakespeare's Mastiff Comedy." *Shakespeare Quarterly* 42, no. 3 (Autumn 1991): 255–75.

Discours de la Vie Abominable, Ruses, Trahisons, Meurtres . . . desquelles a usé & use journellement my Lorde de Lecestre Machiaveliste. Paris (?), 1585.

Donne, John. "The Canonization" (1633). In *John Donne*, edited by Frank Kermode, 95. Oxford: Oxford University Press, 1990.

Donno, Elizabeth Story. Introduction. *Sir John Harington's A New Discourse of A Stale Subject, Called the Metamorphosis of Ajax*, edited by Donno, 1–52. New York: Columbia University Press, 1962.

Doran, Susan. *Monarchy and Matrimony: The Courtships of Elizabeth I*. New York: Routledge, 1996.

Doty, Jeffrey S. *Shakespeare, Popularity, and the Public Sphere*. New York: Cambridge University Press, 2017.

"The Dudley Bear and Ragged Staff." *Notes and Queries* 10, no. 247 (July 22, 1854): 68.

Dudley, Robert. "A Letter from Robert, Earl of Leicester, to a Lady." Edited by Conyers Read. *Huntington Library Bulletin* 9 (April 1936): 14–26.

Du Laurens, André. *A Discourse of the Preservation of the Sight*, translated by Richard Surphlet. London, 1599.

Duncan-Jones, Katherine. *Shakespeare: An Ungentle Life* (2001). Rev. ed. London: Methuen, 2010.

Dust, Philip. "The Kiss in Lyly's *Endymion*." *English Miscellany* 25 (1975/76): 87–95.

Dutton, Richard. "Jonson's Satiric Styles." In *The Cambridge Companion to Ben Jonson*, edited by Richard Harp and Stanley Stuart, 58–72. Cambridge: Cambridge University Press, 2000.

———. *Licensing, Censorship, and Authorship in Early Modern England: Buggeswords.* New York: Palgrave Macmillan, 2000.

———. *Mastering the Revels: The Regulation and Censorship of English Renaissance Drama.* New York: Palgrave Macmillan, 1991.

Dutton, Richard, and Jean E. Howard, eds. *A Companion to Shakespeare's Works.* 4 vols. Malden MA: Blackwell, 2006.

Eggert, Katherine. *Showing Like a Queen: Female Authority and Literary Experiment in Spenser, Shakespeare, and Milton.* Philadelphia: University of Pennsylvania Press, 2000.

Eley, Geoff. "Nations, Publics, and Political Cultures: Placing Habermas in the Nineteenth Century." In *Habermas and the Public Sphere*, edited by Craig Calhoun, 289–339. Cambridge MA: MIT Press, 1992.

Elizabeth I. *Elizabeth I: Collected Works*, edited by Leah S. Marcus, Janel Mueller, and Mary Beth Rose. Chicago: University of Chicago Press, 2000.

Ellis, Anthony. *Old Age, Masculinity, and Early Modern Drama: Comic Elders on the Italian and Shakespearean Stage.* Aldershot: Ashgate, 2009.

Ellis, David. *Shakespeare's Practical Jokes: An Introduction to the Comic in His Work.* Lewisburg PA: Bucknell University Press, 2007.

Elyot, Thomas. *The Castel of Helthe.* London, 1539.

Erickson, Peter. "The Order of the Garter, the Cult of Elizabeth, and Class-Gender Tension in *The Merry Wives of Windsor.*" In *Shakespeare Reproduced: The Text in History and Ideology*, edited by Jean E. Howard and Marion F. O'Connor, 116–40. New York: Routledge, 1987.

———. *Rewriting Shakespeare, Rewriting Ourselves.* Berkeley: University of California Press, 1991.

Feuillerat, Albert. *John Lyly: Contribution a l'Histoire de la Renaissance en Angleterre.* 1910. Reprint. New York: Russel & Russel, 1968.

Fiedler, Leslie A. "Eros and Thanatos: Old Age in Love." In *Aging, Death, and the Completion of Being*, edited by David Van Tassel, 235–54. Philadelphia: University of Pennsylvania Press, 1979.

Fineman, Joel. *Shakespeare's Perjured Eye: The Invention of Poetic Subjectivity in the Sonnets.* Berkeley: University of California Press, 1986.

The First Part of Sir John Oldcastle. London, 1600.

Fitz, L. T. "Egyptian Queens and Male Reviewers: Sexist Attitudes in *Antony and Cleopatra* Criticism." *Shakespeare Quarterly* 28, no. 3 (Summer 1977): 297–316.

Fleetwood, William. "Itinerarium ad Windsor." In *The Name of a Queen: William Fleetwood's "Itinerarium ad Windsor,"* edited by Charles Beem and Dennis Moore, 19–62. New York: Palgrave Macmillan, 2013.

Foxe, John. *Actes and Monuments.* London, 1596.

Fraser, Nancy. "Rethinking the Public Sphere: A Contribution to the Critique of Actually Existing Democracy." In *Habermas and the Public Sphere*, edited by Craig Calhoun, 109–42. Cambridge MA: MIT Press, 1992.

Freedman, Barbara. "Falstaff's Punishment: Buffoonery as Defensive Posture in *The Merry Wives of Windsor*." *Shakespeare Studies* 14 (1981): 163–74.

———. "Shakespearean Chronology, Ideological Complicity, and Floating Texts: Something Is Rotten in Windsor." *Shakespeare Quarterly* 45, no. 2 (Summer 1994): 190–210.

Frye, Northrop. *Anatomy of Criticism* (1957). Edited by Robert D. Denham. Toronto: University of Toronto Press, 2006.

———. *Fools of Time: Studies in Shakespearean Tragedy*. Toronto: University of Toronto Press, 1981.

Frye, Susan. *Elizabeth I: The Competition for Representation*. New York: Oxford University Press, 1993.

Galloway, David, ed. *Records of Early English Drama: Norwich (1540–1642)*. Toronto: University of Toronto Press, 1994.

Gascoigne, George. *The Noble Arte of Venerie or Hunting*. London, 1575.

Gascoigne, William Hunnis, George Ferrers, et al. *The Princely Pleasures at Kenelworth Castle*. In *The Plesauntest Workes of George Gascoigne, Esquire*. London, 1587.

Golding, Arthur. "Prefatory Epistle" (1567). In Ovid, *Metamorphoses*, edited by Jonathan Frederick Sims, translated by Arthur Golding, 405–22. Philadelphia: Paul Dry, 2000.

———. "To the Right Honourable and his Singular Good Lord Robert Dudley Earle of Leicester." In Heinrich Bullinger, *A Confutation of the Popes Bull . . . against Elizabeth*, translated by Golding. London, 1572.

Goldring, Elizabeth. "Portraiture, Patronage, and the Progresses of Robert Dudley, Earl of Leicester, and the Kenilworth Festivities of 1575." In *The Progresses, Pageants, and Entertainments of Elizabeth I*, edited by Jayne Elisabeth Archer, Elizabeth Goldring, and Sarah Knight, 163–87. Oxford: Oxford University Press, 2014.

———. *Robert Dudley, Earl of Leicester, and the World of Elizabethan Art*. New Haven: Yale University Press, 2014.

Gosson, Stephen. *Plays Confuted in Five Actions*. London, 1582.

Gouws, John. "Greville, Fulke, first Baron Brooke of Beauchamps Court (1554–1628)." In *Oxford Dictionary of National Biography*. Accessed November 3, 2017. http://www.oxforddnb.com.

Grady, Hugh. "Shakespeare and Impure Aesthetics: The Case of *A Midsummer Night's Dream*." *Shakespeare Quarterly* 59, no. 3 (Fall 2008): 274–302.

———. *Shakespeare, Machiavelli, and Montaigne: Power and Subjectivity from Richard II to Hamlet*. Oxford: Oxford University Press, 2002.

Gras, Henk. "*Twelfth Night, Every Man Out of His Humour*, and the Middle Temple Revels of 1597–98." *Modern Language Review* 84, no. 3 (July 1989): 545–64.

Greenblatt, Stephen. *Shakespearean Negotiations*. Berkeley: University of California Press, 1988.

———. *Will in the World: How Shakespeare Became Shakespeare*. New York: Norton, 2004.

Greville, Fulke. *Fulke Greville's Life of Sir Philip Sidney (1652)*. Edited by Nowell Smith. Oxford: Clarendon, 1907.

Grigsby, Bryon Lee. *Pestilence in Medieval and Early Modern English Literature*. New York: Routledge, 2004.

Gurr, Andrew. *Playgoing in Shakespeare's London*. Second edition. Cambridge: Cambridge University Press, 1996.

———. "Privy Councilors as Theatre Patrons." In *Shakespeare and Theatrical Patronage in Early Modern England*, edited by Paul Whitfield White and Suzanna R. Westfall, 221–45. Cambridge: Cambridge University Press, 2002.

Guy, John. "The 1590s: The Second Reign of Elizabeth I?" In *The Reign of Elizabeth I: Court and Culture in the Last Decade*, edited by Guy, 1–19. Cambridge: Cambridge University Press, 1995.

———. *Elizabeth: The Later Years*. New York: Viking, 2016.

Habermas, Jürgen. *The Structural Transformation of the Public Sphere: An Inquiry into a Category of Bourgeois Society*. Translated by Thomas Burger. Cambridge MA: MIT Press, 1989.

Hackett, Helen. "Dream-Visions of Elizabeth I." In *Reading the Early Modern Dream*, edited by Katharine Hodgkin, Michelle O'Callaghan, and S. J. Wiseman, 45–66. New York: Routledge, 2008.

———. *Shakespeare and Elizabeth*. Princeton: Princeton University Press, 2009.

———. *Virgin Mother, Maiden Queen: Elizabeth I and the Cult of the Virgin Mary*. London: Palgrave Macmillan, 1995.

Halpin, N. J. *Oberon's Vision in the Mid-summer Night's Dream*. London: Shakespeare Society, 1843.

Hammer, Paul. "'Absolute and Sovereign Mistress of her Grace?' Queen Elizabeth I and her Favourites, 1581–1592." In *The World of the Favourite*, edited by J. H. Elliott and L. W. B. Brockliss, 38–53. New Haven: Yale University Press, 1999.

———. "Devereux, Robert, Second Earl of Essex (1565–1601)." In *Oxford Dictionary of National Biography*. Accessed November 3, 2017. http://www.oxforddnb.com.

Harbage, Alfred. *Shakespeare and the Rival Traditions*. Bloomington: Indiana University Press, 1970.

Harington, Sir John. *A Tract on the Succession to the Crown (1602)*. Edited by Clements R. Markham. London: Roxburghe Club, 1880.

———. *Nugae Antique*. 1804. Reprint. New York: AMS Press, 1966.

BIBLIOGRAPHY

———. *Sir John Harington's A New Discourse of A Stale Subject, Called the Metamorphosis of Ajax*. Edited by Elizabeth Story Donno. New York: Columbia University Press, 1962.
Harris, Nicholas, ed. *Memoirs of the Life and Times of Sir Christopher Hatton, K. G.* London, 1847.
Haynes, Samuel, and William Murdin, eds. "Confession of Arthur Guntor, Concerning Lord Robert Dudley." In *A Collection of State Papers . . . Left by William Cecil, Lord Burghley*. London, 1740.
Helgerson, Richard. *Adulterous Alliances: Home, State, and History in Early Modern European Drama and Painting*. Chicago: University of Chicago Press, 2000.
———. *Forms of Nationhood: The Elizabethan Writing of England*. Chicago: University of Chicago Press, 1992.
Herbert, William. *Englands Sorrowe or A Farewell to Essex*. London, 1606.
Hirsh, James. "Rome and Egypt in *Antony and Cleopatra*." In *Antony and Cleopatra: New Critical Essays*, edited by Sara Deats, 175–92. New York: Routledge, 2005.
Hobbes, Thomas. *The Treatise on Human Nature* (1650). In vol. 4 of *The English Works of Thomas Hobbes*, 1–76. Edited by William Molesworth. London, 1840.
Holinshed, Raphael. *The Third Volume of the Chronicles*. London, 1587.
Hollander, John. "*Twelfth Night* and the Morality of Indulgence." *Sewanee Review* 67, no. 2 (Spring 1959): 220–38.
Hopkins, Lisa. *Drama and the Succession to the Crown, 1561–1633*. Aldershot: Ashgate, 2011.
Hornback, Robert. *The English Clown Tradition from the Middle Ages to Shakespeare*. Cambridge: Brewer, 2009.
Hotson, Leslie. *The First Night of Twelfth Night*. New York: Macmillan, 1955.
Howard, Jean. "Crossdressing, the Theatre, and Gender Struggle in Early Modern England." *Shakespeare Quarterly* 39, no. 4 (Winter 1988): 418–40.
Hughes, Paul L., and James F. Larkin, eds. *Tudor Royal Proclamations*. New Haven: Yale University Press, 1969.
Hunt, Lynn. *The Invention of Pornography: Obscenity and the Origins of Modernity, 1500–1800*. New York: Zone, 1993.
Hunt, Maurice. "The Garter Motto in *The Merry Wives of Windsor*." SEL: *Studies in English Literature 1500–1900* 50, no. 2 (Spring 2010): 383–406.
———. *Shakespeare's Speculative Art*. New York: Palgrave Macmillan, 2011.
Hunter, G. K. "English Folly and Italian Vice: The Moral Landscape of John Marston." In *Jacobean Theatre*, edited by John Russell Brown and Bernard Harris, 85–111. New York: Capricorn, 1967.
———. *John Lyly: The Humanist as Courtier*. Cambridge MA: Harvard University Press, 1962.
———. "Shakespeare's Politics and the Rejection of Falstaff." 1959. In *Henry the Fourth Parts I and II: Critical Essays*, edited by David Bevington, 253–62. New York: Garland, 1986.

BIBLIOGRAPHY

Hurault, André, Sieur de Maisse. *A Journal of All That was Accomplished by Monsieur de Maisse, Ambassador in England from Henry IV to Queen Elizabeth, Anno Domini 1597*. Edited and translated by G. B. Harrison. London: Nonesuch, 1931.

Hyde, E. "The Difference and Disparity between the Estate and the Conditions of George Duke of Buckingham and Robert Earl of Essex." In *Reliquiae Wottonianae, or, A Collection of Lives, Letters [and] Poems*, 184–202. London, 1685.

James I. *Correspondence of King James VI* (1861). Edited by John Bruce. New York: AMS, 1968.

James, Richard, "Epistle-Dedicatory to Sir Henry Bourchier." In *William Shakespeare: A Documentary Life*, William Schoenbaum, 143. New York: Oxford University, 1975.

Jankowski, Theodora. "'As I Am Egypt's Queen': Cleopatra, Elizabeth I, and the Female Body Politic." *Assays: Critical Approaches to Medieval and Renaissance Texts* 5 (1989): 91–110.

Jensen, Phebe. *Religion and Revelry in Shakespeare's Festive World*. Cambridge: Cambridge University Press, 2008.

Jones, Ann Rosalind, and Peter Stallybras. *Renaissance Clothing and the Materials of Memory*. Cambridge: Cambridge University Press, 2000.

Jones, Norman, and Paul Whitfield White. "*Gorboduc* and Royal Marriage Politics: An Elizabethan Playgoer's Report of the Premiere Performance." *English Literary Renaissance* 26, no. 1 (January 1996): 3–16.

Jonson, Ben. *The Works of Ben Jonson*. 7 vols. Edited by David Bevington, Martin Butler, and Ian Donaldson. Cambridge: Cambridge University Press, 2012.

Joubert, Laurent. *Popular Errors* (1578). Translated by Gregory David de Rocher. Tuscaloosa: University of Alabama Press, 1989.

Kamps, Ivo. "Madness and Social Mobility in *Twelfth Night*." In *Twelfth Night: New Critical Essays*, edited by James Schiffer, 229–43. New York: Routledge, 2011.

Karremann, Isabel. "A Passion for the Past: The Politics of Nostalgia on the Early Jacobean Stage." In *Passions and Subjectivity in Early Modern Culture*, edited by Brian Cummings and Freya Sierhuis, 149–64. Burlington VT: Ashgate, 2013.

Kastan, David Scott. *Shakespeare after Theory*. New York: Routledge, 1999.

Kegl, Rosemary. "'The Adoption of Abominable Terms': The Insults that Shape Windsor's Middle Class." *ELH: English Literary History* 61, no. 2 (Summer 1994): 253–78.

Kendall, Alan. *Robert Dudley, Earl of Leicester*. London: Cassell, 1980.

Kermode, Frank. *Shakespeare, Spenser, Donne*. London: Routledge, 1971.

Kerrigan, John. "Secrecy and Gossip in *Twelfth Night*." *Shakespeare Survey* 50 (1997): 65–80.

Kisery, András. *Hamlet's Moment: Drama and Political Knowledge in Early Modern England*. Oxford: Oxford University Press, 2016.

Klause, John. "Shakespeare's *Sonnets*: Age in Love and the Goring of Thoughts." *Studies in Philology* 80, no. 3 (Summer 1983): 300–324.

Klein, Ezra. "Tim Kaine's Feminism." Accessed November 3, 2017. http://www.vox.com/policy-and-politics/2016/10/25/13402422/tim-kaine-man-supporting-woman.

Knowles, John. "*1 Henry IV.*" In vol. 2 of Dutton and Howard, *Companion*, 412–31.

Knox, John. *The First Blast of the Trumpet Against the Monstrous Regiment of Women*. London, 1558.

Kyffin, Maurice. *The Blessedness of Brytaine or a Celebration of the Queen's Holyday*. London, 1588.

Laam, Kevin P. "Aging the Lover: The *Posies* of George Gascoigne." In *Growing Old in Early Modern Europe*, edited by Erin Campbell, 75–94. Aldershot: Ashgate, 2006.

Lake, Peter. *Bad Queen Bess?: Libels, Secret Histories, and the Politics of Publicity in the Reign of Elizabeth I*. Oxford: Oxford University Press, 2016.

———. "From *Leicester his Commonwealth* to *Sejanus his Fall*: Ben Jonson and the Politics of Roman (Catholic) Virtue." In *Catholics and the "Protestant Nation,"* edited by Ethan Shagan, 128–61. Manchester: Manchester University Press, 2005.

———. "The Politics of 'Popularity' and the Public Sphere: The 'Monarchical Republic' of Elizabeth I Defends Itself." In Lake and Steven Pincus, *The Politics of the Public Sphere in Early Modern England*, 59–94. Manchester University Press, 2007.

Lake, Peter, and Steven Pincus. "Rethinking the Public Sphere." In *The Politics of the Public Sphere in Early Modern England*, edited by Lake and Steven Pincus, 1–30. Manchester: Manchester University Press, 2007.

———, eds. *The Politics of the Public Sphere in Early Modern England*. Manchester: Manchester University Press, 2007.

Laneham, Robert (?). *A Letter, Whearin Part of the Entertainment unto the Queenz Maiesty, at Killingworth Castl . . . is signified*. London, 1575.

L'Aubespine-Chateuneuf, Guillaume. "Ambassade de l'Aubespine-Chateauneuf en Angleterre." In vol. 4 of *Relations Politiques de la France et de L'Espagne avec L'Ecosse*, edited by Alexandre Teulet, 61–88. Paris, 1862.

Le Comte, Edward. *Endymion in England: The Literary History of a Greek Myth*. New York: King's Crown, 1944.

Leicester's Commonwealth: The Copy of a Letter Written by a Master of Art of Cambridge. 1584. Edited by D. C. Peck. Athens: Ohio University Press, 1985.

Leicester's Ghost. Edited by Franklin B. Williams Jr. Chicago: University of Chicago Press, 1972.

Leonard, Nancy. "Shakespeare and Jonson Again: The Comic Forms." *Renaissance Drama* n.s. 10 (1979): 45–69.

"'A Letter of Estate': An Elizabethan Libel." Edited by D. C. Peck. *Notes and Queries* 28, no. 226 (Winter 1981): 21–35.

Lever, Ralph. *The Philosopher's Game*. London, 1563.

Levin, Carole. *Dreaming the English Renaissance: Politics and Desire in Court and Culture*. New York: Palgrave MacMillan, 2008.

———. *The Heart and Stomach of a King: Elizabeth I and the Politics of Sex and Power*. Philadelphia: University of Pennsylvania Press, 1994.

Linthicum, M. Channing. "Malvolio's Cross-gartered Yelllow Stockings." *Modern Philology* 25, no. 1 (August 1927): 87–93.

Logan, Robert A. "'High Events as These': Sources, Influences, and the Artistry of *Antony and Cleopatra*." In *Antony and Cleopatra: New Critical Essays*, edited by Sara Deats, 154–74. New York: Routledge, 2005.

Loomis, Catherine. *The Death of Elizabeth I*. New York: Palgrave Macmillan, 2010.

Luce, Alice. Introduction. *The Countess of Pembroke's Antonie*, edited by Luce, 1–51. Weimar, 1897.

Lyly, John. *Endymion*. Edited by David Bevington. Manchester: Manchester University Press, 1996.

MacCaffrey, Wallace. *Elizabeth I: War and Politics, 1588–1603*. Princeton: Princeton University Press, 1992.

———. "Hatton, Sir Christopher (c. 1540–1591)." In *Oxford Dictionary of National Biography*. Accessed November 3, 2017. http://www.oxforddnb.com.

MacFaul, Tom. "'A Kingdom with my Friend': Favorites in Shakespeare." In *Literary Milieux: Essays in Text and Context Presented to Howard Erskine-Hill*, edited by David Womersley and Richard McCabe, 52–71. Newark: University of Delaware Press, 2008.

Machiavelli, Niccolò. *The Prince* (1532). Edited by Peter Bondanella and translated by Bondanella and Mark Musa. 1984. Reprint. New York: Oxford University Press, 1998.

Maclean, Sally-Beth. "Tracking Leicester's Men: The Patronage of a Performance Troupe." In *Shakespeare and Theatrical Patronage in Early Modern England*, edited by Paul Whitfield White and Suzanna R. Westfall, 46–71. Cambridge: Cambridge University Press, 2002.

Malcolmson, Cristina. "'What You Will': Social Mobility and Gender in *Twelfth Night*." In *Twelfth Night: Contemporary Critical Essays*, edited by R. S. White, 160–93. New York: St. Martin's, 1996.

Manningham, John. *The Diary of John Manningham of the Middle Temple, 1602–1603*. Edited by Robert Parker Solien. Hanover NH: University Press of New England, 1976.

Marcus, Leah, "Jonson and the Court." In *The Cambridge Companion to Ben Jonson*, edited by Richard Harp and Stanley Stuart, 30–42. Cambridge: Cambridge University Press, 2000.

———. *Puzzling Shakespeare: Local Reading and its Discontents*. Berkeley: University of California Press, 1988.

Marlowe, Christopher. *The Collected Poems of Christopher Marlowe*. Edited by Patrick Cheney and Brian J. Striar. Oxford: Oxford University Press, 2006.

Marotti, Arthur. "'Love is Not Love': Elizabethan Sonnet Sequences and the Social Order." *ELH: English Literary History* 49, no. 2 (Summer 1982): 396–428.

Martin, Christopher. *Constituting Old Age in Early Modern English Literature*. Amherst: University of Massachusetts Press, 2012.

McCabe, Richard. "Elizabethan Satire and the Bishops' Ban of 1599." *Yearbook of English Studies* 11 (1981): 188–93.

McDonald, Russ. *Shakespeare and Jonson / Jonson and Shakespeare*. Lincoln: University of Nebraska Press, 1988.

McLaren, A. N. *Political Culture in the Reign of Elizabeth I: Queen and Commonwealth, 1558–1585*. Cambridge: Cambridge University Press, 1999.

Middleton, Thomas. *Thomas Middleton: The Collected Works*. Edited by Gary Taylor and John Lavagnino. Oxford: Clarendon, 2007.

Minogue, Sally. "A Woman's Touch: Astrophil, Stella, and 'Queen Vertue's Court.'" *ELH: English Literary History* 63, no. 3 (Fall 1996): 555–70.

Montrose, Louis. *The Purpose of Playing*. Chicago: University of Chicago Press, 1996.

———. "'Shaping Fantasies': Figurations of Gender and Power in Elizabethan Culture." In *Representing the English Renaissance*, edited by Stephen Greenblatt, 31–64. Berkeley: University of California Press, 1988.

———. *The Subject of Elizabeth: Authority, Gender, and Representation*. Chicago: University of Chicago Press, 2006.

Morris, Helen. "Queen Elizabeth I 'Shadowed' in Cleopatra." *Huntington Library Quarterly* 32, no. 2 (May 1969): 271–78.

Mueller, Janel. "Virtue and Virtuality: Gender in the Self-Representations of Queen Elizabeth I." In *Form and Reform in Renaissance England: Essays in Honor of Barbara Kiefer Lewalski*, edited by Amy Boesky and Mary Thomas Crane, 220–46. Newark DE: University of Delaware Press, 2000.

Muir, Kenneth. "Elizabeth I, Jodelle, and Cleopatra." *Renaissance Drama* n.s. 2 (1969): 197–206.

Mullaney, Steven. "Mourning and Misogyny: *Hamlet*, *The Revenger's Tragedy*, and the Final Progress of Elizabeth I." *Shakespeare Quarterly* 45, no. 2 (Summer 1994): 139–62.

———. *The Reformation of Emotions in the Age of Shakespeare*. Chicago: University of Chicago Press, 2015.

Nashe, Thomas. *Pierce Penniless's Supplication to the Devil*. Edited by J. Payne Collier. London, 1842.

Naunton, Robert. *Fragmenta Regalia, or Observations on Queen Elizabeth, Her Times & Favorites*. Edited by John. S. Cerovski. Washington DC: Folger Shakespeare Library, 1985.

Neely, Carol Thomas. *Broken Nuptials in Shakespeare's Plays*. New Haven: Yale University Press, 1985.

Neill, Michael. "Bastardy, Counterfeiting, and Misogyny in *The Revenger's Tragedy*." *SEL: Studies in English Literature, 1500–1900* 36, no. 2 (Spring 1996): 397–416.

Neufeld, Christine M. "Lyly's Chimerical Vision: Witchcraft in *Endymion*." In *John Lyly*, edited by Ruth Lunney, 191–211. Aldershot: Ashgate, 2011.

"*News from Heaven and Hell*: A Defamatory Narrative of the Earl of Leicester." Edited by D. C. Peck. *English Literary Renaissance* 8, no. 2 (March 1978): 141–58.

Nicholls, Mark, and Penry Williams. "Ralegh, Sir Walter (1554–1618)." In *Oxford Dictionary of National Biography*. Accessed November 3, 2017. http://www.oxforddnb.com.

Nichols, John. *The Progresses and Public Processions of Queen Elizabeth*. London: John Nichols & Son, 1823.

Nyquist, Mary. "'Profuse, Proud Cleopatra': 'Barbarism' and Female Rule in Early Modern English Republicanism." *Women's Studies* 24, nos. 1–2 (November 1994): 85–130.

Oeppen, J., L. R. Poos, and R. M. Smith. "Re-assessing Josiah Russell's Measurements of Late Medieval Mortality Using Inquisitions *Post Mortem*." In *The Fifteenth-Century Inquisitions Post Mortem: Source, Process, and Potential*, edited by M. Hicks, 155–68. Rochester NY: Boydell & Brewer, 2012.

Osborne, Laurie. "'The Marriage of True Minds': Amity, Twinning, and Comic Closure in *Twelfth Night*." In *Twelfth Night: New Critical Essays*, edited by James Schiffer, 99–113. New York: Routledge, 2011.

Ovid. *Metamorphoses* (1567). Translated by Arthur Golding. Edited by John Frederick Nims. Philadelphia: Paul Dry, 2000.

Oxford Dictionary of National Biography. Online edition. 2004–. http://www.oxforddnb.com/.

Parker, Patricia. *Shakespeare from the Margins: Language, Culture, Context*. Chicago: University of Chicago Press, 1996.

Paster, Gail Kern. *The Body Embarrassed: Drama and the Disciplines of Shame in Early Modern England*. Ithaca: Cornell University Press, 1993.

Patterson, Annabel. *Censorship and Interpretation: The Conditions of Writing and Reading in Early Modern England*. Madison: University of Wisconsin Press, 1984.

———. *Shakespeare and the Popular Voice*. Cambridge: Blackwell, 1989.

Peck, D. C. Introduction. *Leicester's Commonwealth: The Copy of a Letter Written by a Master of Art of Cambridge*. Edited by Peck, 1–53. Athens: Ohio University Press, 1985.

———. Introduction. "*News from Heaven and Hell Heaven and Hell*: A Defamatory Narrative of the Earl of Leicester." Edited by Peck. *English Literary Renaissance* 8, no. 2 (Spring 1978): 141–43.

Peele, George. *The Arraygnment of Paris* (1581–84). In vol. 1 of *The Works of George Peele*, edited by A. H. Bullen, 1–73. 1888. Reprint. Port Washington NY: Kennikat Press, 1966.

Perry, Curtis. *Literature and Favoritism in Early Modern England.* Cambridge: Cambridge University Press, 2006.

Petowe, Henry. *Elizabetha Quasi Vivens, Eliza's Funerall.* London, 1603.

Petrarch, Francesco. *The Secret.* Edited and translated by Carol E. Quillen. Boston: Bedford-St. Martin's, 2003.

Pincombe, Michael. *The Plays of John Lyly: Eros and Eliza.* Manchester: Manchester University Press, 1996.

Plato, *Symposium.* Translated by Benjamin Jowett. Second edition. New York: Bobbs-Merrill, 1956.

Platter, Thomas. *Thomas Platter's Travels in England, 1599.* Edited by Clare Williams. London: Jonathan Cape, 1937.

Plutarch. "The Life of Marcus Antonius." In *Shakespeare's Plutarch*, edited by T. J. B. Spencer, 175–294. New York: Penguin, 1964.

———. *The Lives of the Noble Grecians and Romans.* Translated by Thomas North. London, 1579.

Poole, Kristin. "Saints Alive! Falstaff, Martin Marprelate, and the Staging of Puritanism." *Shakespeare Quarterly* 46, no. 1 (Spring 1995): 47–75.

Purkiss, Diane. "Medea in the English Renaissance." In *Medea in Performance 1500–2000*, edited by Edith Hall, Fiona Macintosh, and Oliver Taplin, 32–48. Leeds: Legenda–Taylor & Francis, 2000.

———. *The Witch in History: Early Modern and Twentieth-Century Representations.* New York: Routledge, 1996.

Quinn, Michael L. "Celebrity and the Semiotics of Acting." *New Theatre Quarterly* 6, no. 22 (May 1990): 154–61.

Rackin, Phyllis. "Androgyny, Mimesis, and the Marriage of the Boy Heroine on the English Renaissance Stage." *PMLA: Publications of the Modern Language Association of America* 102, no. 1 (January 1987): 29–41.

———. *Shakespeare and Women.* New York: Oxford University Press, 2005.

———. "Shakespeare's Boy Cleopatra, the Decorum of Nature, and the Golden World of Poetry." *PMLA: Publications of the Modern Language Association of America* 87, no. 2 (March 1972): 201–212.

———. *The Stages of History: Shakespeare's English Chronicles.* Ithaca: Cornell University Press, 1990.

Ralegh, Sir Walter, *The History of the World* (1614). Edited by C. A. Patrides. Philadelphia: Temple University Press, 1971.

———. *The Poems of Sir Walter Ralegh: A Historical Edition.* Edited by Michael Rudick. Tempe: Arizona Center for Medieval and Renaissance Studies, 1999.

———. "Ocean to Cynthia." In *Elizabeth I and Her Age*, edited by Donald Stump and Susan M. Felch, 439–52. New York: Norton, 2009.

———. "Sir Walter Ralegh to the Earl of Leicester, 29 March 1586." In *Queen Elizabeth and Her Times*, edited by Thomas Wright, 291. London, 1838.

Ricci, Maria Teresa. "Old Age in Castiglione's *The Book of the Courtier*." In *Growing Old in Early Modern Europe*, edited by Erin Campbell, 57–73. Aldershot: Ashgate, 2006.

Richards, Judith. "Love and a Female Monarch: The Case of Elizabeth Tudor." *Journal of British Studies* 38, no. 2 (April 1999): 133–60.

Riehl, Anna. *The Face of Queenship: Early Modern Representations of Elizabeth I*. New York: Palgrave Macmillan, 2010.

Riggs, David. *Ben Jonson: A Life*. Cambridge MA: Harvard University Press, 1989.

Rinehart, Keith. "Shakespeare's Cleopatra and England's Elizabeth." *Shakespeare Quarterly* 23, no. 1 (Winter 1972): 81–86.

Roach, Joseph. *Cities of the Dead: Circum-Atlantic Performance*. New York: Columbia University Press, 1996.

Rosenberg, Eleanor. *Leicester: Patron of Letters*. New York, 1955.

Roser, Max. "Life Expectancy." Accessed November 3, 2017. https://ourworldindata.org/life-expectancy.

Rowe, Katherine. "Minds in Company: Shakespearean Tragic Emotions." In vol. 1 of *A Companion to Shakespeare's Works*, 4 vols, edited by Richard Dutton and Jean E. Howard, 47–72. Malden MA: Blackwell, 2006.

Rowe, Nicholas. *Some Account of the Life of Mr. William Shakspear* (1709). Edited by. Samuel H. Monk. Ann Arbor MI: Augustan Reprint Society / Edward Brothers, 1948.

Rowlands, Samuel. *Ave Caesar*. London, 1603.

Saccio, Peter. *The Court Comedies of John Lyly*. Princeton: Princeton University Press, 1969.

Schalkwyck, David. "Love and Service in *Twelfth Night* and the *Sonnets*." *Shakespeare Quarterly* 56, no. 1 (Spring 2005): 76–100.

Schiffer, James, ed. *Twelfth Night: New Critical Essays*. New York: Routledge, 2011.

———. "Taking the Long View: *Twelfth Night* Criticism and Performance." In Schiffer, *Twelfth Night: New Critical Essays*, 1–44. New York: Routledge, 2011.

Schleiner, Winfried. "Orsino and Viola: Are the Names of Serious Characters in *Twelfth Night* Meaningful?" *Shakespeare Studies* 16 (1983): 135–41.

Schoenbaum, Samuel. *William Shakespeare: A Documentary Life*. New York: Oxford University, 1975.

Scott-Warren, Jason. "Harington, Sir John (bap. 1560, d. 1612)." In *Oxford Dictionary of National Biography*. Accessed November 3, 2017. http://www.oxforddnb.com.

———. "When Theaters Were Bear-Gardens; Or, What's at Stake in the Comedy of Humors." *Shakespeare Quarterly* 54, no. 1 (Spring 2003): 63–82.

Scragg, Leah. "Shakespeare, Lyly, and Ovid: The Influence of *Gallathea* on *A Midsummer Night's Dream*." *Shakespeare Survey* 30 (1977): 125–34.

———. "The Victim of Fashion? Rereading the Biography of John Lyly." *Medieval and Renaissance Drama in England* 19 (2006): 210–26.

BIBLIOGRAPHY

Shahar, Shulamith. *Growing Old in the Middle Ages*. New York: Routledge, 1997.

Shakespeare, William. *The Riverside Shakespeare*. Second edition. Edited by G. Blakemore Evans. Boston: Houghton Mifflin, 1997.

Shannon, Laurie. *Sovereign Amity: Figures of Friendship in Shakespearean Contexts*. Chicago: University of Chicago Press, 2002.

Shapiro, James. *The Year of Lear: Shakespeare in 1606*. New York: Simon & Schuster, 2015.

Shaw, George Bernard. "Better than Shakespear?" In Shaw, *Three Plays for Puritans*, xxviii-xxxvii. New York: Brentano's, 1919.

Shephard, Alexandra. *Meanings of Manhood in Early Modern England*. Oxford: Oxford University Press, 2003.

Shephard, Robert. "Sexual Rumours in English Politics: The Cases of Elizabeth I and James I." In *Desire and Discipline: Sex and Sexuality in the Premodern West*, edited by Jacqueline Murray and Konrad Eisenbichler, 101–22. Toronto: University of Toronto Press, 1996.

Sidney, Mary, Countess of Pembroke, trans. *The Countess of Pembroke's Antonie*, edited by Alice Luce. Weimar, 1897.

Sidney, Philip. "Defense of Leicester." In *Leicester's Commonwealth: The Copy of a Letter Written by a Master of Art of Cambridge* (1584), edited by D. C. Peck, 249–64. Athens OH: Ohio University Press, 1985.

——. *Sir Philip Sidney: The Major Works*. Edited by Katherine Duncan-Jones. Oxford: Oxford University, 1989.

——. *The Prose Works of Sir Philip Sidney*. Edited by Albert Feuillerat. 1912. Reprint. Cambridge: Cambridge University Press, 1962.

Smith, Bruce. *Shakespeare and Masculinity*. Oxford: Oxford University Press, 2000.

Smith, Hallet. "Bare Ruined Choirs: Shakespearean Variations on the Theme of Old Age." *Huntington Library Quarterly* 39, no. 3 (May 1976): 233–49.

Smith, Lacey Baldwin. *Treason in Tudor England: Politics and Paranoia*. Princeton: Princeton University Press, 1986.

Smith, Logan Pearsall, ed. *The Life and Letters of Sir Henry Wotton*. Clarendon: Oxford, 1907.

Smith, Nowell. Introduction. In *Fulke Greville's Life of Sir Philip Sidney*, edited by Smith, v-xxi. Oxford: Clarendon, 1907.

Smith, Peter. "M. O. I. A. 'What Should That Alphabetical Position Portend?': An Answer to the Metamorphic Malvolio." *Renaissance Quarterly* 51, no. 4 (Winter 1998): 1199–224.

Spenser, Edmund. *Edmund Spenser's Poetry*. Third edition. Edited by Hugh Maclean and Anne Lake Prescott, 655–66. New York: Norton, 1993.

Stanicuković, Goran V. "Masculine Plots in Twelfth Night." In *Twelfth Night: New Critical Essays*, edited by James Schiffer, 114–30. New York: Routledge, 2011.

Starks, Lisa. "'Immortal Longings': The Erotics of Death in *Antony and Cleopatra*." In *Antony and Cleopatra: New Critical Essays*, edited by Sara Deats, 243–58. New York: Routledge, 2005.

Stater, Victor. "Knollys, William, First Earl of Banbury (c. 1545–1632)." In *Oxford Dictionary of National Biography*. Accessed November 3, 2017. http://www.oxforddnb.com.

Steadman, John. "Falstaff as Actaeon: A Dramatic Emblem." *Shakespeare Quarterly* 14, no. 3 (Summer 1963): 231–44.

Steggle, Matthew. "Charles Chester and Ben Jonson." *SEL: Studies in English Literature, 1500–1900* 39, no. 2 (Spring 1999): 313–26.

———. *Laughing and Weeping in Early Modern Theaters*. Aldershot: Ashgate, 2007.

———. *Wars of the Theatres: The Poetics of Personation in the Age of Jonson*. English Literary Studies 75. Victoria BC: University of Victoria Press, 1998.

Stern, Tiffany, and Simon Palfrey. *Shakespeare in Parts*. Oxford: Oxford University Press, 2007.

Stow, John. *The Annales or Generall Chronicle of England*. London, 1615.

Streitberger, William. "Personnel and Professionalization." In *A New History of Early English Drama*, edited by John D. Cox and David Scott Kastan, 337–56. New York: Columbia University Press, 1997.

Strong, Roy. *The Cult of Elizabeth: Elizabethan Portraiture and Pageantry* (1977). London: Random House, 1999.

Stubs, Philip. *The Anatomie of Abuses*. London, 1595.

Sullivan, Garret, Jr. "Sleep, Epic, and Romance in *Antony and Cleopatra*." In *Antony and Cleopatra: New Critical Essays*, edited by Sara Deats, 259–73. New York: Routledge, 2005.

———. *Sleep, Romance, and Human Embodiment: Vitality from Spenser to Milton*. Cambridge: Cambridge University Press, 2012.

Suzuki, Mihoko. "Gender, Class, and the Ideology of Comic Form." In *A Feminist Companion to Shakespeare*, edited by Dympna Callaghan, 139–61. Malden MA: Blackwell, 2000.

Tassi, Marguerite. "O'erpicturing Apelles: Shakespeare's *Paragone* with Painting in *Antony and Cleopatra*." In *Antony and Cleopatra: New Critical Essays*, edited by Sara Deats, 291–307. New York: Routledge, 2005.

Taunton, Nina. *Fictions of Old Age in Early Modern Culture*. New York: Routledge, 2007.

———. "'Time's Whirligig': Images of Old Age in *Coriolanus*, Francis Bacon, and Thomas Newton." In *Growing Old in Early Modern Europe*, edited by Erin Campbell, 22–38. Aldershot: Ashgate, 2006.

Taylor, Charles. "Modern Social Imaginaries." *Public Culture* 14, no. 1 (Winter 2002): 91–124.

Taylor, Gary. "William Shakespeare, Richard James, and the House of Cobham." *Review of English Studies* 38, no. 151 (August 1987): 334–54.

Tennenhouse, Leonard. "Power on Display: The Politics of Shakespeare's Genres." In *Twelfth Night: Contemporary Critical Essays*, edited by R. S. White, 82–91. New York: St. Martin's, 1996.

———. *Power on Display: The Politics of Shakespeare's Genres*. New York: Methuen, 1986.

Thane, Pat. *Old Age in English History*. Oxford: Oxford University Press, 2000.

"Three Merry Men We Be" (1681–84). *English Broadside Ballad Archive*. University of California, Santa Barbara. Accessed November 3, 2017. https://ebba.english.ucsb.edu.

Thomas, Keith. "Age and Authority in Early Modern England." *Proceedings of the British Academy* 62 (1976): 205–48.

Thomas, Susan D. "*Endimion* and Its Sources." *Comparative Literature* 30, no. 1 (Winter 1978): 35–52.

Traub, Valerie. *Desire and Anxiety: Circulations of Sexuality in Shakespearean Drama*. New York: Routledge, 1992.

Tricomi, A. H. "Philip, Earl of Pembroke, and the Analogical Way of Reading Political Tragedy." *Journal of English and Germanic Philology* 85, no. 3 (July 1986): 332–45.

Vanhoutte, Jacqueline. "Antony's 'Secret House of Death': Suicide and Sovereignty in *Antony and Cleopatra*." *Philological Quarterly* 79, no. 2 (Spring 2000): 153–75.

———. "*Itinerarium ad Windsor* and Robert Dudley, Earl of Leicester." In *The Name of a Queen: William Fleetwood's "Itinerarium ad Windsor*," edited by Charles Beem and Dennis Moore, 85–104. New York: Palgrave Macmillan, 2013.

———. *Strange Communion: Motherland and Masculinity in Tudor Plays, Pamphlets, and Politics*. Newark DE: University of Delaware Press, 2003.

Vaughan, William. *Approved Directions for Health, both Naturall and Artificiall*. London, 1612.

Verstegan, Richard. *A Declaration of the True Causes of the Great Troubles*. . . . Antwerp, 1592.

Vickers, Nancy J. "Diana Described: Scattered Woman and Scattered Rhyme." *Critical Inquiry* 8, no. 2 (Winter 1981): 265–79.

Villanova, Arnaldus de. *The Defence of Age and Recovery of Youth*. London, 1550.

Waith, Eugene. *The Herculean Hero in Marlowe, Chapman, Shakespeare, and Dryden*. London: Chatto & Windus, 1962.

Walker, Greg. *Plays of Persuasion*. Cambridge: Cambridge University Press, 1991.

Warner, Michael. *Publics and Counterpublics*. New York: Zone, 2002.

Webster, John. *The White Devil*. In *"The Duchess of Malfi" and Other Plays*, edited by René Weiss, 1–102. Oxford: Oxford University Press, 1996.

White, Paul Whitfield, and Suzanna R. Westfall, eds. *Shakespeare and Theatrical Patronage in Early Modern England*. Cambridge: Cambridge University Press, 2002.

White, R. S., ed. *Twelfth Night: Contemporary Critical Essays*. New York: St. Martin's, 1996.

Whitney, Charles. *Early Responses to Renaissance Drama*. Cambridge: Cambridge University Press, 2006.

Whyte, Rowland. *The Letters of Rowland Whyte (1595–1608)*. Edited by Michael G. Brennan, Noel J. Kinnamon, and Margaret P. Hannay. Philadelphia: American Philosophical Society, 2013.

Wilder, Lina Perkins. "Changeling Bottom: Speech Prefixes, Acting, and Character in *A Midsummer Night's Dream*." *Shakespeare* 4, no. 1 (January 2008): 45–64.

Wiles, David. *Shakespeare's Clown: Actor and Text in the Elizabethan Playhouse*. Cambridge: Cambridge University Press, 1987.

Wilson, Bronwen, and Paul Yachnin. Introduction. *Making Publics in Early Modern Europe: People, Things, Forms of Knowledge*, edited by Bronwen and Yachnin, 1–24. New York: Routledge, 2010.

Wittek, Stephen. *The Media Players: Shakespeare, Middleton, Jonson, and the Idea of the News*. Ann Arbor: University of Michigan Press, 2015.

Woodcock, Matthew. "The Fairy Queen Figure in Elizabethan Entertainments." In *Elizabeth I: Always Her Own Free Woman*, edited by Carole Levin, Jo Eldridge Carney, and Debra Barrett-Graves, 97–115. Aldershot: Ashgate, 2003.

Worden, Blair. "Favourites on the English Stage." In *The World of the Favourite*, edited by J. H. Elliott and L. W. B. Brockliss, 159–83. New Haven: Yale University Press, 1999.

Wright, Thomas, ed. *Queen Elizabeth and Her Times*. London, 1838.

Wyatt, Sir Thomas. "Mine Own John Poyntz." In *Sir Thomas Wyatt: The Complete Poems*, edited by R. A. Rebholz, 186–89. New Haven: Yale University Press, 1978.

Yachnin, Paul. "'Courtiers of Beauteous Freedom': *Antony and Cleopatra* in its Time." *Renaissance and Reformation* 15, no. 1 (Winter 1991): 1–20.

———. "The Populuxe Theatre." In *The Culture of Playgoing in Shakespeare's England: A Collaborative Debate*, edited by Yachnin and Anthony B. Dawson, 38–68. Cambridge: Cambridge University Press, 2001.

———. "Performing Publicity." *Shakespeare Bulletin* 28, no. 2 (Summer 2010), 201–19.

INDEX

Page numbers in italics refer to figures.

Actaeon myth, 65–66, 70, 96, 98, 110, 113–14, 119, 131, 133, 190
Actes and Monuments (Foxe), 100
Adams, Simon, 47, 176, 210n15
Adelman, Janet, 160–61, 175, 181, 183, 200, 201, 206
Admonition to the Nobility and People of England and Ireland (Allen), 30, 35–38, 42–43, 46, 61, 63, 68, 73, 79–80, 132, 184
age-in-love trope: in *Antony and Cleopatra*, 162–63, 181, 183, 186–87, 192–94, 202, 206; definition of, 2; in *Endymion*, 35, 37, 56–57, 69, 74; in *Merry Wives of Windsor*, 2, 84, 110–17; in *News from Heaven and Hell*, 94; and performance, 1–5; and second reign of Elizabeth, 5; Shakespeare's fascination with, 1–4, 12–22, 28–29; in Shakespeare's sonnet sequence, 1–5, 154–58; in *Twelfth Night*, 20, 31, 125, 141–43, 151–53, 156; and vanity, 1, 5, 20, 57, 60, 71, 73, 97, 111, 141, 155–56; and wit, 11
Ajax. See *A New Discourse on a Stale Subject, or the Metamorphosis of Ajax* (Harington)
Alençon, Duke of, 41, 96

Allen, William, 73, 125, 161; *Admonition to the Nobility*, 30, 35–38, 42–43, 46, 61, 63, 68, 73, 79–80, 132, 184. See also *A Briefe Discoverie of Dr. Allen's Seditious Driftes*
amans senex, 5, 9, 19–20, 30–31, 73, 95, 153, 164, 182. See also *senex amans*
androgyny, 2
anticourt polemics, 31, 71, 82, 96, 121, 125, 139, 159–64, 190, 202; as "slanderous devices," 55, 93, 95, 114, 138; suppression of, 53–55. See also *Admonition to the Nobility*; *Leicester's Commonwealth*
Anton, Robert, 201
Antonie and Cleopatra (Greville), 173–74, 196
Antony and Cleopatra (Shakespeare): and age-in-love trope, 162–63, 181, 183, 186–87, 192–94, 202, 206; age of actor playing Antony in, 163, 203; and bearbaiting, 174, 183; and emotion, 165, 179–81, 188–90, 195–203; eulogies of Antony in, 199–200; and "great fairy," 15, 178, 181, 202; judgment in, 185, 188–89; and *Metamorphoses*, 186, 191, 194; and news, 188, 190; and "Life of Marcus Antonius," 31, 166–68, 171–72,

INDEX

Antony and Cleopatra (cont.)
  175–76, 180–82, 184, 187–88, 190–92; and royal favoritism, 164, 166–67, 173–74, 177, 180, 192, 194; and the theater, 167–68, 188–89, 190, 201–2
Arden, Alice, 58–59
Arnold, Janet, 40
Arraygnment of Paris (Peele), 130, 132
As You Like It (Shakespeare), 10, 16–17
Atwood, Margaret, 205
Auden, W. H., 110
Ave Caesar (Rowlands), 195

Bacon, Francis, 8, 42, 59–60, 63, 99, 131, 176, 191, 200, 206
Barber, C. L., 125, 140
Barkan, Leonard, 96, 99, 190
Bartholomew Fair (Jonson), 24
Barthomolaeus Anglicus, 19
Barton, Anne, 140, 194
Barton, John, 140
Bates, Catherine, 22, 175
bearbaiting, 4, 8; bandogs used for, 73; as contests of wit, 82, 84; Leicester's event of, 51–52
bearbaiting trope, 27; in *Antony and Cleopatra*, 174, 183; and Falstaff, 100, 109–17; in *Merry Wives of Windsor*, 9, 31, 110–17; in *News from Heaven and Hell*, 91–93, 112; Shakespeare's earliest reference to, 9; in *Twelfth Night*, 9, 123, 125–26, 135, 138–39, 143–51. *See also* Dudley bear and ragged staff
Berger, Harry, Jr., 82–83
Berry, Philippa, 38
Berry, Ralph, 139, 149, 151
Betts, Hannah, 34
Bevington, David, 25, 66, 71
Bishop's Ban of 1599, 137
Blanchett, Cate, 39

The Blessedness of Brytaine or a Celebration of the Queen's Holyday (Kyffin), 168–69
Blundeville, Thomas, 8, 11, 79
Bond, Sallie, 58
Bono, Barbara, 203
Book of the Courtier (Castiglione): ambiguous references to real persons in, 27; on derisive laughter, 11, 36, 48; on distinction between lust and love, 156; on old men in love, 3, 11, 17, 18, 36, 40, 85; on unbridled desire, 92; on wit and judgment, 82, 84
Boym, Svetlana, 125–26, 132, 152, 153, 166
Bradley, A. C., 193
Breitenberg, Mark, 19
Brennan, Liam, 141
A Briefe Discoverie of Dr. Allen's Seditious Driftes, 80, 82, 100
Bruster, Douglas, 6, 10
Burbage, James, 12, 86
Burbage, Richard, 159, 162–63, 186–87, 200, 203, 208
Burghley, Lord (William Cecil), 3, 45–46, 48, 57, 217n6

Camden, William, 53, 80
Canterbury Tales (Chaucer), 20, 71, 98
Carlson, Marvin, 28, 82, 122
Carroll, Tim, 141
Castiglione, Baldesar. *See Book of the Courtier*
castration, 73, 91, 93, 129, 184. *See also* emasculation
Cather, Willa, 206
Catholics: dissidents, 36, 81; exiled, 9, 36, 38, 42, 83; and *Leicester's Commonwealth*, 6, 35, 94
Cavendish, Margaret, 206
Cecil, William. *See* Burghley, Lord (William Cecil)
Chapman, George, 63

282

INDEX

Charles I of England, 151
Chaucer, Geoffrey, 20, 71, 98
Chronicles (Holinshed), 87, 124
Cicero, 20, 34, 58, 73, 167, 182, 185; *Cato Maior*, 16; on "unadvised adolescencye," 18, 134
Clapham, John, 42
class. *See* social class
Cleopatra (Daniel), 172
Clinton, Hillary, 3, 26, 208
Cobham affair, 100, 109
Collington, Philip, 16
Comedy of Errors (Shakespeare), 26–27
costume and dress: age-expected norms of, 33, 135; and bodily composition, 134–35; changes in, 2, 73, 75, 134; expense of, 86; old clothing as, 86, 102; and "popular breeches," 85, 102, 118; stockings as, 2, 134, 135, 245n65
cross-dressing, 2, 21, 36, 37, 73, 74, 113, 140, 160, 193
cuckoldry, 19–20. *See also senex amans*
Cymbeline (Shakespeare), 206
Cynthia's Revels. *See The Fountaine of Selfe-Love or Cynthia's Revels* (Jonson)

Daniel, Samuel, 172
Dash, Irene, 180
Davison, Francis, 46
"The Dead Man's Right" (anon.), 87, 94
Deats, Sara, 36
de Certeau, Michel, 80, 117
defamation, 10, 53, 105. *See also* libel; slander
deformity: and aging males, 36, 64, 70, 142; and Antony, 186; and Elizabeth's favorites, 36, 64; and *Endymion*, 36, 70; and *Every Man Out of His Humour*, 145, 151; laughter and ridicule at, 36, 70, 125, 134, 148; and love, 36; of texts, 128; and *Twelfth Night*, 125, 128, 134, 142, 150–51

Dekker, Thomas, 144
de Maisse, André Hurault, 37, 43–45, 177
democratization: and age-in-love figures, 12; and the public sphere, 12; and the theater, 10, 84
desire: and age, 1, 17–19, 35, 40, 71–72, 101, 106, 125, 154, 156; "Deep," 34–35, 64, 93, 144, 175; and nostalgia, 200; and public duty, 178–79; and Sonnet 138, 1, 18; transgressive, 65; "unnatural," 69
Devereux, Robert. *See* Essex, Earl of (Robert Devereux)
dotage, 18, 31, 58, 70, 184–86, 194
Doty, Jeffrey S., 6, 10, 12, 85
dress. *See* costume and dress
The Duchess of Malfi (Webster), 138, 206
Dudley, Ambrose. *See* Warwick, Earl of (Ambrose Dudley)
Dudley, John, 47
Dudley, Robert. *See* Leicester, Earl of (Robert Dudley)
Dudley bear and ragged staff, 7, 8, 35, 48, 51–53, 65, 86, 87, 89–91, 101, 103
Dudley family, 47–48
Dutton, Richard, 26, 98, 107
Dyer, Edmund, 21

effeminacy, 16–17, 38, 47, 109, 112, 117, 142, 146, 161, 171, 184
Eggert, Katherine, 22, 163, 165, 177
Elizabeth: accession of, 2–3; age of the court of, 3; death of, 195; and identification with Richard II, 82; length of reign and age of, 41–44; moon cult of, 34, 38, 65, 78, 110, 196; Ovidian allusions to, 4, 35, 36, 38, 56, 63–66, 68, 72, 96–97, 104, 109, 113, 145; pet names for favorites of, 48, 62, 96; portraits of, 169–71; Rainbow Portrait of, 78, 169, *170*, 171; and the Queen's Men, 12–13; second reign of,

283

INDEX

Elizabeth *(cont.)*
5, 20–22; and snake symbolism, 169, *170*, 171; speculation on age of, 42; Tilbury speech of, 164, 176
Ellis, Anthony, 16
emasculation, 52, 67, 93, 96, 113, 150, 173, 186, 190
Endymion (Lyly): and age-in-love trope, 35, 37, 56–57, 69, 74; and aging Elizabethan court, 3, 33, 38, 41–42, 57–75; Bacon on, 59–60; bearbaiting in, 73; deformity in, 36, 70; Earl of Oxford as patron of, 57; as fable about princes and favorites, 59–60; and *Leicester's Commonwealth*, 56–57; male sexuality in, 33–37, 39, 57, 66–75; and *Metamorphoses*, 36, 46, 66, 72; *mundus scenescit* trope in, 57–58; and pastimes, 24–26, 27, 31, 56; and royal favoritism, 24, 30, 33, 36, 58–70, 74; and rumor, 56, 59–60, 68–69; and satire, 37; and scandal, 30, 56, 60; and *senex amans*, 5, 73, 95; on solitary lives of favorites, 61; as source for *Merry Wives of Windsor*, 23, 78; and *Twelfth Night*, 122–25, 130–35, 140, 152–54; and vanity, 71, 73; wind metaphor in, 56
England's Caesar, 195
entertainments: of Ditchley, 59; of Kenilworth, 6, 13, 34, 51, 64, 86–87, 92–93, 97, 132, 153, 175; of Woodstock, 97. *See also* pastimes
Erickson, Peter, 207, 208
Essex, Countess of (Lettice Knollys), 61, 67
Essex, Earl of (Robert Devereux), 8, 26, 27, 117, 165; *Blessedness of Brytaine* dedicated to, 168; and comparisons to Antonius, 172, 180; contemporary public response to, 21; on Elizabeth's age, 41, 42; and Falstaff, 111, 114; historical privileging of, 22, 180, 207–8; as "proto-democratic"

figure, 207; rebellion of, 42, 138, 172–74; and response to Elizabeth's letters, 176; and self-love, 131
eulogies, 199–200
Every Man Out of His Humour (Jonson), 123, 128, 130, 138–40, 144–46, 151

The Faerie Queene (Spenser), 86–87, 92, 96, 97–98
fairies and fairy queens, 25, 71, 74; in *Antony and Cleopatra*, 15, 178, 181, 202; in *Merry Wives of Windsor*, 114, 131; in *Midsummer Night's Dream*, 96–99, 124
fairy tales, 121, 123
Falstaff, 87, 89, 163; in cross-dressing scene, 113, 193; death of, 121; dehumanization of, 110; and desire for new livery, 106; effeminacy of, 110; Elizabeth's connection to, 77–78; in the haunting of *Twelfth Night*, 31, 123, 126, 129, 131–34, 141, 147, 149–50; Jonson's ghosting of, 122; and minion, 78; and the moon, 77–79; in *"Munsur Fatpanche,"* 101; pity for, 109; publicity of, 118; self-description of, 77–78; self-promotion of, 103–4; theatrical ghosting of, 81–82; and transgressions of Elizabethan court, 78, 82; and wit and judgment, 77, 81–84, 101, 112, 147, 149, 181, 182, 187
favoritism. *See* royal favoritism
Fiedler, Leslie A., 2, 124
The First Part of Sir John Oldcastle (anon.), 100, 129
fish: as Elizabeth's caught or tamed favorites, 63–64, 174; as Elizabeth's pet name for Ralegh, 48, 62, 63
Fitz, L. T., 128
The Fountaine of Selfe-Love or Cynthia's Revels (Jonson), 123, 131, 133, 138, 145–46; "popular breeches" in, 85, 102, 118

284

INDEX

Foxe, John, 100
Freedman, Barbara, 106
Frye, Northrop, 141, 148
Frye, Stephen, 141
Frye, Susan, 22

A Game at Chess (Middleton), 26
Garnier, Robert, 172–73
Gascoigne, George, 34, 64, 86, 107; *Noble Arte of Venerie or Hunting*, 86–87, 107, *108*, 114; "Princely Pleasures," 34, 64
gender: bending categories of, 74, 91, 95–96, 140–41; convergence of, 193; and Elizabethan moon cult, 38; Elizabeth's exploitation of, 44; versus generational categories, 192; hierarchies of, 12–13, 48; and judgment, 107, 115; and longing, 12; old men and norms of, 2, 3, 5, 14, 16, 21, 48, 91, 95–96; as political asset, 63, 93; and power, 159, 164, 190; and the public sphere, 12, 84; and social decorum, 12
gerontocracy, 15–16, 20, 190
"Gertrude Talks Back" (Atwood), 205
ghosting, 81–82, 122
Globe, 86, 102, 122, 141, 159, 162
Goddard, William, 144
"Golden Age" (film), 39
Golding, Arthur. See *Metamorphoses* (Ovid), Golding's translation of
Goldring, Elizabeth, 6
Goodman, Godfrey, 42
Gorboduc (Norton and Sackville), 138
gossip, 56, 117, 123, 163, 172, 187, 194; about Hatton, 3–4, 13, 133; about Leicester, 3–4, 84, 87, 93–94, 205; and scandal, 93–94. See also *Leicester's Commonwealth*; rumor; scandal
Gosson, Stephen, 10, 105, 167, 190, 202
Grady, Hugh, 23
Greenblatt, Stephen, 22, 97, 130, 148

Greville, Fulke, 173–74, 184, 196, 197
Guy, John, 176, 207

Habermas, Jürgen, 8, 11, 80
Hackett, Helen, 63, 68, 98
Halpin, N. J., 25
Hamlet (Shakespeare), 4–5, 16, 17, 25, 27–28, 106, 122, 159–63, 178, 185–86, 192, 202, 205–7
Harington, Sir John: on Elizabeth, 43, 64; fishing analogy of, 64; *A New Discourse on a Stale Subject, or the Metamorphosis of Ajax*, 31, 123–24, 136, 137
Harvey, Gabriel, 57
Hatton, Christopher, 13–15, 22, 29, 33–34, 47, 71, 114, 138, 146, 149, 155, 176; and abdication of traditional masculinity, 21, 34, 184; age of, 3–4, 57; on Elizabeth as "fishing" for courtiers, 64, 174; Elizabeth's preference for men like, 180; and *Endymion*, 61–64; John Guy on, 207; as pattern, 176; sheep as Elizabeth's pet name for, 48, 59; theatrical description of, 13–14; and vulnerability to slander, 46
Hawthorne, Nigel, 141
Heminge, John, 86
The Henriad (Shakespeare): *1 Henry IV*, 29, 77, 78, 79, 81–84, 99–104, 106, 109–10, 112, 116–19, 124, 126, 154; *2 Henry IV*, 9, 28, 79, 81, 83, 99–107, 110, 115–17, 121, 141; *Henry V*, 85, 87, 117, 121, 147; *2 Henry VI*, 9; *Richard II*, 81–82; *Richard III*, 45
Herbert, William, 199, 200
Hobbes, Thomas, 105
Holinshed, Raphael, 87, 124
horizontal exchanges, 84
Hornback, Robert, 102
humoral theory of sexuality and aging, 39, 69

285

INDEX

Hunt, Maurice, 23
Hunter, G. K., 72, 74
"Hymnus in Cynthiam" (Chapman), 63

Isle of Dogs (Jonson and Nashe), 24, 144

James I of England (James VI of Scotland), 5, 41, 163, 172, 195–97
James IV of Scotland, 57
James VI of Scotland (James I of England), 5, 41, 163, 172, 195–97
Jankowski, Theodora, 163, 179
Jensen, Phebe, 123, 129
Jones, Rosalind, 86
Jonson, Ben, 24–26; *Bartholomew Fair*, 24; on Elizabeth's age, 42; *Every Man Out of His Humour*, 25, 26, 29, 122–23, 128, 130, 138–40, 144–46, 151; *Fountaine of Selfe-Love or Cynthia's Revels*, 85, 102, 118, 123, 131, 133, 138, 145–46; ghosting of Falstaff by, 122; imprisonment of, 24; *Isle of Dogs*, 24, 144; and "narrow-eyed decipherers," 26, 29; and "popular breeches," 85–86, 102, 118; and Shakespeare, 12, 25, 115, 122–23; *Twelfth Night*'s allusions to works of, 122–23, 128, 130–31, 133, 138–40, 144–46, 151
Jouber, Laurent, 17, 19
judgment. *See* wit and judgment

Kaine, Tim, 3
Kapur, Shekhar, 39
Kastan, David Scott, 78, 81
Kempe, Will, 12, 28, 86, 101–4, 107, 119, 163, 186, 208
King Lear (Shakespeare), 10–11
Kingsley, Ben, 141
Kisery, András, 10, 12
Knights of the Garter, 51, 53, 110–11, 114–15
Knollys, Lettice, 61, 67

Knox, John, 35, 173
Kyd, Thomas, 89

Lake, Peter, 10, 12, 52
Lamb, Charles, 151
Lee, Sir Henry, 57, 58, 59
Leicester, Earl of (Robert Dudley): age of, 3–4; aging body of, 48, 50–53; and bearbaiting event, 51–52; and commissioning of Golding's *Metamorphoses* translation, 97; in "Dead Mans Right," 87, 94; death of, 85; and death of son, 62; as Elizabeth's lapdog, 174, 226n158; Golding's dedicatory letter to, 35, 65, 87; gossip and scandal about, 3–4, 84, 87, 93–94, 205; as governor-general of the Netherlands, 50; and Kenilworth, 6, 13, 34, 51, 64, 86–87, 92–93, 97, 132, 153, 175; libido of, 6, 50–53; marriage of, 61–62; patronage of traveling troupe by, 85; and printing press, 6, 86; Segar's portrait of, 48, *49*; self-promotion of, 85, 87; and slander, 14, 21, 36, 46, 53, 55, 87, 89–90, 101, 104–5, 114; transgressions of, 52, 95, 118; and vanity, 50, 64, 91, 97. *See also Leicester's Commonwealth*
Leicester's Commonwealth (anon.), 62, 82, 90–91, 93–95, 114, 162, 184; anonymous Catholic expatriates as authors of, 6, 35, 94; and court trial, 78–79; and Dudley bear and ragged staff, 51–53, *54*, 89; Elizabeth's attempted suppression of, 56; and *Endymion*, 56–57; as entertainment, 89; as exploitation of public anxiety about favorites, 30, 35; female cameos in, 67; French translation of, 53, *54*; impetus for, 8, 124; influence of, 87; on Leicester's body and libido, 50–53, 55–57; misogynist arguments in, 146–47; popularity of, 52–53

286

INDEX

Leicester's Ghost, 94–95, 199
Leoni, Téa, 26
Levin, Carole, 4, 130, 207
libel, 10, 30, 53, 55, 80, 100. *See also* defamation; slander
life expectancy, 3, 57
Loomis, Catherine, 195, 198, 199
Lord Admiral's Men, 106–17
Lord Chamberlain's Men, 86, 106–7, 122
"A Lover's Complaint" (Shakespeare), 158
Love's Labor's Lost (Shakespeare), 13
Lowin, John, 159, 163
Lyly, John, 3; Earl of Oxford as patron of, 57, 74; and Elizabeth, 74; influence of, 23–24, 74–75. See also *Endymion*

MacFaul, Tom, 14
Machiavelli, Niccolò, 11, 45, 79–80, 89
Madam Secretary (television program), 26
Malcolmson, Cristina, 126, 127
Marc Antoine (Garnier), 172–73
Marcus, Leah, 25, 147
Markham, Robert, 124, 130
Marlowe, Christopher, 46
Marprelate controversy, 100
Marston, John, 137
Martin, Christopher, 16, 40, 157
Mary, Queen of Scots, 41, 57, 67
masculinity, 3, 6, 12–14, 16, 21–22, 205–7; abdication of, 21, 59–61, 73; and Antony, 164–65, 175; feminine perspective of, 195, 201, 202, 206; hyper, 48; and old men, 34, 40, 46, 48, 207; and wit and judgment, 84
A Mastif Whelp with Other Ruff-Island-lik Currs Fetcht from Amongts the Antipedes (Goddard), 144
McLaren, A. N., 93
memory: individual and collective, 126, 200; and the theater, 27–29, 82, 95, 102–4, 111, 122, 123

Merry Wives of Windsor (Shakespeare), 4, 9, 10, 31, 84, 110–17, 122, 194; age-in-love trope in, 2, 84, 110–17; bearbaiting in, 9, 31, 110–17; comparative judgment of, 84, 111–17; Elizabeth's role in writing of, 77; *Endymion* as source for, 23, 78; punishment in, 111–12; and *Twelfth Night*, 131–32, 135
Metamorphoses (Ovid): and *Antony and Cleopatra*, 186, 191, 194; Aurora in, 36, 56, 194; Circe in, 4, 35, 96, 104, 109, 114, 132, 145, 171, 174, 184–85, 190, 193, 203; and Elizabethan allusions, 4, 35, 36, 38, 56, 63–66, 68, 72, 96–97, 104, 109, 113, 145; and *Endymion*, 36, 46, 66, 72; and *Merry Wives of Windsor*, 113; on passion, 186; and royal favorites, 4, 35; Tithonus in, 36, 38, 46
Metamorphoses (Ovid), Golding's translation of: dedicatory letter to Leicester in, 35, 65, 87; Dudley bear and ragged staff displayed on, 35, 65, 87, *88*; Leicester's commissioning of, 97; title page of, 87, *88*
The Metamorphosis of Pygmalions Image (Marston), 137
Microcynicon (Middleton) 144
Middleton, Thomas, 12, 29; *Game at Chess*, 26; influence of Lyly on, 24; *Microcynicon*, 144; *Revenger's Tragedy*, 5, 159–63, 178, 181–82, 185, 188, 189
A Midsummer Night's Dream (Shakespeare), 14, 15, 151–52, 172, 181; Bottom in, 2, 14, 95, 96, 98–101, 107, 115, 124, 163, 181, 182, 202; *Endymion* as source for, 23, 95; Fairy Queen in, 96–99, 124; Kenilworth as inspiration of, 97; and masculine merit versus feminine perspective, 202; and Shakespeare scholars, 22; and women in power, 205

287

miles gloriosus, 71, 73, 95, 113, 129, 182–83
minion, definition of, 78
misogyny, 12, 22, 44, 146, 180, 201, 203, 207, 213–14n58
Montrose, Louis, 14, 22, 25, 37, 38, 41, 44
moon: Elizabeth's cult of, 34, 38, 65, 78, 110, 196; in *Endymion*, 58–59, 62–63, 67, 69, 181; and Falstaff, 78–79; and Isis, 169; minions of, 30, 77
Muir, Kenneth, 178
Mullaney, Steven, 37, 38, 39, 159–60, 201
mundus scenescit (trope), 37, 57–58

Nashe, Thomas: and Bishop's Ban of 1599, 137; *Choice of Valentines*,137; *Isle of Dogs*, 24, 144; *Pierce Penniless's Supplication to the Devil*, 87
Naunton, Robert, 13, 48, 50
Netherlands, 25, 50, 53, 79, 87, 91, 102
Neoplatonism, 37, 40, 65, 69, 124, 162, 183, 193
A New Discourse on a Stale Subject, or the Metamorphosis of Ajax (Harington): bearbaiting in, 123–24; *Twelfth Night*'s allusions to, 31, 123–24, 136, 137
news, 10–11; of Antony, 188, 190; of Falstaff's death, 121; and rumor, 104–5
News from Heaven and Hell (anon.), 90–95, 121, 133; age-in-love trope in, 94; bearbaiting trope in, 91–93, 112; "bere whelp" in, 92, 113, 194; and castration anxiety, 184; on Dudley bear and ragged staff, 90–91, 101; and judgment, 90–95; on Leicester 101, 102, 103; as precedent for Shakespeare, 90; and punishment, 90–95, 106, 112
The Noble Arte of Venerie or Hunting (Gascoigne), 86–87, 107, *108*, 114
North, Sir Thomas, 165–66, 171, 187
Northumberland, Duke of (John Dudley), 47

nostalgia, 31, 125–26, 132, 152, 153, 155, 166, 200
Nunn, Trevor, 140–41
Nyquist, Mary, 175–76

Ocean to Cynthia (Ralegh), 38, 78, 130
Oldcastle, Sir John, 100, 123
Order of the Garter, 51, 53, 110–11, 114–15
Ormond, Earl of, 53
Othello (Shakespeare), 15, 19
Ovid. See *Metamorphoses* (Ovid); *Metamorphoses* (Ovid), Golding's translation of
Owen, Clive, 39
Oxford, Earl of, 57–58, 74

Pack, Roger Lloyd, 141
Palfrey, Simon, 163, 167
Parallel Lives (Plutarch; North's translation), 165–66
Parker, Patricia, 74, 98
Paster, Gail Kern, 136, 139
pastimes: in *Antony and Cleopatra*, 168; definition of, 24; Elizabeth's anxiety regarding, 82; in *Endymion*, 24–26, 27, 31, 56; and Falstaff, 90–100, 109, 110, 114, 116, 119; in *Twelfth Night*, 133, 139, 149–50
patriarchy, 3, 6, 16–17, 19, 61, 161, 164, 181, 190–91, 194, 202, 206
Patterson, Annabel, 27, 216n128
Paulet, Sir Amyas, 57
Peck, D. C., 21, 124
Peele, George, 130, 132
Pembroke, Countess of (Mary Sidney), 172–73
Perry, Curtis, 12, 68, 80, 85, 89, 94, 210n15
personalities, 25, 35
Petrarch, 19, 58, 65, 71, 72, 130, 140, 143–45, 161, 162
Philip II of Spain, 57
Pincus, Steven, 10

288

INDEX

Plato, 128; *Symposium*, 127–28, 194. See also Neoplatonism

Platter, Thomas, 42, 169

Plautus, 15; *Menaechme*, 128; *miles gloriosus*, 71. See also *miles gloriosus*

playgoers: and *Antony and Cleopatra*, 163, 167, 177–79, 181, 183, 185, 187–89, 196, 198, 200, 202; collaboration of, 27, 86, 102, 127, 133, 134, 136, 138–39, 181, 183; and Falstaff, 84, 100, 104–7, 110, 112–18; and laughter, 11, 27, 28, 105, 112, 125, 134, 148, 185, 188; and Shakespeare's allusions to Elizabeth's suitors, 27–29

Plutarch: influence on Shakespeare, 166–67; "Life of Marcus Antonius," 31, 166–68, 171–72, 175–76, 180–82, 184, 187–88, 190–92; *Parallel Lives*, 165–66

Pole, John, 48

"popular breeches," 85, 102, 118

popularity: of anticourt satire, 31, 36, 52; control of, 180; of court materials, 85; definition of, 6, 85; of dream-settings, 68; of Elizabethan moon cult, 38; and Leicester, 6, 87; of lost masculine ideal, 153; of verse satires, 137

printing press, 6, 86, 118

Privy Council, 3, 24, 55, 114, 138, 195

promotion, 85, 87, 103–4

Protestantism: and Falstaff, 100; and Leicester, 8, 25; and *News from Heaven and Hell*, 83, 94; radicals of, 6, 25; and treason, 100

publicity, 6, 8–10, 12, 29–30, 36–37, 86, 94, 118, 179

public-making texts and stories, 28, 90, 166

public punishment, 10, 112

public sphere, 6, 10–12, 15, 80, 84, 89, 93, 150, 180

punishment: charivaris, 20, 214n89; in *Merry Wives of Windsor*, 111–12; in *News from Heaven and Hell*, 90–95, 106, 112; public, 20, 112; in *Twelfth Night*, 106, 139, 149

Purkiss, Diane, 73

Queen's Men, 12–13

Quinn, Michael L., 4

Rainbow Portrait of Elizabeth I, 78, 169, *170*

Ralegh, Sir Walter: and Elizabeth, 21, 38, 39, 41, 42, 47, 48, 62, 63, 65, 172, 174, 175; as Elizabeth's "fish," 48, 62, 63; "Golden Age" portrayal of, 39; and Jonson, 133, 145; as Middle Templar, 138; *Ocean to Cynthia*, 38, 78, 130; "Of Favorites," 142; on old age, 1, 46, 141; as royal minion, 111; and *Twelfth Night*, 125, 130, 132, 133

Revenger's Tragedy (Middleton), 5, 159–63, 178, 181–82, 185, 188, 189

Richard II (Shakespeare), 81–82

Richard III (Shakespeare), 45

Riehl, Anna, 44

Roach, Joseph, 104

Rowe, Nicholas, 77, 118

royal favoritism, 3–4, 306–8; and *Antony and Cleopatra*, 164, 166–67, 173–74, 177, 180, 192, 194; and Elizabeth's names, 48, 62, 96; and *Endymion*, 24, 30, 33, 36, 58–70, 74; and *Hamlet*, 161, 206; and minions, 47, 52, 59, 77–79, 81, 84, 94, 100, 104, 106, 110–11, 113–14, 116–17, 146–47, 200; public anxiety regarding, 30; and the theater, 12–14, 24–25, 26, 29; and transgression, 4, 46, 65, 75, 78; and *Twelfth Night*, 126, 131, 137–38, 142, 147, 148, 153; and vanity, 5, 57, 60, 73, 97, 99, 111, 116, 155

royal interference, 77

INDEX

Rudd, Bishop, 42
rumor, 8, 187, 194, 199; about Elizabeth's love affairs, 4; and *Endymion*, 56, 59–60, 68–69; and Falstaff, 82, 118. *See also* gossip; scandal
Rylance, Mark, 141

scandal, 9, 84, 109; definition of, 93–94; and *Endymion*, 30, 56, 60; and libel legislation, 55; transformation of, 109. *See also* gossip; rumor
Segar, William, 48; portrait of Robert Dudley, Earl of Leicester, *49*
self-promotion, 85, 87, 103–4
senex amans, 30–31, 73, 95, 153, 164, 182; in *Antony and Cleopatra*, 182; definition of, 19–20; and Elizabethan court, 30; in *Endymion*, 5, 73, 95; Shakespeare's fascination with, 9, 20, 95; in *Twelfth Night*, 20, 31, 153, 164
Shakespeare, William: as an actor, 12–13; and age-in-love trope, 1–4, 12–22, 28–29, 206; *As You Like It*, 10, 16–17; *Comedy of Errors*, 26–27; and Jonson, 12, 25, 115, 122–23; *King Lear*, 10–11; *Love's Labor's Lost*, 13; Lyly's influence on, 23; metatheatrical devices of, 10; Othello, 15, 19; and the revision of Plutarch's "Life of Marcus Antonius," 180–81; and *senex amans*, 9, 20, 95. *See also Antony and Cleopatra*; *Hamlet*; *The Henriad*; *The Merry Wives of Windsor*; *A Midsummer Night's Dream*; sonnet sequence; *Twelfth Night*;
Shannon, Laurie, 80
Shapiro, James, 166, 183, 187
Shaw, George Bernard, 121, 201
Sheffield, Douglas, 67
Sheffield, Lady, 61
Shephard, Alexandra, 16
Sidney, Mary, 172–173

Sidney, Philip, 11, 50, 53, 55, 101, 105, 134, 148, 149, 172–75, 208
silence, 2, 56, 196
slander, 194; and antigovernment propaganda, 30, 53, 55, 87, 89–90, 138; devices of, 55, 93, 95, 114, 138; and Falstaff, 101, 104–5, 114, 117; against Hatton, 14, 46; against Leicester, 14, 21, 36, 46, 53, 55, 87, 89–90, 101, 104–5, 114; and pastimes, 150. *See also* defamation; libel
Simier, Jean de, 96
Smith, Mel, 141
Smith, Peter, 136
social class, 11, 13, 16, 30, 34, 75, 84, 89, 105–6, 112, 125, 140, 148
"social imaginary," 21
social mobility, 2, 8, 14, 29, 34, 51, 58, 89, 126–27, 147, 154
sonnet sequence (Shakespeare), 126, 128, 154–58; age-in-love trope in, 1–5, 154–58; Sonnet 2, 155; Sonnet 5, 155; Sonnet 7, 155–56; Sonnet 16, 156; Sonnet 19, 155; Sonnet 20, 128; Sonnet 25, 155; Sonnet 31, 156; Sonnet 34, 56; Sonnet 37, 156; Sonnet 55, 156; Sonnet 60, 157; Sonnet 62, 155; Sonnet 63, 157; Sonnet 64, 155; Sonnet 65, 157; Sonnet 73, 157; Sonnet 76, 129; Sonnet 129, 20; Sonnet 138, 1–2, 15, 18–23, 75, 156; Sonnet 107, 155, 196
The Spanish Tragedy (Kyd), 89
Spenser, Edmund: Epithalamion, 59; *Faerie Queene*, 86–87, 92, 96, 97–98
sport and theater, 14, 26, 28, 84, 115, 118, 123, 144, 148–50, 206
"sportful malice," 26, 149–50, 194
Stallybras, Peter, 86
Stanivuković, Goran, 153
Steggle, Matthew, 25
Stern, Tiffany, 163, 167
Storage, William, 53, 104

290

INDEX

"strippling age," 1
Strong, Sir Roy, 40, 169
subjugation, 84, 190
Sullivan, Garret, 59, 67, 109, 116

Tarleton, Richard, 103, 130
Tassi, Marguerite, 169
Taunton, Nina, 16
Taylor, Charles, 21
Tennenhouse, Leonard, 143, 165
theater, 83–84; and *Antony and Cleopatra*, 167–68, 188–89, 190, 201–2; bearbaiting compared to, 123; commodification of court materials by, 103; democratizing functions of, 10, 24, 105–6; and laughter, 11, 27–28, 105–6, 185; and Leicester, 103–4, 176; and memory, 27–29, 82, 95, 102–4, 111, 122, 123; memory machine aspect of, 28; and pastimes, 24; patronage system of, 12, 74, 106–7, 172; as place of judgment, 10–11; and Privy Council's attempts to restrain, 106–7; and royal favorites, 12–14, 24–25, 26, 29; and shared emotions, 11, 12, 15–17, 28, 147–53, 188–90, 195–200; and sport, 14, 26, 28, 84, 115, 118, 123, 144, 148–50, 194; and *Twelfth Night*, 140–41
theatres: Globe, 86, 102, 122, 141, 159, 162; the Theatre, 12
Thomas, Keith, 3, 15, 16, 19
transgressions: of aging sexuality, 75, 159; and Falstaff, 78, 82, 111; gendered, 92, 149; generational, 78, 141, 149; of Leicester, 52, 95, 118; as resistance, 81; of royal favorites, 4, 46, 65, 75, 78; of *senex amans* figure, 20; social and natural, 52; and Sonnet 138, 1; into transcendence, 15, 158
Twelfth Night (Shakespeare): age-in-love trope in, 20, 31, 125, 141–43, 151–53, 156; allusions to *Ajax* in, 123–24, 136, 137; allusions to *Cynthia's Revels* in, 123, 131, 133, 138, 145–46; allusions to *Endymion* in, 122–25, 130–35, 140, 152–54; allusions to *Every Man Out of His Humour* in, 122–23, 128, 130, 138–40, 144–46, 151; and bearbaiting trope, 9, 123, 125, 143–51; and deformity, 125, 128, 134, 142, 150–51; division and subtraction in, 127–28; dogs and dogging in, 123, 144, 149–51; and emotional response of playgoers, 147–53; Falstaff's haunting of, 31, 123, 126, 129, 131–34, 141, 147, 149–50; fustian riddle in, 127, 136; Jonson as target of, 143–43; and judgment, 137, 139, 142, 144, 147, 149–51; names in, 127; and nostalgia, 125–26; punishment in, 106, 139, 149; Rylance's all-male production of, 141; and satirical norms, 129, 132, 135–37, 139–42, 144–51; *senex amans* in, 20, 31, 153, 164; stagings and productions of, 140–41; twinning and twins in, 125–28, 132, 140–41, 147, 154; and violence, 106, 141, 148, 150–51

United States presidential election of 2016, 208

vanity, 145, 219–20n44; and "age in love," 1, 5, 20, 57, 60, 71, 73, 97, 111, 141, 155–56; and Antony, 166–67; Elizabeth accused of, 38, 40, 45–46; and *Endymion*, 71, 73; and Falstaff, 83, 99, 111; and Leicester, 50, 64, 91, 97; in *Midsummer Night's Dream*, 97; and royal favoritism, 5, 57, 60, 73, 97, 99, 111, 116, 155; and Shakespeare's sonnet sequence, 1, 156; and *Twelfth Night*, 141, 155

INDEX

Vavasour, Anne, 57, 59, 67
Vickers, Nancy J., 65

Waith, Eugene, 189
Walsingham, Sir Francis, 3, 53, 57
Warner, Michael, 12, 28, 55, 83, 90
Warwick, Earl of (Ambrose Dudley), 8–9, 144
Webster, John, 138; *Duchess of Malfi*, 138, 206; *White Devil*, 89
wind 56, 104–5
wit and judgment: and age-in-love trope, 11; bearbaiting as contests of, 123; Castiglione on, 82, 84; and Falstaff, 77, 81–84, 101, 112, 147, 149, 181, 182, 187; and gerontocracy, 15–16, 20, 190; laughter as form of, 11; and masculinity, 84; in *Merry Wives of Windsor*, 115; political, 9, 14–15; for royal favoritism, 68; theater as place of, 9–11; and *Twelfth Night*, 123, 142

Wittek, Stephen, 10
Wotton, Henry, 11, 102
Wyatt, Sir Thomas, 19, 71

Yachnin, Paul, 10, 95, 163, 179

IN THE EARLY MODERN CULTURAL STUDIES SERIES:

Courage and Grief: Women and Sweden's Thirty Years' War
By Mary Elizabeth Ailes

Travel and Travail: Early Modern Women, English Drama, and the Wider World
Edited and with an introduction by Patricia Akhimie and Bernadette Andrea

At the First Table: Food and Social Identity in Early Modern Spain
By Jodi Campbell

Separation Scenes: Domestic Drama in Early Modern England
By Ann C. Christensen

Portrait of an Island: The Architecture and Material Culture of Gorée, Sénégal, 1758–1837
By Mark Hinchman

Producing Early Modern London: A Comedy of Urban Space, 1598–1616
By Kelly J. Stage

Words Like Daggers: Violent Female Speech in Early Modern England
By Kirilka Stavreva

Sacred Seeds: New World Plants in Early Modern English Literature
By Edward McLean Test

My First Booke of My Life
By Alice Thornton
Edited and with an introduction by Raymond A. Anselment

Age in Love: Shakespeare at the Elizabethan Court
By Jacqueline Vanhoutte

The Other Exchange: Women, Servants, and the Urban Underclass in Early Modern English Literature
By Denys Van Renen

To order or obtain more information on these or other University of Nebraska Press titles, visit nebraskapress.unl.edu.

CPSIA information can be obtained
at www.ICGtesting.com
Printed in the USA
LVHW092135240419
615471LV00009B/120/P

9 781496 207593